# DRIVING OFFENCES

# Driving Offences
## Law, Policy and Practice

SALLY CUNNINGHAM
*University of Leicester, UK*

Routledge
Taylor & Francis Group
LONDON AND NEW YORK

First published 2008 by Ashgate Publishing

2 Park Square, Milton Park, Abingdon, Oxfordshire OX14 4RN
711 Third Avenue, New York, NY 10017

*Routledge is an imprint of the Taylor & Francis Group, an informa business*

First issued in paperback 2018



**British Library Cataloguing in Publication Data**
Cunningham, Sally
Driving offences : law, policy and practice
1. Automobiles - Law and legislation - England
2. Automobiles - Law and legislation - Wales 3. Traffic
violations - England 4. Traffic violations - Wales
5. Traffic regulations - England 6. Traffic regulations -
Wales
I. Title
345.4'20247

**Library of Congress Cataloging-in-Publication Data**
Cunningham, Sally.
Driving offences : law, policy, and practice / by Sally Cunningham.
p. cm.
Includes bibliographical references and index.
ISBN 978-0-7546-4905-2 (hardback)
1. Automobiles--Law and legislation--England. 2. Automobiles--Law and legislation--Wales. 3. Traffic violations--England. 4. Traffic violations--Wales. 5. Traffic regulations--Wales. 6. Traffic regulations--England. I. Title.

KF2617.C86 2008
345.73'0247--dc22

2008018065

ISBN 13: 978-0-7546-4905-2 (hbk)
ISBN 13: 978-1-138-37899-5 (pbk)

# Contents

# List of Tables

# Table of Cases

**Swedish Cases**

# Table of Legislation

**Statutes**

**Secondary Legislation**

# Acknowledgements

Thanks go to the University of Leicester for allowing me to take study leave in order to complete the writing of this book. Special thanks go to the Institute of Advanced Motorists Trusts and particularly Bert Morris for providing financial support for the comparative study of the law in Sweden which involved a visit to Sweden in August/September 2007.

The study of Swedish law required the cooperation of a number of individuals, to whom I am very grateful. Dr Josef Zila at Stockholm University was extremely hospitable during my three week stay in Stockholm, and valuable in providing me with contacts for my research. Jonas Fransson provided important and efficient research assistance and linguistic support. The following individuals and organisations deserve my thanks for their willing and candid answers to interview questions: Karin Lindkvist and Thomas Lönnelid at the Swedish Prosecution Authority in Stockholm, Sven-Erik Alhem and Ulla Öhman at the Swedish Prosecution Authority in Malmö, Tommy Stiernelantz at Solna Police, Örjan Brodin at the Swedish National Police Board, Hans Wahlström and Håkan Östlin at the Swedish Road Traffic Inspectorate and Claes Tingwall at the Swedish Road Administration.

The empirical study conducted in England during 2000–2002 required the cooperation and help of several individuals and organisations. Thanks go to police officers and civilian staff working for the three police forces involved in the study – Leicestershire, Lincolnshire and Northamptonshire. These include (but I am sure the list is not exhaustive): the Data Protection Officer from each force; staff from the Road Safety Partnership in Lincolnshire; staff from the Accident Enquiry Unit at Charles Street Police Station, Leicester; staff in the Central Accident Bureau at Mereway, Northampton. Great help was provided to me in the form both of administrative support and cooperation in interviews. I would also like to express gratitude to members of staff at the Crown Prosecution Service, both at headquarters and in each of the three areas, who located files and provided me with a room in which to read them. The contribution from Crown prosecutors in interview was important. The support of the Chief Crown Prosecutor from each area was particularly appreciated.

On a more personal note I would like to thank R.D.R. Kyd, who very efficiently proofread earlier drafts of the text, and Matthew Cunningham, for his continued support. I would also like to thank my colleague at the University of Leicester, Professor C.M.V. Clarkson, whose continued encouragement has been invaluable.

# Chapter 1

# Introduction

## The Scope of this Book

This book aims firstly to set out the law relating to driving offences. Other than practitioner texts there is very little written on offences under statutes such as the Road Traffic Act 1988 and the Road Safety Act 2006. Since driving offences are dealt with by the criminal justice system and are under the jurisdiction of the magistrates' court and Crown Court, they form part of the substantive criminal law. However, driving offences are rarely studied by undergraduate students of law, perhaps due to the perception that they fall outside the 'paradigm' of criminal liability, and, along with other types of offences such as drug offences, are not seen as 'core' crimes (see Husak 2005, 65). Driving offences tend to be regarded as mere regulatory offences, which, as noted by Wells in the context of corporate crime and health and safety offences, leads to them being perceived as 'quasi' crime rather than 'true' crime (Wells 2001, 7). The law relating to road traffic offences is often overlooked by commentators on the criminal law, who tend to focus on the more paradigmatic groups of offences such as homicide offences, offences against the person, sexual offences and property offences. Arguably, however, traffic offences should receive much greater attention, given that it is the one area of the criminal law most likely to touch on the everyday lives of a large majority of the adult population of any industrialized country. Unlike the more paradigmatic types of offences, the average member of the public is conceivably as likely to be a perpetrator of a traffic crime as he or she is to be a victim thereof.

Cars and other motor vehicles have now been around for over a century, with the first car having been imported into England in 1894 (Perkin 1976, 7), and there is no doubt that they have had an enormous impact on both society as a whole and the lives of individuals. As noted by Perkin, the automobile has 'determined where we live and work, and so the shape and character of the human community' (ibid., 129). It has liberated individuals by enabling them to travel where they choose, thus producing freedom of choice as to where they live and work, as well as providing a valuable method of transport for commercial purposes. Yet in addition to numerous advantages created by its invention, the motor vehicle has brought with it disadvantages of equal significance.

Pollution and congestion are two such drawbacks, but perhaps the most damaging feature of motor vehicles is their ability to cause death and injury. The danger caused by motorized traffic was nothing new: before the invention of the car, horse-drawn vehicles had been a cause of death on the roads (Foreman-Peck 1987, 265). But as the car became more popular and affordable and was able to achieve higher speeds, the death rate on the roads soared. In 1913, when there were 106,000 cars on the roads, the number of fatal road traffic accidents was 1,743 (Emsley 1993, 358–9). By 1935, when mass-production and the increase in disposable income of the middle classes allowed more people to afford cars, there were 1,477,000 cars on the roads and 6,437 fatalities (ibid.). Improvements to roads and safety campaigns caused a drop in the fatality rate in the late 1930s until after the war, when cars became available to the masses and fatalities rose to 7,407 in 1973 (Perkin 1976, 227).

It is obvious that the use of motor vehicles incurs a high cost in terms of lives lost, but one should also not overlook the financial expense of traffic collisions. The government has estimated the cost of collisions involving deaths or injuries at £3 billion a year (DETR 2000, para.1.1), although more recent figures have suggested that the total financial cost is much higher, with road traffic collisions costing the NHS £470 million a year and the economy as a whole a further £7.2 billion (Audit Commission 2007, 8).

Given such financial and human losses, Foreman-Peck describes the initial policy reaction to road safety issues as 'strangely muted' (Foreman-Peck 1987, 269). This can be explained, he suggests, by the distribution of costs and benefits of the motor vehicle. As with many new inventions that bring problems as well as benefits (further examples include the railways and industrial machinery and, more recently, networked personal computers, which bring with them dangers posed by paedophiles and fraudsters), laws were passed to regulate the use of motor vehicles, with the aspiration to reduce death and injury.

Such laws, along with engineering innovations, have gone some way to achieving their aims, with the current annual death rate being just over 3,000 (there were 3,201 fatalities in 2004, down from 3,221 in 2003: DfT 2006, 16). In fact Britain, along with the other European countries of Sweden and the Netherlands (see, for example, Koornstra et al. 2002), has one of the lowest death rates from driving in the developed world. Yet death on the roads remains a problem, with 30 per cent of the deaths of young people aged 15–19 years being due to traffic collisions (DfT 2006, 127). In 1987 the government set a target to reduce road casualties by one third by 2000 (DETR 2000, 5). This target was achieved in relation to deaths and serious injuries, which fell by 39 per cent and 45 per cent respectively (ibid.). However, there was not such a dramatic drop in the number of collisions resulting in slight injuries. This suggests that reductions have been achieved through improvements in engineering, vehicle design, legislation (in the form of seat-belt laws) and medical treatment, rather than improved driver behaviour. As noted by Rothengatter, if further reductions in casualties are to be attained, it is necessary to address drivers' behaviour (Rothengatter 2002, 250).

The government has introduced a further initiative, setting new targets for casualty reductions to be achieved by 2010 (DETR 2000). This initiative recognizes Rothengatter's point that part of the solution to the problem is to produce safer drivers, a recognition that underlies two of the ten main themes in the document *Tomorrow's Roads – Safer for Everyone* (ibid.). It identifies seat-belt legislation and changes in attitudes to drink-driving as having helped reduce deaths in the past, and notes that in the wider context tackling road crime such as speeding and dangerous driving is important not only to produce further reductions, but also as an important part of the wider crime-reduction agenda (para.1.10). Following this position paper, the government conducted a review of the penalties for traffic offences (Home Office 2002), and commissioned a report on the current law on dangerous driving (Pearce et al. 2002).

Since then, the Road Traffic Act 2006 has been passed, creating new offences relating to the causing of deaths on the roads. It will be argued that the main motivation behind these reforms was misguided and, if we are to continue to reduce road traffic casualties, efforts should be concentrated on changing attitudes to driving offences generally, rather than directing punitive measures at those alone who kill. The government is right to suggest that there is a need to produce safer drivers, but the question remains as to how such an objective can be achieved. This book looks at what role the criminal law can take in achieving that objective.

Road safety policy generally relies on the three Es for its implementation: 'Engineering', 'Education' (more recently expanded to Education, Training and Publicity, or ETP: Audit Commission 2007) and law 'Enforcement'. Whilst the last of these three will be the focus of this book, one of the points to be made is that enforcement will only ever gain success if promoted alongside driver education. With that in mind, there is considerable discussion in this book of research conducted by psychologists on the issue of driver behaviour (see, in particular, Chapter 6). In contrast to the discipline of law, which has largely ignored driving offences in its research, traffic psychology as a discipline has expanded considerably since the 1980s (Rotthengatter 2002, 249), providing a wealth of information relating to attitudes of drivers and the cognitive task of driving. It is the premise of this book that such research should be used to optimum effect in considering how law enforcement can be utilized to best advantage in seeking to increase the safety rate on Britain's roads.

The first few chapters of this book examine various general driving offences. The focus here is on laws that penalize bad driving because of the risks entailed. The legislation dealing with road traffic offences has been described as 'considerable, technical and complex' (Ormerod 2005, 1005). Whilst other more specific offences exist to promote road safety, such as regulations relating to vehicle test certificates, requirements for minimum treads on tyres, construction and use regulations, vehicle lighting, driver licensing, driver hours and tachograph offences for commercial vehicle drivers and laws relating to seat belts and crash helmets, such offences can involve extremely technical issues and the concern of this book is rather with the task of driving itself, requiring a driver to maintain control of a vehicle and exercise the care of a competent and careful driver. As a result, driver offences such as driving whilst disqualified, without a licence or insurance are also ignored, with the exception of the new causing death offence under the Road Safety Act 2006. This book deals with what Steer and Carr-Hill described as 'driving' as opposed to 'dishonest' offences (Steer and Carr-Hill 1967).

As noted above, driving offences fall outside the realm of 'paradigmatic' crime. Essentially this is because although they seek to prevent physical harm, as do many more traditional offences, they lack the characteristics of paradigmatic crime. It has been suggested that there are two essential elements to paradigmatic crime:

harm and blame (Clarkson 2005, 17). Taking the requirements of some traffic offences at face value, it can be argued that they represent a double departure from this paradigm (ibid.). Driving offences do not require *mens rea* as traditionally defined, although the offences of dangerous driving and careless driving require different degrees of negligence, a more recently recognized species of *mens rea* (Clarkson et al. 2007, 169). On the other side of the equation, the offences of careless and dangerous driving, drink-driving and speeding do not require that physical harm has been caused before criminal liability can be established. They are what are known as endangerment offences, which exist to punish those who take risks, whether or not such risks result in physical harm. Risk-taking is a wrong in itself because of the possibility that it can result in harm, and can be seen as a kind of second-order harm (Gross 1979, 125). That the offences seek to punish behaviour that is wrong is essential in justifying the use of the criminal sanction in attempting to prevent bad driving, and is the issue to be addressed in Chapter 6. Research conducted by psychologists and criminologists is drawn upon to complete the picture, and comparisons with law, policy and practice in other jurisdictions are also considered. Here, the European country of Sweden has been selected for special analysis, chosen because of the excellent road safety record achieved there over recent years.

This is, however, primarily a book on law. Each of the following three chapters sets out the basic requirements contained within the relevant statutes, and examines how these have been interpreted in any existing case law. A word should be said about jurisdiction here. The law in this book is the law as it applies in England and Wales, which operates under a different criminal justice system to that of Scotland. Although statutes such as the Road Traffic Act 1988 apply in Scotland as well as England and Wales, this is not true of all the offences (particularly the common-law offence of manslaughter), and there is a different prosecution procedure north of the border. Some cases interpreting the law do originate from Scotland, however, and when providing statistics it is sometimes necessary to refer to Great Britain or the UK, including Scotland and Northern Ireland, since some of the research does not distinguish between the different jurisdictions. It should be noted that such statistics provide less accurate information than might be desired, given that they originate from a larger geographical area.

The starting point is to look at endangerment offences, or conduct crimes, which penalize risk-taking but do not require the risk to have materialized for liability to be imposed. Following on from the endangerment offences, the focus turns to result crimes. Whilst offences such as careless and dangerous driving, drink-driving and speeding are conduct crimes, which do not require any physical harm to result before a prosecution can be brought, there exist a number of homicide offences specifically created to punish those who cause death by their bad driving. Manslaughter, causing death by dangerous driving, causing death by careless driving, causing death by careless driving whilst under the influence of drink or drugs, causing death by driving whilst uninsured, unlicensed or disqualified and aggravated vehicle taking provide severe penalties for those whose driving causes death. Whether separate homicide offences are justified is one important issue for discussion, and the question of how such offences operate in practice is addressed through analysis of research results on real-life fatal collisions conducted by the author (Cunningham 2004).

## The Importance of Prosecutorial Discretion

No matter how offences are defined in statute, the way they operate in practice will depend on a number of factors. Statutory interpretation by the courts plays an obvious role, but before a case ever gets to court the discretion of lawyers working within the Crown Prosecution Service (CPS) plays a fundamental part in determining the disposal of a particular case. Although the final outcome of a case may depend not only upon the offence for which the defendant is tried but also on the decision-making of his or her peers (either a jury or a bench of magistrates, depending upon the charge), the decisions made at earlier stages of the process, before the case reaches court, can be argued to be the most important, not least due to the high rate of guilty pleas in such cases.

As Fionda points out:

> Such is the unique, central and pivotal position of the prosecutor in the structure of the criminal justice process that practice at that stage can have wide-reaching, reverberating effects on the decision-making practice of all other agencies throughout the process, both at the initial stages (that is, the police) and at the 'back door' of the system (that is, the courts, the probation service and the prison service). (Fionda 1995, 1)

This is recognized by HM CPS Inspectorate as being particularly true of cases arising from fatal road traffic collisions: 'the selection of charge is possibly more significant when dealing with road traffic fatality cases than with most other criminal cases because of the wide divergence between penalties available in respect of offences of causing death by dangerous driving and in summary offences of careless driving' (HM CPS Inspectorate 2002 para.5.11). It is the 'low visibility' decisions made at the early to mid-way stages of the criminal justice process that dictate how the law operates in practice. However, it should also be noted that the effects are reciprocal. Not only does the exercise of discretion by the prosecutor affect decisions taken by the police and courts, but decisions taken by the police, and future decisions likely to be taken by the courts, will affect the way in which the prosecutor exercises his or her discretion in any particular case. Both the police and CPS exercise considerable discretion in determining the way in which a suspect is dealt with. Their decisions are 'low visibility' because they are made privately and, although the parties involved will be informed of such decisions, they will not be party to them and will not necessarily be made aware of the reasoning behind the decision-making. No official statistics are collected providing information about the number of cases in which the police or CPS decide that charges are inappropriate.

Two documents exist to give guidance to the CPS in reaching its decisions. The first is the *Code for Crown Prosecutors*, which the Director of Public Prosecutions (DPP) is required to issue under section 10 of the Prosecution of Offences Act

1985. This document provides guidance on the general principles to be applied in exercising prosecutorial discretion and should be adhered to in all cases. It is currently in its fifth edition, published in 2004. The second document is the *Policy for Prosecuting Cases of Bad Driving*, which has recently replaced a document called the *Driving Offences Charging Standard*. The *Charging Standard* was agreed between the police and CPS, providing guidance to help police and prosecutors when deciding what offence to charge as the result of a driving incident. The new policy appears to replace the *Charging Standard* and is available online as part of Legal Guidance on the CPS website.

The aim of the guidelines provided in the *Charging Standard*, and more recently the prosecution policy, has been to produce more consistent decisions in cases of motoring offences, particularly those causing serious injury or death. The DPP in office at the time of the first publication of the *Charging Standard* welcomed it and stated that it would:

> help police and Crown Prosecutors when identifying appropriate charges to operate to a clear, shared understanding of the legal requirements which must be met and what has to be proved before a prosecution can proceed on each possible charge. This will be particularly helpful where there is a choice of which charge or charges should be brought. (CPS 1996c)

The guidance provided in the *Charging Standard* and *Policy* exists to complement the general principles in the *Code for Crown Prosecutors* and does not replace the tests therein. Specific guidance provided by the *Charging Standard* and *Policy* in relation to various offences will be referred to in the relevant chapters of this book.

The procedure for charging suspects has recently changed under the Criminal Justice Act 2003, with the introduction of a new 'statutory charging scheme' (amending the Police and Criminal Evidence Act (PACE), section 37A). The significance of this new scheme is that the responsibility for deciding what charge to bring now rests squarely with the CPS in most cases. Previously the police would normally charge suspects themselves before forwarding a file to the CPS, who would then review the file to decide whether the correct charge had been chosen. This caused considerable problems for the CPS and the criminal justice system in general, leading to a number of cases where charges were downgraded, or even dropped, because the CPS found that there was insufficient evidence to support the original charge. The aim of the new scheme is for the correct charge to be selected from the outset, with the CPS applying the legal tests contained within the *Code for Crown Prosecutors*.

Those tests are the evidential test and the public interest test. The evidential test requires that there is enough evidence to provide a 'realistic prospect of conviction' against D on the charge (CPS 2004, para.5.2). It is an objective test, which means that 'a jury or bench of magistrates, properly directed in accordance with the law, is more likely than not to convict the defendant of the charge alleged' (ibid., para.5.3). Before the *Code* was produced the previous test of evidential sufficiency applied by the police was known as the 51 per cent rule, but the Explanatory

Memorandum accompanying the third edition of the *Code* made it clear that the test should not be referred to in terms of percentages, as weighing evidence is not a precise science (CPS 1996, para.4.14). The current version of the *Code* attempts to clarify this test by emphasizing that the evidential test for Crown prosecutors is a separate test from the one that the courts themselves apply which involves a stricter test (CPS 2004, para.5.3), with conviction at court requiring that the Crown has proved its case to such a degree for the magistrates or jury 'to be sure' of the defendant's guilt (Judicial Studies Board 2007). (Note that the standard of proof was previously expressed as proof 'beyond all reasonable doubt'.)

The second test within the *Code*, which should only be applied once the evidential test is passed, is the public interest test. The *Code* states that 'a prosecution will usually take place unless there are public interest factors tending against prosecution which clearly outweigh those tending in favour, or it appears more appropriate in all the circumstances of the case to divert the person from prosecution' (CPS 2004, para.5.7). Public interest factors that are likely to have an influence on the decision usually relate to the seriousness of the offence or the characteristics of the offender (ibid., para.5.8). Two non-exhaustive lists providing examples of factors weighing for and against prosecution are given by the *Code*, although cautious use should be made of these factors, as it is made clear that the exercise of discretion does not merely require a mathematical assessment of how many factors there are in favour or against prosecution (ibid., para.5.11).

Thus, in all criminal cases the CPS must apply this guidance in the *Code for Crown Prosecutors*, and in cases involving driving offences they should additionally take heed of the guidance within the prosecution policy (formerly the *Charging Standard*). In serious cases it is now the CPS, rather than the police, who initially decide what charges to bring. The new charging scheme may not amount to a great culture change for Crown prosecutors deciding charges following a fatal road traffic collision in some areas due to there being a high degree of liaison between police and CPS already in existence (Cunningham 2005). However, in less serious cases it may be that the new scheme will not apply at all, since advice issued by the DPP states that the police may, as an exception to the general provisions within section 37A of PACE, decide to prosecute in the following circumstances, without liaison with the CPS:

> Any offence under the Road Traffic Acts or any other offence arising from the presence of a motor vehicle, trailer, or pedal cycle on a road or other public place, except where (and the charge must therefore be determined by a Crown Prosecutor):
>
> The circumstances have resulted in the death of any person; or
>
> There is an allegation of dangerous driving; or
>
> The allegation is one of driving whilst disqualified and there has been no admission in a PACE interview to both the driving and the disqualification; or
>
> The statutory defence to being in charge of a motor vehicle (unfit through drink or drugs or excess alcohol) may be raised under Section 4(3) or 5(2) of the Road Traffic Act 1988; or
>
> There is an allegation of the unlawful taking of a motor vehicle or the aggravated unlawful taking of a motor vehicle (unless the case is suitable for disposal as an early guilty plea in the magistrates' court) (DPP 2007).

The police therefore retain a large degree of discretion in many cases involving road traffic offences, not only under the statutory charging scheme but, in addition, under the fixed penalty notice system. The Road Traffic Offenders Act 1988 allows the police to divert motoring offenders away from the courts by issuing fixed penalties resulting in a fine and, in some cases, endorsement of penalty points on the offender's licence. Fixed penalty notices are not available in relation to most of the offences discussed in this book, however, with the exception of speeding.

The reason for the introduction of the statutory charging scheme under the Criminal Justice Act 2003 stemmed from Lord Justice Auld's finding that 'a significant contributor to delays in entering pleas of guilty and in identifying issues for train and, in consequence, the prolonged and disjointed nature of many criminal proceedings, is "over-charging" by the police and failure by the Crown Prosecution Service to remedy it at an early stage' (Auld 2001, 408). This concern about 'over-charging' was on-going since the Glidewell review a few years earlier, which highlighted driving offences as one particular area where this phenomenon was deemed to be prevalent. The problem with over-charging is that it leads to 'downgrading' of charges. Downgrading occurred either when the CPS decided to alter the charge made by the police, substituting a less serious charge, or when the CPS decided to accept a guilty plea to a lesser charge. Glidewell reported that, although the CPS deny that downgrading occurred due to considerations of cost, factors such as the certainty of a conviction resulting from a guilty plea and the saving of time and effort may have influenced decisions to downgrade charges (Glidewell 1998, para.46). The difficulty in researching this phenomenon is that there are no published statistics dealing with downgrading. Despite failing to reach any firm conclusions in relation to the existence of downgrading, Glidewell considered that a change in practice or even the law may be required once further research had been carried out (ibid.).

Following the Glidewell Report, HM CPS Inspectorate conducted a thorough inspection of the CPS in relation to its prosecutions in cases involving fatal road traffic collisions. Despite the earlier concerns it found a 'high standard of decision-making in the large majority of cases … [and] the vast majority of decisions not to prosecute for any criminal offence to be sound, and the overall attrition rates of cases that were prosecuted were low' (HM CPS Inspectorate 2002, para.2.3). However, it also reported that the decision-making in a small number of cases needed to be improved, although the Inspectorate was considerably less critical than might have been expected, given comments made in previous publications.

Other than HM CPS Inspectorate's review, and a report by the Transport Research Laboratory commissioned by the government (Pearce et al. 2002), little empirical research has been conducted into this area of law. The results of a study conducted by the author have been drawn upon in writing this book, since they give some insight into the operation of the law in this area. The study was conducted over the years 2001–2003, involving fatal road traffic collisions in Lincolnshire, Leicestershire and Northamptonshire that occurred in the years 1999–2000. Access was gained to police files relating to each fatal collision in which there was potential for charges to be brought because one or more of the drivers involved had survived the collision. Where charges were brought CPS files were accessed for information regarding the decision-making of prosecutors and courts. This was coupled with open-ended interviews with Crown prosecutors and police. Some of the results have been published elsewhere (Cunningham 2005; Cunningham 2007), but are used here to illustrate the issues involved in prosecuting the offences under discussion. Whilst this is useful, there is still scope for future empirical research in this area. In particular, questions persist over charging practice in relation to cases where collisions result in only non-serious injury or damage to property, or where offences are committed but luckily no harm at all results because the risk taken does not materialize in a collision. The role of the criminal law in such cases will be a theme recurring throughout this book, but the lack of evidence relating to practice in such cases means that the issue of policy should be considered particularly important.

While reading about the law in relation to each offence set out in the first part of this book, the relevance of prosecutorial discretion in deciding charges should be borne in mind. We start with the offences requiring negligence to be proven to a greater or lesser degree (dangerous driving and careless driving) in Chapter 2, before considering two offences that can be described as 'strict liability' offences (drink-driving and speeding) in Chapter 3. Chapter 4 sets out the law on the various offences that arise out of a fatal collision, before the discussion turns to extra-legal research and the experiences of achieving road safety in a Scandinavian jurisdiction. It should be noted that throughout the book the abbreviations D and V will be used. D denotes the driver at fault in a case, a potential defendant, whilst V refers to the deceased or 'victim' of any case of bad driving. The book culminates in some suggestions for law reform with a view to promoting road safety, drawing on the work of psychologists in so doing.

## Chapter 2

# Dangerous Driving and Careless Driving

The offences discussed in this chapter relate most directly to the prevention of risk-taking and the promotion of safety on the roads. Dangerous driving and careless driving are committed when a driver drives below the required standard of a competent and careful driver; the degree by which he or she fails to meet the requirement will determine which of the offences has been committed. Driving below the required standard is more likely to lead to road traffic collisions, which in turn are likely to cause injury, serious injury or death. The term 'collision' is preferred in this book to that of 'accident' because the latter implies a chance occurrence for which no-one is to blame. It is rare for collisions to be caused in such a way: although mechanical defects and factors such as road and weather conditions may contribute to collisions, the principal reason for collisions is human error. Police forces are moving away from the use of the word 'accident' and replacing it with terms such as 'collision' or, in the case of a fatal collision, 'road death incident'. For example, the guidance provided in the *Road Death Investigation Manual* used by police is based on: 'our perception that there are very few "accidents" on our roads and that most are caused by human error' (ACPO 2004, 2). The CPS are following suit, with a commitment to avoiding use of the term 'accident' and replacing it with 'collision' to refer to bad driving that results in death or serious injury (CPS 2007b, para.6.9).

The word 'accident' does, however, carry legal significance and the fact remains that the Road Traffic Act (RTA) 1988 defines legal obligations in terms of 'accident'. For example, there is a legal obligation to report an 'accident' under section 170 of the Road Traffic Act 1988. Under section 6(5) RTA 1988 a police officer has the power to administer a breath test following an 'accident'. In *Chief Constable of West Midlands Police v Billingham* (1979) it was held that 'accident' was to be given its 'popular' meaning and would include deliberate acts. The word 'accident' is also significant for procedural purposes. The offences discussed in this chapter do not require that a collision or 'accident' occurred as a result of bad driving. However, section 1 of the Road Traffic Offenders Act (RTOA) 1988 requires that a notice of intended prosecution be served on the defendant within 14 days of the commission of the offence. This requirement does not apply, however, if, at the time of the offence or immediately after it, 'an accident occurs owing to the presence on a road of the vehicle in respect of which the offence was committed' (section 2(1) RTOA 1988). In the case of *Currie* (2007) the defendant (D) appealed against his conviction for dangerous driving on the basis that the prosecution had failed to issue a notice of intended prosecution and was obliged to do so as there had been no 'accident'. The Court of Appeal dismissed his appeal. D had been stopped by police and told to get out of the car. D had done so but while the police were talking to his passengers he got back in the car and started the ignition. A police officer attempted to stop him driving away and as she did so D lurched the car forwards towards her. The officer put her hands on the car bonnet and the car again moved forwards towards her. She grabbed hold of the open passenger door but D reversed away. In upholding his conviction the Court of Appeal relied on the Scottish case of *Bemner v Westwater* (1994) in which it was said that the word 'accident' was to be given a commonsense meaning and that it was not restricted to untoward or unintended consequences having an adverse physical effect.

The first offence to be discussed in this chapter is dangerous driving, the more serious of the two offences. Although many of the cases discussed relate to the offence of causing death by dangerous driving, an offence which will be examined in Chapter 4, they are equally relevant to the underlying offence of dangerous driving in interpreting the word 'dangerous'.

## Dangerous Driving

### *Background to the Current Law*

Dangerous driving was first introduced as an offence by the Road Transport Act 1930. At that time it was a matter of contention whether the offence could be sufficiently defined (Emsley 1993, 377) and this issue has endured ever since. The law has been altered several times over the decades, with the current attempt to define the offence originating from a review of traffic offences conducted by the North Commission in1988 which led to the Road Traffic Act 1991 providing amendments to the relevant sections of the RTA 1988.

In 1988 the Road Traffic Law Review Committee headed by Peter North reviewed the existing offences penalizing bad driving. At that time the two general driving offences in existence were reckless driving, the more serious of the two and an offence under section 2 of the Road Traffic Act 1972, and careless driving, the lesser offence under section 3 of the same Act. Various problems were perceived in relation to the existing law, and it was concluded that 'the criminal justice system taken as a whole was not satisfactorily meeting public requirements as regards very bad driving' (Department of Transport 1988, para.4.11).

It was concluded that the structure of bad driving offences should remain the same, namely that there should be two general bad driving offences of different seriousness. Suggestions rejected by the Review included the idea of having one broad offence of bad driving, leaving it to the discretion of the judge to sentence according to the seriousness of an individual case. This was rejected on the basis that it could lead to more inconsistency in sentencing and for the pragmatic reason that it would necessitate trial by jury for every case (ibid., paras.4.15–4.16). At the other extreme it was suggested that a detailed list of specific offences, similar to the rules of the Highway Code and laws of some states in the United States, be introduced. It was recognized that such offences might be easier to prove, but the problem as the Review saw it was that such offences would not obviate the need for general bad driving offences (ibid., para.4.19).

Once the Review had decided to maintain the structure of the law with two general bad driving offences, it faced the task of deciding what those offences should be and how they should be defined. Some suggested that the old offence of dangerous driving, in force prior to the Road Traffic Act 1977, should be reinstated. The Review rejected this on the basis that the old law required the courts merely to look at the nature of the dangerousness of the driving irrespective of whether the conduct of D could be considered blameworthy (ibid., para.5.3).

Conversely, the main problem with the offence of reckless driving was identified as being that to prove recklessness it was necessary to establish what had gone through D's mind at the time of the offence and this was often too difficult. This was required by the test for recklessness laid down in the case of *Lawrence* (1982). This species of 'objective' recklessness has been particularly controversial within the criminal field, and has recently suffered a considerable blow with the case of *G and Another* (2004) reinstating 'subjective' *Cunningham* (1957) recklessness as the required *mens rea* for the offence of criminal damage. In *Lawrence* Lord Diplock laid down the following test for reckless driving:

> First, that the defendant was in fact driving the vehicle in such a manner as to create an obvious and serious risk of causing physical injury to some other person who might happen to be using the road or of doing substantial damage to property; and
>
> Second, that in driving in that manner the defendant did so without having given any thought to the possibility of there being any such risk or, having recognized that there was some risk involved, had nonetheless gone on to take it. (*Lawrence* 1982, 526–7)

It was the second part of this two-part test that caused problems in relation to the offence of reckless driving, since it required proof of the defendant's state of mind at the time of the offence. Thus, unlike the general criticisms of the species of recklessness levelled at it by subjectivists and the House of Lords in *G and Another* that it is wrong to criminalize conduct on the basis of an objective test, in the road traffic sphere it was argued that the test was in fact too subjective to be workable. A purely objective test, where the defendant's state of mind is inconsequential, was preferred by the North Report. The question was then how to construct such a test.

The North Review rejected a number of proposals put forward by other bodies. The Criminal Law Revision Committee's idea of an offence of 'driving in such a way as to show complete disregard for the life and safety of other persons' (CLRC 1980, para.146) was rejected on the basis that the test would be too subjective because of the inclusion of the word 'disregard' (Department of Transport 1988, para.5.17). A proposal which the Review considered contained more merit was that of the Law Commission in its suggestion of an offence of 'driving with criminal negligence' (Law Commission 1985, para.8.24), using the definition of 'criminal negligence' in its draft Criminal Code (Clause 11b). In defining criminal negligence as conduct which is 'a very serious deviation from the standard of care to be expected of a reasonable person' the proposal was seen as having the advantages of being a purely objective test, not being linked to any particular circumstances or results and of indicating what conduct falls within the offence in relation to the general standard (Department of Transport 1988, para.5.19). However, the proposal was rejected on the basis that, firstly, the requirement of a 'serious deviation' might result in some examples of bad driving not being included in the offence and, secondly, it was not clear whether it would include cases involving risk of damage to property as well as to the person and dangers from the state of the vehicle rather than the way in which the vehicle was driven (ibid., para.5.20).

Although *Lawrence* applied in England and Wales, a different approach was taken in Scotland. Since there was much less dissatisfaction with the law in Scotland the North Review used the test in the leading case of *Allen v Patterson* (1980) as a source of inspiration for its proposal. Thus the Review's proposal for an offence of 'very bad driving' was that the new definition should be objective, asking the question 'was the driving really bad?', that it should convey the idea of a serious fall from an accepted norm of behaviour in using the phrase from Scottish law of falling 'far below the standard of driving expected of the competent and careful driver', and that it should necessitate consideration of the quality of driving in relation to the particular circumstances in which it occurred, i.e. 'how would the competent and careful driver have behaved in these circumstances?' (ibid., para.5.22). Because the law had operated successfully in Scotland no consideration seems to have been given to the question of who the competent and careful driver is and whether s/he is recognisable to ordinary members of the driving public. In settling on the definition the Review failed to answer its own criticisms of the other proposals it had considered. If it was concerned that the Law Commission's inclusion of the term 'serious deviation' might exclude from the offence such conduct which it thought ought to be included, why did it think that the same problem would not occur with its own suggestion of a requirement that the driving fell 'far below' a particular standard? Both proposals imply that there is an agreed, accepted and identifiable standard of driving, but find it difficult to define how far removed from such a standard an offence of very bad driving would have to be.

### *The Current Law*

Following the North Report the government published a White Paper entitled The *Road User and the Law* in 1989, leading to the Road Traffic Act 1991. Section 2 states:

> A person who drives a mechanically propelled vehicle dangerously on a road or other public place is guilty of an offence.

This offence is triable either way, meaning that it can be tried at the magistrates' court or at the Crown Court, depending on the seriousness of the particular case.

The prosecution must first of all establish that D was driving. In most cases this will be straightforward, as long as the identity of the driver is clear. In *Attorney-General's Reference (No. 4 of 2000)* a bus driver tried to argue that he was not 'driving' for the purposes of the offence of causing death by dangerous driving (CDDD) when he mistakenly put his foot on the accelerator instead of the brake. His contention was that this was an involuntary act so that he could not be deemed to be 'driving'. At his trial the judge directed the jury to acquit him of CDDD, but the Attorney-General referred the issue as a point of law to the Court of Appeal. The question for the court was 'whether, if a driver causes a vehicle to behave in a most dangerous manner, as this vehicle did, due to his unintentionally pressing the wrong pedal (albeit because of the arrangement of the pedals), is he to be taken still to be driving that vehicle for the purposes of the offence under the Road Traffic Act?' (*A-G's Ref. (No. 4 of 2000)*, para.11).

The Court of Appeal held that it was clear that D was driving. He was conscious of the act his body was performing, and whilst it may have been an unintended action that fact was not relevant to the statutory definition of the offence: 'As we understand the offence of dangerous driving, it is intended to cover occurrences where a driver has made a mistake of this nature' (ibid., para.21). Such a mistake was similarly made by D in the case of *Cambray* (2007) – where D, a learner driver, drove over a kerb 20 cm high and on to a beach, killing a young child – when he claimed that his foot slipped from the brake to the accelerator as he was attempting to park the car. In that case a conviction for CDDD was upheld.

Secondly, the driving must have been of a mechanically propelled vehicle. The leading practitioner text, *Wilkinson's Road Traffic Offences*, notes that the term 'mechanically propelled' is far wider than the previous one used of 'motor vehicle', as it may include vehicles (for example, dumpers and digging machines) not intended for use on the road but that might nevertheless become a danger to other road users (Wallis et al. 2005, para.5.14).

For driving to amount to dangerous driving it must have taken place 'on a road or other public place'. In *Spence* (1999) it was recognized that there is no statutory definition of 'public place', but the Court of Appeal held that the words should be interpreted as being of the same nature as the definition of 'road' within section 192(1) RTA 1988, namely 'any highway and any other road to which the public has access'. The question of whether the public has access is one, the court opined, that depends on there being evidence that the public utilized access to the place in question, and does not depend on the presence or absence of physical obstruction or a notice forbidding entry. In this case a car park in which D had driven was used by employers, customers and other business visitors who formed a 'special class' set apart from the general public, and D's conviction was quashed.

*The meaning of 'dangerous'* According to section 2A of the Road Traffic Act (RTA) 1988, as amended by the 1991 Act, a person is to be regarded as driving dangerously if:

a) the way he drives falls far below what would be expected of a competent and careful driver; and
b) it would be obvious to a competent and careful driver that driving in that way would be dangerous.

'Dangerous' in this context refers to a danger of injury to any person or of serious damage to property (section 2A(3)).

Little guidance has been given by the courts on how bad driving must be before it is considered 'dangerous'. In *Conteh* (2004), for example, D moved into a bus lane to pass a line of traffic in preparation to turn left a short distance ahead. He was driving at about 20 mph in a 30 mph limit. Before the turn there was a pelican crossing, the lights for which were showing green for D. However, out of sight to his off side the deceased (V) and her friend were crossing the road, despite the lights showing red against them. A van in the offside lane had stopped in the slow-moving traffic to let them cross, and they walked directly into the path of D. At trial the prosecution alleged that D had been driving dangerously because he should not have moved into the bus lane, because he was driving too fast for the prevailing road conditions and faster than the traffic in the offside lane and because he took a calculated risk in approaching the pelican crossing along the nearside of the stationary van when he could not be sure that somebody would not cross it. The Court of Appeal quashed the conviction, opining that the judge should have upheld the defence submission of no case to answer.

The court emphasized that dangerous driving involves a high threshold and that the judge should direct the jury that mere breach of the Highway Code does not itself constitute the offence of dangerous driving. This ruling highlights the statement in the Road Traffic Act (RTA) 1988, section 38(7), that:

> A failure on the part of a person to observe a provision of the Highway Code shall not itself render that person liable to criminal proceedings of any kind but any such failure may in any proceedings … be relied upon by any party to the proceedings as tending to establish or negative any liability which is in question in those proceedings.

In *Conteh* the conviction for CDDD was quashed, with the Court commenting that if V had not died it suspected that the prosecution would not have considered a charge of dangerous driving. In another case where D had been drinking and overtook on the brow of a hill in contravention of double white lines in the centre of the road, resulting in a collision with V's car travelling in the opposite direction, D appealed against his conviction for CDDD on the basis that the judge had been wrong to include the Highway Code as the standard by which the jury could assess the definition of a competent and careful driver (*Taylor* 2004). The Court of Appeal upheld the conviction, satisfied that the judge had made appropriate reference to section 38(7) of the RTA 1988. *Wilkinson's Road Traffic Offences* describes the Highway Code as the 'best *guide* for those engaged in dangerous and careless driving cases' (Wallis et al. 2005, para.5.69).

*An objective test* The test involves comparing D to the 'competent and careful driver', someone who might have been referred to as the 'reasonable man' in the past but, as noted in *Wilkinson's*: 'In this age of personal transport the man on the Clapham omnibus appears finally to have given way to his more affluent successor, the man on the North Circular' (Wallis et al. 2005, para.5.05). This description is inaccurate to the extent that the 'competent and careful driver' is just as likely to be a woman as a man and the gender of the suspect is as irrelevant here as it is for most offences. It is true, however, that far more men than women are guilty of driving offences (see Chapter 6).

Other characteristics of the driver are equally immaterial. If a driver is suffering from any impairment or disability that he or she knows could result in the creation of an obvious and serious risk, this acts as evidence of dangerous driving (*Marison* 1997), and will not mitigate the defendant's position as it might do in relation to other criminal offences. In *Marison* D was a diabetic who had suffered several hypoglycaemic attacks rendering him unconscious. A few months before the fatal collision he had been involved in another crash, and ten days before the fatal collision a doctor had been called out to see him at night. The doctor found him to be hypoglycaemic and advised him to contact his surgery for a review of his treatment. On the day of the fatal collision D suffered another attack as he was driving, causing his car to veer across the road into the path of another vehicle, the driver of which died. At trial the judge was asked to rule on whether this could amount to dangerous driving. The judge ruled that it was, and D subsequently changed his plea to guilty of CDDD. D later appealed, arguing that the judge had been wrong to make such a ruling. The Court of Appeal dismissed his appeal on the basis that he had driven in a dangerously defective state, knowing that he might have a hypoglycaemic attack at any moment.

This case was distinguished in *Gilbert* (2006), where a different conclusion was reached. D also suffered a hypoglycaemic episode while driving, causing a fatal collision. In this case it was noted that Type 1 diabetes sufferers were advised to check their blood sugar levels prior to a journey, but the court thought it was unrealistic to expect them to be checked prior to *every* journey. The Court of Appeal ruled that the judge was right to find no case to answer since, unlike *Marison*, D had not been experiencing hypoglycaemic attacks in the run-up to the collision and had no reason to think that she was a danger to other road users. Here it is the doctrine of prior fault that comes into play. One can view cases like this in one of two ways. Either the D in *Gilbert* was not guilty because she did not drive dangerously; she had no reason to believe that it would be dangerous for her to drive on that occasion. Alternatively one can say that she did in fact drive below the standard of the competent and careful driver, since no driver would lose control of their vehicle and veer across the carriageway into on-coming traffic but, although the *actus reus* of the offence is made out, D is not liable because she can rely on the general defence of automatism.

If D's physical movement in driving a vehicle can be said to be involuntary, with D retaining no control over D's actions, D may be able to plead the defence of automatism. The classic example of such a case is that of a driver who is attacked by a swarm of bees, 'so that he is for the time being disabled and prevented from exercising any directional control over the vehicle, and any movements of his arms and legs are solely caused by the action of the bees' (*Hill v Baxter* 1958, 286). A variant of this scenario was put forward by the defendant in *Moses* (2004), in which a bus driver mounted a pavement and killed a child. D pleaded not guilty to CDDD on the basis that a wasp had flown into the cab and he was attempting to wave it away and did not notice that his bus had veered from its path. The prosecution rejected this version of events and claimed that D had become annoyed at a van driver who had pulled in front of him. Whether or not the jury accepted D's story is not clear, but they convicted him of CDDD nevertheless. The prosecution had suggested that even if D's account were true, the appropriate course of action for D would have been to stop the bus and deal with the wasp, rather than drive along without looking where he was going. The Court of Appeal rejected D's application to appeal.

As seen in *Gilbert*, a more likely cause of involuntary action when driving is the effect of a hypoglycaemic attack caused by diabetes. However, for such a defence to be successful, D must not be at fault in inducing such automatism. Thus in *Davies*, although D lost control of his vehicle as a result of a hypoglycaemic attack, D was unable to plead automatism successfully because it was said that he was at fault in not eating properly and failing to maintain his blood sugar levels, and that the collision could have been avoided if he had stopped driving when he first experienced the symptoms. This explains the ruling of the court in *Marison*, where D drove knowing that there was a strong likelihood that he may suffer a hypoglycaemic attack. It was held that this was not a case of automatism because D had committed the offence of dangerous driving before the attack took place, since he had driven when a hypoglycaemic attack was reasonably foreseeable. Similarly, sleep cannot be relied upon as the basis of an automatism plea if D continues to drive when feeling sleepy and subsequently falls asleep at the wheel of his vehicle, since D's failure to stop constitutes the fault necessary to convict D of careless or dangerous driving (*Kay v Butterworth* (1945); *Henderson v Jones* (1955)).

Thus, whilst the driver who is asleep or suffering a hypoglycaemic episode was not at fault at the time of any collision, the fact that driving is an ongoing act means that the courts may look at D's behaviour at an earlier stage and judge whether D was to blame for the bad driving. Where D consciously took the risk of driving knowing that D might become impaired during the journey, or was negligent in preventing the condition that impaired D's driving, D should not be able to rely on the defence of automatism. Where there was no prior fault, on the other hand, D should escape liability. It should be noted that drivers are under a duty to disclose any relevant disability to the Driver Vehicle Licensing Agency (DVLA), and commit an offence under section 94 of the RTA 1988 if they fail to do so without reasonable excuse.

Other cases invoking the doctrine of prior fault include those where D takes drugs and drives under the influence of those drugs. Drink-driving is to be considered in the following chapter, but the ingestion of intoxicants may also be relevant to the offence of dangerous driving. This was confirmed in *McBride* in which Ashworth J stated: 'if a driver is adversely affected by drink, this fact is a circumstance relevant to the issue whether he was driving dangerously. Evidence to this effect is of probative value and is admissible in law' (*McBride* 1962, 172). He went on to qualify this point: such evidence is only probative and therefore admissible if it shows that the amount of drink taken was such as would adversely affect a driver or that the driver was in fact adversely affected. This was applied by the Court of Appeal in *Woodward* (1995) where there was witness evidence that D had been seen with a glass in his hand prior to driving, but no further evidence available to the court about the amount drunk or the level of alcohol in his blood. Here D's conviction for CDDD was quashed. Whilst evidence of consumption of an unquantifiable amount of alcohol is not admissible in a prosecution for dangerous driving, the same is not true of Class A drugs. In *Pleydell* (2006) D lost control of the car he was driving and collided with a parked car, killing his passenger. D was found to have traces of cocaine in his blood, despite a denial from D that he had taken the drug prior to driving. The Court of Appeal distinguished the consumption of Class A drugs from that of alcohol on the basis that although consumption of a small amount of alcohol before driving is permissible, no amount of cocaine can be taken safely before driving since the drug has a tendency or capacity to impair driving ability. It was, therefore, right that the jury should be given access to evidence that D had consumed cocaine as this was relevant to the issue of driving dangerously and D's conviction was upheld.

Ormerod notes that this last case, along with the earlier cases relating to consumption of alcohol, raise 'interesting questions about the logic and coherence of the courts' approaches to the admissibility of intoxicants in these serious driving offences' (Ormerod 2006, 426). On the one hand, the test for dangerous driving is an objective one and it is D's driving that must be assessed by the jury (or magistrates) in objective terms, not the possible causes of D's bad driving. On the other hand, if the courts are to consider those causes as relevant, it is difficult to sustain the distinction they have made between evidence of alcohol intake, for which there must be clear evidence of the amount consumed, and illegal drug intake, for which evidence of any amount of drug ingestion is permitted. Given that any consumption of alcohol may affect driving ability to a greater or lesser extent, Ormerod questions the logic behind the rule that unquantified alcohol consumption is irrelevant (ibid.). The danger is that the admission of evidence of alcohol or drug consumption, which may have impaired D's driving, might lead the jury to conclude that D is guilty of dangerous driving without having regard to the standard of driving D actually displayed. This would turn a crime of negligence into one of strict liability in cases involving alcohol or drugs, and this was certainly not the intention of the North Review when proposing the offence. Thus, the courts must be careful to decide the degree of evidence of intoxicants consumed to be allowed to go to the jury whilst also providing clear directions to the jury about the relevance of that evidence. It is not clear that the courts have yet found this balance.

These cases on impaired drivers suggest a watering down or chipping away at the objective test within s2 RTA 1988 which has taken a worrying turn in the case of *Milton*. This case has a long history and its full impact on the law of dangerous driving is yet to be seen. The case involved PC Milton, a police officer trained to Grade I advanced driver level, who drove an unmarked police car at grossly excessive speeds. On a motorway he drove at an average speed of 148 mph, where the limit was 70 mph; on a trunk road he drove at an average of 114 mph, where the limit was 60 mph; within a built up area he drove at 60 mph, in a 30 mph limit. These speeds were not reached in pursuit of a known suspect, or to reach the scene of an emergency as quickly as possible. The reason D gave for the speed was that he needed to familiarize himself with the vehicle, which he had not driven before.

D was charged with dangerous driving and acquitted at the magistrates' court. The Director of Public Prosecutions (DPP) appealed to the High Court and the appeal was successful. The case was reheard by District Judge Wallis, editor of the principal practitioner's book on traffic law: *Wilkinson's Road Traffic Offences*. DJ Wallis, an expert in the area, convicted D of dangerous driving, although he then sentenced him to an absolute discharge. D in turn appealed to the High Court, which gave its judgment on 16 March 2007. D's conviction was quashed.

At the magistrates' court DJ Wallis had referred to the Government's intention, made clear within the White Paper, *The Road User and the Law*, that the test for dangerous driving should be judged in absolute terms, taking no account of factors such as inexperience, age or disability, and stated that 'exceptional ability is no more relevant than lack of ability' (quoted in *Milton v DPP* 2007 at para.11). He noted that the speed had to be considered in the context of all the circumstances and found that D's driving had fallen far below the standard to be expected of a competent and careful driver and it would have been obvious to a competent and careful driver that PC Milton's driving was dangerous. The basis of the appeal was that PC Milton's special skills as an advanced police driver should be considered as relevant factors when assessing the dangerousness of his driving.

Smith LJ's judgment that DJ Wallis had misdirected himself stem from her interpretation of section 2A(3) RTA 1988, which in explaining the meaning of 'dangerous' states that:

> In subsections (1) and (2) above, 'dangerous' refers to danger either of injury to any person or of serious damage to property; and in determining for the purposes of those subsections what would be expected of, or obvious to, a competent and careful driver in a particular case, regard shall be had not only to the circumstances of which he could be expected to be aware but also to any circumstances shown to have been within the knowledge of the accused.

In the earlier case of *Collins* (1997) another police driver had attempted to rely upon this section to defend a prosecution for CDDD. In this case D had been in pursuit of a suspected stolen car and crossed a junction against a red light at a speed approaching 100 mph. D argued that it was reasonable for him to drive through the junction as he believed that it was being controlled by other police vehicles, as had been the case at junctions earlier in the pursuit, and that the standard of driving against which his driving should be compared was that of a competent and careful police driver engaged in the course of his duties in legitimate pursuit of a suspected offender, rather than that of just a competent and careful driver. The Court of Appeal ruled that D's belief at the time was irrelevant and dismissed the appeal.

In *Milton*, however, Smith LJ took the wording of section 2A(3) to signify that the government had departed from its original position in the White Paper that dangerous driving should be judged in absolute terms, and that it was therefore wrong and misleading of DJ Wallis to have referred to the White Paper. Section 2A(3) should, she opined, be interpreted to mean that both adverse and favourable circumstances can be taken into account. If it is incumbent on the court in a particular case to take account of D's knowledge that D might suffer a hypoglycaemic attack behind the wheel then it is also necessary to consider the fact that D was an advanced police driver. The question in *Milton* was whether it was dangerous for an advanced police driver to drive at such excessive speed. It might be the case that even for an advanced driver such actions could be considered dangerous or, alternatively, that whereas it would be considered dangerous for a driver of ordinary skill, for a driver of exceptional skill it was not. However, Smith LJ was keen to stress that to allow such circumstances to be taken into account 'does not offend against the requirement that the test for dangerous driving is objective. It simply refines the objective test by reference to existing circumstances' (*Milton v DPP* 2007, para.27).

The Crown in *Milton* had argued that to allow D's advanced driving skills to be taken into account would open the floodgates for the court to have to consider the degree of experience and skill possessed by all drivers accused of dangerous driving. Smith LJ refuted this concern and argued that it will only be in cases where driving experience lies at the extremes of the spectrum from 'special skill' to 'almost complete lack of experience' that it will be relevant. It seems rather optimistic to think that this will not take up extra court time in considering the issue, however. It seems more likely that given the precedent set in *Milton* drivers will take every opportunity to defend their case on the basis of their prior driving record (where good), and also perceivable that the prosecution will seek to rely on evidence of bad driving record in arguing its case.

*Dangerousness due to the condition of the vehicle* Driving is not only 'dangerous' because of the manner in which the task is carried out or the condition of the driver; it may also be 'dangerous' due to the condition of the vehicle that is being driven. According to section 2A(2) RTA 1988:

> A person is also to be regarded as driving dangerously for the purposes of sections 1 and 2 above if it would be obvious to a competent and careful driver that driving the vehicle in its current state would be dangerous.

This covers both the mechanical state of the vehicle and the way in which anything is attached to or carried on the vehicle (section 2A(4)). If a prosecution for dangerous driving is founded on the premise that the vehicle itself was inherently dangerous this must be due to some alteration to the vehicle or lack of maintenance; it does not include the manufactured condition of the vehicle (*Marchant and Muntz* 2004).

An example of a case argued on the basis of the way in which a load was attached to the vehicle is *Few* (2005), in which bails of hay fell off D's lorry, causing minor injuries to pedestrians. The prosecution argued that if D had secured the bales properly they would not have fallen off. The fact that they had fallen off suggested in itself that D's act was inherently dangerous. The Court of Appeal rejected this reasoning, however. D had secured the bales in the same way as he had been doing for the past 25 years without incident, and had never been told during visits by the Health and Safety Executive that the system he employed for securing the bales was unsafe. The Court of Appeal quashed D's conviction on the basis that it was perverse to hold that the system was dangerous since if it had been obviously unsafe some incident would have occurred before the present one.

In the case of *Strong* (1995) the words 'obvious at a glance' were used to explain to the jury the test of dangerousness in this context, and have been adopted in subsequent cases. Interestingly, the Court of Appeal in *Marsh* (2002) made it clear that the test of dangerousness in section 2A(2) is entirely separate to the test for dangerous driving under section 2A(1). It is not necessary to consider whether D's act of driving with the vehicle in the current state fell far below the standard of the competent and careful driver. It is only necessary to consider whether it would be obvious to the competent and careful driver that driving the vehicle in its current state would be dangerous. Here, in considering the test of being obvious 'at first glance' used in *Strong,* the court stressed that 'obvious' should be given it's ordinary meaning and that judges should not attempt to define it further.

The requirement is clearly that a driver with no particular expertise would have realized that the vehicle or its load was dangerous. The jury need not hear evidence from experts as to the way in which a particular piece of machinery or load should have been maintained or secured, but often expert evidence is provided in court to help the jury reach their decision. However, section 2A(3) makes it clear that if D has special knowledge about the vehicle in question, this should be attributed to the competent and careful driver for the purposes of the test.

The version of the offence of dangerous driving under section 2A(2) may be committed by accomplices, as well as the driver of the vehicle. Where a vehicle is owned by the employer of a driver and it is the employer who has responsibility for its upkeep it may be that the employer can be held liable for procuring or counselling an offence of dangerous driving. However, the issue here is whether the driver (employee) is also liable for the offence. The employer can only be liable for procuring dangerous driving if the offence of dangerous driving has been committed. This will depend on whether it should have been obvious to D that the vehicle was in a dangerous state. It may be that it was not obvious to D and would not have been obvious to a competent and careful driver that there was something wrong with the vehicle. The problem is that, even where the employer knows that there is a problem with the vehicle and should have taken it off the road for proper maintenance, he or she cannot be held liable for dangerous driving if the employee did not also have knowledge of the fault.

This is the position following the case of *Loukes* (1996). D's employer, L, who was responsible for overseeing the maintenance and servicing of vehicles, had been informed by another driver that there was a strange noise coming from a particular tipper truck. L had told the driver that it would be serviced during the following week and did no more about it. On the day when the service was due, D was driving the truck when a part of the prop shaft broke free and killed a driver travelling in the opposite direction. The evidence at trial suggested that an examination of the underside of the vehicle would have revealed defects and it would have been obvious that there was a danger of that part breaking free and causing an accident. This was, however, unconnected to the whining noise heard by the other driver.

D was prosecuted for CDDD and L was prosecuted for aiding, abetting, counselling or procuring CDDD. However, the judge withdrew the case against D from the jury. His basis for doing so was that although D had committed the *actus reus* of the offence he had no *mens rea*. He identified the *actus reus* of dangerous driving as being 'driving a motor vehicle on a road in a dangerous state' in section 2A(2) of the RTA 1988. The *mens rea* was denoted by the requirement that it would be obvious to a competent and careful driver that driving the vehicle in its current state would be dangerous. L, on the other hand, could be convicted of CDDD because it was open to the jury to decide that he did have the necessary *mens rea* under subsections 2A(2) and (3) because if he did not know of the state of the vehicle he *should*, as the person responsible for maintaining the vehicle, have known of the fault.

The Court of Appeal, however, did not agree with the judge's analysis of the law. The court was of the view that the requirement of 'obviousness' within section 2A(2) is a constituent of the *actus reus* of dangerous driving. In fact, it was held, the offence of dangerous driving is an absolute offence with no requirement of *mens rea* at all. Thus, if D did not meet all the requirements of the offence, and all the requirements of the offence amount to its *actus reus*, he could not be said to have committed the *actus reus* of the offence. If D had not committed the *actus reus* than there was no offence that L could have aided, abetted, counselled or procured. L's conviction for CDDD was therefore quashed.

*Loukes* was applied in the case of *Roberts* (1997) where D was the driver of a tipper truck owned by R. A wheel became detached and hit another vehicle, killing the driver. D had, in accordance with R's instructions, carried out a visual inspection of the wheels every day and physically checked the wheel nuts every week. The Court of Appeal suggested that, in deciding whether the defect would have been obvious to a competent and careful driver, generally speaking it would be wrong to expect D to do more than he was instructed to do, provided that the instructions were apparently reasonable. D could not have been expected to do more than R had told him to do in this case; if the defect was not obvious to him in carrying out these checks he could not be guilty of dangerous driving. Because he was not guilty then neither could R be held guilty. Even if the jury thought that the instructions R gave to D were inadequate and that a more rigorous maintenance system should have been in place, R could not be held liable if D had not committed the offence.

These cases are important in categorizing dangerous driving as a strict liability offence. Arguably they are wrong to do so and the trial judge in *Loukes* was correct in his analysis of the offence in dividing it into *actus reus* and *mens rea* elements. In his commentary to *Roberts* Smith argues that it is certainly better argued as an offence of negligence rather than one of strict liability, although he advises against judges using such terminology in court. The author of this book agrees that dangerous driving is a crime of negligence; it is not enough that D drove in such a way that a risk to other road users was created thereby. This view seems to be supported by recent proposals in the area of gross negligence manslaughter and corporate manslaughter, where the terminology of 'falling below the standard that can be expected' of a person or company in the circumstances has been adopted as a replacement for the current offence of gross negligence manslaughter, which is clearly not an offence of strict liability (Home Office 2000a; Corporate Manslaughter and Corporate Homicide Act 2007, section 1).

The result of cases such as *Loukes* also has a negative impact on the law for policy reasons. It was noted *per curiam* in *Loukes* that if the interpretation given to the law in that case was correct, 'a person who, knowing of the dangerous state of a vehicle, procured another innocent of that dangerous state, to drive it, and where there was no evidence that that state would have been obvious to a competent and careful driver, would escape conviction' (*Loukes* 1996, 445). Whilst it is arguable that *Loukes* is in fact wrong, it has been accepted in subsequent cases. Whether the House of Lords, as a superior authority, would agree with this position is yet to be seen, but in the meantime the Court of Appeal has suggested that the injustice resulting from its interpretation would need to be cured by legislation (ibid.). That it is an injustice is clear; those responsible for the maintenance of vehicles who fail in that duty and cause danger to other road users by allowing a vehicle in a dangerous state to be driven on the roads should not avoid conviction on a technicality. If the law is to encourage safe maintenance of vehicles it seems clear that either new legislation or an alternative judicial interpretation of the current law is needed. In the case of a fatal collision it may now be possible to prosecute an employer company for corporate manslaughter under the Corporate Manslaughter and Corporate Homicide Act 2007 where those in senior management were aware of a defect to the vehicle involved (see Chapter 4).

### *Defences*

The defence of automatism (involuntary conduct) has already been discussed above. Another common-law defence that could be available to a driver charged with dangerous driving, or any other driving offence, is duress of circumstances. In fact duress of circumstances, a relatively modern development within the criminal law, has emerged primarily through the law on driving offences. In the early days of the defence it was sometimes referred to as the defence of 'necessity', but in more recent times this label has been replaced by one of 'duress of circumstances'. Whether 'necessity' and 'duress of circumstances' are the same thing is a moot point (see, for example, Clarkson 2004), but the Court of Appeal has on at least one occasion treated them as one and the same (*Shayler* 2001). The term 'necessity' was used in one of the first cases recognizing such a defence in relation to driving offences (*Willer* 1987). In this case D drove onto the pavement in order to escape a gang of men who were attacking his passengers, and was convicted of reckless driving for so doing. In quashing his conviction, Watkins LJ held that it should have been left to the jury to decide whether the defendant should be able successfully to plead a defence. This defence was also referred to as 'duress' by which the appellant 'was wholly driven by force of circumstances into doing what he did and did not drive the car otherwise than under that form of compulsion' (*Willer* 1987 at 25).

The label of 'duress of circumstances' was then given to the defence by the Court of Appeal in *Conway* (1989) in applying *Willer* to another case of reckless driving. In *Martin* (1989), a case of driving whilst disqualified, it was held that the defence is available if, from an objective standpoint, D can be said to have acted reasonably in order to avoid a threat of death or serious injury.

### *Sentencing*

Dangerous driving is a triable either way offence. If tried at the Crown Court, the maximum penalty is two years' imprisonment; at the magistrates' court it is six months' imprisonment (although this may rise to twelve months if and when section 154 Criminal Justice Act 2003 is brought into force to increase the sentencing powers of magistrates). In addition to any term of imprisonment, disqualification from driving is mandatory.

In the case of *Stokes* (1998) the defendant, who was running late, had driven through the red light of a pelican crossing and collided with two nine-year-old pedestrians, who had suffered serious injuries. D accepted that he was guilty of careless driving, but contested the charge of dangerous driving on the basis that his driving had not fallen *far* below the standard of a competent and careful driver. He was convicted at the Crown Court and sentenced to twelve months' imprisonment and disqualified from driving for three years. D was previously of good character and had a clean licence. The Court of Appeal noted that there were no aggravating factors with regards to D's driving, and that it was a single piece of bad driving. However, the judge had been entitled to take into account the consequences of the bad driving, which were lucky not to have been fatal. However, because the criminality of the driving was 'very much at the bottom end of the scale' (*Stokes* 1998, 285), D's sentence was quashed and replaced with a sentence of eight months' imprisonment and two years' disqualification.

Research by Pearce gives some indication of the sorts of sentences dangerous driving offenders can expect to receive. In a questionnaire of convicted offenders 91 per cent were disqualified from driving, with 52 per cent having to take an extended retest before regaining their licence (Pearce 2004, 31). Fifteen per cent received a prison sentence and two per cent a suspended sentence (ibid.). Fifty-nine per cent of offenders found their sentence to be more severe than expected (ibid.) and 30 per cent lost their job as a result of their penalty (ibid., 32).

*Policy*

Whether the law comes to be applied by the courts as described in the above section will depend on a number of factors, not least the exercise of discretion by Crown prosecutors in their choice of charge. No matter how an offence is defined in statute, the way in which it operates in practice will depend on how those involved in the criminal justice system interpret the requirements, informed by experience and policy imposed from a superior level. The CPS *Policy for Prosecuting Cases of Bad Driving* has recently been published, having undergone a public consultation exercise. This document replaces the previous *Charging Standard* and is incorporated into the online Legal Guidance on Road Traffic Offences. It provides the following as examples of what the CPS is likely to regard as dangerous driving:

- racing or competitive driving;
- speed, which is highly inappropriate for the prevailing road or traffic conditions;
- aggressive driving, such as sudden lane changes, cutting into a line of vehicles, or driving much too close to the vehicle in front;
- disregard of traffic lights and other road signs, which, on an objective analysis, would appear to be deliberate;
- disregard of warnings from fellow passengers;
- overtaking which could not have been carried out safely;
- driving a vehicle with a load which presents a danger to other road users;
- where the driver is suffering from impaired ability, such as having an arm or leg in plaster, or impaired eyesight;
- driving when too tired to stay awake;
- driving a vehicle knowing it has a dangerous defect;
- using a hand-held mobile phone or other hand-held electronic equipment when the driver was avoidably and dangerously distracted by that use;
- reading a newspaper/map;
- talking to and looking at a passenger where the driver was avoidably and dangerously distracted by that;
- selecting and lighting a cigarette, or similar, in circumstances where the driver was avoidably and dangerously distracted by that. (CPS 2007b, para.5.27)

Of these, the last three examples have been added to the list since the public consultation was completed. Previously they had appeared as examples of behaviour that would lead to a charge of careless driving, showing that there has been a shift in attitudes in relation to the behaviour that is deemed serious enough to support a charge of dangerous driving. The CPS was aware of this possibility at the time that it consulted on its policy: ‘It is important to recognize that what society deems acceptable or “careless” may change over the years and come to be considered as “dangerous”’ (CPS 2006, para.133). The CPS specifically asked respondents to consider whether momentary inattention and single misjudgements and speed resulting in a collision should be considered as careless or dangerous (ibid., 23–5). These are areas which, as will be seen below, have caused prosecutors particular difficulties in practice.

The charging policy gives the following guidance on whether speeding should be charged as dangerous driving:

> Evidence of excess speed is another example of this. Where there is evidence of grossly excessive speed, or speed which, although not grossly excessive, is dangerous as a result of the prevailing road conditions, a charge of dangerous driving may be appropriate. Each case will be reviewed according to its particular facts. (CPS 2007b, para.5.42)

The policy stresses that in all cases prosecutors will have to apply the examples according to the circumstances of the particular case, but in response to potential criticism that providing any examples is unhelpful because it may lead prosecutors slavishly to follow the guidance without taking each case on its merits (CPS 2006, para.135), the CPS has suggested that it is appropriate to refer to examples in order to promote consistency in decision-making, and that the examples are intended merely as illustrative (CPS 2007b, para.5.39).

The original *Charging Standard* published in 1996 listed neither fatigue nor using a mobile phone as examples of dangerous driving. In fact, 'nodding off' was listed as an example of conduct supporting a charge of careless driving only (CPS 1996a, para.5.6). The guidance required amendment following the Court of Appeal's implementation of the Sentencing Advisory Panel's guidelines on sentencing for CDDD, which included driving when tired as an aggravating factor (*Cooksley* 2004). The prevalence of sleep-related collisions has been researched by Horne and Reyner, who reported that 16–23 per cent of collisions were sleep related, with the higher percentage relating to motorways (Horne and Reyner 1995). They recommended that public awareness should be drawn to the dangers of driving while sleepy. The Highway Code (Rule 91) now provides drivers with advice about tiredness and driving, incorporating Horne and Reyner's conclusion that the only way to counter sleepiness is to stop and nap, or alternatively drink caffeinated coffee (Horne and Reyner 2001). The change in category of fatigued driving from 'careless' to 'dangerous' seems to have resulted from research findings that suggest that drivers will be provided with forewarning that they may fall asleep through precursory feelings of sleepiness (ibid.), and are blameworthy if they do not take heed by resting. There has also been one particular high-profile case of driver fatigue causing multiple deaths that is likely to have had an effect on policy. Gary Hart was responsible for the Selby rail crash in February 2001, which killed ten people, following which it transpired that he had driven after staying up all night. Hart's application to appeal against his conviction for CDDD, for which he was sentenced to five years' imprisonment, was refused (*Hart* 2003).

The prevention of fatigue is the main reason behind the European drivers' hours regulations, which require drivers of goods and passenger vehicles to take specific periods of rest over the course of a day or week (Regulation (EEC) 3820/85). This has been incorporated into UK law with the Transport Act 1968, section 96(11A) of which makes it an offence to contravene the rules. Compliance can be measured through the examination of tachograph charts, which record the time and movement of vehicles. These regulations do not help combat the problem of car drivers who drive when fatigued, however. In other jurisdictions greater thought has been given to how the law can help prevent sleep-related vehicle collisions. In New Jersey, for example, there is a specific provision made for those who kill as a result of fatigued driving. Known as 'Maggie's Law', the new law amended the provision of the penal code dealing with vehicular homicide (N.J.S.2C:11–5) which reads that 'criminal homicide constitutes vehicular homicide when it is caused by driving a vehicle or vessel recklessly'. In 2003 Maggie's Law added the following meaning of 'recklessly':

> For the purposes of this section, driving a vehicle or vessel while knowingly fatigued shall constitute recklessness. 'Fatigued' as used in this section means having been without sleep for a period in excess of 24 consecutive hours. Proof that the defendant fell asleep while driving or was driving after having been without sleep for a period in excess of 24 consecutive hours may give rise to an inference that the defendant was driving recklessly. (N.J.S.2C:11–5)

The alternative method of establishing a presumption of recklessness is if D was driving under the influence of drugs or alcohol. 'Maggie's Law' is named after the victim of a collision caused by a driver who had not slept for 30 hours, leading to a public campaign for a new offence. Defining 'fatigued' with reference to absence of sleep in a certain time period could be criticized as arbitrary and may make prosecution of the offence difficult, however. A driver who sets out to drive immediately after sleeping for two hours having had no sleep in the preceding 48-hour period would presumably not be covered by this definition of 'fatigued'. Jones et al. have argued that the law should recognize that fatigue is a 'cumulative process in which increasing levels of fatigue lead to increasing levels of impairment' (Jones et al. 2003, 355).

In Finland article 63 of the Road Traffic Act states that a driver who is unfit to drive because of illness or fatigue must not drive (Radun et al., unpublished). Under section 2, Chapter 23 of the Finnish Penal Code the offence of 'causing a serious traffic hazard' is committed when D 'deliberately or grossly negligently' breaches a traffic regulation. The provision lists particular regulations that fall within the scope of this offence (significantly exceeding the speed limit; overtaking when there is insufficient visibility; failure to heed duty to stop or give way), but also includes an open-ended clause allowing D to be convicted if D 'in another comparable manner breaches the traffic regulations, so that the act is conducive to causing serious danger to another's health or safety'. Article 63 of the Road Traffic Act could fall within the meaning of such a regulation, suggesting that a fatigued driver could be convicted of 'causing a serious traffic hazard' (ibid.), carrying a maximum penalty of two years' imprisonment. The courts, however, seem reluctant to recognize cases in which D was suffering from fatigue at the time of the collision. In a sample of nine fatal collisions where there was some indication that D may have fallen asleep, only one case resulted in such a finding by the court, due primarily to the fact that D had admitted to falling asleep (ibid.). There seems no obvious way of dealing with the problem of fatigued driving in law, but it is right that the CPS prosecution policy should include some reference to fatigue in examples of dangerous driving.

Whilst fatigued driving has long been a problem that has only recently been taken seriously, driving whilst using a mobile phone is a modern phenomenon. Although driving whilst using a handheld mobile can provide evidence of dangerous or careless driving (see below) it is of itself an offence under regulation 110 of the Road Vehicles (Construction and Use) Regulations, in force since 1 December 2003. This regulation creates three offences of using a mobile phone whilst driving, causing or permitting the use of a mobile phone by a driver and supervising a provisional licence-holder whilst using a mobile phone. There is a defence to these offences if use of the phone was required in an emergency. The maximum penalty is a fine at level 4, although cases will normally be dealt with by way of fixed penalty notice in the form of a £60 fine and three penalty points.

There is good reason why driving whilst using a mobile phone should be banned. The danger caused by driving whilst talking on a mobile phone is not so much that D has one hand occupied whilst holding the phone to D's ear, but that operating the phone and engaging in conversation increases the cognitive load experienced by D. Groeger explains that even deciding whether or not to answer a ringing phone will increase the involvement of D's prefrontal cortex and, if D is currently engaged in a difficult driving manoeuvre, the level of demand imposed on D might prove greater than that which D can meet safely (Groeger 2000, 109). If D decides to answer the phone, to do so will increase demand on the areas of the brain responsible for motor activity (ibid., 110). How much demand is involved will depend on the nature of the call itself, for example whether matters discussed are intellectually demanding or emotionally arousing (ibid.).

Talking on a mobile phone leads to greater reaction times to hazards, and it has been found that this is true whether D is using a hand-held phone or a hands-free kit (Lamble et al. 1999; Patten et al. 2004). Harbluk et al. carried out a study to assess the theory that hands-free mobile phone kits are not distracting because they allow drivers to use their phones without taking their visual attention away from the road. Drivers who were asked to complete maths problems over the phone whilst driving demonstrated an increased tendency to look straight ahead the more difficult the problems became, with subjects neglecting to use their peripheral vision or check their mirrors (Harbluk et al. 2007). The reason that the ban on mobile phones when driving is confined to hand-held devices has more to do with the enforceability of the law than with underlying safety reasons. Whilst it could be argued that difficulty of driving task might similarly be increased through conversations with passengers, which it would be impossible to outlaw, it has been found that normal in-car conversations are suppressed when the driving task gets too difficult to maintain both the conversation and concentration on the road, since the passenger is able to react to the prevailing road conditions (Crundall et al. 2005). There are therefore clear reasons why use of mobile phones of all types whilst driving ought to be banned, if it is possible to overcome the obvious difficulties of enforcing such an offence. This is an offence that would usually require the police to witness its commission, limiting the number of cases that can be prosecuted, even in relation to hand-held devices. In 2004 there were 789 prosecutions for the offence and 641 convictions, in addition to 73,796 fixed penalty notices issued (Hansard, HC 3 Sep 2007, col.1830W). However, it is not clear that this offence is being taken seriously, with the Department for Transport reporting that 21 per cent of drivers admit to the offence (*BBC News* 27 February 2007) and even government ministers being amongst those found guilty (Bird 2007).

By providing use of a mobile phone as an example of conduct capable of amounting to dangerous driving the CPS will hopefully emphasize to drivers the dangers of committing the offence of using a hand-held mobile phone whilst driving. There have been a few cases where such behaviour has led to a fatal collision and D has been charged with CDDD. In *Payne* (2007) D had been distracted from driving his HGV by using his mobile phone. He failed to notice a queue of traffic ahead and collided with the rear of the queue, killing the occupant of that car. His sentence of four years' imprisonment for CDDD resulting from a guilty plea was upheld by the Court of Appeal. In *Browning* (2002) D was prosecuted for CDDD after trying to send a text as he drove his HGV along a dual carriageway. D veered off the road and collided with two cars that were stationary in a lay-by, killing a man who was standing by the cars. D claimed that he had been distracted by papers fluttering in the wind from the open window of the cab but the judge, in a Newton hearing, found that he had been composing a text message. There was evidence that D had a practice of composing and transmitting text messages whilst driving. The judge described such actions as wicked and sentenced D to five years' imprisonment, upheld on appeal. These cases demonstrate that the courts at least take a dim view of drivers who take obvious risks by using their mobile phones whilst behind the wheel of a vehicle.

## Careless Driving

Careless driving criminaliizes those who drive with a degree of negligence that does not amount to dangerous driving, and cases where dangerous driving is charged and the court is unconvinced that the offence is made out will usually result in a conviction for the lesser offence of careless driving. Unlike dangerous driving, however, the offence attracted little attention from the legislature and was left undefined by statute until the Road Safety Act 2006.

In its review of bad driving offences in 1988, the North Review recognized that it was difficult to define cases that should fall within the definition of 'carelessness' at the bottom end of the scale of seriousness, and passed the buck on this issue by advising that ACPO issue guidelines on what is or is not minor carelessness (Department of Transport 1988, para.5.35). What it did state, however, was that:

> even the most competent and careful driver is unlikely to be perfectly vigilant for every moment of every journey however desirable it may be that they should .... They may be momentarily distracted or may make occasional errors of judgement. Such occasional lapses need not invariably result in criminal charges even if, unfortunately, they result in an accident. (ibid.)

This has left the offence involving a rather 'woolly' concept which, as with dangerous driving, causes difficulties for prosecutors and courts in their application of the law.

*The Law*

'Careless driving' is the shorthand term for the offence of driving without due care and attention. Often it also refers to the offence of driving without reasonable consideration for other road users, or inconsiderate driving. Both offences are provided for in section 3 of the RTA 1988, which provides:

> If a person drives a mechanically propelled vehicle on a road or other public place without due care and attention, or without reasonable consideration for other persons using the road or place, he is guilty of an offence.

Until recently the statute said nothing more about what was meant by 'without due care and attention' or 'without reasonable consideration for other persons'. Under case law, the test was established as: 'was the defendant exercising the degree of care and attention that a reasonable and prudent driver would in the circumstances?' (*Simpson v Peat* 1952). However, section 30 of the RSA 2006 inserts section 3ZA into the RTA 1988 and defines driving without due care and attention as follows:

> (2) A person is to be regarded as driving without due care and attention if (and only if) the way he drives falls below what would be expected of a competent and careful driver.
> (3) In determining for the purposes of subsection (2) above what would be expected of a careful and competent driver in a particular case, regard shall be had not only to the circumstances of which he could be expected to be aware but also to any circumstances shown to have been within the knowledge of the accused.

The definition given to inconsiderate driving under the section is as follows:

> (4) A person is to be regarded as driving without reasonable consideration for other persons only if those persons are inconvenienced by his driving.

Although these provisions now provide a definition of careless and inconsiderate driving in statute, previous case law will continue to apply and will be built upon by cases decided after the new section comes into force. What is clear is that the test, as for dangerous driving, is entirely objective.

With regards to inconsiderate driving the offence is dependent upon other persons using the road at the time. There must be other road users, whether they be pedestrians or drivers, in the vicinity of D in order that someone is inconvenienced by D's driving. Prior to the enactment of the new section 3ZA it was not clear whether D must actually have caused inconvenience to others, or whether it was sufficient that D was inconsiderate in D's actions. Smith argued that careless driving is a conduct crime, rather than a result crime, and so does not require proof of inconvenience to other road users (Smith 2002, 502). In the case of *Dilks v Bowman Shaw* (1981), however, D was acquitted because the other road users involved gave evidence that they had not been inconvenienced by his manoeuvre. The new statutory provision specifically states that the offence is only made out if other persons are inconvenienced by D's driving. This implies that whilst careless driving is correctly viewed as a conduct, or endangerment, offence, *inconsiderate* driving falls within the category of result crimes. *Wilkinson's* suggests that whilst careless driving includes inconsiderate driving, since no competent and careful driver would drive in such a way as to inconvenience other drivers, the reverse is not true and therefore careless driving is a far wider offence than inconsiderate driving (Wallis et al. 2005, para.5.44).

Inconsiderate driving rarely appears in the case reports, since most cases are based on the broader offence of careless driving. One recent example of a case of inconsiderate driving is that of Stephanie Cole, who was disqualified from driving for one week after she pleaded guilty to the offence. D had driven at less than 10 mph along the M32 motorway between the slow lane and the hard shoulder. D suffered from 'fear of driving' and had found her way onto the motorway by mistake. The magistrates imposed the driving ban because they were seriously concerned about D's driving ability, her safety and the safety of other road users. As part of the sentence D must retake her driving test before she can drive again (Pidd 2008).

With regard to careless driving, similar factors to those relevant to dangerous driving will be taken into consideration. The main difference between the two offences is, however, that whilst dangerous driving requires a danger of injury or of serious damage of property to have been created by D's driving, careless driving requires no corresponding risk to have been created. Otherwise, though, the issues are very much the same in proving the offence, but it must be established that D drove below the standard of a competent and careful driver rather than far below that standard. The degree of proficiency or experience attained by D is irrelevant to the question of whether D was exercising the degree of care and attention that a reasonable and prudent driver would exercise in the circumstances (*McCrone v Riding* 1938). D may rely on the same defences as might arise in a case of dangerous driving, such as automatism or what has been referred to as the 'emergency defence' (Spencer 2004).

When D is faced with an emergency D can only be expected to react as the competent and careful driver would. So, for example, where D's lights failed without warning as he was driving along the motorway, and his chosen course of action was to pull onto the hard shoulder, he was not guilty of careless driving when he collided with an unlit vehicle which he could not see parked on the hard shoulder. Since it was reasonable for D to act as he did in the circumstances his conviction for careless driving was quashed (*Jones v Chief Constable of Avon and Somerset* 1996). On the other hand, a competent and careful driver faced with an emergency would remain calm and apply some thought to what the best course of action might be. Slamming on the brakes in reaction to an emergency such as a sudden loss of control, with little regard for the risk of skidding, has been upheld as grounds for conviction for careless driving (*R (on the application of Bingham) v DPP* 2003).

The criminal law borrows the doctrine of *res ipsa loquitur* (the facts speak for themselves) from civil law in cases of careless driving. The courts have attempted to avoid use of the term, since the burden of proof is different in civil and criminal cases, and Smith has noted that references to such concepts of civil law 'are probably best avoided' (Smith 2002, 501 in fn 11). For all intents and purposes, however, the concept is now accepted by those working in the field as a necessary evil. It may be that there are no witnesses to a collision, and that even D is unable to account for the incident due to memory loss resulting from injuries suffered in the crash. However, one can assume that a driver paying due care and attention to the road will not stray over the central white line or leave the road unless affected by a mechanical defect, the actions of a third party or something else beyond his or her control such as an animal in the road. The case of *Watts v Carter* (1959) seems to have been the first case to have dealt with this issue. In this case the Divisional Court held that where a car leaves an empty road for no apparent reason there is a case to answer on a charge of careless driving. This was followed in 1971 in the case, sharing very similar facts, of *Wright v Wenlock* (1971). It was held that a rule similar to *res ipsa loquitur* may apply in criminal proceedings where the defendant offers no explanation. Where D has an explanation it is for the prosecution to disprove it, but in certain circumstances where D is unable to offer an explanation careless driving may be inferred. This was in turn followed in *Rabjohns v Burgar* (1971) later that month, a case where D drove his car into a wall and failed to provide an explanation for doing so. Lord Chief Justice Parker, who also gave the judgment in *Wright v Wenlcock,* held that the case should be sent back to the magistrates' court with a direction to convict, and stressed that *res ipsa loquitur* did not apply in the criminal law but that in a case such as this inferences could be made.

Although the above cases were not cited in the case of *Bensley v Smith* (1972) the following year, the case resulted in the same outcome. D had crossed the double white lines in the centre of the road and collided with an on-coming car. On the basis that a mechanical defect or illness on the part of D could not be ruled out, the justices acquitted D. The Divisional Court sent the case back with a direction to convict, however, on the basis that neither of these defences had been raised by the defence. *Bensley v Smith* was followed in the more recent case of *Mundi v Warwicksire Police* (2001), where D attributed the fact that he had veered across the central line into on-coming traffic to the fact that he had caught sight of a child running down a driveway 20 yards ahead of him on his left-hand side. The child had stopped once she reached the pavement and there was no evidence to suggest that she would have run into the road and, on this basis, D's appeal against conviction for careless driving was dismissed. Thus, where the defendant can put forward a viable explanation for an act such as crossing the central line or leaving the road, then the prosecution must disprove it, but in the absence of such viable explanation the presumption will be that D is guilty of careless driving.

Drivers can often be distracted by what is going on around them, and sometimes such distraction is justified. However, D must always remember to return D's attention to the road and to alter D's speed to take account of the conditions. In *R (on the application of Plunkett) v DPP* (2004) D was again distracted by children near the road. In this case, D had been driving along a dual carriageway and had seen a vehicle stop in the outside lane of the opposite carriageway. Children got out of the car and were on the grass island in the middle of the carriageway and, in paying attention to the children, D failed to notice that traffic ahead of him had come to a standstill and collided with the rear of the vehicle at the back of the queue. The traffic had been stationary for 30–60 seconds and D's speed on impact was 22 mph. The judge concluded that a court must determine on the facts of a particular case whether what occurred amounted to a sufficiently distracting event to result in the absolution of the driver from any ensuing collision. He ruled that D had allowed himself to become distracted for too long and should have reduced his speed further in the circumstances. D's conviction for careless driving was upheld.

The new provision under section 3ZA(3) of the RTA 1988 makes it clear that although it remains an objective test, subjective elements can be taken into consideration insofar as the competent and careful driver is to be attributed with any actual knowledge that D had. D will no doubt be expected to be aware of any characteristic of the road that is the subject of a hazard warning sign (for example, that there is a hidden dip in the road), whether or not D paid attention to the sign as D passed it. On the other hand, if D knew of a hazard that was not the subject of a hazard warning sign but came from D's local knowledge and familiarity with the road that could also be relevant to the test. *Wilkinson's* notes that: 'Normally the justices are the best judges as to the actual facts. The Highway Code is a good guide to whether the motorist has departed from the required standard of driving, but breach of the code is not necessarily conclusive' (Wallis et al. 2005, para.5.43). This last point is confirmed by statute: section 38(7) of the RTA 1988, discussed above in relation to dangerous driving.

The case of *Jeshani* (2005) provides an illustration of how wrong judges can be in attempting to provide guidance to juries on the difference between careless and dangerous driving. In this case the judge provided three directions about the meaning of dangerous driving in a case of CDDD, all three of which had different meanings leaving the jury extremely confused, and only one of which was accurate. He first broached the subject of the distinction between careless and dangerous driving in the following way:

> Where driving is to be criticised, a distinction is to be drawn between careless driving and dangerous driving. The one may encompass a foolish act, or an error of judgment and that might be careless. The other may encompass driving which was reckless, or gravely irresponsible, or driving in a way in which an onlooker could call wicked and that may amount to dangerous driving.
>
> It has been said that dangerous driving is a deliberate choice of a course of driving whereby danger arises.
>
> The primary question for you will be: are you sure that this was the position here? If not, then you go on to consider whether or not what the defendant did amounted to careless driving rather than dangerous driving.

This definition suggests that there is a subjective element to the test, since the judge refers to D taking a 'deliberate choice'. As we have seen, the test is entirely objective and this overstates the level of blameworthiness required.

The judge later said:

> A person who causes the death of another person by driving a mechanically propelled vehicle dangerously on a road, or other public place is guilty of an offence. If the defendant was not exercising the degree of care and attention that a reasonable competent and prudent driver would exercise in the circumstances, he should be found 'guilty'. It is a question of fact for you. If the circumstances show that his driving was not inconsistent with that of a reasonably prudent driver, he should be acquitted.

As the Court of Appeal noted, here the judge waters down the first constituent test of dangerousness, that D's driving must fall far below the standard of a competent and careful driver, and instead provides the test for careless driving. When the judge later returns to the issue he gives a far more accurate meaning of the distinction between the two offences:

> ... if you are sure that his driving fell far below what would be expected of a competent and careful driver in the same circumstances, and that it would be obvious to such a competent and careful driver, that driving in the way would be dangerous, then it is open to you to convict.
>
> Should you be of the view that his driving was careless rather than dangerous, then the proper verdict would be 'not guilty as charged', but 'guilty of careless driving'. It is entirely a matter for you.

This last direction finally provides the jury with the information they need to distinguish between the two offences and reach their verdict. However, given that it contradicts the first two directions they were left confused and, having retired, asked the judge for further clarification. Unfortunately the judge repeated the second of his directions, which is incorrect, and the jury convicted D of CDDD. On appeal the Court of Appeal quashed the conviction and substituted a conviction for careless driving, stressing that in such cases it is preferable for the judge to provide the jury with written directions. This, the court suggested, would improve the chances of the judge getting his directions right, and of the jury understanding them.

### *Sentencing*

Careless and inconsiderate driving are summary offences punishable by a fine of up to £5,000 (this was raised from £2,500 by the RSA 2006, section 23, in force from 24 September 2007), penalty points and possible disqualification. An alternative to prosecution, the National Driver Improvement Scheme (NDIS) may be offered in non-serious cases at the discretion of the police.

Until section 20 of the RSA 2006 comes into force, creating the new offence of causing death by careless driving (CDCD), cases of careless driving resulting in death will be punished in accordance with the maximum penalties set out in the previous paragraph. As will be seen in Chapter 4, the fact that only a fine can be imposed for careless driving causing death, as opposed to a 14-year prison sentence for causing death by dangerous driving, led the government to propose the new offence of CDCD to cover this gap in maximum sentences. The relevanceof the result of death in cases of careless driving has not always been dealt with consistently by the courts in sentencing. In *Krawec* (1985) D was found not guilty of causing death by reckless driving but was convicted of careless driving. He appealed against his sentence of a £350 fine. The Court of Appeal allowed the appeal, and reduced the fine to £250 on the basis that the judge should not have taken into account the death caused as an aggravating factor. It was held that the unforeseen and unexpected results of the carelessness were not in themselves relevant to penalty. However, *Krawec* was overruled by the Court of Appeal in *Simmonds* (1999). In that case D attempted to rely on *Krawec* to appeal against his sentence of £1,000, imposed as a result of his pleading guilty to careless driving. The court dismissed the appeal and held that *Krawec* had been decided in the context of a different statutory regime. Since then, the Road Traffic Act 1991 had replaced reckless driving with dangerous driving, which focused on the quality of the driving, and when death was caused carried a maximum penalty (at that time) of five years' imprisonment. The 1991 Act had also created the new offence of causing death by careless driving whilst under the influence of drink or drugs. At the time of *Simmonds* the maximum penalty for such offences had been increased to 10 years' imprisonment. Given that under the new statutory regime the causing of death was regarded as an aggravating feature, the court thought it would be anomalous if it was obliged to disregard such a death when sentencing for careless driving. Although the defendant's criminality would be the main consideration when passing sentence, the causing of death would be taken into account. *Simmonds* remains good law, although it will become redundant once CDCD comes into force.

Pearce's research shows that 12 per cent of drivers convicted of careless driving were disqualified from driving, but only 4 per cent had to take a re-test before regaining their licence (Pearce 2004, 31). Eighty-six per cent received points on their licence and 88 per cent received a fine. Forty-one per cent found their penalty more severe than they had expected, 23 per cent found their sentence as severe as they had expected and 29 per cent had had no idea what to expect (ibid.). For 39 per cent of offenders the penalty had 'no noticeable effect' on their lives (ibid., 32). This last finding might suggest that for some drivers the penalty for careless driving is insufficiently severe or impressionable to achieve any deterrent or rehabilitative effect and that alternatives to the current penalties should be considered.

In less serious cases it may be possible for D to avoid a criminal record by agreeing to attend a driver training course under the National Driver Improvement Scheme (NDIS), rather than face prosecution. The NDIS was initiated after recommendations made by the North Review, which led to a pilot scheme in Devon and Cornwall known as the Driver Rectification Scheme (Cooper and Orme 2008, 28). These courses provide both driving theory in a classroom and practical driver training supervised by an instructor, and can be offered to those suspected of careless driving as long a the offence did not lead to a fatality or serious injury and D has not attended a similar course in the previous three years (Broughton et al. 2005, 3). D must pay a fee to attend, the average cost of which is £150 (Association of National Driver Improvement Scheme Providers website). The course lasts for a day and half, with the theory part, split into three modules entitled 'In the Driving Seat', 'Hazard Recognition' and 'Crash Investigation', taking place before the practical sessions (Edwards 2005, 20). The stated aims of the course are for participants to improve behaviour, skills and attitude (ibid., 28).

Unfortunately research commissioned by the Department for Transport has shown that the NDIS has not been as successful as one might have hoped. Broughton et al. looked at reconviction rates for drivers who attended the course between July 1998 and June 1999, compared with a control group of drivers who were convicted of careless driving. No significant difference was found in the reconviction rates for careless driving of those who attended the NIDS compared to the control group, although the rate for both groups was low (Broughton et al. 2005, 16). Similarly, a study measuring the effectiveness of the scheme in terms of driver behaviour through the use of self-report questionnaires and on-road driving assessment found no significant improvements in the driving behaviour of course attendees compared to a control group, although there was a modest improvement in attitudes towards safe driving (Conner and Lai 2005).

Other research has found more promising results, however. Edwards found a positive change in attitude in that attendees on a course accepted more responsibility for the incident leading to their referral to the NDIS after they had attended the course and also felt they could have done more to avoid the original incident (Edwards 2005, 25). He was also able to show a significant improvement in participants' observation skills (ibid., 28). However, Edwards notes that the effectiveness of the course may differ according to the type of offender in attendance. It is likely to improve the driving of those who commit 'routine violations' (where a driving pattern, such as excessive speed or close-following has become ingrained), whose habits may be corrected by the course, but may be less effective for those, particularly younger drivers, who commit 'optimizing violations' (where D's driving is motivated by thrill-seeking) (ibid., 29). Based on this Edwards suggests that the content of the course should be changed to address the problem of 'optimizing violations' (ibid., 30). In an earlier unpublished study, Burgess and Webley found that those who attended the NDIS reported small but significant reductions in the commission of driving errors and violations and showed significant improvement in attitude towards traffic violations (Burgess and Webley unpublished).

The government clearly sees that there are benefits to the NDIS, since the RSA 2006 will allow a reduction in penalty points or period of disqualification for drivers convicted of careless driving who attend a course (RSA 2006, sections 34 and 35 to amend the Road Traffic Offenders Act 1988). It would appear that such courses will operate separately to the NDIS but they will be based on the same premise: that it is better to improve driving standards and rectify bad habits than merely to reprimand bad driving. It will be suggested in Chapter 7 that the importance of such courses could be increased yet further.

*Policy*

The CPS *Policy for Prosecuting Cases of Bad Driving* lists the following as examples of careless driving and inconsiderate driving:

Careless driving
- overtaking on the inside;
- driving inappropriately close to another vehicle;
- inadvertently driving through a red light;
- emerging from a side road into the path of another vehicle;
- tuning a car radio;
- using a hand-held mobile phone or other hand-held electronic equipment where the driver was avoidably distracted by that use;
- selecting and lighting a cigarette or similar where the driver was avoidably distracted by that use.

Inconsiderate Driving
- flashing of lights to force other drivers in front to give way;
- misuse of any lane to avoid queuing or gain some other advantage over other drivers;
- unnecessarily remaining in an overtaking lane;
- unnecessarily slow driving or braking without good cause;
- driving with un-dipped headlights which dazzle oncoming drivers;
- driving through a puddle causing pedestrians to be splashed;
- driving a bus in such a way as to alarm passengers. (CPS 2007b, para.5.32)

It was noted above that some of the examples previously listed as careless driving have been upgraded to dangerous driving under the new policy. No new examples of careless driving have been listed, although some extra clarification is given to the guidance provided in comparison to the previous *Charging Standard*. For example, driving through a red light is now only deemed to be careless if this was 'inadvertent' (where it is deliberate it would fall within the scope of dangerous driving),and actions such as using a mobile phone or lighting a cigarette are careless if that leads to the driver becoming 'avoidably distracted'. The policy seems to suggest that using a mobile phone while driving could amount to careless *or* dangerous driving, and it is not clear how a prosecutor would decide between the two charges in any particular case. The policy does make it clear, however, that once CDCD comes into force these examples will apply equally to the new offence (ibid., para.5.31).

## Wanton and Furious Driving

There is one further offence that merits a brief mention in this chapter. Under section 35 of the Offences Against the Person Act (OAPA) 1861:

> Whosoever, having the charge of any carriage or vehicle, shall by wanton or furious driving or racing, or other wilful misconduct, or by wilful neglect, do or cause to be

done any bodily harm to any person whatsoever, shall be guilty of a misdemeanour, and being convicted thereof shall be liable, at the discretion of the court, to be imprisoned for any term not exceeding two years

The offence is triable on indictment and carries a maximum penalty of two years' imprisonment. Unlike careless and dangerous driving this offence was introduced before the motor car and so applies to non-motorized vehicles including bicycles. It also differs in that it is a result crime rather than just a conduct crime since it requires bodily harm to have been caused by driving. This is a rarely used provision: in 2003 it was charged in only 55 cases and in 28 cases the charges were dropped, only 12 ending in conviction (Home Office 2005a, para.3.36). That being the case, there are few modern cases on its meaning. In *Cooke* (1971) the following definitions were given to the ingredients of the offence: 'wilful' meant that D was driving and doing what he intended to do; 'misconduct' had its normal meaning and the jury must decide what conduct on the part of a driver fell below the proper standard of driving so as to be called 'misconduct'. In the case of *Okosi* (1996) the appellant attempted to bring some modern legal terminology into the court's interpretation of the law. D argued that it was wrong for the judge to have directed the jury in terms of objective *Caldwell/Lawrence* recklessness and that they should have been directed in terms of subjective *Cunningham* recklessness. Unfortunately the court did not provide a definitive answer to this question, but upheld D's conviction nonetheless, leaving the *mens rea* of the offence a bit of a mystery. Little clarification came in the case of *Knight* (2004), where it was made clear that the jury should be directed in terms of recklessness (without specifying which species), and that carelessness did not suffice.

The North Report recommended repeal of the offence (Department of Transport 1988) and the government has more recently recommended that the offence be replaced by 'suitable modern provisions' (Home Office 2005a, para.1.19), describing it as 'a relic from a bygone era' (ibid., para.3.36). Despite support for this suggestion (Home Office 2005b, 3), the government decided not to go ahead with abolition because little concern was expressed that the offence needed replacement (ibid., 6). However, section 28 of the RSA 2006 extends the penalties available on conviction to include disqualification from driving. *Wilkinson's* describes the offence as being only of use to deal with horse-drawn carriages and cyclists or cases in which the driving took place somewhere other than on a road or other public place, or where the prosecution have failed to adhere to the rules requiring a notice of intended prosecution for an offence under the RTA 1988 (Wallis et al. 2005, para.5.94). CPS prosecution policy confirms that the CPS will only prosecute the offence in cases where it is not possible to charge under the road traffic legislation for those reasons (CPS 2007b, para.5.33).

There are a few cases regarding sentencing that give some illustration of the type of case in which this offence is likely to be used. The case of *Tindale* (2001) is one of those cases in which it would not have been possible to charge dangerous driving as the incident took place on private land. D drove over V's leg with a tractor on private farm land. D was sentenced to nine months' imprisonment, reduced to 16 weeks on appeal. In other cases section 35 is charged alongside more serious offences such as section 20 OAPA 1861 (malicious wounding or inflicting grievous bodily harm). In *Norman* (2007) it was originally alleged that D deliberately drove at V, but that allegation was dropped and D pleaded guilty to section 35. D was sentenced to a suspended 12 month prison sentence, which was overturned on appeal and replaced with a community rehabilitation order. It should be noted that although the maximum penalty is the same as for dangerous driving, the fact that the offence is indictable guarantees that a case will be tried at the Crown Court rather than the magistrates' court, increasing the likelihood of D receiving a custodial sentence. In *Cashon* (2006), for example, D pleaded guilty to the offence and was sentenced to 18 months' imprisonment. This was a case where there were aggravating factors in sentencing, however, such as the fact that D was also guilty of driving with excess alcohol.

This out-dated offence raises the issue of how the law should deal with cases of bad driving that result in serious injury. At present, dangerous or careless driving resulting in injury falling short of death does not lead to a more serious charge than the conduct crime of dangerous or careless driving, unless it occurs in circumstances in which the CPS deem section 35 OAPA to be applicable. The government questioned whether the law should be changed in this regard by either adding 'serious injury' to the 'causing death offences', creating new offences of causing serious injury by dangerous or careless driving or creating a new requirement for the courts to take injury into account as an aggravating factor when sentencing for dangerous or careless driving (Home Office 2005a, para.3.33). Many of the responses to the consultation noted that the last option was not needed, since the courts already take the consequences of bad driving into account when sentencing (Home Office 2005b). There was some support for a separate causing serious injury offence, most notably from the Association of Chief Police Officers (ibid., 21) and road safety charity BRAKE, who proposed a new offence of 'aggravated bad driving' (ibid., 32). The government concluded that the majority of respondents did not see the need for a new causing injury offence and was satisfied that the best way to deal with the issue would be to work with the Sentencing Guidelines Council to ensure that the courts take injury into account when sentencing in cases of bad driving (ibid., 48).

## Dangerous Driving and Careless Driving: Practice

Reported cases on the law of dangerous and careless driving can, in addition to setting precedents on the way in which the law should be applied and statutes interpreted, provide some indication of the sort of circumstances in which the different offences are charged, particularly when a case report relates to sentencing. However, the 'run-of-the-mill' everyday cases are unlikely to reach the case reports or even newspaper reports and it can be difficult to glean a full understanding of the way in which the law operates in practice without undertaking empirical research. Two research projects will be discussed to provide some insight into the way in which the law is applied by those responsible for the day-to-day workings of the criminal justice system in the field of driving offences.

The first project is one undertaken by the Transport Research Laboratory (TRL) for the Department of Transport, Local Government and the Regions (since replaced by the Department for Transport), leading to a report published in 2002 entitled *Dangerous Driving and the Law* (Pearce et al. 2002). This report marks the government's first step towards creating the offence of causing death by careless driving, to be discussed in detail in Chapter 4. The research conducted by the TRL was used as groundwork for the subsequent consultations that took place on the question of what changes, if any, ought to be made on the law of bad driving as set out in the RTA 1988 amended by the RTA 1991. Two of the research questions for the TRL are worth discussion at this point. The first was whether the RTA 1991 has made a difference to the pattern of prosecutions and convictions for dangerous driving and careless driving; the second was whether there exists 'a problem in the current definitions of Dangerous Driving and Careless Driving which results in the lesser charge of Careless Driving covering a wide range of behaviour from minor inattention to serious negligence?' (Pearce et al. 2002, 11).

The TRL analysed the conviction rate for offences prior to and subsequent to the introduction of the RTA 1991 and found that convictions for careless driving rose slightly from 87 per cent before the Act came into force to 92 per cent after the Act (Pearce et al. 2002, 26). It would seem that this change must have been caused by some factor extraneous to the passing of the Act, since the RTA 1991 made no change to the offence of careless driving. It is perhaps charging practice and the practice of magistrates that is more likely to explain the five per cent increase in conviction rates. The TRL also analysed Home Office statistics to determine conviction and sentencing trends for driving offences. It found that there had been a drop in the number of prosecutions for careless driving but that these prosecutions were more likely to end in conviction than prosecutions for dangerous driving (Pearce et al. 2002, 29–30).

One of the factors that might impact on the way in which a case of careless or dangerous driving is dealt with is the issue of police resources. This issue was commented on by many of the traffic officers interviewed for the TRL project. Whilst a fatal collision is seen to justify the expenditure of closing the road and carrying out a thorough investigation, in the absence of a fatality far less time and money is spent collecting evidence that might be used in a prosecution for careless or dangerous driving. For example, it was noted that in non-fatal cases the police rarely obtain witness statements face to face but instead use forms sent in the post (ibid., 30). This prevents officers from being able to elicit details from witnesses which the latter might not see as important but which are imperative when prosecuting a criminal case. Witness statements will be of particular importance in such cases given that there will be far less physical evidence available to the court; expert evidence from collision investigators is again only usually available in fatal cases.

In relation to the decision to prosecute drivers the TRL found that there was some disagreement between police and CPS as to the correct offence to be charged (ibid., 34). The police view was that the CPS were, at that time at least, over-cautious in their prosecution policy. The CPS view, on the other hand, was that the reason that they were not charging a more serious charge as the police would like was often due to insufficient evidence.

One of the most interesting findings from the TRL report was that representatives of the various agencies (police, CPS, magistrates and judges) failed to respond with consistent answers to questions regarding the type of behaviour needed to be displayed on the part of a driver to secure a conviction for a particular offence. The TRL's questions were based on examples of conduct amounting to careless and dangerous driving contained in the CPS *Charging Standard*. According to the TRL: 'a major difference between Dangerous Driving and Careless Driving rested on whether the behaviour had been deliberate, not in the sense that the driver set out deliberately to cause harm, but that the manoeuvre was carried out with the intention of driving in that particular way' (Pearce et al. 2002, 36). Respondents were asked whether the actions of running a red light and failing to observe a stop sign were required to be deliberate in order to prove dangerous driving. Of the 96 respondents, 23 thought it was necessary so to prove, with further respondents replying that it was 'sometimes' necessary (ibid.). Conversely, it was found that 74 per cent of those questioned felt that it should not be necessary to prove that an action was deliberate in order to prove a charge of dangerous driving. That 74 per cent were right to hold such a view, given that the reasoning of the RTA 1991 in replacing reckless driving with dangerous driving was to remove the need to prove a driver's state of mind and to impose an entirely objective test (see above). That so many respondents were of the belief that a deliberate act was required to prove the offence suggests that the RTA 1991 may not have achieved success in this primary goal. On the other hand, those interviewed seemed to agree that the 1991 legislation has made it easier to prove dangerous driving than it was to prove reckless driving (ibid., 93). The TRL was concerned, however, that his had not translated into higher conviction rates.

When cases get to court the TRL found that there are inconsistencies in the way that lapses in concentration are dealt with by the criminal justice system (Pearce et al. 2002, 47). Speeding was identified as another problematic issue, with the TRL advising that further guidance on the relationship between speeding and dangerous driving was needed (ibid., 52). The objective test for dangerous driving of whether D fell 'below the standard of the competent and careful driver' was chosen for its supposed ease of application. A competent and careful driver pays attention to the road and does not exceed the speed limit or drive at a speed inappropriate in the prevailing conditions. The question is whether those involved in applying the test agree on what is expected of a competent and careful driver. If a case of dangerous driving is heard at the Crown Court then ultimately it is a jury who will decide on this, and the TRL suggested that jurors will use their own competence and carefulness when driving as a yardstick against which to measure the actions of the defendant: 'The fact that "dangerous" is a word in common usage, which most adults feel they understand, may lead juries to apply their own, rather than a legal, interpretation of dangerous' (ibid., 55). The TRL's logic was that if this is what happens, the test of the 'competent and careful driver' becomes the test of the average member of the public. One of the questions asked of the police, lawyers and judges was how many members of the public (and therefore jurors) are, in their view, competent and careful drivers. A few respondents thought that over 91 per cent of the population met this standard, whilst others thought that a much lower percentage, as low as ten per cent in some cases, met the standard (ibid., 56).

The TRL's conclusion was that: 'The definition of Dangerous Driving is such that whilst violators are likely to face that charge, those guilty of serious negligence in their driving face the same charge of Careless Driving as those guilty of very minor offences' (Pearce et al. 2002, 93). The TRL recommended that an intermediate offence of 'negligent driving' should be introduced, which would require bad driving that was more serious than careless driving but less serious than dangerous driving. It did not provide a draft definition and it is difficult to envisage how such an offence would be defined. On this basis the option was rejected by the government, who noted that the offences of careless driving and dangerous driving are contiguous; any perceived gap between them must either stem from the difference in maximum penalties for the two offences or because the language used to label the offences may obstruct their interpretation, given that 'careless' can be potentially 'dangerous' (Home Office 2005a, para.3.9). The addition of a third, intermediate, offence would merely add to the difficult judgements faced by prosecutors and magistrates in deciding into which category a particular case would fall (ibid., para.3.10).

Whilst the TRL report provided some information on the way in which lawyers and judges interpret the law on dangerous and careless driving, and official statistics can give an indication of the number of cases resulting in a conviction for one or other offence, it is impossible to determine from official data the number of cases in which a particular driving offence is suspected of having been committed, unless the case ends in conviction. It is probable that many offences are never detected and, amongst those that are, many may never lead to prosecution because of the exercise of discretion by police and prosecutors. Those that do end in prosecution might end in acquittal or conviction for a lesser offence. In order to establish systematically how many cases there are where either careless or dangerous driving is suspected of having been committed by a driver involved in a fatal collision, the author carried out the study described in Chapter 1.

Although this study was confined to fatal collisions, enabling all such collisions within the geographical location and time frame to be researched, the results give some indication of how prosecutors differentiate between careless driving and dangerous driving generally. It should be remembered that at the time of the study the offence of causing death by careless driving had not yet been created, and although a driver who was guilty of dangerous driving could be prosecuted for CDDD (see Chapter 4 below), a driver whose driving was deemed to be careless could only be convicted of the endangerment offence of careless driving. This explains why these cases will be analysed here rather than in Chapter 4. However, although these cases can tell us something about the difference between careless driving and dangerous driving it should be noted that unless a fatal collision has occurred the quality of evidence available to a prosecutor is likely to be much lower due to the fact that a fatal collision allows the police to close a road in order to carry out a thorough investigation of the scene, a luxury not available where luckily a serious collision has been averted.

The cases have been categorized according to their perceived seriousness. In this chapter there are two borderlines between different standards of driving that are of interest: the borderline between driving that is at the standard of the competent and careful driving (lawful driving) and driving that falls below that standard (careless driving) and the borderline between driving that falls below the standard of the competent and careful driver and driving that falls *far* below that standard (dangerous driving). The discussion starts with a look at the first borderline, where the choice for the police or CPS was between taking no further action (NFA) against the surviving driver and prosecuting for careless driving. Then the discussion proceeds to cases displaying a higher degree of culpability. The individual cases have been given a random number prefixed with the letter A, B or C for ease of reference and to retain anonymity.

*NFA v Careless Driving* Of the 316 cases studied, 190 resulted in no prosecution. In 94 of these cases the lack of prosecution can easily be explained on the basis that the collision was caused by a driver who died and no survivors could be blamed. This often occurred when the driver who died had, for example, lost control of his or her car or motorcycle while attempting to negotiate a bend and crossed into the path of an on-coming vehicle, the driver of which had little or no opportunity to avoid a collision.

When two or more vehicles collide the police will investigate the cause of the collision to establish which of the drivers was at fault. It may be the fault of the deceased (V), or of D, of both, or, very occasionally, of neither. The police point out that collisions are rarely the result of true 'accident' in that they can usually be explained by either human error or the presence of a mechanical defect. In a very small number of cases, however, neither party is to blame and the cause of the collision is attributed to some outside influence. In B15 fault was not attributed to either of two drivers who met on a narrow lane travelling in opposite directions. Having managed to pass each other V lost control of his car, although a possible contributory factor may have been an under-inflated tyre. In A100 the police concluded that the collision was the result of 'accident', the primary contributor being the strong wind which suddenly blew V's motorcycle off course and into the path of an on-coming vehicle.

Motorcyclists are a particularly vulnerable class of road user. In the USA it has been found that motorcyclists are more than twenty times more likely to be fatally injured, per mile travelled, than drivers of other vehicles (Mannering and Grodsky 1995, 21). In Great Britain the statistics give a 'casualty rate' for motorcyclists of 647 (per 100 million vehicle kilometres) and 581 in 1999 and 2000 (the years of the cases in the research sample) respectively (DTLR 2001, Table 1e), as opposed to 55 and 54 in the same years for car users (ibid., Table 1c). Thirty-five of the cases in the author's study where no prosecutions were brought involved the death of a motorcyclist. In 14 of these cases V was seen to be at fault, having lost control of his machine on a bend. Such cases are usually easy to reconstruct, leaving the police with little doubt about blame. However, other types of cases are more difficult to judge. Mannering and Grodsky identify five reasons for motorcyclists' high collision involvement, four of which place the blame with V, but the fifth factor is that car drivers tend to pay less attention to motorcyclists and have conditioned themselves to look only for other automobiles as possible collision dangers. This is probably a significant factor in many of the cases in which motorcyclists were killed in which the decision as to whether to prosecute D was more difficult. In particular, cases involving cars turning across the path of motorcycles were problematic. There were several cases in which V had been riding along a main road, overtaking a line of traffic, when D turned right across V's path, having been at the head of the line which V was overtaking. Other cases involved D turning across the path of V who was travelling in the opposite direction.

In such cases it was often difficult for the police to allocate blame, in that invariably there was a suggestion that V had been riding at excessive speed, and it was difficult to judge the degree to which D was to blame in failing to see the motorcycle before carrying out the manoeuvre or in misjudging V's speed. In such cases the police may have to rely on D's comments in interview concerning what observation D conducted before and during the manoeuvre. Eyewitness statements as to the timing of V's and D's manoeuvres are also important. The problem is that in these cases some degree of blame can usually be apportioned to both parties. The question is whether D's fault is sufficient to warrant criminal proceedings. D should check D's mirrors and blind-spot before performing a right turn, and should ensure that D is not being overtaken. Equally, though, any road-user should not overtake when approaching a junction. Thus, proving careless driving in such circumstances may be difficult. In B38 the Crown prosecutor concluded that it was impossible to say that D was at fault as there were no eyewitnesses to suggest that D had failed to indicate or failed to give sufficient warning when he turned right across V's path.

Pedal cyclists are also vulnerable. However, they are unlikely to contribute to a collision in the same way as motorcyclists. In contrast to motorcyclists they are slow moving, and as such other road-users should have more time to react to their presence. Cyclists themselves are usually aware of their vulnerability and will take suitable precautions in any manoeuvres they carry out. There were nine cases in which, although a cyclist was killed, no prosecutions were brought. In two cases the police concluded that where V and D were travelling in the same direction, V had pulled right into D's path, leaving D no time to react.

However, in A94 the police concluded that D was at fault and there was sufficient evidence to prefer a charge of inconsiderate driving. V had been struck by D's wing mirror as D overtook V in his van. The collision investigator found that V had been positioned close to a white line separating the nearside lane from a bus-stop, suggesting that D had given V insufficient room. However, although it seems that the CPS initially agreed with the police that a prosecution should be brought, in that they sent a fax to the police querying where a summons should be issued, it appears that at some later stage the decision was made not to prosecute. Unfortunately there was no further CPS correspondence on the file explaining this decision, but this case clearly caused difficulties for the decision-makers. It is not clear why the police specified inconsiderate driving rather than careless driving as the appropriate charge, nor whether that preference was adopted by the CPS at later stages.

Similarly, in A30 the police considered that careless driving should be prosecuted but no charges were brought, where D appears to have failed to see a cyclist prior to the collision. In B98 the police disagreed so strongly with the CPS view that there was insufficient evidence to provide a realistic prospect of conviction for inconsiderate driving that a summons was issued against CPS advice. Again, nothing further appears on the file with regards to the prosecution, so it is assumed the case was discontinued by the CPS. Such cases would now be dealt with differently under a change in local charging policy, followed by the introduction of the Statutory Charging Scheme, under which the CPS would have to be the ones to decide to issue a summons in a case involving a fatality (see Cunningham 2005).

Not all cases in which there is equivocal evidence as to the location of V and what happened lead to NFA, though. In B22 V was caught with his pedal cycle in the wheels of an HGV. There was conflicting eyewitness evidence about where V was in relation to the HGV when he was struck and unfortunately the vehicles were moved before the collision investigator arrived at the scene, meaning he was unable to place them exactly. Despite this, a prosecution for careless driving went ahead and was successful. Another successful case of careless driving (B36) involved D failing to give a pedal cyclist sufficient room when attempting to overtake.

When pedestrians are killed on the road different issues must be addressed. Pedestrians will not normally be in the road unless they are attempting to cross it, and so when a pedestrian is killed it raises suspicions about D's level of attention. In the current sample there were 51 cases involving pedestrians in which no prosecution was brought. This might be surprising, given that drivers owe a duty to take particular care when pedestrians are likely to be present. There are various reasons for these types of collisions which explain the lack of prosecutions, however.

Alcohol can be dangerous not only when consumed by drivers, but also when consumed by pedestrians. National statistics show that for the 332 pedestrians killed in 1999 with a known blood/alcohol concentration (BAC), 39 per cent were above the legal limit to drive (80 mg/100 ml) and 24 per cent were above 200 mg/100 ml (TRL 2001). For the 316 pedestrians killed in 2000 with a known BAC, the figures were 35 per cent and 22 per cent respectively (TRL 2002). In twelve of the cases involving pedestrians in the author's study, V was found to have a high level of alcohol in the blood. In these cases the collision took place in darkness, often when V was attempting to walk home late at night on a country road, perhaps attempting to thumb a lift from traffic as it passed and ignorant of the fact that he or she could not be seen by drivers until the last moment.

More worryingly, each of the three counties featured a case in which a young man, walking home at night when drunk, had laid down in the middle of the road in order, it seems, to rest. These cases caused particular problems for the police, who were faced with the need to explain V's presence in the road with no eyewitness testimony to assist. In two of the cases further complications were involved due to evidence that V had been party to an altercation earlier that day. In two of the cases charges were not brought, either because D was judged not to be blameworthy in failing to see V or because there was insufficient evidence to identify who D was. In B37, however, V was run over by a car which had been following an ambulance. The ambulance was able to swerve to avoid V, but the car behind was travelling too close and D's view was restricted by the ambulance. A summons for careless driving was issued against D before CPS advice was obtained, but was later withdrawn.

In another six cases the pedestrians who were killed had been suffering from some kind of mental illness. In some cases it was strongly suspected that V, in effect, took his or her own life by presenting themselves in the path of motor vehicles. In these cases, and others involving pedestrians who appear to have stepped into the paths of vehicles without looking, the police are often able to use various calculations, along with eyewitness testimony, to establish the time it took D to react to the presence of V in the road. In cases where D appears to have reacted fairly promptly, a criminal prosecution will normally be ruled out. In one case, however, the police and CPS disagreed as to whether D's driving fell below the standard of a competent and careful driver. In A76 D could not account for not seeing V sooner. V had stepped off the kerb on D's nearside in daylight. Both the investigating officer in the case and the traffic inspector agreed that D should be prosecuted for careless driving, but the CPS disagreed. Unfortunately the CPS letter of advice did not appear on the file so it is unknown what the exact reasoning behind their decision was. It may be that none of the witnesses appear to have apportioned blame to D, as V stepped off the kerb into D's path. There were several cases with similar facts to this in which the police decided to take NFA, but what appears to distinguish them from this case is that V was highly visible and the collision investigator calculated D's speed as being 36 mph in a 30 mph limit.

There were thirteen cases in which D was convicted of careless driving, having collided with a pedestrian who was attempting to cross the road. The degree of fault on the part of D varied, but in all cases it was agreed by the police and CPS that D failed to react with sufficient promptness to the presence of V. Three cases involved excess speed, with the degree of excess ranging from 5 mph over the limit to 20 mph over. One case (B106) involved D being dazzled by the sun. D was driving in a busy town centre and failed to see V, who had walked out from behind a bus. A major cause, according to the collision investigator, was the low sun. Where drivers are dazzled by either the sun or the lights of other vehicles they are expected to adjust their speed accordingly in order to be able to stop in the distance they can see to be clear. When they fail to do so and this results in a collision they may face prosecution for careless driving. *Wilkinson's* submits that D should stop if the loss of vision lasts for two seconds or more, and if D chooses not to do so and a collision results, D should be found guilty of careless driving at least (Wallis et al. 2005, para.5.74). D was dazzled in a further four cases in the study, two involving pedal cyclists and two involving stationary vehicles. In all cases there was little doubt that D should have taken action to limit the effect of being dazzled.

Occasionally the police may be unable to establish what the cause of a collision was and yet a prosecution against D is brought. This occurs when the police are able to reconstruct the collision in terms of the location of the vehicles and the way in which they collided, but cannot provide a reason for this. CPS charging policy provides the following guidance to prosecutors: 'Occasionally a collision occurs but there is no evidence of any mechanical defect, illness of the driver or other explanation to account for why the collision happened. In these cases, a charge of careless driving may be appropriate, but you should exercise caution' (CPS Legal Guidance online). As discussed above, the courts have accepted a rule similar to the civil law rule of *res ipsa loquitur* applying in cases where there is no explanation for the collision. The basis of the prosecution's case is that in the absence of any other explanation it is inevitable that D must have been driving below the standard expected of a competent and careful driver, since otherwise the collision would not have occurred. This seems to have been the basis of the prosecution case in six of the cases in the sample. In two of these there does seem to have been an explanation in that it is probable that D lost control due to attempting to negotiate a bend too fast. Other cases involved D crossing into the path of an on-coming vehicle for some unexplained reason, and in all cases the prosecution was successful.

*Dangerous driving v careless driving* The statutory definitions of the offences of careless driving and dangerous driving appear, according to some of those interviewed in the course of the study and apparent from the case files studied, to leave a 'grey area' encompassing the lower end of dangerous driving and the upper end of careless driving. This 'grey area' seems to be problematic in fatal cases involving particular features, namely fatigue and excess speed, where the choice for the prosecutor will be whether to charge careless driving or causing death by dangerous driving (CDDD). In future the choice will be between the two causing death offences of causing death by careless driving (CDCD) with a maximum penalty of two years' imprisonment, and CDDD. The TRL's finding that those involved in the prosecution of cases are inconsistent in addressing the question of whether speed is an indication of dangerous driving appears to be borne out to a certain extent by the cases in the author's sample. Of the cases in which excess speed for the conditions was a factor, there were 21 where there was a prosecution for careless driving and eight where the charge was CDDD.

Five cases resulting in prosecutions for careless driving involved speeds well above the speed limit and are perhaps examples of cases at the more serious end of the scale of 'carelessness'. In C18 witnesses described D as travelling at a speed of up to 100 mph on a dual carriageway. The collision investigator was, however, unable to calculate D's speed, and D claimed he did not go above 80 mph. The collision occurred when D came around a bend and was faced with a car which had emerged from a side-road and was attempting to cross the carriageway to turn right on to the opposite carriageway. The driver of this car hesitated when D came into view, not sure as to whether he should continue across to get out of D's way, or stay where he was and let D pass in front of him. He chose to continue across, as D moved into the nearside lane to pass behind him. D managed to pass the car but subsequently lost control, veered across the central reservation and collided with V's car, which was travelling in the opposite direction. Both D and the other driver were prosecuted for careless driving. The investigating officer in the case was of the opinion that of the two, D was more to blame for the collision, as he believed that D had been 'showing off' and did not think that the other driver warranted prosecution. However, he stated that CDDD was not considered as a possible charge against D as a conviction could not be secured on the basis of excessive speed alone. D pleaded guilty to careless driving, whilst the magistrates found no case to answer in relation to the second driver.

A29 and C67 were cases in which D lost control of his car on a bend while driving in excess of the speed limit. In the latter case the collision investigator calculated D's speed to be 75 mph in a 60 mph limit in wet conditions. The critical speed for the bend was 54 mph. Again, it was concluded (by the CPS) that there was insufficient evidence to prosecute D for CDDD, and D was convicted of careless driving. Another two cases (A14 and A97) involved speeds of 44 mph and 45 mph in a 30 mph limit. A97 was probably the more serious of the two cases in that D was driving in the dark, without any illumination on his dashboard, meaning that he was unable to read the speedometer. He collided with an eight-year-old girl who was attempting to cross the road from his offside, and failed to brake until after the collision. The police and CPS agreed that careless driving was the appropriate charge and D pleaded guilty to that offence. It may be that CDDD was given some consideration when the case was reviewed, as there were notes on the file referring to the distinction between careless and dangerous driving, but it appears that it was not deemed serious enough to warrant such a charge. This is clearly an example of a case falling within the 'grey area' and can be compared to a similar case (B108 below) in which a prosecution for CDDD was successful.

All those cases resulting in prosecutions for CDDD which were based on excessive speed involved speeds that were in excess of the speed limit, as well as being inappropriate for the prevailing conditions. However, most of the cases also involved some other factor which contributed to the collision, in addition to speed. Fatigue or inattention combined with speed is obviously a risky combination. There were three cases in which the main contributory factor in proving CDDD was excess speed.

B6 involved what might be described as 'boy-racers'. A group of young people were travelling in a convoy of cars. Witnesses estimated that D was driving at speeds of 70–85 mph on a single-carriageway road, before he attempted to overtake and lost control of his car, which left the road and came to rest in a field. V was D's passenger and friend. This was seen as a relatively clear example of CDDD, and D pleaded guilty to that offence. Another case in which speed was the main cause of danger and yet there was little doubt about the correct charge was C37. D, who was disqualified from driving and did not hold a licence to drive HGVs, took his employers' tractor unit without the latter's consent. He approached a roundabout on a section of dual carriageway at 50 mph in bad weather and failed to negotiate the roundabout, resulting in his passenger being killed when he was ejected from the vehicle and collided with a lamp-post. Again, D pleaded guilty to CDDD.

There was one case (B108) involving speed, however, which fell squarely within the 'grey area' between careless driving and dangerous driving. This can be seen by the fact that the Crown prosecutor advised that careless driving should be charged in addition to CDDD to cover the eventuality that the judge would not allow the case to go to the jury. This was one in which there were no eyewitnesses who saw the collision between D's car and a schoolgirl pedestrian. The collision investigator calculated D's speed to be 43 mph in a 30 mph limit. V was struck as she crossed the road but had almost reached the opposite kerb. The sergeant, in suggesting a charge of CDDD, referred to paragraph 7.7 of the *Charging Standard* (CPS 1996a), which gave excessive speed as an example of driving supporting an allegation of dangerous driving. What may have been an important factor in influencing the decision as to charge, however, was the fact that in interview D had expressly admitted that in his view his driving 'fell far below what would be considered as a competent and careful driver'. D pleaded not guilty to CDDD at trial, but was convicted by a majority of 10–2.

There was a certain technique used by some police officers in interviewing suspects of careless driving and CDDD. This was to ask D to describe D's own standard of driving, and to ask if D thought that D's driving fell below the standard expected of careful and competent driver, and even whether it fell far below the standard. In a few cases in one county in particular it was obvious that officers were wording their questions with the guidelines provided by the *Charging Standard* in mind. If D had a solicitor present at the interview D may have been advised not to answer the question, although some solicitors allowed their clients to fall into the trap. Those without solicitors may not have realized the significance of their admission in agreeing that their driving was dangerous or that it did not meet the standard of a careful and competent driver. In actual fact, D's admission that, in D's own view, D's driving fell far below the standard of a competent and careful driver should not necessarily lead to the conclusion that D's driving did fall below that standard, since the test is an objective one. However, a jury might be influenced by hearing such an admission.

About a third of suspects (7 of 24) subjected to this questioning technique made such an admission. Others were adamant that they had done nothing wrong, and some were not confident about their answer. For example, in B41 D stated that he must be a competent driver, otherwise he would not have passed his test. This particular suspect pleaded not guilty to CDDD at trial but was convicted by the jury. However, even where an admission of dangerous driving was made this did not always guarantee that CDDD would be charged. In C25 D approached an area of road works on the M1 at 56 mph in his HGV. He failed to react to the queue of traffic ahead of him and ploughed into the vehicles, causing two deaths. In interview the police asked D whether he thought these actions, and the fact that D was not in a position to stop, were dangerous. D agreed that it was, but nevertheless the Crown prosecutor concluded that there was insufficient evidence to charge CDDD, presumably on the basis that although D thought his driving was dangerous it was thought more likely than not that a jury would not agree. D was convicted of careless driving.

This last case was one of several in which an HGV driver's inattention, possibly due to fatigue, led to him (all such Ds were male) failing to stop when faced with stationary or slow-moving vehicles ahead of him. There were eleven such cases in the sample, seven of which led to a prosecution for CDDD and four for careless driving. The difficulty with these types of cases is that it is clear that D was not paying sufficient attention to his driving, but it is almost impossible to establish the degree of his inattention. The *Charging Standard* of the time listed 'fatigue/nodding off' as conduct which would support a charge of careless driving (CPS 1996a), but this has now been elevated to being an example of dangerous driving under the new prosecution policy (CPS 2007b). More generally, however, the *Charging Standard* stated that acts caused by something more than momentary inattention would normally lead to a charge of careless driving (CPS 1996a, para.4.3), whilst failure to pay proper attention, amounting to something significantly more than a momentary lapse, would support an allegation of dangerous driving (ibid., para.7.7). The distinction, then, between the degrees of inattention comes with the insertion of the word 'significantly' which was required for dangerous driving. This suggests that a competent and careful driver will occasionally suffer moments of inattention, but no more than that. The longer the duration of the inattention, the further below the standard of the competent and careful driver D will have fallen. With no witnesses to account for D's behaviour behind the wheel in the moments leading up to a collision, such a distinction is extremely difficult to judge or prove. It is perhaps because of this that no mention of this distinction is made in the current prosecution policy.

Perhaps the new prosecution policy will make decisions as to charge less difficult for prosecutors dealing with cases involving fatigue, but at the time of the study such cases were clearly very problematic. A clear example of the problems posed is case C23, which involved a car that had broken down on a dual carriageway. The owner of the car left his wife and two daughters in the car parked in lane one, and went to get assistance. D was driving his HGV along the dual carriageway and failed to see the stationary car ahead of him until it was too late. He collided with the rear of the car, killing the two girls sitting in the rear of the car. The collision investigator calculated that the car would have been visible to D for 21–26 seconds, given that D was travelling at 56 mph according to his tachograph chart. D did not brake until immediately prior to or upon impact. D had failed to take sufficient weekly breaks from his driving. In interview D could not account for his failing to see the car and said he did not remember feeling tired or fatigued. Initially, the prosecutor who provided advice on the case, a senior Crown prosecutor, advised that there was no evidence of fatigue, or that D was driving erratically or had fallen asleep, and so recommended that D be prosecuted for careless driving.

The Chief Crown Prosecutor (CCP) came to review the case as a result of Vs' family expressing concern about this decision. The review was in depth, with the CCP attending the location of the collision to get a good understanding of the road layout. In his view, an estimate of 25 seconds' inattention during which the car was visible to D clearly amounted to something significantly more than momentary inattention, and he decided to charge CDDD. For him, this was not a case falling within the 'grey area' between careless driving and dangerous driving, but a clear case of dangerous driving. Unfortunately his views were never tested in court, as the case was stayed for abuse of process on the basis that the CPS were wrong to review the case at the family's request, and the case reverted to the magistrates' court, where D was convicted of careless driving.

A second case bears almost identical facts to this. In C51 V was a passenger in his father's car, which had stopped in lane one of a dual carriageway behind his mother's car, which had broken down. Again, D failed to see the stationary cars and collided with them. Again, the collision investigator calculated that the cars would have been visible to D for 25 seconds. The Crown prosecutor conducted a thorough review of the case, referring to various paragraphs of the *Charging Standard*, and noting that case law on sentencing indicates that dangerous driving can be a 'one off', for example, briefly dozing at the wheel. He then applied this law to the facts and concluded that both of the evidential and the public interest tests in the *Code for Crown Prosecutors* were met for a prosecution of CDDD, despite the notorious problem of juries adopting a mentality of 'there but for the grace of God go I'. In this case, the jury appeared not to be sympathetic to D, and convicted him of CDDD by a unanimous verdict.

Other cases involved HGV drivers failing to notice that the traffic ahead of them on a motorway had become stationary or very slow-moving due to queues at junctions. In one such case the judge, in sentencing D for three counts of CDDD to which D had pleaded guilty, took into account the special nature of the driving responsibilities of HGV drivers as aggravating factors. Because of the size and weight of HGVs, they pose a greater risk to other road users than do cars. HGV drivers are subject to legislation limiting the number of hours they can drive without resting in order to try to reduce the risk of such drivers becoming victims of fatigue and failing to exercise the degree of attention necessary when driving such dangerous vehicles. They are also subjected to lower speed limits in order to limit the danger they pose to other road users.

A63 is an example of what can occur if both of these regulations are not complied with. D was an HGV driver who had breached the drivers' hours regulations by writing his brother's name on some of his tachograph charts in order to be able to drive more often than he should. He had been driving at 64 mph on a motorway in sleet and rain when he collided with the rear of a queue of traffic. The prosecution was able to rely on a combination of excessive speed and fatigue to secure a conviction for CDDD. Again, this was a case which did not fall within the 'grey area'.

Drivers are sometimes frustrated by the special speed limits for HGVs, as D admitted in B73. This was a case in which prosecution counsel was of the view that D's driving did fall within the 'grey area' between careless and dangerous driving. D had been driving his HGV at 12 mph in excess of its 40 mph speed limit and failed to notice that a car ahead was stationary in the middle of the road waiting to turn right. He drove into the back of the car, shunting it into the path of a van travelling in the opposite direction. D admitted suffering a lapse of concentration, but when asked if he thought it was more than a momentary lapse his response was, 'How long is a piece of string?' The Crown prosecutor advised that there was a *prima facie* case of CDDD and huge public interest to prosecute, but recognized that the jury might return a verdict of not guilty. She advised that careless driving be charged in addition to CDDD. Counsel seems to have been of the opinion that the case fell within the 'grey area' on the basis of D's speed, although following conviction for CDDD by a jury the judge came to the conclusion that D must have fallen asleep.

Although an HGV driver who falls asleep poses a particularly grave danger due to the size of his vehicle, car drivers who fall asleep or are fatigued also create risks. There were three cases in which D was a car driver who had suffered from fatigue, and all three resulted in prosecutions for careless driving. All three Ds had been on their return journey, having driven considerable distances earlier in the day. C62 was perhaps the worst example of driving when tired. D drove to his destination 240 miles from his departure point, arriving shortly after three o'clock in the morning. After a short break he set off for the return journey, the collision occurring not far from his home at seven o'clock in the morning. He said he stopped a few times at service stations, but admitted that he dozed off at the time of the collision. D said that he had felt tired but because he was so close to home he did not want to stop again. The collision occurred when D's car drifted onto the opposite side of the road; D awoke and lost control of the car in attempting to avoid oncoming traffic. D was arrested six days following the collision on suspicion of CDDD, but the CPS advised that there was not a realistic prospect of conviction for CDDD. This was based on a judgment that D was only asleep momentarily and that he had taken some breaks. The decision also appears to have been influenced by D's explanation that he was used to driving long hours with little sleep when working in the army. Quite how this affects his standard of driving as compared to that of a competent and careful driver is unclear. The test is an objective one and any specific reason for D's conduct should not be relevant, despite what was recently decided in *Milton v DPP* (2007).

What these cases seem to suggest is that HGV drivers who suffer from fatigue may be more likely to face charges of CDDD than car drivers. This cannot be explained solely on the basis that HGV drivers have particular responsibilities given the nature of their work. It seems that evidential problems are probably the root of the issue. From examining a tachograph chart the police can establish not only the speed at which D was driving, but also the pattern of D's driving leading up to the collision and can determine at what point, if any, D reacted to the presence of a hazard immediately prior to the collision. When dealing with car drivers, however, the police have no such evidence and must rely on D's account of his driving, any eyewitness evidence, and the presence of any tyre marks on the road surface.

However, even when tachograph evidence is available, it appears that the police or CPS have difficulty in deciding the appropriate charge in cases involving inattention. In the cases of C51 and C23 discussed above the charges for CDDD were based on D having had the hazard in his view for 25 seconds and failing to react. In A34 D drove into the back of a minibus that was stationary at temporary traffic lights for road works. D had driven in the opposite direction earlier that day and so was aware of the presence of road works. However, he could remember nothing of his journey since leaving the motorway, a minute prior to the collision. His tachograph chart showed that he had been exceeding his 40 mph speed limit and that he had not braked at all before impact. The collision investigator found that the road works would have been visible to D for 15 seconds. Sleep specialists Horne and Reyner suggest that where an object is visible for 7–10 seconds and D fails to react to its presence, this implies prolonged inattention rather than momentary distraction (Horne and Reyner 1999). Despite this, and a recommendation from the investigating officer that D be charged with CDDD, D was only prosecuted for careless driving, to which he pleaded guilty. Unfortunately, there was no explanation of this on the file, but there was correspondence between the CPS and V's family, who took the view that the case had not received the attention it ought to have done due to V's racial origin. The CPS responded to these criticisms by stating that the evidence did not support a charge of CDDD and the decision as to charge was based entirely and exclusively on the degree of lapse and standard of D's driving.

Another finding of Horne and Reyner, particularly relevant to the issue of proving CDDD on the basis of D falling asleep at the wheel, is that although drivers are normally aware of the precursory feeling of sleepiness at the time, they may not remember this, or the fact of falling asleep itself, after the collision (Horne and Reyner 2001, 68). Cases involving sleep are thus difficult to identify and distinguish from cases involving mere inattention. One further case from the sample involving inattention warrants discussion. In A114 D collided with V as she was crossing the road at a pelican crossing which displayed a red light to traffic. D was breathalysed and found to be just under the legal drink-drive limit. In interview D said that he did not remember seeing the traffic lights, nor did he remember negotiating the roundabout just prior to the collision scene. It was a route that he took on a daily basis and when asked if he was tired he said that yes, he was tired, as tired as he normally was after a day's work. He did not remember anything other than V hitting his windscreen. D accepted that he was at fault for the collision, but denied that he drove dangerously, stating that he drove in the same way as he always did. The Crown prosecutor concluded that D's attention may only have been distracted for a few seconds and so there was insufficient evidence to charge CDDD. He stated that he had come to the decision with some reluctance, but feared that a prosecution for CDDD would eventually falter at the Crown Court. D pleaded guilty to careless driving.

What is concerning about this case is that it occurred in a residential built-up area with a speed limit of 30 mph. As noted by Horne and Reyner, urban roads provide relatively stimulating driving conditions, meaning that sleep-related collisions are rare (Horne and Reyner 2001, 63). It may be that D in A114 suffered from inattention, rather than falling asleep, but to have failed to see either the red lights of the pelican crossing or the pedestrian in his path suggests that his driving fell far below the standard of the competent and careful driver. The prosecution policy gives disregard for traffic lights as an example of dangerous driving if such disregard appears to be deliberate, and there is no suggestion that that was the case here, but there is no requirement in the statute that an act be deliberate in order that dangerous driving is proved.

One of the results of the TRL study noted above was the finding that some of those involved in the prosecution of bad driving offences are of the opinion that it must be possible to prove that D deliberately drove badly for a charge of dangerous driving to succeed. The law makes no such requirement, but there were some cases in the author's study where a similar view was expressed. One such case was B111, in which D's HGV had been blown into the opposite side of the road and into an HGV driven by V in the opposite direction during stormy weather. D said he had difficulty controlling the lorry and had to compensate for the wind, which was recorded as reaching speeds of 56 mph on the day in question. Earlier in his journey he had seen another lorry that had been blown over. This, one could argue, should have provided him with a warning that it was unsafe to continue in his un-laden vehicle. Yet he deliberately, in the sense that he had control over his actions, continued his journey. This appears to have been a borderline case; the investigating officer suggested a charge of careless driving, but his sergeant thought that a charge of CDDD should be considered. The Crown prosecutor decided not to charge CDDD on the basis that D's bad driving was not deliberate, and D pleaded guilty to careless driving when charged.

In A104 D was convicted of CDDD, having caused two deaths when he attempted to turn his HGV around on a single-carriageway road in thick fog and blocked the road. The HGV was almost invisible, meaning that V collided with the trailer of the truck when it was across the carriageway. D maintained throughout interview that it was not a dangerous manoeuvre, on the basis that if the collision had not occurred he would have 'got round quite comfortably'. He quite obviously embarked upon the manoeuvre deliberately, but it was not his intention, in the sense of either wanting the result or of foreseeing the result as a virtual certainty, to create a risk to other road users. The risk appears to have been created through his complete disregard for other road-users, and was a risk he had not recognized. Despite this, he did eventually plead guilty to two counts of CDDD.

There was one further type of case in which the police and CPS failed to agree on the correct charge. Two cases involved refuse lorries knocking down pedestrians when reversing in the street. The first (C36) occurred in October 1999, when D failed to see V crossing the road behind his truck and she became trapped under the rear wheels of the vehicle. Following a case conference held between the CPS and police, the CPS concluded that there was insufficient evidence to provide a realistic prospect of conviction for careless driving. As a result of this case the council amended its working practice for refuse collectors, providing more detailed advice in relation to reversing. Despite this action, a second fatality (C78) occurred in September 2000, when an elderly pedestrian, who had been walking behind the refuse lorry in the same direction in which it was reversing, was again knocked down and trapped under the rear wheels. In this case the CPS decided that there was sufficient evidence of careless driving, but not of CDDD. The Crown prosecutor retained this view, even after meeting with the collision investigator, who considered D's act to be dangerous and wished to challenge the decision.

Both cases involved a lack of observation on the part of D. The vehicles were equipped with devices to reduce the danger they posed to other road users, with a monitor in the cab displaying a picture from a CCTV camera attached to the rear of the vehicle and a warning alarm which sounded when the vehicle was in reverse. In C36, however, the alarm was defective and D had failed to check that it was working. Perhaps more importantly, in both cases D ignored the advice provided in the council's working practice that another crew member should stand at the rear of the vehicle to assist D when reversing. In both cases, even without a crew member to guide him, the collision investigator concluded that D would have had a view of V in his mirrors and CCTV monitor. The facts of the two cases were extremely similar, and yet a prosecution was brought in the latter but not the former. The one aggravating feature of the second case was, perhaps, that D was reversing for some considerable distance along the road. However, in both cases the ultimate decision made by the CPS as to charge represents a step down from the collision investigator's view of D's guilt in terms of the hierarchy of driving offences.

*Dangerous driving based on the condition of the vehicle* This form of the offence was charged in just two cases (B85 and B94). In B85 D was attempting to carry out a U-turn when V, who was approaching him from behind on his motorcycle, tried to overtake D and collided with D's car. It was found that D's rear offside indicator did not work, and the repeater indicator on the side of the car was fitted with a blue lens which would have rendered it almost invisible. Thus, although D claimed that he had indicated before he commenced the turn, such indication was ineffective and D had failed to see V. D pleaded guilty to CDDD.

In B94 the prosecution for CDDD was unsuccessful. D had been driving a tractor with a particularly wide drill attached to the rear of the vehicle. He had been accompanied by his employer earlier on his journey in order to warn other road users of the vehicle's presence, but when they reached the field that was their destination the gate was locked and D's employer left him in order to enter the field via a different gate and let him in. D continued on to the next gate, which was on the other side of a bend. On the bend D had pulled the tractor over so that it was partly on the road and partly on the verge, although the verge was wide enough to accommodate the whole width of the vehicle. V drove around the bend from the opposite direction, braked and skidded into the tractor. The view around the bend was severely restricted, meaning that the tractor was not visible until V was very close to it.

The charge of CDDD was made on the basis that the drill attached to the tractor was so wide that it was dangerous to drive the tractor in that condition without the safety measures of being accompanied by another vehicle and the displaying of markers, as required by the Motor Vehicles (Authorisation of Special Types) Order 1976. This was aggravated by the fact that D did not pull off the road as he could have done on the bend. At trial D was acquitted of CDDD but convicted of careless driving. Another case in which CDDD could have been alleged was B99, where the Construction and Use Regulations had been breached. However, this was a case in which it was felt that it was not in the public interest to prosecute the driver of the tractor, who turned across the path of a motorcyclist, because both V and D came from a small, close-knit community.

Other cases involved vehicles that were in a dangerous condition and yet CDDD was not charged. In A67 a set of steps fell from a mechanical digger on to the road. As the driver of the digger (D) was reversing back along the verge to retrieve them, V collided with the steps and lost control of his car, colliding with a vehicle travelling in the opposite direction. It was found that the bolts which fixed the steps to the vehicle had not been fitted correctly and one had been missing for some time, and the Vehicle Inspectorate concluded that there were problems with the vehicle's maintenance arrangements. D was arrested at the scene for CDDD based on the condition of the vehicle, but there was no further mention of this offence in subsequent documentation. D faced a prosecution for using a motor vehicle likely to cause injury under section 40A of the RTA 1988, but the case was discontinued. D's employer was convicted of the same offence. It may have been felt that CDDD was not made out because D could not have been expected to have been aware of the defect and the employer could not be held liable for aiding and abetting the offence because of the principle in *Loukes* (see above).

The findings of the author's study confirm those of the TRL that the distinction between careless and dangerous driving is often obscure, and this causes difficulties for police, prosecutors and the courts in determining the appropriate offence for which D should face liability. Further results from this study are discussed in the following two chapters in the context of cases involving speeding and, to a greater extent, in the context of the discussion of vehicular homicide. The cases discussed in this chapter are equally relevant to the discussions that will take place on the appropriateness of a charge of causing death by dangerous driving or causing death by careless driving.

# Chapter 3

# Drink-driving and Speeding

It may not be instantly obvious why the two offences of drink-driving and speeding should be placed together in one chapter. On the one hand drink-driving stands out as the one driving offence that carries with it a degree of stigma usually attached to more paradigmatic criminal offences. Speeding, on the other hand, is a far more accepted practice, hardly deemed to be a criminal offence at all in the eyes of even the most respectable 'law-abiding' citizen. That these attitudes prevail is in itself interesting, and is an issue that will be addressed throughout the chapter, with reference to research conducted by psychologists and criminologists, and one that will be returned to in Chapters 6 and 7. However, whilst the popular view is that these offences are completely diverse, from a legal perspective there is much to compare them. Both are 'strict liability' offences requiring no proof of *mens rea*, even in the form of negligence, as is required in relation to the offences discussed in Chapter 2. Both offences, instead of relying on proof of the driver's standard of driving, instead usually rely on technological devices to provide evidence of a particular state of affairs: either that the defendant had alcohol or drugs in his or her body, or that the vehicle was driven at a speed above a particular limit.

It should be noted that there are various 'moving' or 'driver' offences under statute which will not be discussed in this book. These include failing to comply with a road sign under section 36(1) of the Road Traffic Act (RTA) 1988, which makes it a criminal offence to disobey signs including red traffic lights, 'stop' and 'give way' signs and double white lines, amongst others. Such an offence could in itself amount to careless or dangerous driving depending on the circumstances of the particular case.

## Drink-driving

An upper legal limit for the amount of alcohol permitted to be consumed before driving was first introduced in the UK in 1967. However, prior to this the offence of driving while unfit through drink or drugs was already in existence. Thus the term 'drink-driving' is a term which could be used to describe one of two offences: driving with excess alcohol and driving while unfit.

### *The Law*

This book is not concerned with the issue of evidential propriety of blood or breath specimens, which themselves provide a considerable amount of work for the courts. Instead, the focus is on the requirements of the substantive law in establishing an offence under either section 4 or section 5 of the RTA 1988. Section 5 will be dealt with first, as it is the more straightforward of the two offences.

*Section 5 Road Traffic Act 1988: Excess alcohol*

> (1) If a person –
> (a) drives or attempts to drive a motor vehicle on a road or other public place, or
> (b) is in charge of a motor vehicle on a road or other public place,
> after consuming so much alcohol that the proportion of it in his breath, blood or urine exceeds the prescribed limit he is guilty of an offence.
> (2) It is a defence for a person charged with an offence under subsection (1)(b) above to prove that at the time he is alleged to have committed the offence the circumstances were such that there was no likelihood of his driving the vehicle whilst the proportion of alcohol in his breath, blood or urine remained likely to exceed the prescribed limit.
> (3) The court may, in determining whether there was such a likelihood as is mentioned in subsection (2) above, disregard any injury to him and any damage to the vehicle.

The prescribed limit of alcohol is currently 35 micrograms of alcohol in 100 millilitres (35 μg/100 ml) of breath, 80 milligrams of alcohol in 100 millilitres (80 mg/100 ml) of blood, or 107 milligrams of alcohol in 100 millilitres (107 mg/100 ml) of urine (RTA 1988, section 11). In order for a police officer to be able to collect the necessary evidence to prove such an offence, there are various statutory provisions dealing with the power to require a driver to submit to a test. The police may require a preliminary test to be taken if D has committed a moving traffic offence, has been involved in an accident, or has provided the police with reasonable suspicion that he or she is under the influence of drink or drugs and has been driving (RTA 1988, section 6). It is an offence for a driver to fail to submit to such a test in those circumstances (RTA 1988, section 6(6)). The type of preliminary test used will depend on whether D is suspected of being drunk or having taken drugs. If the former is the case, D will be required to take a breathalyser test under section 6A, whilst in the latter case (in which case the offence suspected would be that under section 4) D will be required to undertake a 'preliminary impairment' test under section 6B. A preliminary impairment test involves the officer observing D undertaking a number of tasks at the officer's request, and is governed by a code of practice issued by the Secretary of State. Although section 6C provides for the possibility of administering a preliminary drugs test through the taking of a sample of sweat or saliva for analysis, there is currently no suitable analytical device approved by the Secretary of State for that purpose (Wallis et al. 2005, para.4.35).

Thus, for a preliminary test to be carried out, one of the three 'trigger events' must be reasonably suspected by a police officer, who must be in uniform (section 6(7)). There is currently in the UK no power for the police to carry out random testing, as is permitted in other jurisdictions such as Sweden (see Chapter 5 below).

It is not possible for the police to set up road blocks and systematically test drivers as they pass through the block. However, it is possible for the police to circumvent this prohibition on random testing to some extent. It has been confirmed by the Divisional Court that it is permissible for the police to stop cars randomly and, if they suspect that a particular driver is under the influence of drink or drugs (for example, because of D's demeanour or the smell of alcohol), they are then afforded the necessary suspicion to carry out a preliminary test under section 6 (*Chief Constable of Gwent v Dash* 1986).

Section 5 actually creates six offences: three of 'driving' and three of 'attempting to drive'. The prosecution must specify whether the excess alcohol was in the (i) breath, (ii) blood or (iii) urine (*Bolton JJ, ex p. Khan* 1999). The alcohol must be measured in a specific way using an approved device, the detailed requirements of which will not be discussed here but can be found in *Wilkinson's Road Traffic Offences*, chapter 4 (Wallis et al. 2005). Section 7(3) dictates that the normal routine will be to require two breath tests, and that a requirement to provide a specimen of blood or urine cannot be made unless one of five circumstances prevail. These are: first, that there are medical reasons why a specimen of breath cannot be provided or should not be required (for example, D may suffer from asthma); second, that an approved device for testing breath is not available; third, that an approved device has been used to test a specimen of breath and this has not provided a reliable reading; fourth, that a preliminary drug test has proved positive, necessitating the blood or urine to be tested for drugs; fifth, that a medical practitioner has advised the constable that the condition of D might be due to some drug.

So, if a driver suspected of drink-driving is stopped by the police and asked to take a preliminary breath test and the test proves positive, D will be arrested and taken to a police station, where D will be required to provide a further two specimens of breath for evidential purposes, unless a specimen of blood or urine can be required for one of the above reasons. In future it will be possible for the police to avoid this time-consuming exercise, as section 154 of the Serious Organised Crime and Police Act 2005 amends section 6D RTA 1988 to allow roadside evidential breath tests. However, until a suitable portable breath-testing device has obtained type approval this power cannot be activated (DfT 2007c, para.165).

If, when stopped by the police, D refuses to provide a specimen of breath, D will be committing an offence under section 6(6). If D fails to provide a specimen of breath when required to do so at the police station, D will be committing an offence under section 7(6). Of the two specimens of breath required at the police station, the lower of the two is, under section 8(1), to be used for the purposes of prosecution and the higher measure disregarded. If one of the two specimens of breath provided by D is no more than 50 micrograms of alcohol in 100 millilitres (50 µg/100 ml) of breath, D can request that D give a specimen of blood or urine to replace both the breath tests. Testing of blood and urine is often more reliable than breath testing, but clearly if D asserts this right D risks the blood or urine analysis providing even stronger evidence of D's guilt.

If the required test proves positive, in that the amount of alcohol exceeds the limits set out in section 11 RTA (see above), the presumption is that the proportion of alcohol in D's breath, blood, or urine at the time of driving was not less that shown in the specimen (section 15(2) of the Road Traffic Offenders Act 1988). With the exception that D can prove that D took alcohol after the alleged offence took place and before providing the specimen, and that had D not done so the alcohol in the specimen would not have exceeded the prescribed limit (section 15(3) of the Road Traffic Offenders Act 1988), the presumption is irrebuttable (*Beauchamp-Thompson v DPP* 1988), and the fact that it is irrebuttable does not breach D's rights under Article 6 European Convention of Human Rights (ECHR) (*Parker v DPP* 2001; *Griffiths v DPP* 2002).

It may be that there has been a delay between D driving and the police being in a position to take the relevant specimen. If D was injured in a collision, or if D initially managed to evade the police before being apprehended, several hours may have passed. Given that the alcohol level in the body declines with the passage of time, the specimen might come back negative, despite the fact that D was over the limit at the time of driving. The police may therefore attempt to produce a back-calculation of alcohol from the specimen and the Crown may use the results in a subsequent prosecution (*Gumbley v Cunningham* 1989). To produce a back-calculation is a difficult task, because the rate of decline in the level of alcohol in a person's blood can be affected by a multitude of factors; any back-calculation is only likely to provide a comparatively imprecise prediction of D's alcohol level at the time of driving (Wallis et al. 2005, para.4.186). In using a back-calculation as part of the prosecution case the Crown may find it difficult to prove their case beyond all reasonable doubt, unless there is unequivocal expert forensic evidence on the issue.

### *Section 4 Road Traffic Act 1988: Driving while unfit*

(1) A person who, when driving or attempting to drive a mechanically propelled vehicle on a road or other public place, is unfit to drive through drink or drugs is guilty of an offence.
(2) Without prejudice to subsection (1) above, a person who, when in charge of a mechanically propelled vehicle which is on a road or other public place, is unfit to drive through drink or drugs is guilty of an offence.
(3) For the purposes of subsection (2) above, a person shall be deemed not to have been in charge of a mechanically propelled vehicle if he proves that at the material time the circumstances were such that there was no likelihood of his driving it so long as he remained unfit to drive through drink or drugs.
(4) The court may, in determining whether there was such a likelihood as is mentioned in subsection (3) above, disregard any injury to him and any damage to the vehicle.
(5) For the purposes of this section, a person shall be taken to be unfit to drive if his ability to drive properly is for the time being impaired.

Historically this offence was first introduced before analysis of bodily fluids or breath was possible to establish how much D had had to drink. The original ancestor of the offence can be found under section 12 of the Licensing Act 1872:

> Every person who is drunk while in charge on any highway or other public place of any carriage, horse, cattle, or steam engine, or who is drunk when in possession of any loaded firearms, … shall be liable to a penalty not exceeding level 1 on the standard scale, or in the discretion of the court to imprisonment for any term not exceeding one month.

Following the introduction of the motor car to the masses, section 15 of the Road Traffic Act 1930 made it an offence to drive or attempt to drive or to be in charge of a motor vehicle on a road or other public place when under the influence of drink or drugs to such an extent as to be incapable of having proper control of the vehicle, and it was not until the 1960s that exceeding a prescribed limit could be proven by the use of scientific methods. Rather than replacing the existing law based on unfitness to drive, however, the new laws setting limits were added alongside existing offences. These different approaches to proving drink-driving have been described as the 'impairment approach' and the 'per se approach', and whilst the law in England and Wales takes both approaches, in other jurisdictions (for examples some US states) either one or the other applies (see Austrian Road Safety Board 2003, para.3.2).

Nowadays, the offence under section 4 can be used where D is suspected of being over the prescribed limit for alcohol, but has failed to submit to be tested under section 7 RTA 1988 and so there is insufficient evidence to prosecute D under section 5. It is also the appropriate offence where D has not been drinking but is impaired through consumption of some other drug. There must be evidence of both impairment in D's ability to drive properly and of that impairment stemming from drink or drugs. This may come from a doctor, who will normally be called to examine a driver suspected of the offence (Wallis et al. 2005, para.4.104).

The word 'drugs' under section 4 includes medicines (*Armstrong v Clark* 1957), as well as prohibited drugs. Section 11 of the RTA 1988 defines a drug as including 'any intoxicant other than alcohol'. Drivers who are on medication prescribed or otherwise should read the instructions on taking their medicine clearly, and should desist from driving if warned against it by the drug manufacturer. Although it is not technically a criminal offence in England and Wales to take controlled drugs such as cannabis and methamphetamine (ecstasy), only to possess (Misuse of Drugs Act 1971, section 5) or supply (Misuse of Drugs Act 1971, section 4) them, users of such drugs will be committing a criminal offence as soon as they attempt to drive a motor vehicle whilst under their influence.

*Defences* Section 5(2) and section 4(3) provide a defence to D if D can show that at the time of being found 'in charge' of a vehicle and either over the limit or 'unfit' there was no likelihood of D driving. D might claim that D was taking refuge in the vehicle from the weather and intended to sleep until the alcohol had worn off before driving home. However, the burden of proof is on D to provide convincing evidence of such a story, not on the prosecution to prove otherwise.

The House of Lords has held that this does not breach Article 6(2) of the ECHR (presumption of innocence) (*Sheldrake v DPP* 2005). Lord Bingham noted that previous incarnations of these offences were strict liability to the extent of providing no such defence, and that in introducing the defence in favour of the defendant there was no reason why the burden should not rest with D:

> This is not in my view an oppressive outcome, since a person in charge of a car when unfit to drive it may properly be expected to divest himself of the power to do so (as by giving the keys to someone else) or put it out of his power to do so (as by going well away). (Ibid. at [40])

He went on to explain his decision against the background of the Strasbourg jurisprudence on the issue of reverse burdens of proof:

> It may not be very profitable to debate whether section 5(2) infringes the presumption of innocence. It may be assumed that it does. Plainly the provision is directed to a legitimate object: the prevention of death, injury and damage caused by unfit drivers. Does the provision meet the tests of acceptability identified in the Strasbourg jurisprudence? In my view, it plainly does. I do not regard the burden placed on the defendant as beyond reasonable limits or in any way arbitrary. It is not objectionable to criminalise a defendant's conduct in these circumstances without requiring a prosecutor to prove criminal intent. The defendant has a full opportunity to show that there was no likelihood of his driving, a matter so closely conditioned by his own knowledge and state of mind at the material time as to make it much more appropriate for him to prove on the balance of probabilities that he would not have been likely to drive than for the prosecutor to prove, beyond reasonable doubt, that he would. I do not think that imposition of a legal burden went beyond what was necessary. If a driver tries and fails to establish a defence under section 5(2), I would not regard the resulting conviction as unfair … (Ibid. at [41])

Lord Carswell justified the reverse burden on the basis that it was 'quite easy' for the defendant to establish the defence on the balance of probabilities, whereas it would be 'difficult' for the prosecution to prove beyond all reasonable doubt that it did not apply (ibid. at [84]).

Beyond this statutory defence, D may be able to plead a common-law defence if the circumstances allow. The general defence of duress of circumstances discussed in Chapter 2 has been raised in relation to charges of drink-driving in a number of cases, but has often failed. For example, in *DPP v Jones* (1990) D was acquitted of drink-driving after raising the defence of what was referred to as 'necessity' (another label for duress of circumstances) at trial. D had been confronted by another man in the car park of a public house and hit on the head. D had sought refuge in his car and, after his assailant had directed blows at the car, had decided that his only means of escape was to drive home. This secured his acquittal at the magistrates' court, but on appeal to the Divisional Court it was held that although the defence may have been available to D to make good his escape, there was no need for him to drive the full one and a half miles to his home and the case was sent back to the magistrates' court with a direction to convict.

In a case with similar facts (*DPP v Bell* 1992), the Divisional Court dismissed the appeal by the prosecution against the acquittal of D, who had, unlike the defendant in *Jones*, stopped his car once he had made good his escape from a nightclub car park. In this case it was held that the fact that D may have intended to drive home from the club after drinking even before the violent incident started was irrelevant, since the requirements of the defence were met.

One of the requirements of the defence is an objective test that a sober person of reasonable firmness sharing D's characteristics would have responded to the threat in the way that D did (*Graham* 1982). In any case where D is pleading duress of circumstances as a defence to drink-driving D will not share the characteristic of being 'sober' which could lead to failure in the defence. For example, in *DPP v Tomkinson* (2001) it was said that there was no basis for the magistrates' conclusion that a sober woman of reasonable firmness would have driven 72 miles whilst over the limit, as the defendant had done in attempting to escape her violent husband. The objective nature of the test was similarly highlighted in the cases of *DPP v Davis* and *DPP v Pitway* (1994).

*Penalties* In addition to a fine of up to £5000 and a possible sentence of six months' imprisonment for a first offence, the offences of driving or attempting to drive under sections 4 and 5 lead to obligatory disqualification under section 34 Road Traffic Offenders Act (RTOA) 1988, whilst disqualification for the 'being in charge' offences is discretionary. In 2004, 90,300 persons were disqualified for driving after consuming alcohol or taking drugs (Home Office 2006, 13). The minimum term for disqualification is twelve months, unless there are special reasons for imposing a shorter period of disqualification or no disqualification at all (section 34(1)). Where D has a previous conviction for drink-driving within the past ten years, the minimum period of disqualification rises to three years (section 34(3)).

D may try to argue that there are special reasons for not imposing the minimum twelve months' disqualification. Reasons listed by the Judicial Studies Board which might amount to a special reason include that D's drink was laced:

> The defendant will need to establish:
> (a) His drink was 'laced'.
> (b) He did not know or suspect that it was 'laced', and
> (c) If his drink had not been 'laced', the alcohol level in his breath would not have exceeded the prescribed limit.
>
> The defendant must establish (c) with medical or scientific evidence unless it is obvious to a layman that the added drink explains the excess while with (b) there must come a point at which the court takes the view that the reading is so high or the level of impairment so substantial that the defendant must have realised he was affected by drink. (JSB 2005, 119)

Given that drink-driving is a strict liability offence the only way of taking into consideration D's claim that D did not know that D was over the limit is at the sentencing stage. It is clearly going to be rare that such a plea succeeds, however. In other cases there is another way in which D can reduce the period of disqualification. Under section 34A, where the period of disqualification is at least twelve months, D can receive a reduction of between at least three months and no more than a quarter of the period, (so, for example, a disqualification period of twelve months is reduced to nine months) if D attends an approved course. These courses aim to educate drivers on the dangers involved in drinking and driving to help prevent re-offending (see below).

An additional method of reducing the period of disqualification that will be available in future is through the use of alcohol ignition interlocks. Section 15 of the Road Safety Act (RSA) 2006 introduces section 34D into the RTOA 1988, and allows a disqualification period of not less than two years to be reduced by between at least twelve months and not more than one half of the unreduced period if the court also imposes an 'alcohol ignition interlock programme order' requiring the offender to comply with the alcohol ignition interlock conditions. If D contravenes those conditions the disqualification period that must be served reverts to the original period that was to be imposed by the court. The main condition is that D must not drive a motor vehicle during the period that the order applies unless it is fitted with an alcohol ignition interlock in good working order.

Alcohol ignition interlocks, or 'alcolocks', have been pioneered in Sweden, where, in addition to being used in an attempt to help rehabilitate drink-drive offenders, they are also used by companies to ensure that their drivers are not drink-driving. Drivers are required to provide a specimen of breath into the interlock device and only if the result is negative will it be possible to start the engine. Under section 34D Road Traffic Offenders Act (RTOA) 1988 the device to be used in England and Wales must be such that it requires a specimen of breath to be provided not only at the start of a journey but also at regular intervals while driving (section 34D(9)). The limit prescribed by section 34 is nine micrograms of alcohol in one hundred millilitres (9 µg/100 ml) of breath, which is far lower than the general legal limit for driving (35 µg/100 ml). In order to deter abuse of the system, section 34(12) creates two offences. The first is the offence of interfering with an alcolock to cause it not to function properly, which is an offence that might be committed by any person, not only the driver. The second is the offence of providing a specimen of breath for the purposes of the alcolock with the intent to enable the offender to drive, which is necessarily committed by someone other than D. This is to prevent D asking a friend to provide a clear specimen of breath when D knows that he himself would provide a positive specimen. The provisions under section 15 RSA 2006 are to be introduced for an experimental period in the first instance. They will not apply after the year 2010 unless they prove to be a success and the Secretary of State orders that they may continue (section 16 RSA 2006).

### *Policy and Practice*

There is no doubt that driving whilst impaired through drink should be discouraged, and it is well accepted that the use of criminal sanctions to deter drink-driving is justified. Currently, around 10 per cent of fatal road traffic collisions in Great Britain are attributed to impairment by alcohol (DfT 2007a, Table 4b). In the

Europe-wide public opinion survey of SARTRE 3, less than 2 per cent of British interviewees thought that the legal blood alcohol level should be higher than at present and a tiny fraction (0.16 per cent) thought that drivers should be able to drink as much as they liked before driving (Dahlstedt 2006, Table 68). There are clear physiological reasons why drinking and driving do not mix:

> The immediate effects of alcohol on the brain are either depressing or stimulating in nature, depending on the quantity consumed .... Either way, alcohol results in impairment which increases the likelihood of a crash since it produces poor judgement, increased reaction time, lower vigilance and decreased visual acuity. Physiologically, alcohol also lowers blood pressure and depresses consciousness and respiration. Alcohol also has analgesic and general anaesthetic properties. Alcohol can impair judgement and increase crash risk even at relatively low BAC levels. However, the effects become progressively worse as the BAC increases. Not only do judgement and reaction time suffer, but vision also deteriorates. Apart from its direct impact on crash outcomes, alcohol is believed to affect other aspects of driver safety such as seat-belt wearing, helmet use, and speed choice. (GRSP 2007, para.1.2.10)

Whilst it is clear that an offence of drink-driving should exist, the question remains as to what level should be set for the legal blood alcohol concentration (BAC). The level of 80 mg/100 ml is fairly high compared to the level in other European countries. The United Kingdom, Ireland, Malta and Luxembourg are the only EU member states to have such a high BAC limit. Fifteen EU Member States have now adopted a legal BAC limit of 50 mg/100 ml (Austria, Belgium, Bulgaria, Cyprus, Denmark, Finland, France, Germany, Greece, Italy, Latvia, the Netherlands, Portugal, Slovenia and Spain). Some have gone even further with a level as low as 20 mg/100 ml (Poland and Sweden) whilst others apply a zero policy with a legal BAC of 0 g/100 ml (Czech Republic, Estonia, Hungary and Slovakia) (European Road Safety Observatory website). The European Commission recommends that all member states of the EU should set a legal BAC of 50 mg/100 ml or lower (2001/116/EC).

Whilst it might be seen to be rather extreme to adopt a legal BAC of zero, as has been done in some of the eastern European countries, research shows that even the smallest amount of alcohol can affect a driver's performance. A BAC of 10–50 mg/100 ml leads to: increase in heart and respiration rates; decrease in various brain centre functions; inconsistent effects on behavioural task performances; decrease in judgement and inhibitions; mild sense of elation, relaxation and pleasure. A BAC of 60–100 mg/100 ml leads to: physiological sedation of nearly all systems; decreased attention and alertness, slowed reactions, impaired coordination, and reduced muscle strength; reduced ability to make rational decisions or exercise good judgement; increase in anxiety and depression; decrease in patience. As we have seen, most European countries set a BAC somewhere below this level. Above the maximum legal BAC, a BAC of 100–150 mg/100 ml leads to: dramatic slowing of reactions; impairment of balance and movement; impairment of some visual functions; slurred speech; vomiting, especially if this BAC is reached rapidly (GRSP 2007, Table 1.1).

In 1964 the Grand Rapids study carried out in Michigan in the United States showed that drivers who had consumed alcohol had a much higher risk of involvement in crashes than those with a zero BAC, and that this risk increased rapidly with increasing blood alcohol levels (GRSP 2007, Box 1.2). Those with a BAC of 60 mg/100 ml were twice as likely to cause a collision than those with a BAC of zero. This rose to six times more likely with a BAC of 100 mg/100 ml and 25 times more likely with a BAC of 150 mg/100 ml (Austrian Road Safety Board 2003, para.3.4.1.2).

Some consideration of lowering the legal BAC has been given by the UK parliament (see, for example, debates on the Road Safety Bill in Hansard, HC October 9, 2006, column 74). At a time when it was thought that a European Directive on the matter was imminent, the government stated that it was minded to reduce the BAC limit to 50 mg/100 ml (DETR 1998), but when the European Commission passed a recommendation on the matter instead of a Directive (2001/116/EC) the reform was shelved. In answering questions posed by the House of Lords Select Committee on Europe, the government indicated that the main reason for not following the advice of the European Commission was that it was feared that a debate on the question of reducing the permitted BAC would imply that there was an acceptable level below which it is safe to drink and drive, and the government strongly endorsed the view that motorists should not drink and drive at all (House of Lords Select Committee 2002, para.36). In addition, there was concern that reduction of the permitted legal limit would lead to violations of this lower limit being seen as a 'lesser offence', resulting in pressure to reduce the penalties for drink-driving (ibid., para.37).

The House of Lords Select Committee, in recommending a reduction in the legal BAC level to 50 mg/100 ml, noted that:

> The current 80 mg/100 ml level encourages a popular rule-of-thumb assessment about how much a person can drink before the limit is reached. The effect of alcohol on a person's ability to drive varies considerably. A reduction of the BAC limit to 50 mg/100 ml would reduce the level at which the rule-of-thumb assessment operated and would possibly convince many drivers that the only way they could be certain of not breaking the limit would be to avoid alcohol entirely when driving. (para.42)

Another excuse provided by the government for not lowering the limit was that there was insufficient support for such a move. This is contrary to the responses collected to the government's 1998 consultation paper on the matter: of the 401 responses 206 were in favour of the reduction compared to 163 who argued for retaining the existing 80 mg/100 ml limit. Of the 206 in favour, 170 supported the proposed 50 mg/100 ml limit, a further 28 supported it as a first step towards an even greater reduction, and another eight favoured a zero limit. This positive reaction to the proposal is supported by other research: almost 19 per cent of British interviewees in SARTRE 3 thought that the legal BAC should be lower than it is at present, and as many as 51 per cent thought that drivers should be permitted to drink no alcohol at all (Dahlstedt 2006, Table 68). Another survey found that 62 per cent of respondents were in favour of a lower BAC limit (Home Office 2004).

Other jurisdictions have been successful in lowering their legal BAC level in recent years. In 2002, French President Jacques Chirac declared publicly that road safety would be one of the three major priorities, and a number of initiatives were introduced. At that time the legal BAC was 70 mg/100 ml, having been dropped from 80 mg/100 ml in 1995, and this was further reduced to 50 mg/100 ml (and 20 mg/100 ml for bus drivers, as recommended by the European Commission). This was coupled with an increase in both enforcement levels and the penalties for drink-driving. Breath tests were increased by 15 per cent and penalty points were increased from three to six for a BAC between 50 mg/100 ml and 80 mg/100 ml (as in Great Britain, in France 12 points lead to disqualification). The results appear to be extremely positive, with road deaths decreasing by 32 per cent between 2002 and 2004 and the number of incidents of drink-driving falling by almost 40 per cent from 2003 to 2004 (GRSP 2007, Box 1.6).

The government has itself predicted similar benefits of reducing the BAC in Great Britain. An estimated 50 lives could be saved each year if the legal BAC level was reduced to 50 mg/100 ml (DETR 1998). Despite this, there seems little likelihood that a lowering of the legal BAC will occur unless the European Commission imposes a directive to that effect.

Despite Britain lagging behind other countries with respect to its substantive law on drink-driving in terms of the legal BAC limit, it is often thought that the law has been a successful deterrent to drink-drivers. The results of research are, however, somewhat mixed. A Home Office self-report study of drivers conducted in 2002 found that 44 per cent of drivers admitted to driving after drinking some alcohol in the previous year, and 12 per cent admitted to doing so when they believed they had been over the limit (Home Office 2004). This can be compared to the 22 per cent of men who admitted to driving when they knew they were over the limit in the 1984 British Crime Survey (Riley 1985, 246). Of those who admitted to driving when over the limit in the 2002 survey, 18 per cent claimed that they did so once a month or more (Home Office 2004). Of those who said they had driven after drinking but thought themselves under the limit, 31 per cent said they did so once a month or more. Within this last group it might be possible that some of the drivers were actually over the limit when driving, given that it is difficult to estimate whether one has drunk enough to take oneself over the limit, since this can be affected by a number of factors.

The main reason given for drink-driving was that drivers 'felt safe to drive' despite being over the limit: 49 per cent of drivers admitting to driving when over the limit gave this as their reason (ibid.). This finding would seem to conflict with attitudes expressed in the same survey suggesting that drink-driving was viewed very negatively and 63 per cent of respondents, including 53 per cent of those who admitted driving over the limit, believed that drink-driving was 'very often' or 'always' a factor in accidents. Although the message that drinking and driving is dangerous is getting through, it would seem that some drivers fail to take the message on board in modifying their own behaviour.

The number of disqualifications for drink-driving peaked at 103,000 in 1989 and steadily declined until 1994. Since then it has been relatively stable, although 2004 saw a rise of 3,300 disqualifications for drink-driving from the previous year (Home Office 2006, 12). The number of disqualifications is a good indication of the number of offenders convicted, since disqualification is mandatory. A better indication of the number of drink-drivers stopped by the police is probably a combination of the number of positive breath tests undertaken coupled with the number of tests refused. This has shown a dramatic drop since 1979, when 51 per cent of those stopped were either positive, refused to be tested, or were unable to be tested. The year 1994 experienced the lowest level of positive or refused breath tests (14 per cent), whilst the proportion of positive or refused tests in 2004 was 18 per cent (ibid., 17).

There is clearly a need to reduce this figure below 18 per cent, and research has been conducted both in the UK and internationally to establish who needs to be targeted in any measures aimed at doing so. Generally, research has shown that drivers more likely to drink-drive are characterized as being:

- male
- aged 18–24 years old
- from a low socio-economic grouping
- single or divorced
- in a blue collar occupation
- of low education and limited literacy
- of low self-esteem. (GRSP 2007, para.1.3.1)

In the UK specifically, it has been reported that a quarter of 16- to 29-year-olds admitted to driving whilst over the limit in the previous year (Home Office 2004). Breath-test statistics show that young men under 21 comprise around 12 per cent of drink-driving offenders, a percentage greatly disproportionate to the number of licence-holders of that age (House of Commons Transport Committee 2007, 34). It has also been reported that young drivers aged 17–19 are 10 times as likely to have a drink-drive crash and young drivers aged 20–24 are 4.5 times as likely to have a drink-drive crash per mile driven than the driver population as a whole (ibid.).

There are a number of initiatives that might help address drink-driving amongst those groups shown to be the most common offenders. In the United States, 30 states have enacted lower BAC limits (typically 0–20 mg/100 ml) for young drivers (GRSP 2007, 79), as a result of the US Congress passing a law requiring zero tolerance laws for drivers below the age of 21 (Fell and Voas 2006, 239). One of the reasons for this change was that in many states the legal age for drinking is 21, several years higher than the legal driving age, and it 'seemed logical that underage drivers should have no alcohol in their systems whey they drove' (ibid.). A more universal reason for such a law is evidence that young men are the group most likely to drink and drive. One study which evaluated the effects on drinking and driving of lowered BAC limits for drivers younger than 21 years between 1984 and 1998 showed that the new laws were followed by statistically significant decreases (19 per cent) in the amount of driving after drinking (GRSP 2007, 76). However, it should be noted that the lower BAC levels for young drivers are just one element in a policy directed towards reducing young drink-drivers. One of the main reasons for a minimum legal drinking age of 21 is itself to reduce the numbers of young people who drink and drive. Voas et al. note that although minimum legal drinking age laws are only weakly enforced the very existence of the legislation may be influencing normative changes in drinking and driving attitudes (Voas et al. 2003, 586).

In the UK, the House of Commons Transport Committee, in looking at the problem of risk-taking amongst novice drivers, has made the following recommendation:

> Based on the evidence available, we believe there is a case for reducing the permitted blood alcohol concentration from 0.8 g/l to zero (or 0.2 g/l, which in practice is effectively zero) for novice drivers. If the Department [for Transport] introduces a lower permitted blood alcohol concentration for novice drivers it must be assiduous in countering any impression that it is acceptable for more experienced drivers to drive under the influence of alcohol. We understand that the Department is to shortly consult on proposals to address the problem of drink-drive collisions. We welcome this much needed investigation and look forward to a thorough examination of what should be the permitted blood alcohol concentration for drivers. The Department for Transport must tackle drink-driving through ongoing publicity and enforcement campaigns targeted at all drivers, including the young and newly-qualified. (House of Commons Transport Committee 2007, para.110)

There are several options for the UK parliament with regards to the legal BAC limit. It could leave it as it is at 80 mg/100 ml, it could reduce it to 50 mg/100 ml for all drivers, or it could reduce the legal BAC limit to 0–20 mg/100 ml for young drivers, leaving a higher level (either the current 80 mg/100 ml or a reduced 50 mg/100 ml) to apply to other drivers. Given that most EU member states now have a legal BAC of 50 mg/100 ml it may be unlikely that the European Commission will find it necessary to pass a Directive on this matter. Nevertheless, there is strong evidence that such a change would have a positive effect on the number of collisions resulting from drink-driving and this fact, irrespective of the Commission's decision, should be enough to encourage the British government to initiate the change.

In order to maximize the effects of a lower legal BAC limit, the government might also wish to reconsider its policy with regards to enforcement. Currently there is a huge variance in the likelihood of being detected for drink-driving depending on regional location. In 2004, for example, there were 255 tests carried out per 100,000 population in the West Midlands, compared to 3,600 tests carried out per 100,000 population in North Wales. For the purposes of deterrence rather than enforcement, perhaps what is more important than the number of tests carried out is the public's perception of the likelihood that they will be caught, although this must bear some relation to the actual threat posed to effect enduring deterrence (Corbett 2003, 94). When asked how likely it was for a drink-driver to be caught if driving over the legal limit once a week for a year, half of the respondents in a public survey thought it was unlikely or very unlikely that they would be caught (Home Office 2004). Greater consistency in the numbers of screening tests carried out is likely to increase the deterrent effect, and ideally a change in law should allow for random breath testing.

Random breath testing has been the principal method of drink-drive law enforcement in Australia since 1982 (Briscoe 2004). Unlike in the UK, police in Australia have the power to breathalyse any driver regardless of whether they suspect an offence has been committed. Random breath-testing programmes use roving cars and buses to stop drivers, rather than stationary check-points, which increases visibility of enforcement measures (Peek-Asa 1999, 65). The Australian policy of random breath testing is modelled on deterrence principles and aims to increase drivers' perceived risk of apprehension through highly visible and well-publicized patrols that breath test a large proportion of the motoring population selected at random (Briscoe 2004). The results appear to be positive: following the introduction of random breath testing in New South Wales serious injury accidents fell by 19 per cent, fatalities fell by 48 per cent and single-vehicle night-time collisions (often caused by drink-driving) fell be 26 per cent (ibid.). These effects appear to persist over the long term, unlike many initiatives that show an immediate effect followed by a gradual wearing-off.

Random breath testing occurs in several other jurisdictions, such as Sweden (see Chapter 5), where it can take the form of 'sobriety checks' or road blocks. Unlike in Australia, these involve stopping every vehicle at a particular location in order to conduct breath tests of the drivers. A review of the studies on the effectiveness of random breath testing found that overall fatalities measured before and after implementation of random breath testing showed reductions ranging from 16.2 per cent to 29 per cent (Peek-Asa 1999, 59). Those studies that related to Australia tended to show a higher decline in alcohol-related fatalities than those studies that related to the United States, where sobriety checkpoints are more common (ibid., 63). This suggests that the long-term use of random breath testing in Australia is more effective than the short 'blitz' effect of sobriety checkpoints in the US. (It should be noted, however, that US sobriety checkpoints require the police to have reasonable suspicion that D has been drinking before they can require a breath test, which is perhaps more similar to the law in the UK than somewhere like Sweden, where true random testing operates.)

Given the positive results in other jurisdictions, it might be advantageous to introduce random breath testing in the UK. Support for random testing in one form or another exists amongst the British public: 86 per cent of drivers were in favour of random breath testing in one survey, including 70 per cent of drivers who admitted to driving over the limit (Home Office 2004). Although an amendment to the Road Safety Bill 2006 was tabled in the House of Lords to allow for random breath testing, it was never passed. This would have allowed the police to undertake targeted breath testing for a maximum of 24 hours where an inspector believed that drinking and driving may be taking place (Hansard, HL November 22, 2005, column 1523). Lord Davies of Oldham, speaking on behalf of the government, stated that:

> while it was suggested by some that this proposal would not go far enough ... for the Government it is a step too far, given the current practice of the police in their enforcement procedures against drink-driving. The police are content with their existing powers in this area and we would not wish to widen them. (Ibid., column 1525)

A separate issue is that of driving under the influence of drugs, which currently cannot be detected through the use of breath tests and must be prosecuted under section 4 RTA 1988 (driving while unfit). Whilst the incidence of drink-driving has been reducing until very recently, drug-driving increased by a factor of approximately three between the late 1980s and 2000 (Tunbridge et al. 2001, 5). Other countries take a different approach to drug-driving in contrast to the UK. For example, in 1999 Sweden introduced a law imposing a zero limit on narcotics in the blood. Belgium intended to pass a similar law the same year, but the government rejected a zero limit and insisted on setting limits similar to those imposed for drink-driving. Under the Belgian law the legal limits for most drugs found in blood are set at 50 ng/ml, with the exception of cannabis (2 ng/ml) and morphine (20 ng/ml) (Austrian Road Safety Board 2003, para.3.3.2.2).

Britain continues to rely on the impairment approach in legislating on drug-driving, rather than taking a '*per se*' approach. However, in most cases a blood sample testing positive for drugs will go a long way towards proving the offence under section 4, as long as it can be shown that D's driving was affected by the drugs. A zero tolerance approach has been proposed, and an amendment to Road Safety Bill 2006 was tabled to create an offence of 'driving with illegal drugs':

> A person who when driving or attempting to drive a mechanically propelled vehicle on a road or other place is found to have traces of an illegal drug in his body shall be guilty of an offence.

The government was, however, opposed to this offence on the basis that it would prefer to set limits for drug-driving similar to those for drink-driving, but thought it impossible to do so until such time as effective detecting devices could be used (Hansard, HC October 9, 2006, column 85). There does not appear to be the need for a change in the law at the moment, since it has been found that the general medical examination and standardized impairment testing applied by police surgeons are generally effective in determining impairment, at least in relation to cannabis consumption (Sexton et al. 2002).

Research on the effects of illegal substances on driving ability is mixed. Some research shows that there is an increased risk of collisions and injuries for all substances, whilst conflicting research exists suggesting that there is no increased risk for some substances. Insufficient studies have been carried out to assess the effects of specific concentrations of different drugs on driving ability (Austrian Road Safety Board 2003, para.3.4.2.3). Given that it has not been established that driving with only the smallest amount of drugs in the body is dangerous, a common argument is that the law would not be justified in taking a zero tolerance approach and until such time as science provides a validated limit it is better to continue with 'driving when unfit' offences (ibid. para.3.4.2.4.2). An additional problem is the issue of traceability. Many illegal drugs (particularly cannabis) can be detected in the body for a long time after the intoxicating effects have worn off, meaning that under a zero tolerance approach drivers could be found guilty of an offence even though they had not driven whilst under the influence of drugs (ibid.). Until much more is known about the characteristics of different drugs and their effects on driving, it is unlikely that the law will be changed and section 4 will remain the relevant offence in cases of drug-driving.

The two offences under sections 4 and 5 are 'closely inter-related' (Wallis et al. 2005, paras 4.28 and 4.98), and whilst cases of drug-driving can only lead to a charge under section 4, in many cases of drink-driving it may be appropriate for offences under both sections 4 and 5 to be charged. Although random testing is not yet permitted in the UK, the number of screening tests recorded in 2004 was up 8 per cent from the previous year, although the figure of 578,000 was far lower then when the number peaked in 1998 at about 800,000 (Home Office 2006, 16). Police forces often conduct campaigns at specific times of year when a far higher number of breath tests are likely to take place. Campaigns at Christmas are commonplace, and in 2004 15 per cent of screening tests were carried out during December (ibid., 17). Campaigns at other times of year also take place, however. In 2007 many police forces ran a summer drink-drive campaign to tackle drink-driving by those enjoying the warm weather. Interestingly, however, the highest number of refused or positive breath tests take place in the months of October and November rather than during the summer or Christmas period (ibid.).

Thus far the issue of detecting and deterring single instances of drink-driving have been discussed. Research has found that one of the characteristics shared by those who tend to drink-drive is that they drink more in proportion to the rest of the population (Home Office 2004). Given that there is evidence that many offenders are alcoholics, it may be beneficial to try to address the underlying causes of drink-driving once offenders have been detected. With this in mind, the High Risk Offender Scheme was introduced in 1983 (Inwood et al. 2007) in an attempt to rehabilitate drink-drivers.

Under the High Risk Offender Scheme those convicted of a drink-drive offence may, in certain circumstances, be classified as a high risk offender (HRO). This means that, if D is disqualified for the offence, D's driving licence will not automatically be returned to D at the end of the period of disqualification. The High Risk Offenders Scheme is intended to deal with drivers whose apparent dependency on alcohol presents a risk to road safety.

This scheme covers people in the following categories:

1) Those disqualified twice, within a ten-year period, for any drink-drive offence.
2) Those disqualified for having a proportion of alcohol in the body two and a half, or more, times the legal limit, which therefore equalled or exceeded:
   (i) 87.5 mg/100 ml of breath, or
   (ii) 200 mg/100 ml of blood, or
   (iii) 267.5 mg/100 ml of urine.

3) Those disqualified for failing without reasonable cause to provide a specimen for analysis.

Under the High Risk Offenders Scheme offenders are required to satisfy the Medical Advisor at the Driver and Vehicle Licensing Agency (DVLA) that they do not have a drink problem and are fit to drive before their licence is returned.

Although it is necessary for HROs to undergo a positive assessment of fitness to drive before their licence is returned to them, there is little compulsion to address their problems beyond this. All drink-drivers, whether HROs or first offenders may, since January 2000, be offered attendance on a drink-drive rehabilitation course after sentence by the court (Inwood et al. 2007, 1). These courses are similar to speed awareness courses (see below) and must be paid for by the offender. In return, D may receive up to a 25 per cent reduction in the period of disqualification to which D has been sentenced. If D has been sentenced to the minimum of 12 months' disqualification, D will receive a discount of three months and suffer disqualification for nine months only, on completion of the course. It is a question for D as to whether D decides to accept the offer or not. There is no set format to the courses, although the most common format is one session a week (ibid., 10).

The take-up rate for the drink-drive rehabilitation courses has been found to be around 45 per cent (Inwood et al. 2007, 6), but only 30–40 per cent of HROs attended. Those more likely to attend the course were women, offenders aged 40 or more and offenders from a higher social status (ibid., 16). The main reasons given for not attending were that D did not want to drive, or that D could not afford the course fee (ibid., 15). Other reasons given were practical ones relating to transport problems in getting to the course venue, work or family duties and the reported inconvenient location of the courses. It is unfortunate that HROs are less likely to attend the courses, given that for those who choose to attend the courses appear to have positive results, particularly for HROs, younger drivers and male drivers (ibid., 17). Inwood et al. calculate that course attendees are around 44 per cent less likely than non-attendees to be reconvicted of a drink-drive offence within five years (ibid., 7). However, it is unclear from their findings whether these positive results stem from attendance on the course itself, or from feelings of guilt because of the fact of being involved in an a collision, since it was found that those drink-drivers who were apprehended by the police at the scene of a collision were more likely than others to attend the course (ibid., 13). Inwood et al. recommend that attendance on a drink-drive rehabilitation course should be mandatory, to ensure that those most in need of it benefit (ibid., 19).

Beyond the law there are a number of ways that drink-driving could be addressed, particularly through education. Inwood et al. suggest that the following measures, amongst others, should be introduced:

- Alcohol knowledge could be brought into the school curriculum as part of general health education. There seems to be a lot of focus on the use of drugs but alcohol use is still prevalent.

- Information about the risks of drinking and driving could be provided during the training of driving instructors so that they can disseminate the information to pupils.
- More serious consequences for drink-drive offences could be introduced and publicised. (Inwood et al. 2007, 20)

It may be that, in relation to the final suggestion, increased penalties are not needed, but that the authorities should concentrate on publicizing the current penalties, given that there is widespread ignorance on the subject. When asked about different initiatives that might help reduce drink-driving, more than 80 per cent of offenders in Inwood et al.'s survey agreed that both the legal consequences and the social consequences of drink-driving should be better advertised, and 80 per cent thought that the alcohol content of drinks should be better advertised. Around 50 per cent agreed that cheaper non-alcoholic drinks would be beneficial, and in confirmation of other research referred to above, 60 per cent thought that making it illegal to drink any alcohol before driving would help. Around 50 per cent agreed that lowering the legal BAC would likewise be a positive step (ibid., 16).

## Speeding

The term 'speeding' is here used to denote the offence of driving in excess of the speed limit. It is sometimes used in other contexts to mean driving at a speed that is inappropriate for the prevailing conditions, but that is not the meaning employed here.

### *The Law*

Driving at excess speed is an offence under section 89(1) of the Road Traffic Regulations Act (RTRA) 1984:

> (1) A person who drives a motor vehicle on a road at a speed exceeding a limit imposed by or under any enactment to which this section applies shall be guilty of an offence.

In addition to this, there are specific offences of driving at excess speed found in sections 81 (exceeding the speed limit of 30 mph on restricted roads), 86 (speed limits for different classes of vehicles), and 88 (temporary speed limits) of the RTRA 1984.

A restricted road is one where the street lamps are not more than 200 yards apart, or one which has been designated as a restricted road by the traffic authority, and is usually in a 'built-up' area. Thus, unless there are signs to the contrary, a driver should presume that the speed limit for a particular road is 30 mph, even if there is not a sign to that effect, if the street lamps are less than 200 yards (183 metres) apart. The fact that any sign confirming this is obscured from view will not provide a defence (*Hood v Lewis* 1976). A driver should therefore pay attention to his or her surroundings, since the strictness of the law is confounded by the fact that speed limit repeater signs are prohibited on a restricted road with street lamps at 200 yard intervals (SI 2002/3113, reg.11), so that if the first speed limit sign is missed D will not pass further signs indicating that the speed limit is 30 mph. In addition to roads with street lamps at the specified intervals any other road can be designated as a restricted road by the traffic authority. Where a 30 mph limit has been imposed on a road without street lamps it must be ensured that the signage indicating the limit is visible to drivers in good time to allow them to reduce their speed to 30 mph before entering the zone (*Coombes v DPP* 2006). Where signs have become obscured by overgrowing vegetation this could provide D with a defence, and any local knowledge that D has of the existence of the speed limit will not be taken into account (ibid.).

Not only do different speed limits apply on different classes of road, but also to different classes of vehicle. Although the speed limit for a car on a motorway is 70 mph, the speed limit for HGVs (goods vehicles exceeding 7.5 tonnes laden weight) on a motorway is 60 mph. On single-carriageway roads where the speed limit for cars is 60 mph, the limit for HGVs is only 40 mph and for other goods vehicles (not exceeding 7.5 tonnes laden weight), buses (including minibuses) and coaches is 50 mph. If D is driving a class of vehicle which D is not used to driving, it is incumbent on D to know the speed limit applying to that class of vehicle on the particular road on which D is driving.

For a prosecution under section 89 to succeed, section 89(2) RTRA 1984 requires corroboration that D was exceeding the speed limit: the evidence of more than one witness (for example, a police officer) whose opinion it is that D was speeding is needed. Corroboration could be provided by the eye-witness testimony of a second police officer, but is usually provided by some form of speed detection device. However, it is also possible for forensic evidence collected during the aftermath of a collision to act as corroboration. Skid marks and damage caused to vehicles can help the police reconstruct the collision and calculate the speed of the vehicles upon impact, and this can provide sufficient evidence for a conviction of speeding (*Crossland v DPP* 1988).

Where automated speed cameras are in use evidence of speeding does not require corroboration, and section 20 of the Road Traffic Offenders Act (RTOA) 1988 governs the admissibility of evidence from automatic devices detecting excess speed, amongst other offences (other devices included within the remit of section 20 are those which detect a failure to stop at a red light or the use of a bus lane by another vehicle). Such evidence must take the form of a record produced by a prescribed device along with a certificate as to the circumstances in which the record was produced. A prescribed device is one approved by the Secretary of State, and must be operated under the conditions imposed upon its use by such approval. In addition to devices such as radar and laser speed measuring devices, which have been used for many years, the police may also, since 1999, use a device which captures and records images of motor vehicles at two positions on the road and calculates the average speed of the vehicles between those positions (SI 1999/162). These cameras, known as SPECS, have proved particularly effective in reducing speeds and collisions where they have been in use. The advantage of

SPECS is that the system avoids the 'yo-yoing' effect of drivers slowing down for a camera only to speed up once safely past the threat of detection. The uptake of permanent SPECS installations has been slow, with only seven permanent SPECS sites as of November 2007 (Collins 2007). This may be because unlike the traditional speed cameras they are not expected to pay for themselves and have been reserved for locations where there has been a history of collisions along a particular route (rather than at just one 'black spot') (ibid.). Permanent SPECS installations have led to a reduction of between 49.2 and 100 per cent in fatal and serious injury collisions (ibid.). They have also been used at the sites of major road works on motorways, where, in addition to casualty reductions, the cameras have had the benefit of improving the flow of traffic and reducing speed limit offences. On the M8, for example, compliance with the 40 mph speed limit at road works in 2007 was 99.7 per cent, with the average recorded speed being 38 mph (ibid.).

Section 41C of the RTA 1988, as inserted by section 18 of the RSA 2006, creates a new offence of contravening or failing to comply with a construction or use requirement as to speed assessment equipment detection devices. This provision makes possible the ban on vehicles being fitted with, or a person using a vehicle carrying, speed assessment equipment detection devices. It is unclear what specific devices will be prohibited, since these will be identified in future regulations, but the government notes that it is not intended to prohibit those devices that only contain information about published camera site locations (DfT 2007c, para.211). Such devices, whilst being advertised as useful for road safety purposes, are increasingly used by those in opposition to the enforcement of speed cameras to avoid detection with little doubt that manufacturers are well aware of, and indeed happy to benefit from, the desire to evade speed enforcement amongst many drivers.

Section 89(4) RTRA 1984 explicitly provides for the issue of procuring an offence of speeding:

> (4) If a person who employs other persons to drive motor vehicles on roads publishes or issues any time-table or schedule, or gives any directions, under which any journey, or any stage or part of any journey, is to be completed within some specified time, and it is not practicable in the circumstances of the case for that journey (or that stage or part of it) to be completed in the specified time without the commission of such an offence as is mentioned in subsection (1) above, the publication or issue of the time-table or schedule, or the giving of the directions, may be produced as prima facie evidence that the employer procured or (as the case may be) incited the persons employed by him to drive the vehicles to commit such an offence.

This is an offence that could be committed by employers of commercial drivers or those whose jobs necessitate travelling by car between meetings. However, where an employer gives only verbal directions concerning the time in which a journey is to be completed, it will be difficult to provide sufficient evidence of the offence.

There is one group of drivers who drive for work which may be exempt from the law on speed limits. Section 9 of the RSA 2006 amends section 87 RTRA 1984 to read:

> (1) No statutory provision imposing a speed limit on motor vehicles shall apply to any vehicle on an occasion when—
> (a) it is being used for fire and rescue authority purposes or for or in connection with the exercise of any function of a relevant authority as defined in section 6 of the Fire (Scotland) Act 2005, for ambulance purposes or for police or Serious Organised Crime Agency purposes,
> (b) it is being used for other prescribed purposes in such circumstances as may be prescribed, or
> (c) it is being used for training persons to drive vehicles for use for any of the purposes mentioned in paragraph (a) or (b) above, if the observance of that provision would be likely to hinder the use of the vehicle for the purpose for which it is being used on that occasion.

This provision only applies to those who have completed a course of training in the driving of vehicles at high speed, or who are driving a vehicle as part of such a course (section 87(2)).

*Penalties* Speeding is an offence which is usually dealt with by way of a fixed penalty notice. The fixed penalty is £60 and three penalty points, but if D wishes to contest D's guilt and go to court the sentence on conviction is three to six penalty points, or disqualification in the very worst cases, and a fine of up to £1000 (or £2500 if the offence is committed on a motorway). In bad cases of speeding the police may wish not to offer a fixed penalty, but to prosecute D at court to enable the penalty imposed to be higher. The average fine for speeding at the magistrates' court in 2004 was £119 (Home Office 2006, 12). Disqualification for speeding is discretionary, but rarely used. It is more likely that D will lose D's licence under the 'totting' rules in section 35 RTOA 1988, according to which:

> 35 (1) Where—
> (a) a person is convicted of an offence to which this subsection applies, and
> (b) the penalty points to be taken into account on that occasion number twelve or more,
>
> the court must order him to be disqualified for not less than the minimum period unless the court is satisfied, having regard to all the circumstances, that there are grounds for mitigating the normal consequences of the conviction and thinks fit to order him to be disqualified for a shorter period or not to order him to be disqualified.

The minimum period is six months if D has not been disqualified before, one year if D has been disqualified once in the last three years and two years if D has been disqualified twice or more in the past three years.

The *Magistrates' Court Sentencing Guidelines* suggest that the number of points endorsed will depend on the degree by which D exceeded the speed limit. A speed limit of 30 mph, if exceeded by up to 10 mph, will normally result in three penalty points. If a 30 mph limit is exceeded by 21–30 mph the magistrates might choose to impose six penalty points or disqualify D for up to 56 days. Where the limit is 70 mph, D will have to have exceeded it by at least 30 mph for the most severe approach to sentencing to be adopted (Magistrates' Association 2004, 75). In addition to taking into account the degree by which D exceeded the limit, the magistrates will also consider whether any mitigating or aggravating circumstances exist. The only mitigating circumstance listed is that it has been established that D was driving in an emergency, whereas the following non-exhaustive examples of aggravating factors are provided: D was driving a goods vehicle, bus or taxi; time of day, location and visibility; serious risk created; D was towing a caravan or trailer.

In most cases though, a case will not go to trial and a fixed penalty will be issued, which takes the form of a 'conditional offer' sent to the registered keeper of a vehicle caught speeding by an automatic device. Under section 75(7) RTOA 1988:

> (7) A conditional offer must –
> (a) give such particulars of the circumstances alleged to constitute the offence to which it relates as are necessary for giving reasonable information about the alleged offence,
> (b) state the amount of the fixed penalty for that offence, and
> (c) state that proceedings against the alleged offender cannot be commenced in respect of that offence until the end of the period of twenty-eight days following the date on which the conditional offer was issued or such longer period as may be specified in the conditional offer.

The registered keeper of a vehicle has an obligation to provide the police with the name and address of the driver of a car caught speeding by an automated speed camera, and commits an offence if he or she fails to do so under Section 172 of the RTA 1988:

> (2) Where the driver of a vehicle is alleged to be guilty of an offence to which this section applies—
> (a) the person keeping the vehicle shall give such information as to the identity of the driver as he may be required to give by or on behalf of a chief officer of police, and
> (b) any other person shall if required as stated above give any information which it is in his power to give and may lead to identification of the driver.
> (3) Subject to the following provisions, a person who fails to comply with a requirement under subsection (2) above shall be guilty of an offence.

The section applies to most of the offences contained within the RTA 1988, including the drink-driving offences discussed above, as well as manslaughter by the driver of a motor vehicle (section 172(1)).

A general principle of criminal law is the privilege against self-incrimination, which means that 'a suspect cannot be required to provide the authorities with information that might be used against him in a criminal trial' (Redmayne 2007,

209). This privilege can be seen to be connected to the presumption of innocence, although this connection has been questioned by Redmayne (Ashworth and Redmayne 2005, 133; Redmayne 2007, 218–19), who notes that it is almost impossible to provide a compelling rationale for the privilege (Redmayne 2007, 210). The presumption of innocence means that the burden of proof in a criminal trial is on the prosecution, who must prove beyond all reasonable doubt that the defendant committed the offence charged. It is not for the defendant to prove that he or she is innocent. Making the prosecution's task easier by requiring the suspect to provide information does not, in itself, alter that burden of proof (Redmayne 2007, 218).

Ashworth and Redmayne describe the privilege against self-incrimination more accurately as a method of governing the relationship between individual citizens and the state:

> the basic principle is that a suspect should not be required to cooperate with the authorities who are prosecuting him. This reflects the common intuition that the privilege is connected to the proper relationship between State and citizen. The principle is valuable in that it limits State power in criminal prosecution, and allows the suspect to preserve some distance between himself and the State. (Ashworth and Redmayne 2005, 133)

Punishing individuals for failing to cooperate with the police can be seen as a 'misplaced use of coercive power by the state' (Redmayne 2007, 228).

How, then, can the requirement under section 172 be reconciled with this privilege against self-incrimination? The Privy Council has dealt with the issue in relation to a drunk-driver in the case of *Brown v Stott* (2003), in which D admitted to driving to a shop where she had been found shoplifting and under the influence of alcohol. In ruling that section 172 was not a breach of D's right to a fair trial under Article 6 ECHR, Lord Bingham identified a number of justifications for the provision. Firstly, he noted that section 172 requires D to answer a simple question and that the answer to that question 'cannot of itself incriminate the suspect, since it is not without more an offence to drive a car' (at 705). Failure to answer the question leads to a moderate and non-custodial penalty (a fine), rather than some greater punishment. Secondly, Lord Bingham compared answering a question to submitting to a breath test, and could find no reason why it should be objectionable to answer a question but not to undergo a breath test. Finally, Lord Bingham highlighted the fact that section 172 forms part of a regulatory regime applying to a group of the public who voluntarily subject themselves to the rules of the regime by choosing to own a motor car. This regime is in place because of the recognized potential for cars to cause grave injury. He concluded:

> If, viewing this situation in the round, one asks whether section 172 represents a disproportionate legislative response to the problem of maintaining road safety, whether the balance between the interests of the community at large and the interests of the individual is struck in a manner unduly prejudicial to the individual, whether (in short) the leading of this evidence would infringe a basic human right of the defendant, I would feel bound to give negative answers. (at 705–6)

Redmayne has argued that the reasoning that the goal of maintaining road safety justifies a breach of the privilege against self-incrimination should be avoided, since it could justify an exception to the privilege in relation to a multitude of contexts (Redmayne 2007, 229). He prefers the alternative (rather than additional) reasoning that the RTA 1988 forms part of a regulatory regime for car owners, who must accept the duties and obligations imposed upon them if they wish to drive (ibid.).

In *Brown v Stott* the defendant was attempting to argue that it would be against her right to a fair trial under Article 6(1) ECHR for the prosecution to be able to rely on her admission that she had driven, which was obtained under section 172(2)(a). Until recently, however, this particular issue had not been directly considered by the European Court of Human Rights (ECtHR). In *Weh v Austria* (2005) the ECtHR was asked to consider the question of whether a provision under Austrian law, the equivalent of section 172, breached Article 6(1). The court held that, although the privilege against self-incrimination is protected by Article 6, the applicant's rights were not threatened in the case because the applicant had not been prosecuted for speeding, but was instead fined for providing inaccurate information when asked who had been driving his car at the time that it was recorded exceeding the speed limit.

The recent case of *O'Halloran and Francis v UK* (2007) enabled the ECtHR to give a more definitive position on the compatibility of section 172 with Article 6. In this case the first applicant had been prosecuted for speeding after he had admitted he was driving his car when it was caught doing 69 mph in a 40 mph zone. At trial he pleaded not guilty and argued that his admission should be excluded because his privilege against self-incrimination had been breached. His application to the ECtHR was joined with that of the second applicant, whose circumstances were slightly different. Unlike the first applicant, the second applicant refused to provide the police with details of the driver of his car at the time his car had been caught doing 47 mph in a 30 mph zone. As a result, the Crown had insufficient evidence to prosecute him for speeding and he was instead prosecuted for the offence under section 172. Both applicants were convicted of the offences charged and sentenced to a fine and penalty points. They applied to the ECtHR on the basis that their rights under Article 6 had been breached. The ECtHR ruled fifteen votes to two that there had been no violation of Article 6(1). It ruled that there were various factors that must be considered in determining if a compulsion to provide information amounted to a violation of the Article and held that there was no such violation on the basis that: as recognized by the Privy Council in *Brown v Stott*, the compulsion to provide information was part of a regulatory scheme that fairly imposes obligations on drivers in order to promote safety on the roads; the information required is the simple, specific and restricted fact of who was driving; the offence under section 172 is not entirely absolute, in that it contains a safeguard in the form of a due diligence defence.

Ashworth has questioned the robustness of the arguments used in *O'Halloran and Francis v UK*, suggesting that a clear rationale for the privilege against self-incrimination is lacking (Ashworth 2007). However, the case provides confirmation to road users that the obligation under section 172 is a lawful one which cannot be evaded in the hope that the Human Rights Act 1998 can be used to escape liability. The case does, however, illustrate the public's opposition to speed cameras, which are seen as a method of criminalizing the 'law-abiding majority', as will be discussed further below.

### *Policy and Practice*

In a survey asking the public about the issues needed to be tackled to improve quality of life, speeding and volume of traffic were identified by around one fifth of people (Audit Commission 2006). Exceeding the speed limit was a contributory factor in 5 per cent of all accidents in 2006, a figure that rises to 14 per cent when looking at fatal accidents (DfT 2007a, Table 4b), and it has been reported that accidents that involve exceeding the speed limit as a contributory factor are over twice as likely to result in at least one fatality compared to those that do not (Robinson and Campbell 2006, 15). It has been calculated that 90 per cent of pedestrians hit by a car travelling at 40 mph are killed, compared to 20 per cent when the car is travelling at 30 mph (House of Commons Transport Committee 2004, 30). Thus, not only does speeding increase the frequency of collisions, it is also a factor increasing the severity of any collision that occurs. There is clear evidence that speeding is dangerous, but little acceptance of this fact amongst drivers.

This denial of fact is problematic in that it is one of the causes of a common conception that many people, even those involved in the prosecution of offences, do not see speeding as a 'real' crime (Corbett et al. 1998. See further Chapter 6 below). Since speeding is not 'really' a crime, any method of detecting offending behaviour is resented. Corbett carried out a study of driver attitudes at the time of the introduction of some of the first automated speed cameras along the A40 in 1992, showing that around half the drivers' self-reported behaviour was affected by the presence of the cameras (Corbett 1995). Forty-five per cent claimed to be unaffected by the installation of the cameras, although 6 per cent were not aware of their existence (ibid., 347). Fifty-four per cent slowed down to differing degrees, with 10 per cent admitting to slowing down for the cameras and speeding up where no cameras were situated (ibid.). This last group, labelled 'manipulators', tended to be drivers who drove the fastest generally (ibid., 348) and, in turn, they were the group who were the most frequent users of the road (ibid. 349). In a later study Corbett expanded on this research, looking at the effects of speed cameras on the attitudes and perceptions of the four different groups she had identified and labelled as 'conformers', 'deterred', 'manipulators' and 'defiers'. The conclusion was that:

> While overall the results on perceptions, beliefs and attitudes towards cameras were promising, there may nonetheless be an element of 'preaching to the converted'. The drivers most in favour of cameras, and most fearful and respectful of them, were those who are probably least likely to fall foul of them, i.e. conformers. At the other extreme, those who present the main problem to road safety planners – defiers and

> manipulators – seem the least respectful and fearful of cameras and least attitudinally influenced by them. (Corbett and Simon 1999, 6)

A particularly interesting finding in Corbett's original A40 study was that the closer drivers kept to the speed limits, the more likely they were to say that they did not know where the cameras were situated and could not estimate their number (Corbett 1995, 349). Corbett notes that this was not a causal relationship: drivers did not drive at slower speeds because they were worried about being caught speeding unawares (ibid., 350). One of Corbett's conclusions was that if uniform slow speeds were the objective of speed camera enforcement, greater uncertainty about the location of the cameras was needed. If, on the other hand, the objective was to reduce speeds at accident black spots, this was already being achieved by drivers slowing down for the cameras (ibid., 353). The government seems to have taken the second option as their main objective, as speed cameras have become more (rather than less) visible since the research was carried out, and mobile cameras, rather than being a means of catching drivers speeding unawares and thus encouraging a uniform low speed as Corbett suggested, actually have their location advertised by the local media.

Perhaps the reason for this choice of tactic is that, as predicted by Corbett (ibid.), the driving public's contentment with the cameras when they were first introduced quickly faded and was replaced by alienation. Attitudes to speed cameras, reflecting attitudes towards speed limits, are often negative. A change in attitudes could achieve a far higher observance of the speed limit, but this has been identified as being 'one of the most difficult tasks' (Parker et al. 1996, 15). The question is whether the law, rather than some other mechanism, can be successful in changing such attitudes:

> Experience has shown that the role of health education in bringing about behavioural change is likely to be subtle and indirect. For example, in the domain of driver behaviour, considerable effort was put into encouraging the voluntary use of seatbelts. Disappointingly, research suggested that such campaigns were largely unsuccessful in changing behaviour ... Nevertheless, when the wearing of seatbelts became a legal requirement in the UK, the level of compliance with the new law was immediately very high. The extensive publicity given to the beneficial effects of wearing a seatbelt not only prepared the public to accept legislation that would otherwise have been fairly unpopular, but also paved the way for an immediate change in behaviour on the introduction of legislation. (Parker et al. 1996, 16)

Can law enforcement combined with campaigns to educate drivers on the risks of speeding achieve success in altering attitudes towards speeding behaviour? Parker et al. were confident that by identifying the key determinants of speeding behaviour and then trying to modify those determinants, behaviour can be modified (ibid.). Of four videos designed to challenge attitudes to speeding, two were found by Parker et al. to have 'genuine potential to bring about changes in the desired direction in beliefs and/or attitudes concerning speeding at 40 mph (65 kph) in a 30 mph (48 kph) zone' (ibid., 14). These videos focused on 'normative beliefs' and 'anticipated regret'. The 'anticipated regret' video attempted to portray speeding as inherently wrong, whether or not harm results, whilst the 'normative beliefs' video focused on the attitudes of close relatives to D's speeding behaviour, suggesting that they might disapprove of it, in the hope that these people would have a strong influence on the behaviour of D.

In addition to 'significant others' having the potential to influence driving behaviour, other drivers may also be important. Haglund and Åberg found that family members were not particularly important for decisions about speed; rather, drivers were more concerned about other road users in their choice of speed:

> A driver's own behaviour is intimately related to the behaviour of other drivers. A driver who perceives others to drive at excessive speeds is also more likely to drive fast than a driver who perceives others to comply with the limits. It thus seems as though speed choice in driving is a behaviour largely influenced by people immediately present, such as other drivers, and not by non-present persons that might normally be prominent in other areas of the driver's life (Haglund and Åberg 2000, 49).

The problem for changing attitudes is that drivers overestimate the rate of speeding amongst other drivers. Haglund and Åberg conclude that drivers should be supplied with information about the average speed or the proportion of drivers keeping to the speed limit (ibid.). This might be a dangerous tactic, however, given that 60 per cent of the drivers in Haglund and Åberg's sample actually exceeded the speed limit (ibid., 43). In Great Britain in 2005, 56 per cent of drivers on motorways exceeded the 70 mph limit, and 50 per cent exceeded the 30 mph limit in built-up areas (DfT 2006b, 3).

In addition to communicating to drivers how other people feel about speeding, it may also be effective to educate them on the dangers of speed, and the underlying reasons for the existence of speed limits. Speed can be dangerous for a number of reasons, but primarily it creates a risk because it is the key determinant of task difficulty of driving (Fuller et al. 2006, 70). The speed at which D drives will determine the 'time window' available to identify and react to events on the road, and if the 'time window' is too short because D is driving too fast, the task demand will be pushed beyond the capability of the driver (ibid.). Fuller et al. provide three ways of defining what an inappropriate high speed is (or what is 'driving too fast for the conditions'). First, in cases where a collision has been caused, one can look at the causes of the collision and determine that one of the contributory factors in the collision was driving too fast for the conditions so that D lost control of the vehicle. Second, even in the absence of a collision D may have been driving beyond D's capability:

> we might still describe the speed as inappropriately high, despite the absence of a crash outcome … because at such a speed the driver is driving close to the threshold where task demand might exceed capability. Under these conditions there is no room for error or unexpected events, there is no margin of safety, for example taking account of varying road surface conditions. (Fuller et al. 2006, 71)

The only difference between the first and second definition of inappropriate high speed is whether D managed to escape a collision or not. Third, one can define inappropriate high speed simply by reference to the speed limit imposed (ibid.). However, whilst driving at a speed in excess of the speed limit can be defined as 'inappropriate', it does not follow that D will be driving at the limits of the task demand at such a speed. The converse is also true: the limits of the task demand might be reached at a speed lower than the legal limit.

That the legal speed limit does not necessarily correlate to the first and second definition of 'inappropriate high speed' might be a key to explaining why the law seems to be failing to deter many drivers from exceeding the limit. As will be discussed at greater length in Chapter 6 below, research has found that drivers often prefer to drive according to their own personal code, rather than being dictated to by the Highway Code and traffic regulations (Corbett and Simon 1992a). Such drivers do not necessarily simply choose to violate the law, however. It may be that there is a psychological reason why drivers decide the speed at which they will drive for themselves. Fuller et al. note that:

> Compliance with a speed limit often involves the switching of control decisions from one key mode to a rather different one: our conceptualisation, from control by task difficulty or feelings of risk to control by speedometer read-out. … [T]he speed limit system requires a kind of 'double standard' in driver control. Speed limits provide only a rough guide to the speed at which the driver can maintain control of the driving task. … [W]here the speed limit is actually lower than the speed which road and traffic conditions would dictate, drivers are forced into conflict with the law – unless, of course, they switch control to feedback from the speedometer. (Fuller et al. 2006, 71)

If this is an accurate picture of how drivers carry out the driving task, it may be that many drivers find it difficult to keep switching control between task difficulty and the legal speed limit. But this will only be required at the top end of the limit, where traffic is free flowing and D will have to check that acceleration does not take D above the limit. This in itself should not be too complex a task, although D might then feel pressure from other vehicles travelling in the vicinity to exceed the limit to keep up with the flow of traffic (Haglund and Åberg 2000). It may take some willpower for drivers to keep within the limit in such circumstances, and the question is what motivation can be found to best reinforce such willpower.

One of the problems faced by the authorities in using automated speed cameras in enforcing speed limits is that they are sometimes seen to be used for purposes of money-making rather than road safety. Section 38 of the Vehicle (Crimes) Act 2001 made provision for the funding of speed cameras, using what is referred to as the 'netting off' scheme. This enabled Safety Camera Partnerships (set up between the local police and council) to spend the revenue collected from speeding fines on further safety cameras, rather than all the money going straight to the Treasury, as was previously the position. One might have thought that the use of the revenue in this way would be applauded by the motoring public, but suspicions remained amongst many people, with Corbett noting that 'there is a suspicion among some that cameras are deployed as an easy "money earner" or "stealth tax"' (Corbett 2006, 9). The House of Commons Transport Committee suggests that the guidelines for the use of speed cameras have 'backfired' and 'reinforced the supposition that speeding is only really illegal in particular places' (House of Commons Transport Committee 2004, 31). The netting-off scheme ended in 2007, when there was a switch to cameras being funded by extra allocations to councils over four years, with the aim of integrating cameras into wider road safety activity (Audit Commission 2007, para.41). It is unlikely that this will change public attitudes, however.

Public attitude is the main obstacle to be overcome in ensuring effective enforcement of speeds. The Audit Commission note that paradoxical views on road safety are often expressed by road users. Whilst 72 per cent of drivers support speed restrictions of 20 mph in residential areas, only 43 per cent of drivers favour speed bumps used to enforce this lower limit (Audit Commission 2007, para.23). Having an accident is what concerns drivers the least, with traffic congestion and financial cost being rated as greater concerns (ibid., para.24).

It is clear that the government cannot be sure about how best to deal with the speeding problem. It was recently announced that a new consultation on the question of raising penalties for speeding offences would take place (*Guardian* 9 November 2007). The Road Safety Minister was reported as suggesting that a possible reduction in the penalty for minor offences (such as travelling at 75 mph on the motorway) from three to two points could be offset by an increase to six penalty points for the worst offenders (ibid.). Such proposals seem designed to placate the otherwise 'law-abiding majority' of speeding motorists whilst targeting those most likely to be a danger to the public. Whether or not the public will be in favour of such a change is yet to be seen, as the consultation process is yet to get under way at the time of writing.

As a result of widespread acceptance of speeding in society, speeding is the largest offence group dealt with by the police: in 2004 there were 2.1 million offences of speeding (Home Office 2006, 4). Ninety-one per cent of these offences were dealt with by way of fixed penalty notice, down from 92 per cent the previous year (ibid., 7). The proportion of cases being taken to court, whilst small, is rising. There were 172,300 speeding cases dealt with in court in 2004, a 4 per cent rise from the 165,500 prosecutions in 2003 (ibid., 11). Evidence of the offence was provided by camera devices in 88 per cent of cases in 2004 (ibid., 14).

The police have introduced thresholds for determining whether the law should be enforced in response to a speeding offence. Technically, travelling at 31 mph in a 30 mph zone constitutes a speeding offence, but there may be several reasons why such an offence would not be prosecuted. The Association of Chief Police Officers (ACPO) has set in place various threshold levels as guidance to police forces as to when and how speeding should be enforced. The bottom level threshold that ACPO has set provides a limit below which speed offences should not be prosecuted. This is to allow for equipment inaccuracy, speedometer inaccuracy and human error interpreting a speedometer. ACPO advises that prosecutions below this level should be undertaken by way of careless driving or other offences, not a speed offence alone (ACPO 2006, 4). This, it is assumed, would usually require some element of bad driving in addition to the excess speed. Currently, the bottom level threshold is '10% + 2' (ibid.), meaning that D will not be prosecuted unless D's speed is at least 10 per cent above the speed limit plus an additional two miles per hour above that. So if the speed limit is 30 mph, speeding will only be prosecuted if it is 35 mph or higher (10 per cent of 30 is 3: 30 + 3 + 2 = 35). It has been recommended that the threshold level for enforcement is reduced and that such a reduction be well publicized, since it was predicted that this would lead to more speed reductions and only some slight loss of approval in attitudes towards speed cameras (DfT 1999, 8). The problem with the current thresholds is that some perceive that driving up to 10 mph above the speed limit as complying with the law (ibid.).

The majority of cases of speeding are now detected by the use of automated cameras. In 1998 there were 403,800 offences of speeding detected in this way, rising to 1,913,700 in 2004 (Home Office 2006, Table D). Speeding might also be detected by the police out on patrol, or could be found to be a factor in a collision once the police have investigated and reconstructed the crash. In the author's study of charges arising from fatal road traffic collisions, three cases resulted in prosecutions for speeding. The question for prosecutors in such cases is whether D's speeding may have contributed to the collision and the fatality, in which case it might be more appropriate to charge causing death by careless or dangerous driving, depending on the severity of the offence. All three cases involved HGV drivers whose speed could be determined from examination of the vehicle's tachograph, which records the hours driven by the HGV and the speed at which it is driven. In B44 D had exceeded his speed limit by 20 mph and, although he would not have been able to avoid a collision if travelling at a slower speed, the Crown prosecutor pointed out that his speed would have increased the severity of the impact and was so significantly over the limit that the offence should be marked. In A74 and B57 it was felt that the main responsibility for the collision lay either with V or with another driver, but in both cases D had been driving at 56 mph when his vehicle was restricted to a 40 mph limit.

Although, as noted above, it is possible to bring a case of speeding based on evidence of skid marks and damage to vehicles (*Crossland v DPP* 1988), to the knowledge of the author such an approach was not taken in any of the cases studied, although the speed of vehicles was provided in support of charges of careless driving or causing death by dangerous driving (CDDD). There were thirteen cases resulting in prosecutions for careless driving in which excessive speed was the main contributory factor in the collision, according to the collision investigator. In four of these cases D was not driving in excess of the speed limit, but at a speed which was inappropriate for the prevailing conditions. In another eight cases of careless driving speed was a contributory factor, but other factors were seen as the main reason for the collision. As noted in Chapter 2, the CPS Legal Guidance and charging policy suggest that 'speed which is highly inappropriate for the prevailing road or traffic conditions' is an example of driving which may support an allegation of dangerous driving (CPS 2007b, para.5.27). Depending on the circumstances of a case, then, speed can provide evidence of careless and dangerous driving (see, for example, *DPP v Milton* 2006 involving a police driver, although this conviction was overturned on a second appeal to the Divisional Court in *Milton v DPP* 2007).

In addition, it is also pointed out in the Legal Guidance that under section 38(7) RTA 1988 a failure to observe a provision of the Highway Code may constitute evidence of careless or dangerous driving. Clearly, exceeding the speed limit is acting in breach of Rule 124 of the Highway Code. Exceeding the speed limit does not automatically constitute careless driving, but equally it is clear that driving at a speed within the speed limit does not exclude a possibility of careless or even dangerous driving having been committed due to excessive speed for the prevailing road or traffic conditions.

In the cases in the author's study that involved speed there was some discrepancy in the way the cases were handled and in the approach taken by the police and CPS. In B44 the officer in charge of the case (OIC) and his sergeant recommended that no further action be taken against D, whereas the inspector suggested that D should be prosecuted and the CPS agreed. Similarly in C57 the OIC made no recommendation in relation to the prosecution of D, whilst the CPS advised that D should be prosecuted for speeding. In Case A74, however, the OIC suggested that careless driving might be prosecuted, but his inspector disagreed and commenced a prosecution for speeding only. Whilst these all resulted in a prosecution for speeding there were further cases in which no further action was taken where there was proof that D had exceeded the speed limit. Again, all of these involved HGV drivers. In two cases (C16 and C24) D was found to have exceeded his speed limit by 10 mph and V, travelling in the opposite direction to D, had crossed the carriageway into D's path. D's speed was not seen to be contributory to the collision. In C21 D was again exceeding his speed limit but this was not seen to be a contributory factor as V, who was suffering from depression, walked into D's path. In another five cases D had exceeded the speed limit by 10–17 mph and the file was sent to the CPS for advice. In one of these (C60) V was a pedestrian who was drunk and walking on a dark road, wearing dark clothing and trying to thumb a lift. D was travelling at 12 mph above his 40 mph limit and did not see V at any stage but heard a bang as he collided with V. The collision investigator was unable to say whether D would have seen V had he been travelling at a slower speed and the CPS concluded there was insufficient evidence to provide a realistic prospect of conviction. In another two cases V attempted to overtake when it was unsafe to do so, and collided with D's HGV travelling in the opposite direction. D's speed was not seen as contributory and, as a result, no prosecution took place. What is unclear is how these cases can be distinguished from those three cases mentioned above in which it was decided that although D's speed did not contribute to the collision, he should be punished for speeding.

Although speed limits have become increasingly easy to enforce with the introduction of new technologies, it may be that the fixed penalty notice or prosecution is not the best disposal for someone found speeding. Police forces are increasingly diverting cases away from the criminal justice system by way of providing 'speed awareness courses' (SACs) as an alternative to punishment, forming an extension of the National Driver Improvement Scheme discussed in Chapter 2. The idea is that someone caught speeding might well accept points on his or her licence and pay a fine, without thinking much more about the matter.

Those who can afford fines will not necessarily change their driving behaviour in future unless the number of points endorsed on their licence is nearing the twelve point maximum and they are afraid of losing their licence. Given that speed limits exist to improve road safety, and the prevention of excess speed creating a danger to other road users can be seen as the *raison d'être* of speed limits, it can be seen as more effective to use the detection of a speeding offence as a trigger to provide an opportunity to the police to underline the reason why speed limits exist. Thus, the police are more and more employing 'education' rather than 'enforcement' to combat excess speed, through the provision of SACs.

ACPO has produced guidelines on introducing SACs at a national level. Several forces had begun to implement SACs on a local level, and the need was felt to provide some consistency between areas so as not to undermine the fairness of the system. The ACPO guidance underlines the fact that the disposal of speed offences is at the discretion of the police service in the area where the offence was committed. It is a question for each participating police force whether a speed awareness course is to be offered. ACPO provides three central rules to be adopted by each force in implementing the National Speed Awareness Scheme:

> Rule 1 Courses provided under the scheme will have a minimum content provided in this document as a course specification (appendix A)
>
> Rule 2 National Speed Awareness Courses will not be offered to offenders who were travelling at a speed greater than 10% + 6 above the posted speed limit.
>
> Rule 3 The offender must agree to attend the course within the terms of the offer.
>
> Below 10% + 6 a police force can implement national speed awareness at any level (enforcement level) that is below their agreed prosecution level. Nothing in this document will stop a prosecution under 10% + 6, or no action, if the situation is appropriate (ACPO 2006, 1).

The 'enforcement level' is the level above which all drivers who are found committing a speed violation will be enforced against in some way or another, whether that be by way of warning, caution, SAC, fixed penalty or court summons. Distinct from this is the 'prosecution level', which is a level above the enforcement level, assuming speed awareness has been adopted, after which a driver will be prosecuted by fixed penalty or summons. Although the minimum enforcement level set by ACPO is currently 10% + 2 (see above), ACPO warn that it may not be advisable to prosecute all cases above this threshold, since this could lead to loss of support for speed cameras from the public (ACPO 2006, 4). Offering an SAC at the bottom threshold is seen as an alternative which may provide the best of both worlds: the motoring public will hopefully maintain a degree of support for speed cameras but can be educated on the risks of speeding if they exceed that limit. The upper threshold for offering an SAC is 10% + 6 (39 mph in a 30 mph zone) (ACPO 2006, 9). Normally, then, a first offence of speeding at 35 mph–39 mph in a 30 mph limit will receive an offer of SAC attendance rather than prosecution in areas where the scheme is operational. ACPO stresses that the police retain discretion in deciding the best disposal in any particular case, however. Where D has already attended one SAC in the previous three years only a fixed penalty notice may be offered as an alternative to prosecution (ibid.). SACs are not currently offered in relation to violations of 20 mph limits (ACPO 2006, 4).

**Table 3.1 ACPO's guidance on dealing with particular incidents of speeding**

| Speed limit | ACPO bottom level threshold [10% + 2] | Speed awareness level not more than [10% + 6] | Summons after |
|---|---|---|---|
| 20 | 25 | Nil | 35 |
| 30 | 35 | 39 | 50 |
| 40 | 46 | 50 | 66 |
| 50 | 57 | 61 | 76 |
| 60 | 68 | 72 | 86 |
| 70 | 79 | 83 | 96 |

*Source*: ACPO 2006, 10.

Table 3.1 sets out ACPO's guidance on how a particular incident of speeding should be dealt with, depending on the severity of the violation, although ACPO also stresses that this does not prohibit prosecution below the limit of 10%+6.

SACs have the following aims and objectives:

**Aims**

By the end of the course drivers should be able to identify:

- What causes them to speed?
- The consequences of misusing speed
- Strategies for coping with speed related issues, and
- Demonstrate an understanding of the correct use of speed for a variety of hazards

**Objectives**

1. Develop correct attitudes and behaviour
2. To identify the benefits of compliance with National Speed Limit requirements
3. Ensure drivers leave the course having gained the correct attitudes and beliefs towards the misuse of speed
4. To recognise different speed limit areas
5. Identify the consequences of speeding – identifying the benefits and disbenefits of speeding
6. Recognise absolute personal responsibility for speed
7. To develop practical skills to reaffirm their attitude towards driving at the correct speed subject to the circumstances

8. To facilitate the clients with an opportunity to examine their attitude towards hazard perception with a view to behavioural change in practical driving. (ACPO 2006, 13)

Courses should last for two and a half hours, and involve a variety of methods. The ACPO guidance sets out a list of exercises that could be carried out. The first takes the form of a discussion of why the 'clients' are present: details of the speeding offence they committed. They are then asked to reflect on reasons for speeding, and are pointed towards the conclusion that whatever reasons or excuses might be given it is they, the drivers, who are the common factor. The second exercise involves identifying the consequences of speeding, both for the drivers themselves and for third parties. ACPO advises that personal testimony of those who have suffered as a result of speeding drivers in the form of a video 'may be used to good effect' (ACPO 2006, 19). Having identified their reasons for speeding, drivers are asked in the third exercise to think of ways to cope with those causes. The final suggested exercise aims to facilitate drivers with an ability to develop their hazard awareness skills and perception in relation to speed, and the session concludes with a reinforcement of the lessons learnt during the session. In addition to this theoretical session, ACPO also envisages a three-hour practical session which will involve one-to-one or one-to-two assessment and instruction with an approved driving instructor.

ACPO stipulates that SACs should be offered on a non-profit basis and costs should be kept as low as possible, although there will be some administration costs incurred by the police force and the need to pay for recording the completion of a SAC on the DVLA database (ACPO 2006, 8). Most forces charge a fee of £60, the equivalent of the fine element of a fixed penalty notice, so that what D is really avoiding is the endorsement of three penalty points on D's licence. Currently between a third and a half of police forces in England and Wales offer an SAC as an alternative to a fixed penalty notice or prosecution (source: Association of National Driver Improvement Scheme Providers website). The plan for ACPO, however, is that the scheme will be rolled out nationwide as soon as possible, to enable offenders to attend a course locally even if their offence took place in another locality (ACPO 2006, 6).

Fylan et al. (2006) have carried out some research into how SACs are run, in order to assess the extent to which they utilize evidence-based methods of behavioural change identified by psychologists as being most effective in addressing offending speeding behaviour. The courses attended during the research were probably ones organized on an *ad hoc* basis by safety camera partnerships (made up of the local council and police) before the ACPO guidance discussed above was available. Fylan et al.'s assessment of the courses was that:

> Courses make use of several effective means of behavioural change, such as information to change attitudes towards speeding and to increase threat appraisals. However, most neglect the affective correlates of speeding, such as feelings of thrill and excitement and worry or anxiety, and none makes use of implementation intentions. Despite group discussions and problem-solving exercises being an effective means of achieving

> behavioural change, there is a large variation in the extent to which these are employed. Drivers' self-efficacy in complying with the speed limit is also addressed to a variable extent. (Fylan et al. 2006, 100)

The ACPO guidance might go some way to reducing the variation across courses and ensure a more consistent use of methodologies at SACs.

Although speeding continues to be the most prevalent of criminal offences and not seen as 'real' crime, the government's policy does seem to be having positive effects, showing, with the exception of speeds of HGVs on rural roads, a downward trend in speeding:

- The percentage of vehicles that exceed the speed limit on 30 mph roads has fallen over the last 10 years. The proportion of cars exceeding the speed limit in 1996 was almost three quarters; in 2006 this had fallen to a half.
- In 1996, 11 per cent of articulated HGVs exceed the speed limit of 60 mph on motorways. In 2006 this figure had fallen to just 2 per cent. However over the same period, the proportion of articulated HGVs exceeding the speed limit (40 mph) on single carriageway non-built-up roads has increased from 72 to 76 per cent.
- Sixty-one per cent of 2-axle rigid HGVs were travelling faster than the limit on 30 mph roads in 1996 and this number fell to 46 per cent in 2006. On 40 mph roads however, the proportion of speeding vehicles increased from 16 to 24 per cent over the same period.
- The proportion of motorcycles speeding on 30 mph roads has fallen from 56 per cent in 1996 and 63 per cent in 1998 to 51 per cent in 2006. (DfT 2007b, 49)

Whilst these findings show that speeding enforcement may be having a positive effect, the fact remains that many lives could be saved if speeding behaviour were eradicated from Britain's roads. Speed cameras achieve a reduction in speeding offences primarily by way of deterrence methods which are often resented by the motoring public. It may be that a reduction in the tolerance levels applied by police when enforcing speed limits could provide a short-term bolster to the deterrent effects of the law, but the likelihood is that this alone will only provoke further contempt for speed cameras and the law.

Corbett suggests that education is the most likely of the three 'E's to provide a long-term solution to problems of speeding, but cautions that sustained efforts will be needed (Corbett 2003, 124). Ideally, a way must be found to increase the numbers of 'conformers' rather than 'deterreds' (to use Corbett's terminology) amongst drivers, and the only way to do this is likely to be by changing attitudes. The use of speed awareness courses is a positive step in this direction, combining the two 'E's of 'enforcement' and 'education'. Further consideration will be given to the need to change drivers' attitudes to traffic law generally in Chapter 6.

## Chapter 4

# Homicide Offences

### Introduction

The ultimate harm that the criminal law is seeking to prevent in criminalizing risk-taking in the form of bad driving with the offences discussed in Chapters 2 and 3 is that of death. Harm falling short of death, such as serious bodily harm, is equally in need of prevention, but there are no specific offences of causing bodily harm by means of driving (with the exception of wanton and furious driving under the Offences Against the Person Act 1861, discussed briefly in Chapter 2) and any cases where a collision has resulted in harm falling short of death will have to be prosecuted for the relevant endangerment offence according to the circumstances of the case. Dangerous driving or careless driving causing serious harm is likely to attract harsher penalties than instances of those offences where some lesser harm is caused, given that the *Magistrates' Court Sentencing Guidelines* suggest that 'serious injury or damage is capable of being aggravation' (Magistrates' Association 2004, 67–8), but D's conviction will not reflect the fact that serious harm has been caused and will be indistinguishable in offence label from cases where a risk has been created but has not materialized. In contrast, because of the significance that humans attach to the ending of life, the law has dealt separately with drivers who kill.

A number of 'constructive' crimes have been created that use some of the offences already discussed in previous chapters on which to build separate, more serious offences usually labelled in terms of 'causing death'. Causing death by dangerous driving (CDDD) was the first of these to be created, in 1956, for reasons to be considered shortly. Some time later, in 1991, the offence of causing death by careless driving whilst under the influence of drink or drugs (CDCDUI) was created, constructing a homicide offence from two driving offences (careless driving and drink-driving). Causing death by careless driving in the absence of alcohol or drug impairment has only recently been passed into law in the Road Safety Act (RSA) 2006, although at the time of writing it has not yet come into force. At the same time, an offence of causing death whilst driving when uninsured, disqualified or without a licence (to be referred to here as causing death by unlawful driving or CDUD) was created. Although the underlying offences of driving whilst uninsured, driving without a licence and driving whilst disqualified upon which this offence is constructed are not discussed in this book, the offence of CDUD will be examined here for reasons of completeness.

There is one other offence which punishes more harshly a driver whose driving results in death. This is the offence of aggravated vehicle taking under the Theft

Act 1968. Again, although the offence of taking a vehicle without consent (or TWOC) is not included in this book since it falls more obviously within the law of property offences than driving offences, because the aggravated form of the offence punishes someone for the materialization of a risk taken behind the wheel it would be anomalous not to discuss it here.

In addition to these specially created constructive homicide offences, a driver whose bad driving causes death might also face a charge of manslaughter. The statutory offences have not replaced the common law of manslaughter in cases involving driving, but can be seen as additional accompaniments to existing case law. 'Motor manslaughter', as it is sometimes called, is not a separate species of manslaughter and it is preferable to drop the 'motor' reference altogether in order to avoid confusion. Manslaughter is a charge reserved for the most serious cases and is a rare occurrence in cases involving driving, but this may be set to change in future. Another likely development in the near future is the prosecutions of companies for manslaughter under the Corporate Manslaughter and Corporate Homicide Act 2007. This is an offence that could be charged in cases of fatal road traffic collisions, and warrants consideration here.

The other common-law homicide offence of some, albeit limited, relevance is, of course, murder. Murder will not be a suitable charge in cases where D has taken a risk in order to get ahead, or has caused death by bad driving, no matter how appalling that driving was. Murder can only ever be considered as a possible charge in a driving case where there is evidence that D used a car or other vehicle as a weapon of assault and drove at V intending to kill or cause grievous bodily harm. Its relevance as an offence to a book on driving offences may be doubtful, but there appear to be reasons surrounding the cultural place that driving has in our society for murder by motor vehicle being treated differently to other murders and in that respect it is worth exploring.

The law on each offence will be set out in turn before issues relating to policy and practice are explored. This chapter is structured differently to the previous two chapters, primarily because when death is involved in a case this becomes the starting point around which an investigation and any subsequent prosecution is based. There is considerable overlap between many of the offences to be discussed, and how the law operates in practice will only become comprehensible once the law on each has been set out.

## Causing Death by Dangerous Driving (CDDD)

CDDD was the first specific statutory offence of vehicular homicide to be created by parliament. In order to understand how the law operates it is necessary to explore the reasons behind its creation.

### *Background to the Offence*

Until 1956 a death resulting from bad driving amounted to manslaughter. The law was changed in that year because it was feared that many drivers who killed whilst driving badly escaped liability because juries were reluctant to convict them of manslaughter. This reluctance stemmed from a feeling that it could just as easily be the jurors themselves who were in the dock, and luck was between them and the label of 'manslayer'. This mentality of 'there but for the grace of God go I' was to be cured by creating a new offence, bearing a succinct description of what the offender had done. Thus, the Road Traffic Act 1956 created the offence of causing death by reckless or dangerous driving. Although the new legislation may have been more acceptable to jurors, some academics were less than impressed (e.g. MacKenna 1970). Over the years, several bodies have suggested reform of the law, for example, both the James Committee on the Distribution of Criminal Business between the Crown Court and the Magistrates' Courts (1975), and the Criminal Law Revision Committee (1976) recommended that the offence be repealed. Although these recommendations were not adopted, a number of statutes have made various alterations to the law, including the Criminal Law Act 1977. This statute abolished the offences of dangerous driving and causing death by dangerous driving, but preserved the offence of causing death by reckless driving.

Nevertheless, dissatisfaction with the law persisted because of difficulties in defining recklessness, particularly following the decision of the House of Lords in *Seymour* (1983). Here, the House of Lords addressed the question of the necessary *mens rea* to be proved in cases of motor manslaughter. It was held in *Seymour* that in all cases of manslaughter, including motor manslaughter, the jury should be directed in terms of objective *Lawrence* (1982) recklessness. Lord Roskill also stated that because this meant that the *mens rea* element of both the statutory offence of causing death by reckless driving and common-law manslaughter was the same, a judge would not be able to direct a jury as to the difference between the two offences, and as a result he opined that alternative charges of causing death by reckless driving and manslaughter should not be brought.

Lord Roskill stated that recklessness should carry the same meaning whether the charge was manslaughter or causing death by reckless driving. This apparently created an overlap between the two offences, Lord Roskill opining that manslaughter should only be charged in cases of death resulting from reckless driving when the risk of death (created by the defendant's driving) was 'very high'. This requirement was necessary if a higher maximum penalty of life imprisonment could be justified for manslaughter (the maximum penalty for the statutory offence then being five years' imprisonment).

When the North Committee came to review the law in 1988 it favoured the retention of a causing death offence, but argued that such an offence should not overlap with the offence of manslaughter (Department of Transport 1988, para.6.12). It felt that since it was recommending a change in the basic driving offence from 'reckless' to 'very bad' (dangerous) driving, the overlap would be alleviated despite its proposal to retain a causing death offence (ibid., para.6.13). This, it was claimed, would avoid the problem of the prosecution having to prove the state of mind of the driver at the time of the offence. However, it stressed that where it was possible to prove recklessness, manslaughter should be charged as the more serious offence. Further consideration is given to this point in the discussion on manslaughter below.

*Current Law*

Some of the North Report's recommendations were put into practice by the Road Traffic Act 1991, amending the Road Traffic Act 1988 (hereafter RTA 1988), and creating a new offence of CDDD. Section 1 of the RTA 1988 states that:

> A person who causes the death of another person by driving a mechanically propelled vehicle dangerously on a road or other public place is guilty of an offence.

The law on dangerous driving was explained in Chapter 2 above, and all that is needed for an offence of CDDD is that an instance of dangerous driving resulted in a fatal road traffic collision. An important element of the offence, but one that is usually easily proved, is causation: it was D's dangerous driving that caused the death of V. According to the Court of Appeal in *Hennigan* (1971) the driving need not be a substantial or major cause of death. All that is needed is that the dangerous driving is a cause, and something more than *de minimis*. Thus, where an offence of dangerous driving as described in Chapter 2 is committed and it can be proved that this was a cause of death, there is no more to be proven. The key to the offence is in establishing that driving was bad enough to amount to dangerous driving in that D's driving fell far below the standard of the competent and careful driver.

*Sentencing*

When CDDD was first created it carried a maximum penalty of five years' imprisonment, in addition to obligatory disqualification from driving. The penalty of disqualification has as its primary purpose protection of the public from future risk (Sentencing Advisory Panel 2008, para.101). The maximum period of imprisonment for the offence was increased firstly to ten years by the Criminal Justice Act 1993, section 67(1), and more recently to 14 years by the Criminal Justice Act 2003, section 285(3). The more recent increase in penalty seems ill timed, given that the change came shortly after the Court of Appeal adopted the advice of the Sentencing Advisory Panel (SAP) in setting out guidelines for sentencing in such cases, based on the ten-year maximum (*Cooksley* 2004). Such guidance was long overdue, since prior to this the guidance for such cases came from *Boswell* (1984), a case of causing death by reckless driving, for which the maximum sentence was five years' imprisonment. However, given the second increase in penalty the issue had to be revisited by the Court of Appeal in *Richardson* (2007). Yet further consideration is being given to the matter by the Sentencing Guidelines Council (SGC), on the advice of the SAP, following the enactment of the RSA 2006.

Between 1999 and 2003, even before the Criminal Justice Act increased the maximum sentence, the average sentence for CDDD had already increased from 34.3 months' imprisonment in 1999 to 43 months in 2003 (SAP 2007, 45). In *Cooksley* the Court of Appeal agreed with the SAP that culpability should be the dominant factor when sentencing for cases of CDDD, and went on to provide the following guidance:

The Panel sets out a series of aggravating and mitigating factors... We adopt them but stress that they should not be regarded as an exhaustive statement of the factors. In addition it is important to appreciate that the significance of the factors can differ. There can be cases with three or more aggravating factors, which are not as serious as a case providing a bad example of one factor. They are as follows:

**Aggravating Factors**

*Highly culpable standard of driving at time of offence*

(a) the consumption of drugs (including legal medication known to cause drowsiness) or of alcohol, ranging from a couple of drinks to a 'motorised pub crawl';
(b) greatly excessive speed; racing; competitive driving against another vehicle; 'showing off";
(c) disregard of warnings from fellow passengers;
(d) a prolonged, persistent and deliberate course of very bad driving;
(e) aggressive driving (such as driving much too close to the vehicle in front, persistent inappropriate attempts to overtake, or cutting in after overtaking);
(f) driving while the driver's attention is avoidably distracted, *e.g.* by reading or by use of a mobile phone (especially if hand-held);
(g) driving when knowingly suffering from a medical condition which significantly impairs the offender's driving skills;
(h) driving when knowingly deprived of adequate sleep or rest;
(i) driving a poorly maintained or dangerously loaded vehicle, especially where this has been motivated by commercial concerns.

*Driving habitually below acceptable standard*

(j) other offences committed at the same time, such as driving without ever having held a licence; driving while disqualified; driving without insurance; driving while a learner without supervision; taking a vehicle without consent; driving a stolen vehicle;
(k) previous convictions for motoring offences, particularly offences which involve bad driving or the consumption of excessive alcohol before driving.

*Outcome of offence*

(l) more than one person killed as a result of the offence (especially if the offender knowingly put more than one person at risk or the occurrence of multiple deaths was foreseeable);
(m) serious injury to one or more victims, in addition to the death(s).

*Irresponsible behaviour at time of offence*

(n) behaviour at the time of the offence, such as failing to stop, falsely claiming that one of the victims was responsible for the crash, or trying to throw the victim off the bonnet of the car by swerving in order to escape;
(o) causing death in the course of dangerous driving in an attempt to avoid detection or apprehension;

(p) offence committed while the offender was on bail.

**Mitigating Factors**

(a) a good driving record;
(b) the absence of previous convictions;
(c) a timely plea of guilty;
(d) genuine shock or remorse (which may be greater if the victim is either a close relation or a friend);
(e) the offender's age (but only in cases where lack of driving experience has contributed to the commission of the offence); and
(f) the fact that the offender has also been seriously injured as a result of the accident caused by the dangerous driving.' (Cooksley 2004, para.15)

...

**Starting Points**

We have set out four starting points; no aggravating circumstances – 12 to 18 months; intermediate culpability – 2 to 3 years; higher culpability – 4 or 5 years and most serious culpability – 6 years or over. We make clear that starting points only indicate where a person sentencing should start from when seeking to determine what should be the appropriate sentence. There is, however, a danger in relation to the higher starting points of the sentencer, if he is not careful, double accounting. The sentencer must be careful not to use the same aggravating factors to place the sentence in a higher category and then add to it because of the very same aggravating features. (*Cooksley* 2004, para.32)

Following the increase in the maximum penalty to 14 years' imprisonment, the question for the Court of Appeal in *Richardson* was whether this increase should only affect those sentences at the top end of the scale, or whether it should result in a slight increase in sentences throughout the scale. It was submitted that the increase was enacted in order to cater for cases such as *Noble* (2003), in which the court wished to sentence D to longer than ten years' imprisonment due to the number of aggravating factors coupled with the fact that multiple deaths were caused. In that case, the sentence of 15 years, based on consecutive sentences, was quashed because the sentences could only be concurrent, and reduced to the maximum of ten years. However, the Court of Appeal in *Richardson* was of the opinion that whilst it was probably correct that the main purpose of the amendment was to increase sentencing powers at the top end, there should be some corresponding increase in sentences continuing down the scale. As a result, the starting points laid down in *Cooksley* should be reassessed as follows:

i) No aggravating circumstances – 12 months to two years' imprisonment;
ii) Intermediate culpability – two to four and a half years' imprisonment;
iii) Higher culpability – four-and-a-half to seven years' imprisonment;
iv) Most serious culpability – seven to fourteen years' imprisonment. (*Richardson* 2007, para.19)

The Court of Appeal also expressed a desire to add a further mitigating factor to the non-exhaustive list set out in *Cooksley*. Where D acted responsibly at the scene of the collision, by providing assistance to victims, this is also a mitigating factor (ibid., para.31).

The SAP, in its advice to the Sentencing Guidelines Council (SGC) following a consultation in 2007, decided to draw a distinction between two different types of aggravating factors: those factors that are intrinsic to the quality of driving, which it labelled 'determinants of seriousness', and those that are not, which it labelled 'aggravating factors' (SAP 2008, para.49). The following were categorized as determinants of seriousness:

1) awareness of risk (a prolonged, persistent and deliberate course of very bad driving);
2) dffect of alcohol or drugs;
3) inappropriate speed of vehicle;
4) seriously culpable behaviour of offender (including using a hand-held mobile phone and factors (e), (f), (g), (h) and (i) from *Cooksley* above);
5) victim (failure to have proper regard to vulnerable road users) (ibid., para.69).

Most of the other factors listed in *Cooksley* would amount to aggravating factors. The main ones were identified as: bad driving record; outcome of the offence (multiple deaths or serious injury caused in addition to death; irresponsible behaviour at the time of the offence (ibid., para.82). New mitigating factors include that the victim was a close friend or relative, that the actions of the victim or a third party contributed to the commission of the offence and that drugs or alcohol were consumed unwittingly (ibid., para.98).

The Court of Appeal has so far only suggested appropriate sentencing *ranges* for cases of varying gravity of CDDD. The SAP, in its 2007 Consultation Paper, suggested that it would be appropriate to provide a *fixed starting point* for sentencing in CDDD. In its advice to the SGC it built on this change by suggesting that factors amounting to 'determinants of seriousness' should dictate what the starting point in a particular case should be, whilst aggravating factors could then determine whether an increase in the range from the starting point was warranted. Where enough aggravating factors were present this might elevate the case into the next sentencing range (ibid., para.50).

The SAP set out four levels of seriousness for sentencing starting points and ranges. Level one is the most serious, involving 'a deliberate decision to ignore (or a flagrant disregard for) the rules of the road and an apparent disregard for the great danger being caused to others' (ibid., 27). Level two involves a 'substantial risk', and level three a 'significant risk' of danger. Level four is described as 'likely to be characterised by driving which creates a brief but obvious danger resulting from a single dangerous manoeuvre or from being momentarily (but avoidably) distracted' (ibid.). However, the SGC, whilst adopting most of the SAP's recommendations, has chosen to drop the level four category, leaving the current consultation guideline with three levels of seriousness. The starting points and sentencing ranges otherwise follow the SAP's advice. A level one offence would have a starting point of eight years' imprisonment and a range of seven to 14 years. A level two offence would have a starting point of five years' imprisonment and a range of four to seven years. A level three offence would have a starting point of three years' imprisonment and a range of two to five years (SGC 2008, 12; SAP 2008, 28).

It is clear that sentencing practice in this area is extremely difficult and provides a lot of work for the courts. Cases of CDDD and CDCDUI are among those most frequently referred by the Attorney-General to the Court of Appeal on the basis that the sentence was unduly lenient, according to research conducted by Shute (1999). Since *Cooksley* was decided there have been many cases of appeal against sentence by both the prosecution and the defence: the *Westlaw* database lists (as of November 2007) 37 cases where *Cooksley* has been applied, seven cases where it has been followed, and 39 cases where it has been considered (including *Richardson*). There is no guarantee that the SGC's forthcoming definitive guidance on the matter will bring any stability to this area of law.

## Causing Death by Careless Driving whilst under the Influence of Drink or Drugs (CDCDUI)

### *Background to the Law*

CDCDUI was first introduced following recommendations made in the North Report. In its proposals relating to the new offence of CDCDUI the North Review looked to public opinion as the rationalization of its recommendation. The justification for introducing a new offence of causing death by drink-driving was that there was public revulsion that innocent lives could be lost due to drink-driving. It also suggested that 'the availability of such a specific offence would be of real value in further marking out the dangers to the community of drinking and driving' (Department of Transport 1988, para.6.20).

Prior to the RTA 1991, because of the difficulty in proving reckless driving, drunk-drivers who caused a fatal collision were often only prosecuted for drink-driving (ibid., para.6.18). The North Review considered that more drunk-drivers were likely to come within the definition of its proposed bad driving offence (which later became dangerous driving), but was concerned that 'those whose driving could only be said to be bad, but not very bad …, will still only be liable to be charged with a drink driving offence' (ibid., para.6.19). After rejecting options involving the creation of an absolute offence of drink-driving causing death, the North Review settled on an offence requiring two elements: drink-driving and careless driving. This was to protect from prosecution those drivers who are over the alcohol limit but whose standard of driving had no part in causing death (ibid., para.6.23).

*Current law*

The offence of CDCDUI was introduced by the Road Traffic Act 1991, inserting s.3A into the RTA 1988. Section 3A provides:

> 3A(1) If a person causes the death of another person by driving a mechanically propelled vehicle on a road or other public place without due care and attention or without reasonable consideration for other persons using the road or place and –
> (a) he is, at the time when he is driving, unfit to drive through drink or drugs, or
> (b) he has consumed so much alcohol that the proportion of it in his breath, blood or urine at the time exceeds the prescribed limit, or
> (c) he is, within 18 hours after that time, required to provide a specimen in pursuance of section 7 of this Act, but without reasonable cause fails to provide it,
> (d) he is required by a constable to give his permission for a laboratory test of a specimen of blood taken from him under section 7A of this Act, but without reasonable excuse fails to do so,
> he is guilty of an offence.

Both the elements of drink-driving and careless driving must be proved. If D's driving fell below the standard of a competent and careful driver and D was either unfit through drink or drugs, found to be over the legal BAC limit or D failed to provide a specimen, CDCDUI can be charged. However, if the standard of D's driving is bad enough to amount to dangerous driving, a charge of CDDD may be brought instead of CDCDUI. The intentions of the North Review seem to have been that CDDD should be charged where it can be proved, whether or not alcohol or drugs are involved (Department of Transport 1988, para.6.19). An example of a case of CDDD where D was under the influence of drugs is *Gilmartin* (2001).

In relation to the drink-driving element of CDCDUI, although the offence can be proved in one of three ways it will normally be proved through the second option, involving a positive test for alcohol in the breath, blood or urine of D. A breath test may be requested under section 6 of the RTA 1988 following a collision, and it is usual for such a request to be made to all drivers involved in a collision. An exception would be where D was unable to complete the test due to injuries sustained in the collision, which would provide 'reasonable excuse' for not providing a sample under section 6(6). If the test proves to be positive, the police officer will normally arrest D and a blood sample will be taken to provide further evidence that D was driving over the limit. This should normally be done at a hospital (section 7(3)), and where D is already receiving treatment in hospital due to injuries sustained in the collision the medical practitioner who is treating D must be informed, and may object on medical grounds (section 9).

Prior to the Police Reform Act 2002 it was necessary that D consented to the taking of a blood sample (section 11(4)). However, this caused problems in cases in which D was unconscious for some time following the collision, and thus unable to give consent. The Police Reform Act 2002 has inserted section 7A into the RTA 1988 allowing a police officer to request a medical practitioner to take a specimen of blood from a person where that person is medically incapable of giving such consent. The sample should be kept until such time as D is able to give permission to have the sample tested, and it is an offence under section 7A(6) not to give such permission. In a case involving a fatal collision where D fails to provide such permission D can, following the coming into force of section 31 of the RSA 2006 on 24 September 2007, be charged with CDCDUI. This will solve the problem experienced by police officers that a driver involved in a fatal crash and suffering loss of consciousness could, prior to the RSA, refuse to allow a sample of blood taken from D whilst unconscious to be tested for alcohol or drugs, resulting in the CPS obtaining insufficient evidence to charge CDCDUI and having instead to charge the far less serious offences of careless driving and failing to submit to a blood test.

If D's specimen shows that the level of alcohol in his body was over the legal limit, then the drunkenness part of CDCDUI is easily proved. The prescribed limits were set out in Chapter 3 and are provided here as a reminder:

> 35 micrograms of alcohol in 100 millilitres of breath;
> 80 milligrams of alcohol in 100 millilitres of blood;
> 107 milligrams of alcohol in 100 millilitres of urine (section 11(2) RTA 1988).

If, however, it is impossible to obtain evidence that D was over the prescribed limit because D refuses to provide a relevant specimen, this in itself will be taken as proof that D was under the influence of alcohol under section 3A(c). Otherwise, were this not possible, anyone involved in a fatal collision whilst under the influence of alcohol could attempt to escape liability by simply refusing to cooperate with the police.

Where drugs rather than alcohol are involved, however, the task of the police and prosecution in providing evidence on which to base a charge of CDCDUI is more difficult. As noted in Chapter 3, there are no statutory limits for the amount of drugs allowed to be present in one's body when driving, and if CDCDUI is alleged on the basis of drugs rather than drink, it will have to be proved under section 3A(a). The drugs in question could be either illegal or prescribed, and where any drugs are suspected to have influenced D it would be normal for a specimen of blood to be taken under section 7(3)(c) for analysis once a doctor has given an opinion that a possible cause for D's condition may be drugs. Any results showing the presence of a large quantity of drugs within the blood could be persuasive, but difficulties arise in relation to some drugs, particularly cannabis, which remain in the blood stream for lengthy periods after their intoxicating effects have worn off.

Problems occur in relation to blood analysis for drink or drugs in cases in which such an analysis is not obtained for several hours following the collision. In a case where D leaves the scene of the collision, knowing that D is likely to be over the prescribed limit and wanting to hide the evidence by sobering up before being apprehended by police, it may take several hours for the police to locate D. It may be that when the specimen is obtained it shows the presence of drink or drugs but at a lower level than would have been present at the time of the collision, because the passing of time has led to a reduction in the proportion of drink or drugs in the blood. As explained in Chapter 3, in such cases it is possible for expert witnesses to provide evidence of an estimated level of drink or drugs in the blood at the time of the collision by way of back-calculation (*Gumbley v Cunningham* 1989). Expert evidence of this kind is provided fairly frequently in cases of fatal collisions, given the likely delays in obtaining a specimen in the circumstances of such cases.

In *Millington* (1996) the defendant, who admitted to drinking six vodkas and two pints of beer, argued that his driving had not been adversely affected by this quantity of drink in defending himself against a charge of CDCDUI. D had collided with a pedestrian who had also been under the influence of alcohol, having just left the pub. The Court of Appeal held that the fact that D had been shown to be driving at almost double the permitted BAC, along with D's own evidence about the amount he had drunk, was evidence that the jury could, by the exercise of common sense, use to determine the likelihood that D's driving had been so adversely affected that he had been driving without due care and attention: 'the jury is entitled to look at all the circumstances of the case. They included evidence which is relevant in proving a fact which tends to show that it was more likely than not that the driver drove without due care and attention' (*Millington* 1996, 83). Although there is no requirement that it was the alcohol that caused D to drive carelessly (*Shepherd* 1994), evidence of alcohol level can be relevant to the question of whether D's driving fell below that of a competent and careful driver (*Millington* 1996, 85).

### *Sentencing*

The maximum sentence for CDCDUI is fourteen years' imprisonment, raised from ten years' imprisonment by the Criminal Justice Act 2003, section 285, along with obligatory disqualification from driving. It is an offence on a par with CDDD in terms of seriousness, if offence seriousness is to be judged by sentencing practice. This was confirmed by the Court of Appeal in *Cooksley*, where it was decided that the sentencing task should be approached in the same way for CDCDUI as for CDDD. The issue was given more consideration in *Richardson*, where the Court of Appeal suggested that a case of CDCDUI would fall within one of the ranges in *Cooksley*, depending on the degree by which D exceeded the legal BAC level.

Unlike CDDD, however, the average sentence for CDCDUI has remained fairly static over the years 1999–2003, with an average custody length of 41.7 months in 1999 and 44 months in 2003 (SAP 2007, 45). A key question for the SAP in its review of the guidelines for driving offences causing death was whether it is satisfactory for the courts to continue to adapt the guidelines for CDDD when sentencing in cases of CDCDUI, or whether a separate guideline should be drafted (SAP 2007, para.34), and concluded that the second option was preferable.

Following consultation, the SAP proposed a guideline based both on the level of alcohol or drug consumption and the degree of carelessness. In the most serious cases, where D may be three times over the legal BAC level, the SAP agreed with the Court of Appeal in *Richardson* that this was likely to amount to dangerous driving and a charge of CDDD, and thus suggested that three sentencing categories were needed (SAP 2008, para.117). The proposals were made on the basis of a breath (rather than blood) test result and have been adopted by the SGC (see Table 4.1).

## Aggravated Vehicle-taking

### *Background to the Offence*

The offence of taking a vehicle without consent (TWOC) was introduced into law in order to deal with the social problem of 'joy-riding'. The term 'joy-riding' originates in the United States and came to the UK in 1912, when it was used to describe 'leisure drivers' who enjoyed driving at high speed (O'Connell 2006, 457). At that time the term did not necessarily involve any criminal activity beyond bad driving; there were very few cars on the roads, and only the rich could afford the luxury of owning a motor vehicle. From there, the term developed to describe those who drove vehicles belonging to others. Where offenders stole cars for no other purpose than to use them as a bit of fun in tearing around the streets it was sometimes difficult to prove the offence of theft because in most cases D could argue that D did not possess the necessary intention of permanent deprivation required for that offence. D may abandon the car once finished with it, claiming that it could be retrieved by the owner and that effectively D had just 'borrowed' it. O'Connell reports a case in 1913 in Belfast of an employee who took his employer's car and managed to avoid conviction for larceny by stating that he did not intend to steal it (ibid.). In the early days few would have had the skill to drive, and it was often chauffeurs who were accused of driving their employers' vehicles outside their hours of employment. The gap in the law was first closed with the Road Traffic Act 1930 making it an offence to take and drive away a vehicle without the owner's consent. Over the decades, as car culture developed and cars became more available, the nature of joy-riding changed and by the 1970s there were 'real' criminals who took cars in order to goad the police into chasing them, knowing that if they stole high-performance cars the police would have little chance of apprehending them (O'Connell 2006, 464). Such drivers will have little regard to the rules of the road, and may create a real danger for other road users. Pressure groups have attempted to change the terminology used in relation to such offenders by re-labelling 'joy-riders' as 'death drivers' or 'grief riders' (ibid., 456).

The current version of the TWOC offence appears in section 12 of the Theft Act 1968. The offence is triable summarily only and, following media attention on the issue of joy-riding and its consequences, moral panic led to the view that the maximum penalty of six months' imprisonment was inadequate in cases causing damage or injury, leading to a change in the law in 1992 (Corbett 2003, 40). The Aggravated Vehicle-Taking Act 1992 inserted section 12A into the Theft Act 1968 to create an aggravated form of TWOC which can be likened to constructive manslaughter. Because, as noted below, driving offences cannot be relied upon as the unlawful and dangerous act needed to prove constructive manslaughter

**Table 4.1** Sentencing Guidelines Council Consultation Guidelines for CDCDUI

| The legal limit of alcohol is 35µg breath (80mg in blood and 107mg in urine) | Careless/inconsiderate driving arising from momentary inattention with no aggravating factors | Other cases of careless/inconsiderate driving | Careless/inconsiderate driving falling not far short of dangerousness |
|---|---|---|---|
| 71µg or above of alcohol/high quantity of drugs OR deliberate non-provision of specimen where evidence of serious impairment | Starting point – 6 years imprisonment<br>Sentencing range: 5 to 10 years imprisonment | Starting point – 7 years imprisonment<br>Sentencing range: 6 to 12 years imprisonment | Starting point – 8 years imprisonment<br>Sentencing range: 7 to 14 years imprisonment |
| 51–70 µg of alcohol/moderate quantity of drugs OR deliberate non-provision of specimen | Starting point – 4 years imprisonment<br>Sentencing range: 3 to 7 years imprisonment | Starting point – 5 years imprisonment<br>Sentencing range: 4 to 8 years imprisonment | Starting point – 6 years<br>Sentencing range: 5 to 9 years imprisonment |
| 35–50 µg of alcohol/minimum quantity of drugs OR test refused because of honestly held but unreasonable belief | Starting point – 18 months imprisonment<br>Sentencing range: 6 months to 4 years imprisonment | Starting point – 3 years imprisonment<br>Sentencing range: 2 to 5 years imprisonment | Starting point – 4 years imprisonment<br>Sentencing range: 3 to 6 years imprisonment |

*Source*: SGC 2008, 14.

it was felt that this new offence was needed to provide a higher penalty for joyriders who cause death whilst seeking the thrill of driving stolen cars. Unlike most driving offences which are not seen as 'real' crime, offences such as taking a vehicle without consent are committed by 'criminals' who may then go on to drive in such a way as to cause harm to others. Indeed, the very fact that D is driving a car not belonging to D may encourage D to take risks when driving, since D will not be concerned about damaging the vehicle, and may feel under pressure to take risks if D becomes the subject of a police pursuit. In some cases, the danger of a police pursuit may be the very motivation for taking the car in the first place.

Such offenders fall into Steer and Carr-Hill's typology of 'dishonest' offenders (Steer and Car-Hill 1967). Steer and Carr-Hill categorized road traffic offences as either 'dishonest' or 'driving'. Although they did not discuss the offence of TWOC it is assumed that because the offence involves calculated dishonesty and is not connected, *prima facie*, with the way in which a vehicle is driven, it would fall within the category of dishonest offences, along with driving without insurance or whilst disqualified (indeed, the offence leads to the commission of other offences such as driving without insurance). This book is primarily concerned with 'driving' offences creating a risk to other road users that could lead to death. Aggravated TWOC, as a 'dishonest' offence, is included for the purposes of exploring the charging options open to the prosecution in a case in which such a risk has materialized in death. Unlike 'driving' offences, such as dangerous driving or drink-driving, which according to Steer and Carr-Hill are committed by 'average motorists', 'dishonest' offences are committed by offenders who are often involved in other criminal activities and are seen as more blameworthy by members of the public, warranting greater condemnation (ibid., 222). It is not clear whether Steer and Car-Hill's typology has withstood the test of time, however, given that in relation to drink-driving at least, there have been clear changes in public attitudes since 1967. (This issue will receive greater attention in Chapter 6.)

### *Current Law*

The basic offence upon which aggravated TWOC is founded is that of TWOC under Theft Act 1968, section 12, which provides that:

> 12 (1) a person shall be guilty of an offence if, without having the consent of the owner or other lawful authority, he takes any conveyance for his or another's use or, knowing that any conveyance has been taken without such authority, drives it or allows himself to be carried in it.

Section 12A specifically provides that:

> (1) …, a person is guilty of aggravated taking of a vehicle if –
> (a) he commits an offence under section 12(1) above (in this section referred to as a 'basic offence') in relation to a mechanically propelled vehicle; and
> (b) it is proved that, at any time after the vehicle was unlawfully taken (whether by him or another) and before it was recovered, the vehicle was driven, or injury or

damage was caused, in one or more of the circumstances set out in paragraphs (a) to (d) of subsection (2) below.

(2) The circumstances referred to in subsection (1)(b) above are –
(a) that the vehicle was driven dangerously on a road or other public place;
(b) that, owing to the driving of the vehicle, an accident occurred by which injury was caused to any person;
(c) that, owing to the driving of the vehicle, an accident occurred by which damage was caused to any property, other than the vehicle;
(d) that damage was caused to the vehicle.

The penalty is provided by subsection (4), which in itself creates a separate offence of *causing death* by aggravated TWOC (*Sherwood and Button* 1995):

> (4) A person guilty of an offence under this section shall be liable on conviction on indictment to imprisonment for a term not exceeding two years or, if it is proved that, in circumstances falling within subsection (2)(b) above, the accident caused the death of the person concerned, fourteen years.

Thus, aggravated TWOC causing death exists inasmuch as a separate penalty is provided for causing death as opposed to injury.

It should be noted that this offence can be committed by passengers as well as drivers, if such a passenger knows that the vehicle has been taken without the owner's consent. The reason behind this is to avoid the occupants of the car, when apprehended by the police, from claiming that they were all passengers and denying that they were driving, thus avoiding liability for the offence. It extends constructive liability even further than CDCDUI, in that all that is required is that a vehicle which has been taken without the owner's consent is involved in a fatal collision; there is no need to prove that the standard of driving fell below that of a competent and careful driver; no fault element whatsoever is required (*Marsh* 1997). The offences under section 12A have been described as 'draconian, and have features that depart markedly from the principles that ordinarily govern liability at least for serious crimes' (Ormerod 2005, 728).

### *Sentencing*

The offence carries obligatory disqualification of at least 12 months and a maximum sentence of 14 years' imprisonment where death is caused, or two years where only damage or injury short of death results. Aggravated TWOC is a triable either way offence, meaning that the maximum penalty of fourteen years' imprisonment can only be passed if it is tried at the Crown Court. For the longer sentence to apply, care must be taken in drafting the indictment to specify that death has been caused as a result of aggravated TWOC (*Sherwood and Button* 1995). As with the other 'causing death' offences discussed above, the penalty for causing death has been subjected to an increase by the Criminal Justice Act 2003, s.285(1). This suggests that the offence is deemed as serious as CDDD and CDCDUI, despite the fact that D need not be culpable in relation to the way D drove. Prior to the enactment of the Criminal Justice Act 2003, aggravated TWOC carried a significantly lower maximum penalty than CDDD and in cases where dangerous driving could be proved it could be charged (for example, as in *Adams* 2002). This remains true following the enactment of the Criminal Justice Act 2003, although the incentive for charging CDDD is now lost since the maximum penalty is the same and although CDDD might be perceived as a more serious offence, given the need to prove the fault element of 'dangerous' driving, the ease with which aggravated TWOC can be proven is likely to make it a popular option. Despite this, the offence is comparatively rare. In 2004 there were 19 cases of aggravated TWOC causing death dealt with by the Crown Court in England and Wales, of which 13 led to conviction (Fiti et al. 2006, Table 7). A further three offenders were convicted at the magistrates' court (the offence being triable either way) (ibid., Table 3), probably by way of guilty plea. In three cases an immediate unsuspended period of imprisonment was imposed by the Crown Court, varying in length from between six and 12 months to between three and five years (ibid., Table 9). A further seven cases resulted in incarceration at young offenders institutions across a similar range of sentence lengths (ibid., Table 10a).

## Causing Death by Careless Driving

CDCD can be seen as the corollary of CDDD in that is creates a specific homicide offence by taking the conduct crime or endangerment offence of careless driving and stating that if this leads to a fatal collision a more serious offence has been committed. It is an offence created by the Road Safety Act 2006, following public consultation. It comes exactly 50 years after the creation of CDDD, with little serious consideration having been given to the possibility of creating such an offence until fairly recently.

### *Background to the Offence*

The North Committee paid less attention to the offence of careless driving than dangerous driving, but it did give some consideration to whether a new offence of CDCD should be introduced, including the matter in its consultation. The results of the consultation reflect very closely the responses to the Home Office's consultation on bad driving in 2005 which led to the Road Safety Act 2006. In 1988 the responses fell into two camps: those for and those against CDCD:

> 6.15 ... The exposure of this idea in our first Consultation Document drew a mixed response. Quite a large number of commentators supported the introduction of such an offence, although many of these appeared to have been influenced by a general concern over what they saw as inadequate treatments in the courts of bad cases of careless driving causing death. The arguments advanced in favour of such an offence were that it would help to meet the public sense of outrage at any death caused by bad driving and would, presumably by raising the penalty available, make it possible to give a more appropriate punishment to a careless driver who killed. It was felt by some that a causing death offence linked to careless driving would fill the gap between

reckless driving, which was difficult to prove, and ordinary careless driving, which was insufficiently serious a charge for those who killed.

> 6.16 Of those who opposed the introduction of a causing death by careless driving offence, some argued that it was simply wrong in principle to look to consequences rather than culpability as an ingredient of an offence. These commentators opposed any causing death offence. Others felt that, even if such an offence were justified in relation to reckless driving, this principle could not be extended to careless driving, which was different in kind from reckless driving. Moral blameworthiness might attach to the latter but not to the former. A crime based on consequences might, it was said, be justified where the level of culpability was high but not in the case of carelessness. Carelessness might amount to no more than a minor error of judgement or a moment's inattention, and the offence should not be made more serious because a death resulted. It was also said that the introduction of such an offence would make the law more complex to no good effect, and that its existence would be unlikely to act as a deterrent. (Department of Transport 1988)

On this occasion the North Review was persuaded by those opposed to the offence, and did not recommend the creation of CDCD. This was partly based on an argument that its recommendations for redefining the offence which later became dangerous driving would meet many of the concerns expressed by those in favour of the offence (para.6.17). That optimism seems not to have come to fruition, however, given that a great deal of criticism has been levelled at the CPS's practice in prosecuting dangerous driving since the Road Traffic Act 1991.

The North Review's discussion of careless driving identified one problem which still exists today. It was said that the issues relating to the offence are confused by the shorthand term used of 'careless driving' (North Report 1988, para.5.31). This conveys the message that the offence only requires 'carelessness' and that anyone guilty of it was only 'careless'. The root of the problem is that members of the public see the use of the word as downgrading the conduct of offenders, through their understanding of the word 'carelessness' in everyday language. This is particularly true of cases resulting in death, and was something highlighted by several of the victims' families in the cases in the author's own study. The effect of the law could probably be much improved through a change in the way the offence is described by abandoning the shorthand term and, even if a new definition is not introduced, by referring to the offence using its full requirement of 'driving without due care and attention'. Such a change would clearly not require new legislation but could be achieved through an agreement from ACPO and the CPS that the term 'careless driving' would not be used in any documentation or dealings with the public. ACPO has attempted a similar measure in relation to the word 'accident', replacing it with the word 'collision'. Although the government has given some consideration to changing the terminology to replace careless driving with an offence of 'negligent driving' (with 'grossly negligent driving' to replace dangerous driving), the option was rejected on the basis that it would create 'too much uncertainty in interpretation, for too little potential gain' (Home Office 2005a, para.3.16).

Instead, the government felt that the way to handle public pressure to deal more severely with drivers who kill was to create a new homicide offence. Based on the fact that the courts have accepted that the results of bad driving in the form of multiple deaths can provide aggravating factors in sentencing for CDDD (*Cooksley*), the government took the view that this should also be possible when dealing with cases of death arising from careless driving, and that a mere increase in fine imposed for the result of death was inadequate (Home Office 2005a, para.3.23). It was argued that consequences are as relevant to the culpability of careless drivers as they are to dangerous drivers, and on that basis an offence of CDCD with a maximum penalty of five years' imprisonment ought to be introduced (ibid., para.3.31).

As at the time of the North Review, a clear division can be seen in the responses to this proposal at consultation stage. On the one side were the public and road safety organizations in favour of the new offence, whilst on the other side the legal profession (with the exception of the CPS) opposed it quite strongly (Home Office 2005b, 5). It may be that the government's eventual action on this says more about the prevailing political climate than the force of the arguments put forward, but it is unsurprising that, given that the consultation paper had advanced a view in favour of the offence, the legal profession were unable to dissuade it against the support from the public and others.

### *Current Law*

Section 2B of the RTA 1988 is inserted by the RSA 2006, section 20:

> 2B Causing death by careless, or inconsiderate, driving
> A person who causes the death of another person by driving a mechanically propelled vehicle on a road or other public place without due care and attention, or without reasonable consideration for other persons using the road or place, is guilty of an offence.

This is a triable either way offence with a maximum penalty of five years' imprisonment when tried at the Crown Court, and disqualification is mandatory following conviction. It is unclear when the provision is to come into force, although one newspaper has reported that it will be brought into effect by Easter 2008 (Gibb 2008) (this had not happened by April 2008). The Sentencing Advisory Panel (SAP) and CPS have taken steps towards amending sentencing and prosecution policy to cater for the new offence, with consultation exercises carried out during 2007. The Sentencing Guidelines Council (SGC) has, after receiving advice from the SAP, published a sentencing guideline which is currently undergoing a further consultation process. The SAP, through the analysis of CPS data, has estimated that 70 cases a year will be charged as CDCD (SAP 2008, para.158).

### *Sentencing*

As with any other offence, the SAP is guided by two factors affecting the seriousness of the offence in providing guidance on sentencing: the harm (actual or foreseeable) caused by the offence and the culpability of the offender in relation to that harm (SAP 2007, para.45). In the case of CDCD, however, the SAP notes that: 'This new offence is likely to encounter a particular difficulty in this respect because of the considerable gap between the outcome of the offence (the death of at least one person) and the degree of the offender's culpability' (ibid., para.46). The SAP provisionally proposed four starting points for sentencing CDCD, which were reduced to three following consultation (see Table 4.2). Predictably the lowest sentencing range would not lead to imprisonment but to a community order, something which will no doubt disappoint many of those who were in favour of the creation of the new offence, but which is entirely justified given the low level of offender culpability involved. At the other end of the scale, however, the SAP reduced the sentencing range it had provisionally proposed in its consultation. In the most serious cases it had originally suggested a starting point of three years' imprisonment and a range of two to five years (SAP 2007, 32), but in its advice to the SGC reduced this to a starting point of 15 months and a range of 36 weeks to three years. However, it states that 'the range still leaves scope, within the 5 year maximum, to impose longer sentences where the case is particularly serious' (SAP 2008, para.135), although it is not clear why this should not mean that the range at the top end should read '36 weeks to five years'.

## Causing Death by Unlawful Driving (CDUD)

Another new homicide offence created by the RSA 2006 is the offence of CDUD, which has been described as 'an egregious example of constructive crime' (Dennis 2007, 254).

### *Background to the Offence*

When considering the introduction of CDCDUI the North Review considered the possibility of having an absolute offence of killing someone while driving with more than the legal limit of alcohol in the body or while unfit to drive through drink or drugs, under which it would be enough to prove involvement by a drunk-driver in a fatal collision, and where it would be no defence that the standard of driving had not contributed to the death (Department of Transport 1988, para.6.22). This option was rejected on the basis that 'it is easy to visualize circumstances where an accident leading to a death may have occurred and yet the drinking driver was not in any way to blame. Where, for example, a drunken pedestrian dashes out in front of a car in circumstances such that no driver could have avoided him, it would seem unduly harsh to charge the driver not only with the drink offence but also with a new causing death offence' (ibid.). In contrast to the North Review, the government in 2005 had no such qualms in proposing an offence of causing death where, in fact, no causation is needed between D's standard of driving and the result of death.

In its 2005 review of bad driving offences, the government was concerned not only about offences of bad driving, but also about the problems that illegal driving poses. The three offences of illegal driving it was concerned about were

**Table 4.2 Sentencing Guidelines Council Consultation Guidelines for CDCD**

| Nature of offence | Sentencing range |
|---|---|
| Careless or inconsiderate driving falling not far short of dangerous driving | Starting point – 15 months imprisonment<br>Sentencing range – 36 weeks to 3 years imprisonment |
| Other cases of careless or inconsiderate driving | Starting point – 36 weeks imprisonment<br>Sentencing range – Community Order (HIGH) to 2 years imprisonment |
| Careless or inconsiderate driving arising from momentary inattention with no aggravating factors | Starting point – Community Order (MEDIUM)<br>Sentencing range – Community Order (LOW) to (HIGH) |
| **Additional aggravating factors** | **Additional mitigating factors** |
| (a) other offences committed at the same time, such as driving other than in accordance with the terms of a valid licence; driving while disqualified; driving without insurance; driving while a learner without supervision; taking a vehicle without consent; driving a stolen vehicle<br>(b) previous convictions for motoring offences, particularly offences that involve bad driving<br>(c) more than one person was killed as a result of the offence<br>(d) serious injury to one or more persons in addition to the death(s)<br>(e) irresponsible behaviour, such as failing to stop or falsely claiming that one of the victims was responsible for the collision | (a) offender seriously injured in the collision<br>(b) the victim was a close friend or relative<br>(c) the actions of the victim or a third party contributed to the commission of the offence<br>(d) the offender's lack of driving experience contributed significantly to the likelihood of a collision occurring and/or death resulting<br>(e) the driving was in response to a proven and genuine emergency falling short of a defence<br>**Personal mitigation**<br>(f) the offender gave direct, positive, assistance at the scene to victim(s)<br>(g) the offender has an exemplary driving record |

*Source*: SGC 2008, 16.

driving whilst disqualified, driving without an appropriate licence, and driving whilst uninsured. Each of these raises slightly different issues. In relation to disqualified driving the government pointed out that disqualification is a penalty imposed on those who have committed driving offences and have already posed a risk to other road users, which would suggest that those who are disqualified can be equated to careless drivers: 'The mere act of taking a vehicle on to the road when disqualified is, in the Government's view, as negligent of the safety of others as is any example of driving below the standard expected of a competent driver, even if the disqualified driver, at a particular time, is driving at an acceptable standard' (Home Office 2005a, para.4.2). The problem with using disqualification as a penalty for driving is that its desired consequences can easily be circumvented by the offender continuing to drive despite the disqualification, in the hope that the offence of driving whilst disqualified will not be detected by the police. The penalty for driving whilst disqualified is a maximum of six months' imprisonment, and the government noted that in 2002 around half of the 30,415 people convicted of the offence were sentenced to imprisonment (ibid., para.4.4). However, the government was of the opinion that a longer sentence would be deserved in cases where death resulted from a piece of disqualified driving.

Unlicensed driving, albeit carrying a non-custodial penalty, was likened to disqualified driving and deemed to demonstrate the same level of culpability. There is admittedly a link between disqualified or unlicensed driving and road safety. A system of driving licenses exists in order to try to ensure that only those who have met a certain level of competence in driving should be able legally to drive on public roads. The link between uninsured driving and road safety is, however, rather more tenuous. There is a good reason why insurance is obligatory, but this has to do with dealing with the aftermath of collisions rather than preventing their occurrence. This has been noted by Duff:

> There is of course *some* connection between being unlicensed, or disqualified, and driving dangerously: under an appropriate system, being licensed gives both drivers and others some assurance that drivers are competent to drive safely, and being disqualified is often the result of driving dangerously or being incompetent to drive safely. However, there is no such connection between being uninsured and driving dangerously, because insurance has to do with paying for harm caused rather than with avoiding causing it; and even in the cases of driving when unlicensed or disqualified it is far from clear that the connection is close enough to treat the causation of death as the actualisation of a risk that made the driving wrongful in the first place. (Duff 2008)

The government suggested that a link does in fact exist: 'there are grounds for believing that uninsured drivers are more likely to be involved in collisions, and to disregard road traffic requirements and obligations, than the general driver population' (Home Office 2005a, para.4.8). In recognition of this rather weak justification for holding drivers who drive whilst uninsured responsible for any unfortunate death resulting from such driving, the government admitted that it was not convinced that it was right to do so and welcomed views on the issue (ibid., para.4.10).

Those who drive whilst disqualified or without a licence will inevitably also commit the offence of driving without insurance, since it is impossible to insure a vehicle without a valid licence. However, there are those who might in all other respects follow the letter of the law, but who for some reason fail to ensure that they are insured to drive a particular vehicle. In some instances this omission may be deliberate, but in others it might be an oversight on the part of D, who has failed to ensure that a policy up for renewal has been dealt with, or has been assured by the vehicle's owner that D will be covered under the owner's insurance. In his report on uninsured driving for the government, Greenaway noted that an example of unintentional uninsured driving is caused by: 'drivers misunderstanding the nature of the cover they require for the type of driving they do: a not unusual occurrence given the existence of no fewer than nine (sometimes subtly different) types of cover offered by the market' (Greenaway 2004, para.3.2). Whilst it remains incumbent on a driver to make certain that a valid insurance policy applies, it does not follow that a failure to do so displays the degree of culpability that should lead to more than the financial penalty provided by law for the offence of uninsured driving. Greenaway suggested in his report that uninsured drivers might experience a higher risk of collision involvement than the 'average' driver, given that such drivers might not have a valid licence or the car they are driving might not have a valid MOT certificate. He admitted, however, that there is no independent research in the UK to support this assumption (ibid., para.3.12). If Greenaway is right, this does not justify the addition of driving without insurance as one of the unlawful acts of driving covered by CDUD, since a driver in such a position would fall under the heading of 'unlicensed driving' and if a vehicle does not have an MOT certificate this could amount to dangerous driving based on the condition of the vehicle.

The responses to the proposed CDUD offence were mixed (Home Office 2005b, 7). The police, for example, although against the creation of CDCD, were in favour of CDUD and were of the opinion that unlawful driving is more culpable than careless driving (ibid.). A response from Cambridgeshire Constabulary gave the opinion that 'all persons getting into a car knowing they are breaking the law before they turn on the ignition, should be dealt with in a manner that is robust and provides a visible deterrent to all other would be uninsured/disqualified drivers' (ibid., 23). Others were also in favour of the offence although, as with CDCD, the legal profession were very much against it. Some suggested that a more effective way of dealing with the problem of disqualified drivers would be to increase the penalty for disqualified driving (ibid., 7). Little more was said in relation to uninsured driving, although the government became convinced that it was right to include this within a new offence of CDUD on the basis that 'driving without insurance is reprehensible and shows clear disregard for the welfare and safety of others' (ibid., 8). This view seems to tally with that of the general public. The SAP commissioned independent research to test public opinion on CDUD, amongst other offences, in preparing its advice to the SGC on sentencing. It was found that those taking part in the research considered CDUD to be more serious than CDCD and only marginally less serious than CDDD, and were astonished by the low maximum penalty (SAP 2008, para.145). The SAP attributes this response to the fact that this offence includes 'an inherent avoidance or disobedience of the law which is deemed highly culpable' (ibid.).

*Current Law*

Section 21 RSA 2006 inserts a new section 3ZB into the RTA 1988:

> 3ZB Causing death by driving: unlicensed, disqualified or uninsured drivers
> A person is guilty of an offence under this section if he causes the death of another person by driving a motor vehicle on a road and, at the time when he is driving, the circumstances are such that he is committing an offence under –
> (a) section 87(1) of this Act (driving otherwise than in accordance with a licence),
> (b) section 103(1)(b) of this Act (driving while disqualified), or
> (c) section 143 of this Act (using motor vehicle while uninsured or unsecured against third party risks).

All that is needed to be proven is that D was driving when D ought not to have been because D does not hold a valid licence or insurance or has been disqualified from driving, and was involved in a fatal collision. Even if D's driving was faultless and the collision was the result of another driver's bad driving, D will be convicted of the statutory homicide offence.

A major problem with this offence is that it appears to reject the normal principles of criminal liability in favour of public appeasement. Criminal liability is usually based on two elements: *actus reus* and *mens rea*. The offences discussed in this book represent a departure from this paradigm in either requiring no harm to have been caused (endangerment offences or conduct crimes such as careless driving or speeding) or do not require the normal intention or recklessness required by traditional criminal offences (the result crimes discussed in this chapter). CDUD, on the face of it, is only a departure in terms of *mens rea*: it is a strict liability offence requiring no intention or foresight with regards to the consequences of the defendant's act. However, as with the other offences discussed in this chapter, it does require a particular result to have occurred: death. Unlike the offences of CDDD and CDCD, however, one cannot really bring this result within the legal term of *actus reus*. For the *actus reus* of causing another's death to be proven in relation to CDDD it was noted that D's act must be a cause, albeit not the only cause, of death. It is not evident that this principle will apply to CDUD, although the government has attempted to quell such concerns by suggesting that some degree of causation would be needed to prove CDUD:

> The offence will apply where 'but for' the defendant's car being on the road the person would not have been killed. For example, if the defendant caused a ten car pile up then he could be charged in relation to the death of a person in the tenth car, even though he might not have made contact with that car. Conversely, if he was unavoidably involved in the pile up but it would have occurred even if he had not been present, then he could not be held responsible for any deaths. (Home Office 2005b, 8)

However, this does not explain how the collision has been caused by the defendant's disqualified, unlicensed or uninsured driving. It supposes that D's driving caused death and D should not have been driving, but it does not necessarily follow that D caused death *because* D had been disqualified from driving or was driving without a licence or insurance. As noted by Dennis, the offence is 'founded on an extremely attenuated notion of causation', requiring only the most basic 'but for' causation' (Dennis 2007, 254).

### *Sentencing*

CDUD is triable either way, with a maximum penalty of two years' imprisonment when tried on indictment, and mandatory disqualification. The SAP notes that the sentencing task is even more difficult in relation to CDUD than CDCD, given that in relation to CDCD some degree of bad driving is required to have caused death, whereas there is no need for any bad driving to be a factor in causing a death for the purposes of CDUD (SAP 2007, para.65): 'there is an enormous mismatch between the culpability involved when driving while prohibited from doing so and the harm caused by this offence, which results in a death being caused' (ibid., para.66). Dennis has taken such comments as indicating the SAP's disapproval of parliament's decision to create such an offence (Dennis 2007, 254).

In formulating sentencing guidelines which should reflect the culpability of those convicted for an offence which is difficult to justify, the SAP must have faced a difficult task. As noted by Dennis, in reading the SAP's paper 'one senses a distaste for the job' (Dennis 2007, 254). The SAP deems driving whilst disqualified to be more serious than driving whilst uninsured or without a licence, and so recommends a higher starting point when D was disqualified from driving at the time of the offence (SAP 2008, para.148). Table 4.3 sets out the consultation guidelines for sentencing in cases of CDUD, as proposed by the SAP and adopted by the SGC.

## **Manslaughter**

In addition to the above, the common-law offence of manslaughter remains a possible charge in cases of fatal road traffic collisions. Manslaughter could take the form of either constructive (unlawful act) manslaughter or gross negligence manslaughter, depending on the circumstances of the case.

### *Constructive Manslaughter*

Constructive manslaughter requires that D committed an unlawful act which was dangerous and that the act caused V's death. Of these two elements, it is the former which will be the key to determining whether a driver can be prosecuted for manslaughter. This is because an act falling within the category of 'unlawful' acts for the purposes of manslaughter must be criminal for some reason other than that it was negligently performed. Thus, although dangerous driving and careless driving are crimes, they do not constitute 'unlawful' acts for the purposes

**Table 4.3 Sentencing Guidelines Council Consultation Guidelines for CDUD**

| **Nature of offence** | **Sentencing range** |
|---|---|
| The offender was disqualified from driving<br>OR<br>The offender was unlicensed or uninsured plus 2 or more aggravating factors from the list below | Starting point – 12 months imprisonment<br>Sentencing range – 36 weeks to 2 years imprisonment |
| The offender was unlicensed or uninsured plus at least 1 aggravating factor from the list below | Starting point – 26 weeks imprisonment<br>Sentencing range – Community Order (HIGH) to 36 weeks imprisonment |
| The offender was unlicensed or uninsured – no aggravating factors | Starting point – Community Order (MEDIUM)<br>Sentencing range – Community Order (LOW) to (HIGH) |
| **Additional aggravating factors** | **Additional mitigating factors** |
| (a) previous convictions for motoring offences, whether involving bad driving or involving an offence of the same kind that forms part of the present conviction (i.e. unlicensed, disqualified or uninsured driving)<br>(b) more than one person was killed as a result of the offence<br>(c) serious injury to one or more persons in addition to the death(s)<br>(d) irresponsible behaviour such as failing to stop or falsely claiming that someone else was driving | (a) the decision to drive was brought about by a proven and genuine emergency falling short of a defence<br>(b) the offender genuinely believed that he or she was insured or licensed to drive<br>(c) the offender was seriously injured as a result of the collision<br>(d) the victim was a close friend or relative<br>(e) the actions of the victim or a third party contributed to the commission of the offence<br>**Personal mitigation**<br>(f) the offender gave direct, positive, assistance at the scene to victim(s)<br>(g) the offender has an exemplary driving record |

*Source*: SGC 2008, 18.

of manslaughter, since driving is a lawful activity. This was made clear by Lord Atkin in the case of *DPP v Andrews*:

> There is an obvious difference in the law of manslaughter between doing an unlawful act and doing a lawful act with a degree of carelessness which the legislature makes criminal. If it were otherwise a man who killed another while driving without due care and attention would *ex necessitate* commit manslaughter. (*DPP v Andrews* 1937, 585)

It has always been assumed that this reasoning would extend to other offences, such as drink-driving. It could be argued, however, that due to the innumerable legal requirements for driving to be legal, the reasoning in *Andrews* is not as valid as it once was (Cunningham 2008). Conversely, if such a position were to change then arguably the law in *Andrews* would also have to be reversed in relation to other activities regulated by strict liability offences. One could argue that in circumstances where the harm risked by breaching such regulations is death such an approach would be justifiable. On the other hand, there is much controversy surrounding the continued existence of constructive manslaughter generally, and the Law Commission has proposed that it be replaced by a statutory offence of manslaughter requiring intent to cause injury or an awareness of the risk of causing injury (Law Commission 2006, para.1.67). In these circumstances it would be a backwards step to alter the position in *Andrews*.

It has also been held that an omission will not suffice for unlawful act manslaughter (*Lowe* 1973). Under current law, then, constructive manslaughter is only likely to be charged where a vehicle is used as a weapon of assault, for example when D has driven D's car at V in order to frighten V, resulting in V's death. Assault is a common-law offence, the *actus reus* of which involves the defendant doing something to cause the victim to apprehend imminent force.

The second element of constructive manslaughter is that the unlawful act must also be dangerous. The test of dangerousness for this purpose was set out in the case of *Church* (1966): 'the unlawful act must be such as all sober and reasonable people would inevitably recognise must subject the other person to, at least, the risk of some harm resulting therefrom, albeit not serious harm'. This is a purely objective test – there is no requirement that D realized either that D was committing an unlawful act, or that the act created a risk of harm to others. Driving a vehicle directly at someone in order to frighten them (the unlawful act of assault) will clearly meet the test laid down in *Church*. The only other *mens rea* element required is that D had the necessary *mens rea* of the underlying unlawful act (*DPP v Newbury* 1977). The *mens rea* of common assault is that D must intend or foresee (subjective recklessness) that V will apprehend the infliction of imminent force (*Venna* 1976).

There has been an increase of reported cases (mostly appealed on the issue of appropriate sentence) of manslaughter by motor vehicle in recent years. Sometimes it is not always obvious the basis on which the manslaughter charge has been brought, or manslaughter plea accepted (on a charge of murder). For example, in *Brown* D pleaded guilty to manslaughter after driving the wrong way down a motorway in an attempt to commit suicide, resulting in a clearly foreseeable head-on collision with another car and the death of a passenger. In this case the judge opined that what D did was more serious than CDDD, given the manslaughter charge, and described D as using his car as a weapon to kill himself 'where it was bound to be an awful weapon against others' (*Brown* 2006, para.8). The issue of the basis upon which D pleaded guilty to manslaughter was not discussed in his appeal against sentence, but from the terminology used it is assumed that D was seen to assault other drivers with the necessary *mens rea* of assault. D's state of mind, beyond intending to kill himself, appears not to have been explored in any detail, but it is inevitable that he must have intended to apply unlawful force to others in the course of his actions. His sentence of ten years' detention was upheld by the Court of Appeal.

Similarly, in *Rule* (2003) D pleaded guilty to manslaughter in circumstances in which it is difficult to be sure of the basis of such a plea. D clearly demonstrated culpability of a level deserving a manslaughter conviction, but it is not clear whether his plea was on the basis of constructive manslaughter or gross negligence manslaughter. D was driving whilst disqualified when a police officer attempted to stop him for speeding. D, knowing that a prison sentence was inevitable if he was caught driving whilst disqualified, accelerated towards the officer who was indicating to him to stop. In his appeal against sentence D claimed that he had tried to avoid the officer, and was merely attempting to escape apprehension without any intention to harm or frighten V. If that was true (and he also did not foresee that his actions would frighten V) then he would not be guilty of assault, suggesting that his manslaughter conviction could not be based on constructive manslaughter and would instead have to fall within gross negligence manslaughter. It is not clear whether this was indeed the interpretation the Court of Appeal gave to the case, although it dismissed D's appeal against his sentence of nine years' imprisonment. Discussion of this case in *Parfitt* (2005) would suggest that the court rejected D's claim and upheld the sentence on the basis that D had in fact intended to frighten V.

Other reported cases in recent years where a manslaughter conviction on the basis of an unlawful and dangerous act has resulted have stemmed from cases in which murder has been charged, such as *Attorney-General's Reference (No. 64 of 2001)* (2002), *Franks* (2004), *Wright* (2004), *Ballard* (2005), and *Parfitt* (2005). In all of these cases D had used a car as a weapon of assault but either the Crown accepted a guilty plea to manslaughter or the case went to trial and the jury found that D lacked the necessary intent for murder. Sentences in these cases ranged from four and a half years' to twelve years' imprisonment. Another case is *Dwyer* (2005), in which D drove away from a petrol station with the car's owner hanging from the car's bonnet. V had been giving D a lift but had stopped to make a purchase at the petrol station. As he returned to the car he saw D driving it away, and jumped on the bonnet to prevent her doing so. D continued to drive and weaved in and out of traffic with the appearance of attempting to dislodge V, who was clinging to the driver's door. V fell from the vehicle and died. D was charged with manslaughter and murder, and pleaded guilty to the former, denying that she had intended to remove V from the car or had realized that he had fallen from it. Her sentence of seven years' detention in a Young Offenders' Institution was reduced to five on appeal.

### *Gross Negligence Manslaughter*

In *Andrews*, although Lord Atkin held that constructive manslaughter would not apply, he confirmed that the law in relation to gross negligence manslaughter would apply in a case of death caused by very bad driving. This was almost 20 years before the offence of CDDD was created, and the case of *Bateman* had set out the law on gross negligence manslaughter to be applied. Lord Hewitt CJ in *Bateman* laid down the following test for gross negligence:

> In order to establish criminal liability the facts must be such that, in the opinion of the jury, the negligence of the accused went beyond a mere matter of compensation between subjects and showed such disregard for the life and safety of others as to amount to a crime against the state and conduct deserving of punishment. (*Bateman* 1925, 11–12)

This case has been built upon in the ensuing 80 years. Once CDDD was introduced it was not clear whether the existence of the new statutory offence replaced gross negligence manslaughter in cases of death caused by very bad driving. It was confirmed in *Governor of Holloway Prison, ex p. Jennings* (1983) that motor manslaughter had not been impliedly repealed by the Road Traffic Act 1956. At that time, however, the causing death offence under operation was that of causing death by reckless, rather than dangerous, driving. Problems arose in the definition of 'recklessness' for the purposes of the offence which were addressed to some extent in the case of *Seymour* (1983). Here it was held that in cases of manslaughter, including motor manslaughter, the jury should be directed in terms of objective *Lawrence* (1982) recklessness.

A decade later, after causing death by reckless driving had been replaced by CDDD by the RTA 1991, *Adomako* (1995) reversed the decision in *Seymour* by replacing the test of objective recklessness with one of gross negligence. The House of Lords in *Adomako* confirmed that motor manslaughter should apply the same test as any other form of manslaughter, with Lord Mackay approving of the cases of *Bateman* and *Andrews*. Lord Mackay laid down the following test to be applied in all cases of gross negligence manslaughter:

1) D must have breached a duty of care towards the victim who has died.
2) That breach must have caused the death of the victim.
3) The jury must consider whether that breach of duty should be characterized as gross negligence and therefore as a crime (*Adomako* 1995, 187).

Lord Mackay noted that as a result of applying this test, cases of motor manslaughter might become rare (ibid.). It does not automatically follow from the test laid down that this should be so. In a case of manslaughter involving motor vehicles it can be argued that all drivers owe a duty of care to other road users, whether they are pedestrians, cyclists or other drivers, and thus the first part of the test will always be met. The second part of the test is a simple question of causation. It appears, then, that it is the final part of the test which led Lord Mackay to suggest that motor manslaughter would become rare. This test has been criticized as being 'circular' in nature: the jury should convict D if they think that D's behaviour was so bad that it is deserving of conviction. The circularity of test was a feature recognized by Lord Mackay in laying down the test, but he did not see it as fatal to its success (*Adomako* 1995, 187). Subsequent challenges to the lawfulness of the test have been unsuccessful (*Misra and Srivastava* 2005). The guidance provided in *Adomako* is such that juries should be instructed to consider the extent to which D's conduct departed from the proper standard of care incumbent upon D, having regard to the risk of death involved. As with CDDD, in a case of driving the question will be how far below the standard expected of a competent and careful driver did D's driving fall. What distinguishes the test for manslaughter from that of CDDD is that the jury must have regard to the risk of death involved, whereas for CDDD the relevant risk is that of serious injury or damage to property (RTA 1988, section 2A(3)).

There have been a few reported cases of manslaughter based on grossly negligent driving in recent years. It is worth taking a closer look at them in considering what, beyond the requirement that D's driving fell 'far below the standard of a competent and careful driver' needed for CDDD, is seen to be required for a prosecution of manslaughter. In *Attorney-General's Reference (No. 14 of 2001)* (2002) D had defective vision and drove in darkness without his spectacles, and collided with a pedestrian crossing the road. Although D should have been wearing his glasses, since his vision was blurred at a distance of about 30 centimetres without them, it was accepted at trial that even if he had been wearing them he probably could not have avoided the collision with V, who was wearing dark clothing on a poorly lit road. Despite this, the jury were directed that they could not convict D of either CDDD or manslaughter unless they were satisfied that D had not been wearing his glasses. D had fled the scene of the collision and set fire to the car, for which he did not have valid insurance. D was convicted of manslaughter and on appeal D's sentence of three years' imprisonment was increased to four years and three months' imprisonment.

In *Attorney-General's Reference (No. 134 of 2004)* (2005) D was the driver of a car transporter who reported to his employers the fact that he had defective brakes following a minor collision. He was told that if the vehicle was investigated and found to have nothing wrong with its brakes, D would be held responsible for the crash and face dismissal. D chose not to push the issue and continued to drive the vehicle. When his brakes again failed he mounted the pavement to avoid colliding with stationary traffic at a pedestrian crossing and instead hit a pedestrian who died instantly. D pleaded guilty to manslaughter at the earliest opportunity and was sentenced to twelve months' imprisonment, held not to be unduly lenient by the Court of Appeal. The owner and foreman of the firm who employed D were also prosecuted for manslaughter but found not guilty. It would appear that the main reason why D was prosecuted for manslaughter rather than CDDD in this case was the hope that this would strengthen the case against his employers for manslaughter. It is unusual that D chose to plead guilty to that offence, but it is unlikely that he would have received a lower sentence for CDDD and it is the difference in offence label, rather than sentence, which is most striking. This is a case which now would likely be prosecuted under the Corporate Manslaughter and Corporate Homicide Act 2007 (see below).

Sometimes it is not possible to charge CDDD because death was caused by driving somewhere other than on a road or other public place. This appears to be the main reason for a charge of manslaughter in the case of *Barker* (2003). D drove his partner and three children and a friend to an old chalk pit filled with water. D had no licence or insurance, and had never taken a driving test. At the lake D accidentally drove the car over the edge of the cliff into the lake and the three children drowned. D admitted that the accelerator had got stuck because he had 'floored it' and so had not been driving properly but claimed that he did not mean to drive over the cliff. The Court of Appeal described D's negligence as 'very gross indeed', but reduced his sentence of five years' imprisonment to one of three years' imprisonment. It is unclear whether the main reason for the charge of manslaughter rather than CDDD was that the incident occurred on private property or the degree of negligence involved. The facts of the case can be likened to those in *Cambray* (2007) in which D, an unlicensed driver, drove his car over the wall of a beach-front car park (a public place) and landed on a two-year-old boy, killing him. D claimed that he had accidentally hit the accelerator instead of the brake. D was charged with and convicted of CDDD and sentenced to eight years' imprisonment, reduced to six on appeal. The sentence would suggest that D was even more culpable than the defendant in *Barker*, but he was prosecuted for what is seen as a less serious offence.

In *Attorney-General's Reference (No. 111 of 2006)* (2007) D was a taxi driver who was working in the early hours of the morning. A group of men attempted to hail the taxi but D did not stop, but executed a U-turn and drove back towards the group of men. V was standing in the road and stepped into D's path. D slowed down, but did not stop, whilst V placed his hands on the bonnet of the taxi. V lost his footing and fell under the front of the taxi and, rather than stopping, D accelerated away, with V trapped under his vehicle. V was dragged for about a mile before becoming dislodged, at which point D drove on. D was indicted for murder but a guilty plea to manslaughter was accepted on the second day of the trial. D was sentenced to three years' imprisonment, increased to five on appeal. The basis of the plea was one of gross negligence rather than unlawful act manslaughter, assuming that D's blame lay in his actions once V had become trapped under his vehicle rather than for the way in which V had come to be under the vehicle. This marks it out as an unusual case, since ordinarily a plea of guilty to manslaughter on a murder charge would be based on D admitting using his vehicle as a weapon of offence but not intending to cause death or grievous bodily harm (see Cunningham 2001).

There is one final category of case involving the possibility of a manslaughter charge which is one that the preceding case could have fallen within. *Wilkinson's Road Traffic Offences* suggests that manslaughter might possibly be committed by a hit-and-run driver (Wallis et al. 2005, para.5.40). It is unclear what species of manslaughter this suggestion covers. It is true that section 170 RTA 1988 imposes a duty on all motorists to stop after an accident and *Wilkinson's* submits that one of the purposes behind this provision is the saving of life. It goes on to state:

> If therefore a motorist, knowing serious injury and the risk of death if not medically attended, fails to stop or fails to report the accident and as a result of that failure the person whom he has hit with his motor vehicle dies, it could be argued that his deliberate or reckless failure to comply with the positive duty placed upon him by section 170 might be sufficient to warrant a charge of manslaughter even if there is no evidence of the manner of the defendant's driving. (ibid.)

The wording of this suggestion implies that the species of manslaughter committed is subjective reckless manslaughter, requiring proof that D foresaw the risk of serious harm or death being caused through lack of medical help but decided to take that risk by not stopping. Given that constructive manslaughter cannot be based on an omission (*Lowe* 1973), the only other possibility is that this would amount to gross negligence manslaughter. There are no officially reported instances of such a case, although a prosecution in Yorkshire in 2007 has facts similar to those described in *Wilkinson's*. Andrew Bennett, who had never held a driving licence, lost control of his car on the brow of a hill and ploughed into trees causing his passenger, who had not been wearing a seatbelt, to be flung through the windscreen. D then arranged for V to be driven to his house in another car and more than thirty minutes elapsed before medical help was sought. D pleaded guilty to manslaughter, driving while disqualified and conspiracy to pervert the course of justice. DI Tom Whitely of South Yorkshire Police, who oversaw the investigation, said:

> This is an unusual case that started out as an investigation into a road traffic accident... It was originally dealt with as causing death by dangerous driving but as the full circumstances emerged, particularly the actions of Andrew Bennett, it became clear this was unlawful killing. Following a road traffic accident where a young girl was unconscious an ambulance should have been summoned immediately – there is no question about that. Should she have received immediate medical attention an expert has assessed that [the deceased] would have had an 85 per cent chance of survival. (*Sheffield Today* 9 August 2007)

In 2005/06 there were 14 cases recorded as homicide (meaning murder, manslaughter or infanticide) where the 'apparent method' of killing is stated to be 'motor vehicle' (Coleman et al. 2007, Table 1.03). This is the lowest rate in the past five years, with the number staying at between 20 and 23 in the years 2001/02 to 2003/04. Prior to the start of this century the numbers stayed around the low teens, following a rise from two to twelve between 1996 and 1997. This suggests that there has been a surge in the number of deaths caused by motor vehicle in which the police and/or CPS have judged there to be sufficient evidence to suggest a murder or manslaughter charge after 2000, although it is yet to be seen whether the most recent number, showing a sudden decrease, will be replicated in future years. It would appear more likely that the figure will again increase, given a slight change in CPS policy to encourage charges of manslaughter in appropriate cases, with an alternative charge of CDDD. This has been made possible following the enactment of the RSA 2006. Section 33 of the RSA amends section 24 of the Road Traffic Offenders Act 1988 to allow the Crown to charge manslaughter with the safety net that a jury can return a verdict of guilty of CDDD if they decide that the elements of manslaughter are not made out.

## Corporate Manslaughter

The Corporate Manslaughter and Corporate Homicide Act 2007 creates a new statutory offence of corporate manslaughter. Whilst it has for many years been possible to convict companies for manslaughter based on the common law, such convictions were very rare due to the difficulties involved in proving the necessary fault on the part of the company through the application of what is known as the 'identification doctrine' (*Tesco Supermarkets Ltd v Nattrass* 1972). The Law Commission first recommended the introduction of a new offence of Corporate Killing in 1996, with the government adopting the suggestion in 2000. A draft Corporate Manslaughter Bill was introduced in 2005 and, after a long drawn-out exercise of parliamentary scrutiny, the Act was finally passed in July 2007.

The new offence is set out in section 1 of the Corporate Manslaughter and Corporate Homicide Act 2007:

> (1) An organisation to which this section applies is guilty of an offence if the way in which its activities are managed or organised –
> (a) causes a person's death, and
> (b) amounts to a gross breach of a relevant duty of care owed by the organisation to the deceased.
> (2) The organisations to which this section applies are –
> (a) a corporation;
> (b) a department or other body listed in Schedule 1;
> (c) a police force;
> (d) a partnership, or a trade union or employers' association, that is an employer.
> (3) An organisation is guilty of an offence under this section only if the way in which its activities are managed or organised by its senior management is a substantial element in the breach referred to in subsection (1).
> (4) For the purposes of this Act –
> (a) 'relevant duty of care' has the meaning given by section 2, read with sections 3 to 7;
> (b) a breach of a duty of care by an organisation is a 'gross' breach if the conduct alleged to amount to a breach of that duty falls far below what can reasonably be expected of the organisation in the circumstances;
> (c) 'senior management', in relation to an organisation, means the persons who play significant roles in –
> (i) the making of decisions about how the whole or a substantial part of its activities are to be managed or organised, or

(ii) the actual managing or organising of the whole or a substantial part of those activities.

Where, during the course of a company's business, it employs drivers to drive vehicles, the company could become susceptible to prosecution for corporate manslaughter if a death is caused by a driver employee involved in a fatal road traffic collision. It is yet to be seen how far the offence will extend, but it is conceivable that where a company failed to maintain its vehicles correctly, to the knowledge of the 'senior management', and one such vehicle caused a collision due to its condition, the company could be liable. Similarly, a company whose managers were aware that to meet tight deadlines set for the delivery of goods between destinations of great distance a driver might have to exceed the speed limit or miss scheduled breaks required under drivers' hours regulations could also face prosecution if a driver subsequently caused a fatal collision through fatigue or driving too fast for the conditions.

It should be noted that the offence does not only apply to private companies but also to organizations such as the Highways Authority and police. Any corporation that employs drivers is likely to need to review training practices for its drivers to ensure a good safety culture with regards to driving activities. The nature of duties owed by the Highways Agency to members of the public is different. The Highways Agency might conceivably come under the definition of corporate manslaughter if it failed in one of its statutory duties, such as the duty to maintain the highway under section 41 of the Highways Act 1980. If a collision occurred as the result of a poorly maintained road and this amounted to a 'gross breach' of which senior management was aware, corporate manslaughter might apply. The same would be true in relation to a failure to comply with the New Roads and Streetworks Act 1991, for example if insufficient signage or lighting was provided at the scene of road works, leading to a fatal collision.

Although the police are included within bodies to which the new 2007 Act applies, a number of exemptions are provided under section 5 of the Act, one of which operates to exclude circumstances where the pursuit of law enforcement activities has resulted in a fatality to a member of the public, which has been stated to cover the activities of traffic officers (Home Office 2007, para.31). Further, section 6 clarifies that the offence does not apply to emergency services when responding to emergencies. This latter exemption does not relieve organizations of their responsibilities to provide safe working conditions, however, and is designed to exclude from the offence matters such as the timeliness of a response to an emergency, the level of response and the effectiveness of the way in which the emergency is tackled (ibid., para.34). Emergency vehicles involved in a fatal collision whilst on their way to respond to an emergency call are not necessarily covered by the exemption, it is assumed, although it must be shown that the corporation involved owed a relevant duty of care under section 2 of the Act to the person who died.

For a charge of corporate manslaughter to succeed, there must have been a management failure that caused death and that can be categorized as 'gross'. In deciding whether the breach was gross, section 8 specifies that the jury may take account of whether the company failed to comply with any health and safety guidance. The jury may also take into account any other matters they consider relevant.

The penalty for the offence, given that the offender is a company and not an individual who may be incarcerated, is an unlimited fine. Section 9 of the Act also allows the court to make a remedial order to ensure that future deaths are avoided by the taking of appropriate steps to remedy any failings leading to the death in the case. In addition, the court can make a publicity order to bring to the attention of the public the fact that a corporation has been convicted of the offence. This may help in terms of deterrence to encourage companies to take all available measures to avoid conviction for the offence, as long as they do not operate on the basis that any publicity is good publicity.

The issue of corporate manslaughter has proved to be extremely controversial in all respects, and it is indeed surprising that the Act succeeded in gaining Royal Assent. It is too early to know for sure how the offence will operate when it comes into force on 6 April 2008, particularly in relation to fatal road traffic collisions, but it is possible to envisage the type of case where it might be a useful charge for the Crown to bring. Under the common law, before the offence was introduced, there had already been a few reported cases of companies being held liable for manslaughter as the result of a fatal collision.

One such case is that of Keymark Services, which pleaded guilty to two counts of manslaughter in 2004 (*BBC News Online* 3 December 2004). In that case the court heard how the haulage company falsified tachograph charts so that its drivers could work long hours without any breaks, and also encouraged its drivers to falsify records. One of its drivers was involved in a seven-vehicle pile-up on the M1 motorway when he fell asleep at the wheel of his lorry. The director of the company was also convicted of manslaughter and imprisoned for seven years. Another driving-related case of manslaughter resulting in the successful prosecution of a company was that of Dennis Clothier and Sons, convicted of manslaughter in 2002 (Centre for Corporate Accountability website). V died when he was hit by a 20-tonne trailer which became detached from a tractor because it was dangerously loaded and the hitch mechanism connecting the trailer to the tractor was badly worn, which would have been obvious to those responsible for maintaining the vehicle. Other cases in which individual directors of companies were prosecuted in circumstances similar to those in the Keymark Services case could similarly result in corporate manslaughter convictions under the new law.

There have been other reported cases where a charge of corporate manslaughter might have been viable, but where the Crown has sought only to prosecute individuals within a company. One example is the case of *Coates and Graves* (2004). In this case D was an HGV driver convicted of CDDD after falling asleep and colliding with a car that had broken down on a dual carriageway. The driver of the car had just got out of it, and was killed instantly when struck by D's vehicle. D had been working a 20-hour day and pleaded guilty to falsifying his tachograph. G was the owner of the haulage company for whom D worked and was accused of manslaughter on the basis that he negligently caused or permitted his drivers, particularly D, to falsify their tachograph records to enable them to work longer than the permitted driving hours and become so tired that they were a danger to other road users. G denied this charge and claimed that he took reasonable care to ensure that his drivers kept within their permitted working hours, although he acknowledged that all but one of his drivers had been falsifying their tachograph records. G claimed that he was unaware of this at the time, and denied falsifying his own tachograph records so as to give a bad example to his employees. After a seven month long trial the jury returned a verdict of guilty and G was sentenced to four years' imprisonment. This was the kind of case which might also have seen a successful prosecution of G's company, given that he could be described as the 'directing mind' of the company and could be identified with it. However, this was an extremely complex case and it may be that it was felt that holding G liable for manslaughter was a sufficiently effective way of dealing with the company's responsibility.

During the author's research into prosecutions brought in fatal collisions in the East Midlands, a few cases could have been candidates for the new corporate manslaughter case. The first involved the death of an employee who lost control of his car because the trailer which he was towing, loaded with another car, was too heavy. The vehicle became unstable because the recommended towing weight was exceeded by 59 per cent. V was transporting the car for his employer, who had provided him with the trailer and should have been aware that it was not suitable for that purpose. No training had been given to V about loading or towing a trailer. No prosecution was commenced, although this might have been different under the new law.

One case in which it appears that serious consideration was given to a charge of manslaughter was C1. In this case V was an HGV driver who regularly drove in contravention of drivers' hours legislation. He fell asleep at the wheel, colliding with the rear of a crane travelling slowly on the M1. V's employer was arrested (for attempting to pervert the course of justice) and interviewed. He claimed that he had not put pressure on V to exceed his hours, and had in fact reprimanded him on each occasion that he discovered V had done so. The police searched V's employer's house and found tachograph charts that had been missing from his place of work showing infringements of drivers' hours regulations. V's wife claimed that his employer had contacted her to ask her to lie about the length of time V had been driving his truck and to meet in order to get their stories straight. V's employer denied this. V's wife also said that V felt under pressure to work long hours as he was concerned that if he did not he would be replaced, and if he missed a delivery he would not get paid. A meeting took place between the police and CPS to consider the available evidence, but no prosecutions were brought. The case occurred before that of Keymark Services and it may be that, following a successful conviction in that case and the coming into force of the Corporate Manslaughter and Corporate Homicide Act 2007, prosecutors may be more confident in prosecuting haulage companies in these circumstances in future.

## Murder

Murder is committed when D kills with the *mens rea* of 'malice aforethought'. Malice aforethought means that either D intended to kill or intended to cause grievous bodily harm (*Vickers* 1957). Where D chooses a motor vehicle as a lethal weapon there is no reason why murder should not be charged, provided that the prosecution can prove the necessary malice aforethought, where 'intention' includes both direct and oblique intention under the *Woollin* test of foresight of death or grievous bodily harm as a virtual certainty (*Woollin* 1999).

However, research has shown that murder is rarely charged in cases involving motor vehicles. Writing in 1985, Spencer found that 'murder charges are usually not pressed where they could be' in cases where D had driven at a pedestrian or cyclist (Spencer 1985, 33), and that such cases 'usually seem to be charged with manslaughter at most' (ibid.). In a more recent study it was found that in many cases where murder is charged the lesser offence of CDDD is charged in the alternative (Cunningham 2001). Of the 13 cases where murder was charged by the police as the result of someone being struck by a motor vehicle, only one resulted in a conviction for murder. In seven of the 13 cases CDDD appeared alongside murder on the indictment, and in four cases where the police first charged murder the final conviction was for CDDD (the other three cases resulting in manslaughter convictions) (ibid., 685). In the cases in which murder was charged D either knew his (all the defendants were male) victim or had had an altercation with the victim immediately preceding the attack (ibid., 686). In the one case where a murder conviction was secured, D had mounted the pavement and struck a pedestrian, something that occurred in several of the other cases. What distinguishes this case from others, however, was the fact that unlike other defendants D denied that he had driven at his victim intentionally, instead claiming that he had lost control of the car when an object was thrown at it. It would seem that this implausible explanation was his downfall; had he admitted to driving the car at the victim intending only to frighten and not to injure, the chances are that he would have escaped a murder conviction and been convicted of manslaughter, as occurred in several of the other cases (ibid., 687). An even more favourable defence amongst the cases involved D claiming that V had been standing in the middle of the road and had lurched towards D's car as he drove past, painting V as the aggressor and denying any malice towards V at all. Such cases were likely to end in convictions for CDDD (ibid.).

Murder charges in driving cases remain rare, although they do occur occasionally, but convictions are even rarer (see above for cases resulting in convictions for manslaughter on a murder charge). In 2005 Leayon Dudley was convicted of the murder of PC Moore and the manslaughter of PC Munn. Dudley had collided with the two officers when trying to evade police who had earlier seen him driving at 70 mph in a 30 mph zone. He had been drinking and was later found to have a BAC of at least twice the legal limit. PCs Munn and Moore were attempting to intercept D with the use of a stinger device on a dual carriageway when the collision occurred. The officers had stopped in a lay-by and were preparing the device when D struck them whilst travelling at 78 mph.

Although Dudley was originally convicted of the murder of one of the officers, his appeal against conviction on the basis that he should have been permitted to call expert evidence to explain that the collision had been an 'accident' was successful (*Dudley* 2004). Following this successful appeal the Crown accepted pleas to manslaughter on the basis of unlawful act manslaughter. D was sentenced to 14 years' imprisonment, upheld on appeal (*Dudley* 2006).

## Policy and Practice

The priority for road safety policy is to prevent the ultimate harm of death and, when that ultimate harm which it seeks to prevent arises, it is not surprising that attitudes towards offending changes in reaction to it. The statutory offences discussed in this chapter can be seen as 'hybrid' offences. They are constructed on underlying driving offences which are in themselves conduct crimes (dangerous driving; careless driving; disqualified driving, etc.), but because they are result crimes they also fall within the more traditional field of crime: homicide. Killing is wrong: there is no question over the moral quality of such an act. Driving offences such as careless driving, however, struggle to be recognized as a moral wrong in the same way. When careless driving results in the causing of death, what is the moral quality of such an act and should the criminal law seek to punish for the wrong of causing death? These questions will be explored in greater detail in subsequent chapters, but at this stage it is necessary to establish how the offences operate in practice. Only once this is understood can any real analysis of the justification for the offences take place.

### *Police Investigations of Homicide Cases*

The role for the police in investigating a fatal road traffic collision is quite different from other forms of road policing. A *Road Death Investigation Manual* was introduced by the Association of Chief Police Officers (ACPO) in 2001. The aim of the manual is to standardize the way in which the police investigate road death incidents and serious injury collisions (ACPO 2001, 13). It is based on, and is complementary to, the *Murder Investigation Manual*, which was published in 2000. According to the *Road Death Investigation Manual*: '[t]his manual consolidates many good practices already adopted by police forces and investigative agencies throughout the United Kingdom and provides a definitive document to assist all those involved in the investigation of a road death. It is a dynamic document and will be amended as and when necessary' (ibid.). One emphasis placed on road death investigations is that each case should be treated as a potential murder or manslaughter ('unlawful killing') until such evidence is collected that proves to the contrary. The manual gives such details as the need to deploy sufficient family liaison officers and the role of those involved such as the senior investigating officer (SIO) and collision investigator. It is now in its third edition.

The police will follow a fairly uniform procedure in the initial stages of the investigation into a fatal or potentially fatal collision. Local police officers will be called to the scene and either the control room or an officer first at the scene will request the attendance of a traffic officer once it becomes clear that the collision involves serious injuries. An SIO will oversee the investigation, acting as leader of the team of police investigators and scene manager. The SIO will normally be an officer of the rank of sergeant or inspector (ACPO 2004, 13), and will normally attend the scene (ibid., 15). A collision investigator will attend the scene whenever the collision is seen to be potentially fatal. Some police forces employ civilian collision investigators, whose sole job is to investigate collisions, whilst others use specially trained police officers who may be called away from other operational policing duties to attend the scene of a collision.

The fact that a death has occurred will be important because not only will the police be investigating the possibility that an offence has been committed; they will also be collecting evidence for the purposes of an inquest. The coroner will rely heavily on evidence collected by the police; officers involved in the investigation of fatal collisions will have this in mind when carrying out the investigation. Even if they decide that no further action is appropriate as far as criminal liability is concerned, they will still need to provide a detailed file for the coroner (ibid., 63). Whereas in cases of non-fatal collisions any investigation will be for the purpose of establishing criminal liability only, in a fatal case the necessity of an inquest will guarantee that it is thoroughly investigated. An officer interviewed in the course of the author's research expressed an element of conflict between his role as criminal investigator and coroner's officer, since the purpose of collecting evidence is different for each role. Additionally, the rules of evidence are also different, in that they are less strict in coroners' courts. He pointed out that the quality of evidence submitted to the coroner is far higher than that required, since the police are also investigating the possibility of a criminal offence having been committed.

In many cases the evidence of the collision investigator will be crucial, particularly if the collision took place in the absence of any eyewitnesses. Although the evidence of the collision investigator can be conclusive and reliable, there are cases in which the collision investigator is unable to determine from the evidence available at the scene what the exact cause of the collision was. In other cases defence expert witnesses may disagree with the seemingly irrefutable evidence of the collision investigator. In such cases it will normally be left to the CPS to determine whether the case is strong enough to go to court. That said, such instances are relatively rare. Much can be determined from the presence of tyre marks at the scene, damage to the vehicles and the position of debris along the road. Unlike the evidence in other types of crimes, such evidence tells a story where motive and opportunity are irrelevant to the construction of a case.

In one particular case (A5) in the author's research, the role of the collision investigator came into question. The police completed their investigations and sent an advice file to the CPS, who advised that prosecution for CDDD should go ahead. However, the prosecutor was concerned that there might be difficulty in proving causation and thus asked for clarification of a particular point in the collision investigation report. It was a case in which D had overtaken a vehicle on the approach to a bend. According to an independent eyewitness D had only just managed to regain his correct side of the carriageway when a car, driven by V, passed him coming in the opposite direction and immediately lost control, veering across the road into a car behind D. There was no impact between D's and V's cars and the collision investigator found very little physical evidence on the road. The prosecutor asked the collision investigator to clarify evidence of coarse steering, what effect this would have had, and what, in his opinion, led to such manner of driving. The question was whether D's driving was a possible cause to which V was reacting.

In response (a memo was sent from the collision investigator to his chief inspector) the collision investigator suggested that the Crown prosecutor had not appreciated the collision investigator's role in the investigation of collisions. He saw his loyalty as being to the court as an independent witness, rather than to his 'instructing solicitor'. It is true that an expert's duty is to assist the court in resolving issues, and that this duty takes priority over any duty to the client (Dennis 2002, 711). The collision investigator stated that his role was to reconstruct an accident and to show the behaviour of the vehicles and people involved prior to, during and after the collision from physical evidence at the scene, which is impartial and independent of evidence from witnesses. It was not, in his view, for him to comment on the eyewitness evidence. He seems to have been concerned about his ability to comment on such matters because of cases in which collision investigators have been openly criticized by trial judges. He referred, in particular, to the civil case of *Liddell v Middleton* (1996), in which an expert witness concluded that the defendant in the case was grossly negligent in failing to observe the plaintiff (a pedestrian crossing the road ahead of him at night) and that had he done so and taken appropriate action the collision would never have occurred. Lord Justice Smith criticized the expert witness's evidence, referring to the Civil Evidence Act 1972 and stating that an expert is only qualified to give evidence on a relevant matter, if his knowledge and expertise relate to a matter which is outside the knowledge and experience of a layman.

The point made in this case was that expert witnesses must provide evidence deduced from his or her scientific expertise and not from consideration of eyewitness evidence. An expert is not entitled to give an opinion as to how a defendant should have acted or whether a party was negligent. This is because it breaches the 'ultimate issue' rule. The 'ultimate issue' rule exists to ensure that questions of fact arising in a trial should be left to the fact-finders (the jury or magistrates in a criminal trial), and that an expert does not give his opinion on the ultimate issue which is for the court to decide. However, the fact that *Liddell v Middleton* was a civil case is probably relevant. Although Smith LJ stated that in personal injury cases involving road traffic collisions it is the exception rather than the rule that expert witnesses are required, this is not necessarily true of criminal prosecutions involving fatal collisions, in which the Collision Investigation Report is crucial to the prosecution of a case (Pearce et al. 2002, 31). In criminal cases it has been accepted that an expert may give an opinion on the ultimate issue, provided that he or she is qualified to give such an opinion, the jury are directed that they are not obliged to accept it, and the witness does not 'overstep the line which separates his province from that of the jury' (Dennis 2002, 713). Furthermore, the questions asked by the prosecutor in case A5 seem to have been asked on the basis that the collision investigator would have knowledge of the cause and effect of coarse steering outside the knowledge of the layman, and in this sense did not risk breaching the rule laid down in *Liddell v Middleton* as the collision investigator feared. In other cases in the author's research the collision investigator did in fact, to a greater or lesser degree, give an opinion concerning who was at fault. In one force in particular the collision investigator was expected to recommend what action, if any, should be taken against D, and the investigating officer would merely adopt this recommendation. Such an approach is not accepted in other forces, where the collision investigator is seen to be entirely separate from the rest of the investigation. Since these cases the publication of the *Road Death Investigation Manual* may have brought greater consistency between forces in the way in which fatal collisions are investigated.

### *CPS Charging Decisions in Homicide Cases*

Once the police have completed their investigations they will send a file to the CPS for a decision to be made as to charge. As with non-fatal driving offences, the CPS will be guided by what used to be known as the *Driving Offences Charging Standard*, a document that has recently undergone rigorous revisions as the result of the RSA 2006 and has been republished as the *Policy for Prosecuting Cases of Bad Driving*. The guidance contained therein is also incorporated into the road traffic offences section of the 'Legal Guidance' website.

The new policy recognizes that some sections of the public are of the opinion that manslaughter should often be charged instead of CDDD (CPS 2007b, para.5.2). The CPS's current policy is that 'before a charge of gross negligence manslaughter will be preferred, there must be something to set the case apart from one where one of the statutory offences can be proved' (ibid., para.5.14). This is because gross negligence is more difficult than CDDD to prove, particularly because it requires proof of an obvious and serious risk of death (ibid., para.5.15). Although the maximum penalty for manslaughter is higher than for CDDD, the CPS point to sentencing practice to justify the approach that CDDD ought to be charged on the basis that D will likely receive an equally severe sentence for CDDD as for manslaughter (ibid., para.5.16), and so manslaughter will be reserved for cases of the 'utmost gravity' involving a 'very high risk of death' (ibid., para.5.17). Although, following the RSA 2006, the Crown can now charge manslaughter in the knowledge that the jury can return an alternative verdict of CDDD or CDCDUI, this has not had as much an effect on charging policy as one might have expected. The policy remains that CDDD will be the appropriate charge in most cases (ibid., para.5.20). This is on the basis that manslaughter can only be charged where there is evidence supporting a realistic prospect of conviction (ibid., para.5.19), implying that the CPS remains of the opinion that juries are unlikely to convict drivers of manslaughter. As will be discussed further in Chapter 7, there may be more support for manslaughter in driving cases than the CPS is ready to acknowledge and it is suggested that in many cases of CDDD the risk of death involved will have been such as to support a charge of manslaughter.

Little more is said in the policy about choosing a charge in relation to one of the statutory offences, beyond reference to the standard of driving required for each underlying offence (see Chapter 2). In relation to CDUD, the CPS stresses that where D drove below the required standard, then a charge of CDDD or CDCD is likely to be preferred (ibid., para.5.24). This is also the position in relation to aggravated TWOC (ibid., para.5.37).

One further significant change brought in by the 2007 version of the policy is that 'nearest and dearest' cases will no longer be treated as they once were. Nearest and dearest cases are those where the person who died in the collision was a close relative, or possibly friend, of D. It was formerly CPS policy to approach these cases differently to most, based on the principle that D has 'suffered such enormous personal loss that it would be oppressive and insensitive to prosecute the driver for the bad driving offence that led to the death' (CPS 2007b, para.4.11). This policy meant that D was unlikely to face charges of CDDD if no other person had been killed in the collision, but would instead be prosecuted, if at all, for dangerous driving under section 2 RTA 1988 if D was thought to be a continuing danger on the roads. CDDD would only be charged where D drove in such a way as to show serious disregard for lives of 'nearest and dearest' or other road users. A similar approach was taken in relation to CDCDUI. This approach has been replaced by one where the normal approach will be to prosecute for the relevant causing death offence (CPS 2007b, para.4.12). The one exception to this is where D is suspected of CDUD, in which case the CPS may exercise its discretion not to prosecute 'in cases where the degree of culpability on the part of the driver is low, or where the circumstances of the case would make it unjust to prosecute' (ibid., para.4.13).

The author's research into fatal road traffic collisions was conducted before the RSA 2006 was passed, and the offences of CDCD and CDUD had not been created. It is presumed that those cases discussed in Chapter 2 where the CPS decision was to prosecute for careless driving would now be prosecuted instead for CDCD, once section 20 RSA 2006 is brought into force, since they all involved death. It is astonishing to think that those offenders would, if they had committed their offences several years later, have been convicted of an offence carrying a maximum penalty of five years' imprisonment instead of the fine to which they were subjected. Many of the cases of CDDD were also discussed in Chapter 2, to compare the different standards of careless and dangerous driving, but those falling at the more serious end of the scale will be discussed here.

Before looking at the results of the author's own research, it is worth considering other findings in relation to road death incidents. From the 5,870 police files relating to fatal collisions examined by the Transport Research Laboratory (TRL) in their report for the Department for Transport, the following information was extracted:

- In 44 per cent of cases the driver at fault was killed
- In 20 per cent a pedestrian at fault was killed

- In 10 per cent a driver was reported for CDDD or causing death by reckless driving (where the fatal collision occurred before 1991)
- In 20 per cent a driver was reported for careless driving
- In one per cent a driver was reported for dangerous driving or reckless driving
- In four per cent the file was simply marked as no prosecution
- In two per cent other offences were reported which may have been unconnected to the accident but which were detected during the investigation. (Pearce et al. 2002, 25–6)

In the author's own research, just over a third of cases resulted in prosecution for one of the relevant offences (126 of 316 cases). In many of the cases where there was no prosecution this was because the driver at fault had died. It should also be remembered that any single-vehicle collisions (other than those with pedestrians) were excluded from the sample. None of the cases resulted in a charge of dangerous driving, since this would only be appropriate where causation between D's act and V's death could not be proved. In an earlier research project there was one such case where D was convicted of dangerous driving after the jury decided that D could not be held guilty for murder or CDDD because of medical negligence on the part of hospital staff in failing to recognize that a chest drain had been incorrectly inserted (Cunningham 2001, 685). This case was unusual, since medical negligence very rarely breaks the chain of causation: 'it will only be in the most extraordinary and unusual case that such treatment can be said to be so independent of the acts of the accused that it could be regarded in law as the cause of the victim's death to the exclusion of the accused's acts' (*Cheshire* 1991, 257).

In the author's study of prosecutions in cases of fatal road traffic collisions, 29 cases involved charges of CDDD, there were seven cases of CDCDUI and five of aggravated TWOC. Of the 29 cases of CDDD, 24 resulted in convictions for that offence, either following trial or in consequence of a guilty plea being entered. This success rate of 83 per cent is in fact far higher than the national average for the relevant years (1999 and 2000), with official statistics showing that of the 623 proceedings for trial on a charge of CDDD, 400 (64 per cent) resulted in conviction (Home Office 2000b and 2001, Table 7). The TRL found that 79 per cent of drivers prosecuted for CDDD were convicted of that offence, suggesting that the success rate for CDDD is lower than that for the previous offence of causing death by reckless driving, the conviction rate for which stood at 89 per cent (Pearce et al. 2002). This finding may be seen as surprising, given that the very reason the law was changed was that reckless driving was seen as difficult to prove and the objective test for dangerous driving was expected to be an easier one to apply than *Lawrence* recklessness.

Of the 24 convictions in the author's study, 18 were the result of D pleading guilty to CDDD. Of these, not all pleaded guilty at the first opportunity. There were at least six 'cracked trials', in which D pleaded not guilty at the plea and directions hearing, but changed his plea before his trial commenced. The obvious advantage of pleading guilty is that it will be seen as a mitigating factor in sentencing (*Richardson* 2007), but much of the benefit of any sentencing discount may be lost if the plea is not timely. In cases of CDDD, cracked trials may occur due to the delay in D obtaining the report of a defence expert.

Unlike other classes of criminal offence, the issue in all of the cases of CDDD was not whether or not D was the perpetrator of a known crime for which the police sought to apprehend a suspect. It is extremely rare for D to claim that it is a case of mistaken identity and that the police have got the wrong person. D will normally admit that D drove the vehicle involved in the collision, but may dispute whether the way in which the vehicle was driven fell far below the standard of a competent and careful driver. In preparing D's defence D may call upon the services of an independent expert in collision reconstruction in the hope that such an expert will be able to challenge the evidence of the police collision investigator. However, if the defence expert agrees with the collision investigator, D is left with little in the form of a defence. D may therefore change D's plea from not guilty to guilty in order to secure at least some sentencing discount.

None of the cases resulted in prosecution for manslaughter. It is worth considering the degree of blameworthiness displayed in some of the more serious cases to understand how a Crown prosecutor makes the decision concerning what is to be the appropriate charge.

### *Manslaughter v CDDD*

Arguably, any of the cases in which CDDD was charged could have led to prosecutions for manslaughter. This is based on the argument that there is very little to distinguish between the tests for gross negligence manslaughter and CDDD. Apart from manslaughter applying to driving on private property as well as public roads, the main difference between the offences is that manslaughter requires a risk of death, rather than a risk of injury or damage to property, to be considered. This suggests that the test for manslaughter is slightly higher, leaving a choice for prosecutors between manslaughter and CDDD in the most serious cases. However, the *Charging Standard* in operation at the time of the cases advised that manslaughter will rarely be appropriate (para.11.5), and should be considered in cases where the vehicle was used as a weapon of attack (para.11.6) or where the driving occurred other than on a road or other public place (para.11.7).

All of the cases in the sample occurred either on a road or public place. In fact, all but two cases occurred on a road. A119 took place on wasteland where travellers were residing and A120 involved D riding a motorcycle through a public park. Despite occurring in a public place, however, A120 appears to be a prime candidate for a manslaughter charge. D was riding a stolen motorcycle through a park in darkness with no lights. D initially denied being the driver, claiming that V was driving whilst he was riding as pillion passenger, later admitting that the positions were reversed. D had no licence, no insurance, neither he nor V were wearing helmets and D said that he may have been under the influence of cannabis and had also had some beer. D collided with a bollard positioned in the middle of the path, causing both V and D to fall from the machine. D admitted that what he did was dangerous and pleaded guilty to CDDD. The degree of blameworthiness displayed by D in this case does, however, suggest that a jury might not have been unwilling to convict him manslaughter. The attitude of 'there but for the grace of God go I' clearly would not feature in such a case.

There were no cases in the sample which were interpreted as involving a vehicle being used as a weapon of assault. A80 was a case in which there may have been a strong element of intimidatory and aggressive driving, but no evidence that D had gone as far as using his car as a weapon of attack. The case involved two cars which came into conflict initially when, according to the occupants of the second car, D had pulled in front of the second car at traffic lights. Some verbal abuse seems to have been exchanged between the occupants of the cars, and gestures were made. At a second set of traffic lights this continued, and it appears that D decided to chase after the other car. He was seen to overtake other vehicles on the inside, and one of his passengers claimed he was travelling at 70 mph (the speed limit for the road was 50 mph). As D caught up with the other car he caught a glancing blow against the concrete central reservation, lost control, and collided with the fence on the nearside of the road. V was a passenger in D's car. D had taken his father's car without consent, and at court the prosecution accepted a guilty plea to aggravated TWOC, meaning that D avoided conviction for CDDD.

Other cases, however, involved such a high degree of risk-taking that manslaughter may not have been an inappropriate charge. One of those was A32, a case involving fatigue on the part of an HGV driver, who ploughed into the rear of a queue of traffic, killing two other drivers. What sets this case apart from similar cases is that D had been told by both his GP and a specialist doctor not to drive. He had recently been diagnosed with obstructive sleep-apnoea, a condition which causes sufferers involuntarily and unconsciously to wake themselves up at regular intervals during the night when they stop breathing, leading to them feeling extremely tired during the day. D had been offered treatment for the condition but had declined, it seems, because he wanted to continue work until his HGV driver's licence expired the following month. He had even experienced a near miss in the previous month when he had fallen asleep and left the road, coming to rest in a field. Thus, in this case, D took a conscious risk to continue driving, despite the warnings he had received, putting his own life and those of others at risk. D denied that he had thought, 'I'm ill, I'm going to work regardless,' and said that he viewed what had happened as an accident. However, he was charged with CDDD, based on the fact that his doctors had told him not to drive, and he pleaded guilty. It appears that manslaughter was never considered as an appropriate charge, in this case or any others in the sample.

As noted above, *Wilkinson's* suggests that manslaughter may be committed in 'hit and run' cases. There were seven 'non-stop' cases in the sample. In four of the cases manslaughter would have been difficult to prove, since the accident occurred at a location where there were other people present, meaning that D could assume that medical help would be summoned. In A117 such a charge might have been possible, but the driver of the vehicle causing death was never traced. In another two cases, A116 and C32, where suspects were apprehended and charged with careless driving, failing to stop and failing to report; and aggravated TWOC, failing to stop, failing to report and other 'dishonest' offences respectively, manslaughter might have been a possible charge if what is suggested in *Wilkinson's* is correct.

C32 involved D, the rider of a motorcycle, leaving his pillion passenger, V, at the scene of the collision in the early hours of the morning, rather than summoning an ambulance. He admitted that he knew he should have called for an ambulance but stated that he was afraid that the police would catch him and in any case he heard sirens shortly afterwards, presuming that V was getting help. D had stolen the motorcycle earlier in the evening and pleaded guilty to aggravated TWOC.

In A116, V was found at the side of a dual carriageway near to his parked car, where he had stopped to change a wheel. D, an HGV driver, failed to stop after hitting V and his car. D said that he had not seen V at any point, but had assumed that the car would have been occupied. He pulled into a lay-by further down the road but was too frightened to go back to the scene and failed to report the incident to the police. The difficulty with proving manslaughter would have been causation. In many cases it may be difficult to prove that D's failure to call for help caused the death of V, and in some cases such causation could be ruled out if it was found that V died instantaneously on impact (as was the case in A116). It would be illogical to hold one driver who did not stop after a collision resulting in life-threatening injuries responsible for manslaughter where death resulted, but not do the same in a case where D stopping could not have helped V, who was already dead.

### *Cases Involving Drugs or Alcohol*

Ten of the cases resulting in prosecutions involved alcohol and one (C69) involved the drug MDMA (ecstasy). Although CDCDUI exists to cover instances in which a driver kills when drink- or drug-driving carelessly, this offence was charged in only seven of these 11 cases, and in one of these cases (C82) it was charged alongside CDDD. CDDD was charged on its own in a further two cases (B24 and C41), and in another two cases only careless driving was charged (A51 and A114).

The reason why D was charged only with careless driving and not with CDCDUI in A51 appears to have been that although D was believed to have been drunk and under the influence of drugs when he lost control of his car, colliding with a house and killing his passenger, he was seriously injured in the collision and the police were unable to test him for drink or drugs. However, there was no discussion of CDCDUI on the file and a prosecution very nearly did not take place due to D's mental state and the fact that he was not able to be interviewed for several months following the collision. This case occurred before the change to the law introduced by section 56 of the Police Reform Act 2002, which inserted a new section 7A into the RTA 1988 and allows the police to obtain a specimen of blood from a suspect who is incapable of consenting. This provision, along with the recent amendment made by section 31 RSA 2006, would mean that a case such as A51 would now result in prosecution for CDCDUI, given that the police could take a blood sample whilst D was incapacitated and have it tested at a later time.

A114 was a case in which D was breathalysed at the police station following the collision, where his breath alcohol measured 31 µg/100 ml (the legal limit is

35 μg/100 ml). D declined to provide a specimen of blood, from which it might have been possible to back-calculate his BAC at the time of the collision, meaning that there was insufficient evidence to show that D was over the limit at the time of the offence.

The CPS Legal Guidance advises that in cases involving drink or drugs, CDDD should be charged if it can be proved. It also states that where a case is borderline between dangerous and careless driving when the prosecution is likely to have to elect on which offence to proceed, CDCDUI should be charged, provided that all the elements of the offence can be proved. This is because the prospects of conviction are supposedly greater but the court's sentencing power is equal. The two cases in which CDDD was charged, rather than CDCDUI, were cases which would probably have resulted in a CDDD charge in the absence of any alcohol. Both were cases of dangerous overtaking, and although in C41 D's defence was that the back-calculation of his BAC was inaccurate, the fact that his driving was so objectively dangerous is probably what ultimately led him to plead guilty to CDDD. In B24 D had a back-calculated BAC of 118 mg/100 ml (where the legal limit is 80 mg/100 ml) and he pleaded guilty to CDDD.

C82 was a particularly serious case, in which CDDD, CDCDUI and aggravated TWOC were all charged. The case might have warranted an additional charge of manslaughter, given the high level of blameworthiness on the part of D. CDCDUI was included in the indictment because, although the CPS felt that the case for CDDD was strong, they wanted to provide an alternative verdict in case the jury failed to convict for CDDD. This implies that, no matter how strong evidence of CDDD is, there will always be some concern on the part of the CPS that the jury will fail to convict. It suggests that they fear that the mentality of 'there but for the grace of God go I', which in the past led to juries being reluctant to convict drivers of manslaughter, has transferred to the offence of CDDD. It is not clear that such fears are well founded. The Legal Guidance advises that where cases are borderline, a choice should be made between CDDD and CDCDUI as otherwise the prosecution is likely to be put to election. This case was arguably far from borderline, with a total of eight aggravating features identified by the CPS. However, the Crown prosecutor was concerned that although he felt strongly that the case ought to go to trial on the charge of CDDD, because of the identical maximum sentences for CDDD and CDCDUI the Crown might face difficulties in seeking permission from the judge to continue on such a charge if D offered a guilty plea to CDCDUI. Counsel confirmed that a plea to CDCDUI was not acceptable as the case clearly did not fall within the 'grey area' between dangerous driving and careless driving. In this case the views of V's family were also sought, with V's father being adamant that CDDD should be charged (V's father was a solicitor and so had knowledge of the legal requirements).

In this case D's parents were away on holiday and had hidden the keys to the car in their bedroom, which they had locked. They did so because D had in the past taken the car without their consent and they wanted to prevent him from doing so again, particularly because he only held a provisional driver's licence. However, D managed to gain entrance to the room through the loft-space and, after spending much of the afternoon drinking, took the car for a drive with some friends. Two of D's passengers died, but the surviving passenger, who appears to have been reluctant to get in the car, provided evidence of D's driving. This witness had asked D to slow down, but D ignored his pleas, reaching speeds of up to 100 mph on a single-carriageway road. D lost control of the car on a bend and collided with a tree. D's BAC was 82 mg/100 ml, and although the collision investigator was unable to calculate D's speed with any accuracy, he was of the opinion that it was well in excess of 80mph at the time of the collision. D eventually pleaded guilty to both two counts of CDDD and two counts of CDCDUI. He pleaded not guilty to aggravated TWOC, which was to remain on file.

Other cases in which CDCDUI was charged involved much less serious examples of bad driving. In some of these cases, for example C49, a case of CDCDUI was made out on the basis that without any further explanation for D's vehicle having crossed the centre-line or left the road he must have been driving without due care and attention, and his BAC was clearly above the legal limit. However, prosecutors did sometimes face difficulties in proving such charges. A89 highlights the need for prosecutors to be sure that they select the correct charge. The initial advice from the CPS was to issue summons for driving with excess alcohol only. The collision investigator asked the CPS to reconsider this advice, as a result of which the CPS recommended a prosecution for CDCDUI. However, when the case came to trial the prosecution realized that they were not able to prove that D was over the limit at the time of the collision, as the forensic scientist was only able to provide a back-calculation which estimated D's blood alcohol level at between 76 mg/100 ml and 133 mg/100 ml. If the correct measurement was at the bottom end of this scale, D was not guilty. This case resulted in a judge-ordered acquittal, with the CPS apologizing to V's family for their mistake. The correct charge would have been careless driving (and presumably under the new law, CDCD).

Where drugs are involved it may not be such a clear-cut case as where alcohol is involved. Where alcohol is involved it is fairly straightforward to establish D's liability, if it is possible to take a blood sample soon after the collision. The prosecution may use such evidence to show that the amount of drink taken was such as would adversely affect a driver, or, alternatively, that the driver was in fact adversely affected (*Millington* 1996). It is well known that different levels of alcohol in the blood have different effects on driving ability. However, in C69 the drug which it was alleged D had taken was MDMA (ecstasy). D and some friends had spent the previous day and much of the night at a festival where drug-taking was commonplace. D denied having taken any drugs, but analysis of his blood detected the presence of MDMA. D's passenger died when his car drifted off the road when driving on a dual carriageway. The CPS charged CDCDUI, D was convicted, and his conviction was upheld on appeal. The issue in this case was whether the prosecution had proved that the collision resulted from D's drug intake, with the defence arguing that it was possible that D had fallen asleep naturally and that there was no evidence of a link between his impairment and the drugs. This argument failed, with prosecution experts arguing that drowsiness is one of the symptoms experienced by those who take MDMA as the drug wears off. Given that less is known about the effects of MDMA on driving, however, the task for the prosecution in this case was more difficult than it would have been had D consumed alcohol.

Finally, there was one case (C13) involving alcohol in which D refused to provide a specimen of breath. The police and CPS were able to use this refusal as a basis for proving CDCDUI under section 3A(1)(c) RTA 1988. In this case the officers attending the scene formed the impression that D had been drinking and the police surgeon later agreed that he smelt alcohol on D's breath. D refused to submit to a breath test but eventually admitted to drinking four bottles of lager in the pub that afternoon. Without the provision of section 3A(1)(c), however, it would have been very difficult to prove CDCDUI.

*Cases involving TWOC*

There were seven cases in the sample in which the car D was driving had been taken without the owner's consent. In such cases the prosecution's choice as to charge depends not only on D's standard of driving, since the offence of causing death by aggravated vehicle taking is available, requiring no proof of the matter. In two cases (C82 and C49) the facts were further complicated by D's consumption of alcohol, and CDCDUI was charged in addition to offences reflecting that TWOC had been committed. In C82 CDDD, CDCDUI and aggravated TWOC were all charged. It is not clear, however, why in C49, in addition to CDCDUI, simple TWOC was charged rather than aggravated TWOC. In this case the letter of advice from the CPS recommended charging CDCDUI rather than aggravated TWOC because the former offence could be made out and was more serious, leading to a higher penalty. (It was only later that the maximum penalty for aggravated TWOC was increased to 14 years' imprisonment in line with CDDD and CDCDUI.) Some time later, however, it was deemed appropriate to charge TWOC in addition to this.

A92 and C62 resulted in charges of careless driving only. In A92 D took his brother's car without his consent, but the brother did not wish the issue of the TWOC to be taken any further. In C62, although the car was in fact taken without the owner's consent, D believed that the owner had given his consent to drive the car and so D was afforded a defence under section 12(6) of the Theft Act 1968. The issue in this case was not that of whether aggravated TWOC was the appropriate charge, but whether CDDD might have been proved due to D having driven whilst fatigued.

In two cases, C37 and A80, CDDD was charged alongside aggravated TWOC. In A80 the owner of the car was D's father, but unlike D's brother in A92, he was not against D being prosecuted for vehicle-taking. This was the one case in the sample in which a plea to a lesser offence was accepted by the prosecution. Although the Crown prosecutor was of the opinion that a charge of CDDD was made out, counsel appears to have been less confident, and a plea to aggravated TWOC was accepted. It is unclear the extent to which the CPS was involved in the decision to accept the plea, but earlier correspondence between the CPS and counsel showed counsel's reluctance to continue with the more serious charge.

In C37 a trial on the two charges did not go ahead because D pleaded guilty to CDDD.

## Conclusion

The pervasive use of the motor vehicle has not only resulted in the creation of a huge body of regulatory legislation to help minimize the inherent dangers involved in moving large lumps of metal around at high speed; it has also changed the landscape of the law of homicide with the creation of a number of statutory offences to penalize those whose driving causes death. The culpability involved in such offences ranges from that which more or less equates to the blameworthiness displayed by someone guilty of manslaughter to that which amounts to questionable justification for attaching liability for death. The rationalization put forward in relation to each newly created offence has been the need to deter drivers from causing death. Chapters 6 and 7 will explore further whether this reasoning is sound, drawing upon the work of psychologists and criminologists to establish whether law-making is likely to be successful in preventing road deaths.

# Chapter 5

# A Comparative Study: Traffic Law in Sweden

## Introduction

Sweden, along with the UK and the Netherlands, is among the European countries with the lowest road traffic fatality rate. In 2004 the number of people killed on the roads dropped to 480, the lowest since 1946. This is, of course, a huge difference compared to the number killed on Britain's roads, which in 2004 stood at 3,201. However, it must be remembered that the population of Sweden is far lower than Great Britain (approximately 9 million compared to 60.5 million the UK). Thus, relative to the population, fatality rates in the two countries are fairly similar. In Sweden in 2004 there were 5.3 fatalities per 100,000 population; 0.9 fatalities per 10,000 vehicles and 6.3 fatalities per billion vehicle kilometres. In Great Britain in 2004 the fatality rate was 5.5 per 100,000 population; there were 1.0 fatalities per 10,000 vehicles and 6.5 fatalities per billion vehicle kilometres (DfT 2006a, Table 51). The only European country with a lower death rate on the roads *per capita* is the Netherlands, with 4.9 road deaths per 100,000 population in 2004 (ibid.). These three countries of Sweden, the UK and the Netherlands make up the SUN countries, the subject of a comparative study of road traffic safety published in 2002, subsidized by the European Commission, with the aim of improving current safety practice in each of them and providing guidance to other European countries seeking to reduce road deaths (Koornstra et al. 2002). The SUNflower project included analysis of road traffic enforcement policies among other factors, and will be referred to in this chapter.

In order better to understand the traffic law enforcement culture in Sweden the author has carried out her own comparative study, involving an examination of Swedish legislation and case law, and interviews with those involved in policy development and traffic law enforcement in Sweden. The objective of this study was to discover if there is anything that Britain can learn from Sweden in relation to using law enforcement as a method of reducing road deaths. Open-ended semi-structured interviews were conducted with: two public prosecutors from Stockholm; two public prosecutors from the Prosecution Development Centre at the Malmö office for public prosecutors, including the Chief Public Prosecutor; an inspector in a local traffic police unit in Stockholm; a representative from the Swedish National Police Board; two representatives (including a legal advisor) from the Swedish Road Traffic Inspectorate; the Director of Safety at the Swedish Road Administration. The questions posed at these interviews differed according to the particular expertise of the interviewee, but the overall objective was to gain some insight into the workings of the law with regard to traffic offences in Sweden against the background of road safety policy generally, and to understand the priorities for those who work within the system. An account will be given of the relevant offences in Sweden, with reference to how law enforcement forms part of the internationally renowned road traffic safety policy of 'Vision Zero'.

## The Swedish Criminal Justice System

Before the law is set out, however, it should be noted that the criminal justice system in Sweden differs in many respects from that of England and Wales. Consequently, such differences serve as one of several variables contributing to divergence in the way that offending drivers are dealt with in Sweden compared to England and Wales. Sweden is a civil law jurisdiction and one might expect criminal trials there to adopt a more inquisitorial model than the truly adversarial model seen in common law jurisdictions. This, however, would not be an entirely accurate view: the Swedish criminal process has in fact been described as having a 'distinctive adversarial character' and as resembling the criminal procedure known in common law countries quite closely (Zila 2006, 287). A more striking difference is that prosecutorial discretion is more limited in Sweden than England and Wales, and could be said to represent more closely the legality principle rather than the expediency principle, or opportunity principle as it is referred to by Fionda (Fionda 1995, 9).

The legality principle requires that the police must initiate an investigation in any case where there is reason to believe that an offence has been committed, and the public prosecution service must initiate a prosecution in any case where there is sufficient evidence to prosecute. However, the police may use their discretion to decide that a case is of a trivial nature and it is obvious that D would only be fined if convicted of the offence. If this is the case, the officer may refrain from reporting the offence (Zila 2006, 296). In any case reported by the police to the public prosecution service there is an 'absolute requirement to prosecute' as long as the prosecutor believes that an offence has been committed and there is 'sufficient evidence' against the suspect to establish guilt (Åklagarmyndigheten, 6). Thus, at first glance at least, one of the main differences between prosecutions in Sweden and in England and Wales is that in Sweden there is only one test applied by prosecutors when deciding to prosecute: an evidential test but no 'public interest' test.

This obligation to prosecute is offset to some degree by the fact that public prosecutors in Sweden enjoy a wide judicial power and may, if certain conditions are met, impose a summary judgment in the form of a penal order (*strafföreläggande*) on a suspect, avoiding the need for a trial. Such a penal order can only be imposed if the offence involved is one punishable by fines among other penalties (Zila 2006, 292). The only punishment that can be imposed by way of penal order is a fine or a conditional sentence (similar to a suspended sentence in England and Wales). Such an order might be appropriate in a case of *carelessness in traffic*, for which the penalty is a fine only, but could also be used in a case of *causing death or injury*, provided that the offence deserves nothing more than a conditional sentence. The penal order only takes effect once the suspect has accepted it; if D wishes to contest D's guilt D may ignore the order and a prosecution will be instituted. However, approval of the penal order by D does not in itself amount to a confession (Zila 2006, 293). In fact, it is impossible for a suspect to plead guilty to an offence in Sweden. As a result, the phenomenon of plea bargaining experienced in England and Wales does not exist in Sweden.

In addition to the power to issue a penal order, prosecutors in Sweden can also decide on a waiver of prosecution (*åtalsunderlåtelse*) (Zila 2006, 293). This may be applied in cases similar to those in England and Wales where the evidential test in the Code for Crown Prosecutors has been passed but it is decided that it is not in the public interest to prosecute. This can be seen from the fact that a waiver of prosecution should be distinguished from dropping a prosecution, the latter occurring where there is insufficient evidence to succeed (ibid., 294). However, the public interest test is also incorporated into Swedish law as part of the substantive criminal law in some cases. For example, for the offence of *causing injury* under section 7, Chapter 3 of the Penal Code (see below), prosecution requires that there is a substantial public interest in prosecution (ibid., 164).

As in England and Wales, the police in Sweden have the power to impose fines for minor offences. In Sweden the procedure for doing so is referred to as the summary fines order, which can be applied to offences listed in a particular regulation. These are offences which are punished only by way of a fixed fine (Zila 2006, 295), and thus broadly equate to a fixed penalty notice in England and Wales (for speeding, for example). Summary fines orders are commonly used in relation to road traffic offences, and where D fails to consent to the order the case is forwarded to the public prosecutors (ibid., 296). There is not yet any equivalent in Sweden to the National Driver Improvement Scheme in England, or any opportunity for the police to offer a speeding offender a course on speed awareness rather than face a fine. Whilst the police, particularly those in post as traffic officers, do their best to convey the message that speeding is wrong because it is dangerous through dialogue with offenders on the streets, the official response to offending is either a fine or nothing.

The powers granted to the public prosecutors and police in Sweden mean that in practice only 17 per cent of cases in 2002 judged to pass the evidential test were dealt with by the courts, and 12 per cent were dealt with by way of penal order imposed by the public prosecutors (Zila 2006, 295).

The Swedish prosecution authority (*Åklagarmyndigheten*) has development centres at Malmö, Göteborg, Stockholm and Umeå, where prosecution policy for different types of offences is decided. The centre at Malmö has responsibility for policy in road traffic offences, and produces a Memorandum similar to the CPS's *Charging Standard* to assist prosecutors throughout Sweden in their decision-making. In addition to this, the Development Centre at Malmö also receives appeals from victims and relatives unhappy with a prosecution decision not to prosecute. Prosecutors at the Centre review the evidence available and may alter the original decision if they judge that there is sufficient evidence to prosecute.

As under the statutory charging scheme in England and Wales, the Swedish prosecution procedure requires a close working relationship between police and prosecutors. Unlike under the statutory charging scheme, however, there is not a clear cut-off point when a case is transferred from the competence of the police to that of the public prosecution service. In most cases the police are responsible for investigation of an offence and the collection of evidence, but the preliminary investigation can also fall under the responsibility of the prosecutor. It is not always clear who should be responsible for the preliminary investigation, since the key criterion is whether the matter is of a 'simple nature' or not (Zila 2006, 298). Where it is of a 'simple nature' it will be the police who lead the investigation. However, the Prosecutor General has issued guidance on this question, and agreements on the division of competence are usually made at a local level (ibid., 299). It is usual for the police to be the lead investigators in the case of a road traffic offence, unless the offence involved is *causing another's death or injury* under the Penal Code. 14.7 per cent of investigations of offences classified as road traffic crimes are led by prosecutors, whereas 88.4 per cent of cases of causing another's injury and 76.2 per cent of cases of causing another's death are investigated by prosecutors (ibid., 300).

The uncertain division of labour between the police and public prosecution service has, in the past at least, caused some problems. These stem primarily from resource issues: the police and *Åklagarmyndigheten* have their own individual budgets and it is possible for the police to refuse to assist in an investigation led by the *Åklagarmyndigheten* on the basis of a lack of resources (Zila 2006, 301). From discussions with the police and prosecutors in Stockholm, it would appear that in the case of a road traffic offence it is normal for the police to lead the investigation and for the prosecutor to take over once the investigation is completed. This is equally true of cases involving fatalities, although in particularly complex cases (an example given was of a mother whose daughter was unrestrained and died when the mother crashed her car) the prosecutor may take the lead and become involved in the case at an earlier stage.

A final difference between the role of prosecutor in Sweden and in England and Wales is that, due to the fact that the Swedish system is less adversarial than the English system, the role of the prosecutor in Sweden is seen to be entirely neutral. Although the prosecutor must bring charges in cases where there is sufficient evidence to predict conviction, in theory at least, a case in which a prosecutor did not bring charges or gain a conviction would not be viewed as a 'failure' as it might be in England or Wales. An aspect of the role of prosecutor which might be presumed to undermine this neutral position is that unlike in England and Wales, where the criminal and civil justice systems are entirely separate and the victim of a road traffic collision must start an action in the civil courts if he or she wishes to sue for damages, in Sweden private claims are often settled at the same time as the criminal trial and if the victim takes this opportunity the prosecutor must present the victim's action in conjunction with the prosecution (Zila 2006, 307).

## The Law

The relevant driving offences are contained within the Traffic Offence Act 1951, which has been amended several times in the past fifty years, most recently in 1994. Unfortunately the statute is not available in an official English translation, so what appears below can be seen as a loose translation. Many of these offences are punishable by way of imprisonment or the use of fines. In Sweden, as in some other Scandinavian countries, use is made of what are referred to as 'day fines'. These determine the amount of fine payable by way of a percentage of the offender's daily income.

### *Carelessness in Traffic (vårdslöshet i trafik) and Gross Carelessness in Traffic (grov vårdslöshet i trafik)*

As under the Road Traffic Act 1988 in England and Wales, there are two general driving offences under the Swedish Traffic Offence Act (1951:649), section 1:

> A road user, or a person who operates a tram or who somewhere other than on a road drives a motor vehicle, who gravely fails in the care and caution required in the circumstances to prevent a traffic accident, commits *carelessness in traffic* and may be sentenced to a fine proportionate to his daily income.
>
> A person who, while driving a motor vehicle or a tram, is guilty of gross carelessness or displays an obvious indifference for another person's life or property, is guilty of *gross carelessness in traffic* and may be sentenced to up to two years' imprisonment.

These two offences can be likened to the English offences of careless driving and dangerous driving, one requiring a higher degree of negligence than the other. However, from looking at the case law it becomes clear that, as in England and Wales, prosecutors and courts find the critical terminology, taking the form of the words 'gravely fails' in Sweden, difficult to interpret.

In the prosecutors' Memorandum, reference is made to parliament's intentions in the Bill debated in 1994, when the Act was last amended. From this it can be seen that the intentions of the Swedish parliament were quite different to those of the North Report which recommended the current test of dangerous driving in English law (Department of Transport 1988). For example, it is suggested that any misjudgements caused by momentary inattention or lack of ability should be excluded from the meaning of 'carelessness'. Whilst the former might be excluded from careless driving under English law, the latter would depend on whether the lack of ability could be attributed to a known medical condition or not (see Chapter 2 above).

Looking at cases provides some idea of what degree of inattention is required before a conviction for carelessness in traffic is likely. Allowing oneself to become distracted by something inside the vehicle, such as fast-forwarding a cassette in the car's stereo whilst driving on a motorway at 100 kmph causing one to drive on to the opposite carriageway and collide with oncoming traffic can amount to carelessness in traffic as in the case of *RH 1996:92*. However, this case can be contrasted with one in which D, whilst answering his mobile phone, took his eyes off the road and crashed into a car parked at the side of the road. The District Court held that this amounted to a temporary loss of attention rather than intentional risk-taking, and ruled that D had not gravely failed in his care and caution, and dismissed the case (*District Court Örebro, judgment of 2005–06–21, case number B 1911-05*).

It is perhaps difficult to distinguish between these two cases, both of which involved D allowing himself to be distracted from the road. It should be noted that talking on a mobile phone whilst driving is not yet an offence in Sweden as it is in England and Wales, but that would not in itself prevent a case for carelessness in traffic being based on an accusation that D was using his phone whilst driving. It seems clear, though, that where D is trying to carry out more than one task in addition to driving, D is likely to be guilty of carelessness in traffic. In *RH 2001:19* the driver caused a collision after trying to drive whilst smoking a cigarette and answering his mobile phone and was convicted of that offence.

Particularly interesting is the guidance given in the prosecutors' Memorandum that responsibility for carelessness in traffic should concern actions that are 'careless/reckless in a real sense', no matter if a collision results or not. This makes it clear that whether a collision results from the carelessness is, in law, irrelevant to the question of criminal liability, which is also true under English law. However, it is probable that in practice criminal charges are unlikely to be brought unless a collision has occurred, as in England. From discussions with prosecutors it also became clear that the guidance provided specifying that driving is required to be 'careless/reckless in a real sense' is of little or no help to those deciding whether to prosecute in a case, whether or not a collision has occurred.

The guidance from the Swedish parliament included in the prosecutors' Memorandum suggests that carelessness in traffic would include any instance of intentional risk-taking. In addition, the following are listed as examples of acts which would normally fall within the offence:

- driving when tired;
- dangerous overtaking;
- breaching the duty to stop at a stop sign;
- driving through a red light, when it caused or could have caused danger to others;
- severe speeding in dangerous traffic conditions;
- driving a vehicle in a dangerous condition;
- negligence by a driver who has a special responsibility, such as driving a school bus.

The following are listed as acts which would normally not be seen as carelessness in traffic:

- bumping into a car in a built-up area due to lack of observation;

- disregarding the duty to give way (including the duty to give way to cars coming from the right) or the duty to keep sufficient distance from the car in front;
- single vehicle accidents outside built-up areas which are not due to a tired driver or a dangerous vehicle;
- cases where the road conditions suddenly change, such as the weather conditions; fog; blinding sun.

The second of these examples of what would *not* normally amount to carelessness in traffic appears to be particularly surprising. If D failed to give way or tailgated another vehicle in many circumstances one would expect this to amount to careless driving in Britain. One particular type of difficult case with which the Swedish courts have had to deal is that of a driver who has collided with a pedestrian on a pedestrian crossing. An example is *RH 1998:70* where D failed to stop to give way to a pedestrian on a pedestrian crossing. The circumstances were that the road was slippery, D was driving at high speed and another car had already stopped to give way to the pedestrian who had started to cross. The Court of Appeal found that the driver had shown a severe lack of attention and he was found guilty of carelessness in traffic and sentence to a 40 day fine proportionate to his daily income.

However, a more recent case has cast doubt over the evidence required to convict a driver of carelessness in traffic. In *Supreme Court judgment 2007-01-12, case number B 1170-05* D failed to notice a pedestrian crossing the road at a pedestrian crossing, having been blinded by the sun. D collided with and injured the pedestrian, and was charged with carelessness in traffic, but was acquitted. The case was appealed to the Supreme Court, which confirmed the judgment of the lower courts. The Court found that the facts were that D had been blinded by the sun 30–50 metres from the crossing. She had then pulled down the sun visor and reduced her speed. D thought she had seen something in front of the car, but she had not seen the crossing, the car that had stopped in the opposite direction nor the pedestrian. D was travelling at a speed of 7–8 kmph when she hit the pedestrian. The Court held that D had taken such precautions as could be expected in the circumstances. The fact that she had continued to drive in the belief that she had sufficient visibility amounted to a misjudgement, but it could not be seen as intentional risk-taking. Even though she had to some degree failed in care and caution, her action could not be seen as careless within the meaning of the law; her misjudgement of the situation was not of the kind that could lead to conviction for carelessness in traffic.

This case has caused some consternation amongst those responsible for enforcing and prosecuting traffic offences. In England such a case would probably result in a conviction for careless driving (see Chapter 2), although such cases are by no means clear-cut. In Sweden, since 1994, to establish carelessness in traffic it has been necessary to prove 'something more than mere carelessness, on the verge of being intentional' (according to one prosecutor interviewed). It was suggested in interviews that a driver must be aware of his or her carelessness for a charge of carelessness in traffic to succeed. This case of the driver blinded by the sun was used as an illustration of the degree of wrongdoing required under the 1994 law, which is higher than previously required. If this is accurate, one might liken the offence of carelessness in traffic to the old offence of reckless driving under English law which was replaced by dangerous driving because it was thought that having to prove a driver's state of mind was too difficult. In Sweden, however, at least one prosecutor interviewed actually preferred the new situation, since under the previous law 'a lot of time and money was wasted taking cases to court which were not really crimes'.

This demonstrates that at least some of those involved in the enforcement and prosecution of traffic offences in Sweden hold a view common to that held by many in England and Wales that traffic offences are not 'real' crime and do not have stigma attached to them. This will be discussed further below, but it is inevitable that the way in which a law is interpreted and applied will depend on the views held by those working with such offences. This view is not shared by everyone, however. There were others within the justice system, including prosecutors at the Prosecution Development Centre in Malmö, who were similarly convinced of the need to change the law from the previous position, when it was possible to bring criminal charges in the most minor of collisions, but who were concerned that there is a balance to be struck. The way in which the Supreme Court has interpreted the law in cases such as the one involving the driver blinded by the sun is too limiting, in their view. It is now difficult to predict how the courts will deal with future cases.

Although parliament provided the above list of examples of what it expected would and would not normally fall within the meaning of carelessness in traffic, the courts have not always been consistent in dealing with such cases. As in England and Wales, the issue of excess speed and whether it amounts to carelessness is a particularly difficult question. It would seem that something more than driving well above the speed limit is required: usually some other factor is needed to elevate a case from mere speeding to carelessness in traffic. For example, prior to the 1994 change in the law the case of *NJA 1979 s 274* held that driving at 95 kmph in a built-up area where the limit was 50 kmph and there were pedestrian crossings and a school nearby did amount to carelessness in traffic. However, more recently in *NJA 2001 s 286* it was held that driving at 189 kmph when the limit was 110 kmph did not amount to carelessness in traffic. Here it would seem that there was no danger caused to others, and this was the key factor. This can be compared to a case where carelessness in traffic was found to be present. D had driven at 202 kmph within a 110 kmph limit in wet conditions with other road users on the road, and had overtaken at least ten cars (*District Court of Trelleborg, judgment of 2005–06–15, case number B 432–05*).

As noted in Chapter 2, in addition to cases involving speeding, cases of driver fatigue cause particular problems for prosecutors in England and Wales. In Sweden this may also be true to some degree, but it would appear that the courts have been more willing to find fatigued drivers guilty of carelessness in traffic and the more serious offence of gross carelessness in traffic. The Supreme Court decided two cases in *NJA 1973 s 449 I and II*. In the first of these cases D argued that he had fallen asleep without any prior feeling of tiredness before the crash. This argument was rejected out of hand as being too unlikely to be true, and the

Supreme Court held that the collision could only be explained by D's inattention and that he must have fallen asleep. D was found guilty of gross carelessness in traffic (see also *RH 1995:74*). In the second case D admitted that he had begun to feel tired but was unable to stop immediately and had therefore planned to drive for a short distance to find an appropriate place to stop and rest. The Supreme Court held that D was not negligent in deciding to continue until he was able to stop, but that he had been negligent in failing to increase his attention to the level that the circumstances demanded. This case appears to give mixed signals to fatigued drivers, since it has been consistently found by researchers that the only way to prevent feelings of tiredness is to stop and rest; techniques such as opening the window or turning up music are unlikely to assist in keeping a tired driver alert (Horne and Reyner 2001).

In addition to the offence of carelessness in traffic there is also the aggravated form of the offence, known as *gross* carelessness in traffic, the offence convicted in the first of these two fatigued driver cases. Whilst carelessness in traffic carries with it only the penalty of a fine, gross carelessness is, like dangerous driving in England and Wales, punishable by up to two years' imprisonment. One might expect, therefore, that in terms of what is required in law to prove the respective offences, carelessness in traffic would equate to careless driving and gross carelessness in traffic would equate to dangerous driving. Given the high degree of carelessness needed to establish carelessness in traffic it is, however, more difficult to prove gross carelessness in traffic than it might be to prove dangerous driving in England and Wales. From looking at the cases it would appear that carelessness in traffic is more akin to dangerous driving than careless driving, and it then becomes difficult to imagine the level of blameworthiness required for gross carelessness in traffic. There is no definition of 'gross' in the legislation or in case law, but some examples provide an illustration of the kind of cases falling within this offence.

In *NJA 1978 s 251* D had driven through a red light at a speed of 130 kmph and although there was no collision, the court recognized that there had been a clear risk of collision. D was found guilty of gross carelessness in traffic and sentenced to two years' suspended sentence and a fine. In *RH 2004:86*, D, a motorcyclist, had been speeding at a minimum of 230 kmph on a major road and had overtaken several cars when overtaking was forbidden. He continued at the same speed on a busy motorway and had been weaving in and out of traffic. The Court of Appeal, in finding him guilty of gross carelessness in traffic, sentenced him to two months' imprisonment and held that the crime was equal to gross drink-driving (see below).

The statute provides two ways of establishing the aggravated form of carelessness in traffic. The first is on the basis of gross carelessness in traffic which, as noted, remains undefined. The additional or alternative basis is to establish that D was indifferent to the lives of others. This was tested in the case of *RH 1999:149*. D had overtaken another vehicle on a blind bend causing a head-on collision with a car travelling in the opposite direction. The District Court held that D had shown clear indifference for other people's lives and property and found him guilty of gross carelessness in traffic. The Court of Appeal upheld the conviction, but reduced D's sentence from one month imprisonment to two years' suspended sentence combined with community service. The Court of Appeal, unlike the District Court, did not find that the driver had been indifferent to other people's life or property. Thus, in this case the Court of Appeal must have been satisfied that the driving was sufficiently bad to amount to gross carelessness in traffic in the absence of such indifference. It is far from clear, however, how the relevant standard is to be measured. 'Indifference' under Swedish law suggests that if D were attributed with the knowledge that he might kill someone if he continued in his actions he would, at the time and with this knowledge, have continued in what he was doing (*RH 1988:23; District Court of Handen judgment 2005–12–22, case number B 1260–05*).

It would appear from talking to prosecutors that a charge of gross carelessness in traffic would be fairly rare. Those that would clearly fall within the offence often involve vehicles pursued by the police, where there is plenty of evidence of the standard of driving from police eyewitness evidence and perhaps video evidence from a camera in the police vehicle. Racing has also been held to amount to gross carelessness in traffic (*RH 1995:46*). However, most of the reported cases took place before the enactment of the 1994 amendments, and it is not clear that they would be decided in the same way today. According to official statistics there were 1,021 reported cases of gross carelessness in traffic in 2005, in which a decision to prosecute was taken in only 375 cases (BRÅ, Table 170). Of the 375 cases prosecuted, 53 resulted in sentences of imprisonment (ibid., Table 420). It should be noted, however, that where death or injury is caused by bad driving, prosecutors will find it easier to charge under the Penal Code (see below).

### *Drink-driving (rattfylleri)*

Drink-driving is one area of traffic law enforcement at which Sweden has excelled. Sweden first introduced a legal blood alcohol limit for drivers in 1951, sixteen years before the UK did so. Whilst it is commonly accepted in the UK that drinking and driving is wrong, there is even less tolerance for it in Sweden. Whilst someone in England might drive to a pub and consume a pint of beer before driving home, even this is frowned upon in Sweden. In the third European-wide survey of public attitudes to road safety (SARTRE 3), the number of Swedish drivers surveyed who admitted to driving after drinking even a small amount of alcohol was far lower than the number of drivers in Great Britain who admitted to doing the same (Dahlstedt 2006, Table 66). The law itself is particularly strict in Sweden, with the blood alcohol concentration (BAC) required for a conviction of drink-driving under section 4 of the Traffic Offence Act being fixed at 20 mg per 100 ml (lowered from 50 mg in 1990). Those convicted of drink-driving face a fine and up to six months' imprisonment. However, in addition to this method of proving the offence it is also possible to establish guilt if a driver is found to be driving under the influence of drink or drugs 'to the extent that it can be presumed that he or she cannot drive the vehicle in a safe manner'.

Another difference between Swedish and English law is that drink-driving is not a strict liability offence in the same way that it is in England and Wales.

According to case *RH 1976:81* the offence can only be proven if D intentionally drove whilst drunk. One might expect the rule emanating from this case to cause problems for prosecutors, with offenders claiming that they did not mean to get so drunk that they were over the legal limit, but the anecdotal evidence is that in practice such defences are not raised. The rule suggests that, unlike in England and Wales, if D's drink was spiked and D had no idea that D had consumed alcohol, D could not be convicted of drink-driving if later found to be over the prescribed limit. In most cases where D knowingly drank some alcohol a defence will not be available, given that the legal BAC is so low that D will know that even the smallest amount of alcohol might take D over the limit.

As explained above, the police and public prosecutors have a broad discretion in deciding the disposal of cases under Swedish law, particularly in relation to traffic offences. In 2002 there were 18,800 suspected cases of drink-driving, of which 11,162 (59.4 per cent) were taken to trial, 500 (2.7 per cent) resulted in waiver of prosecution, and 4,004 (21.3 per cent) resulted in a penal order (Zila 2006, 305–6). The proportion of drivers who are over the legal limit and themselves die in a collision is similar to that in Great Britain, with twenty per cent of car-driver fatalities being above the legal limit in both countries (Koornstra et al. 2002, 43; 45), although the legal limit is of course higher in Great Britain.

Under section 4a of the Traffic Offences Act an aggravated form of drink-driving exists to penalize those who are guilty of *gross* drink-driving, the sentence for which is increased to a maximum of two years' imprisonment with a minimum twelve-month driving ban. According to the statute:

The following, in particular, shall be taken into consideration in determining whether the crime is gross:

1) the driver has had at least 1.0 ‰ alcohol concentration in the blood or 0.50 milligram per litre in the breath;
2) the driver has in any case been gravely influenced by alcohol or some other substance; or
3) the operation of the vehicle has led to an apparent danger to road safety.

The easiest way to establish gross drunk driving is through evidence of a BAC of 100 mg per 100ml or higher, but where the BAC is between 20 mg and 100 mg it would remain possible to prove gross drink-driving under one of the other two headings. For example, excess speed combined with a BAC falling between the two limits has been held to amount to gross drink-driving under the third heading (*RH 1991:90*). The converse of this approach is also true; just because someone was found to be driving with a BAC of over 100 mg prosecutors will not automatically charge the aggravated form of the offence, since it will depend on the circumstances of the case. This can be seen in *NJA 2003 s 67*, where D moved his car four metres in a car park. Even though the alcohol concentration was above the limit for gross drink-driving according to section 4a, he was only found guilty of drink-driving under section 4 and sentenced to pay a fine.

Where gross drink-driving is charged it would appear that it is common to charge it alongside gross carelessness in traffic. In all four cases cited in the prosecutors' Memorandum where gross drink-driving was charged, D was also found guilty of gross carelessness in traffic. In the cases in which death was caused as a result, gross causing another's death under section 7 of the Penal Code was added as a third charge (see below).

Drink-driving can be detected through the operation of random breath testing, with the police operating 'control stops' at the road-side. Unlike in England and Wales there is no provision to create an offence of failing to submit to a breath test. The reason for this is that such failures are virtually non-existent. If a driver at the road-side refuses to submit to a breathalyser test, it is possible for the police to use such force as is necessary to take the driver to the police station, where a blood test will be taken (Law 1976:1090). There is no requirement of reasonable suspicion in such cases.

*Speeding (fortkörning)*

In contrast to the Swedish position on drink-driving, the enforcement of speed limits in Sweden has lagged behind the UK's approach to the problem. As of 2006 there were 350 fixed camera devices installed at locations with a high death rate (ETSC 2006, 88). In comparison, in England and Wales there were 2,544 fixed camera sites in 2006 (Hansard, HC 4 June 2007, column 111W). One problem that faces police and prosecutors in enforcing speed limits is that, unlike in England and Wales, Swedish car owners are under no obligation to volunteer information concerning the identity of the driver of a vehicle caught by a speed camera. It must be possible to establish the identity of the driver from the photograph taken by the camera, which can become particularly difficult if the driver is wearing a cap or has lowered the sun visor, and impossible if D has consciously taken steps to hide D's identity for the purposes of avoiding detection. Despite the recent ruling of the European Court of Human Rights in *O'Halloran and Francis v UK* (see Chapter 3 above) it seems unlikely that Sweden will change its position on this in the near future, since it would be a radical departure from tradition to allow the principle against self-incrimination to be restricted in this way.

In his commentary to *O'Halloran and Francis v UK*, Ashworth notes the need to deal with traffic offences differently to other offences and the fact that most countries in Europe impose some kind of compulsion for drivers in these circumstances. Some countries presume the owner to have been the driver unless the owner proves otherwise, which Ashworth suggests compromises the presumption of innocence, whilst others allow adverse inferences to be drawn if the owner fails to respond to a notice requesting the name of the driver in time, a method which Ashworth suggests might threaten the right to silence (Ashworth 2007, 898). Lord Bingham in *Brown v Stott* also gave examples of Spain, Belgium and France as jurisdictions in which the registered owner of a vehicle is assumed to be the driver guilty of a traffic infraction unless he or she shows that some other person was behind the wheel (*Brown v Stott* 2003, 704). Sweden seems to represent a departure from this tendency for authorities to provide exceptions to the privilege against self-incrimination for speeding offences. It is particularly surprising that Sweden does not allow for such presumptions, since in the context of drink-driving there seems to be little concern about endangering the principle against self-incrimination in requiring drivers to submit to a breath test. This displays a clear divergence of views with regards to the way in which the different traffic offences should be dealt.

Penalties in Sweden do not work in quite the same way as in England and Wales. Drivers are fined for speeding but there is no penalty points system as such. Where a driver has been reported for speeding the agency responsible for the issue of driving licences may send a warning to the offender in the case of a first offence, and may revoke the licence on subsequent occasions. In severe cases, the licence may be revoked on the first occasion.

*Causing Death or Injury (vållande till annans död; vållande till kroppsskada)*

In England and Wales the law has traditionally been reluctant to impose liability for death upon those whose negligence contributes to the death, unless such negligence can be established as being gross. We have seen in Chapter 4, however, that this position has been relaxed in relation to negligent driving, with the enactment of homicide offences first of causing death by careless driving while under the influence of drink or drugs and, more recently, the offence of causing death by careless driving under the Road Safety Act 2006. In contrast to the law in England and Wales, the law in Sweden allows liability for those who cause death through mere (as opposed to gross) negligence to be established fairly easily, under Chapter 3, section 7 of the Penal Code (1962:700):

> A person who through carelessness causes the death of another shall be sentenced for causing another's death to imprisonment for at most two years or, if the crime is petty, to a fine.
>
> If the crime is gross, imprisonment shall be imposed for at least six months and at most six years. If the act was committed by driving a motor vehicle, special consideration shall be given, in assessing whether the crime is gross, to whether the sentenced person was under the influence of alcohol or other substance.

This offence is not specific to the context of road deaths, and can be committed in any number of ways. However, statistics are collected on the number of cases where the offence is committed in connection with a road traffic collision. The other context in which the offence is likely to be committed is in an industrial accident. Thus, in 2005 there were 174 reported offences of causing another's death, of which 97 were connected to a road traffic collision and 22 to an industrial accident. Of the 97 resulting in the road traffic context, 50 resulted in a decision to prosecute (BRÅ 2005, Table 420). In 2006, the figures were 96 reported cases and 67 decisions to prosecute in cases involving driving (BRÅ 2006, Table 420).

These figures appear relatively low, if one takes into account the comparative ease with which the offence can be proven. An example may suffice by way of illustration. In the *Svea Court of Appeal judgment 2004–10–28, case number B 322–04* D was prosecuted for carelessness in traffic and causing another person's death. D had been driving a lorry and failed to notice pedestrians on a crossing until it was too late to stop. The lorry hit and killed a wheel-chair user. The District Court found D guilty of both crimes and sentenced him to two years' suspended sentence and a 40 day fine. The Court of Appeal, however, dismissed the case for carelessness in traffic and found him guilty of causing another person's death. The Court held D had been lacking in attention as he should have noticed V before V started to cross the road, but ruled that this inattention was only temporary and not sufficiently grave to convict D of carelessness in traffic (although the sentence was unaltered).

Thus, whilst carelessness in traffic requires something more than negligence, since the defendant must have 'gravely failed' in his or her duty to other road users, this extra element is not required for causing another's death; simple negligence will suffice. In all cases where death has resulted from a collision where carelessness in traffic can be proven, causing another's death under the Penal Code will be available as an additional or alternative charge. Where gross carelessness in traffic or gross drink-driving can be proved, it will also be possible to charge the aggravated form of the causing death offence, carrying a minimum penalty of six months' imprisonment and a maximum penalty of six years' imprisonment.

Despite this maximum penalty, however, severe sentences appear to be rare. One example of the offence is the judgment of the *Skåne and Blekinge Court of Appeal judgment 1998–04–28, case number B 1169–97*. In this case D had been driving at very high speed when he lost control of his vehicle and collided with a car and a lorry travelling in the opposite direction, killing two of the occupants of the car. D was found guilty of gross carelessness in traffic, gross drink-driving, gross causing another person's death and causing another person's injury. He was sentenced to 15 months' imprisonment.

It should be noted that in Sweden the possibility for a driver who has caused a fatal collision to be guilty of murder is far higher than in England and Wales. This is because Swedish law recognizes three forms of intention, or *uppsåt*. The third of these is known as 'indifference intention', which under English law would amount to no more than subjective recklessness, although it broadly corresponds to proposals made by the Law Commission for a *mens rea* term of 'reckless indifference' to suffice for the offence of second degree murder (Law Commission 2005). An example that might fall within such a state of *mens rea* is that of a person, D, who wants to escape from the police using a car. If a police officer were to block D's path and D failed to take evasive action and ran over the officer it could be said that D was indifferent to the fact that the officer might get killed, and can be found guilty of murder. This was a scenario presented in the course of interviews as one in which murder might be considered as the appropriate charge, although there appear to be no reported cases with such facts. It would seem unlikely that murder would be charged in any case of a motor vehicle being used as a weapon of offence unless the victim was a police officer or there was clear evidence from eye-witnesses since, as has been the case in England and Wales in the past, it would be unlikely that the death would be investigated as anything other than a traffic collision.

In a survey of reported cases and newspaper reports, only one case of murder by motor vehicle could be found in recent years. This was the judgment of the

Court of Appeal in *Västra Sverige* dated 12 May 2004, in which a 74-year-old man was sentenced to seven years' imprisonment for the murder of his wife. D's wife had been out jogging close to her home when she was hit from behind by a car and was subsequently run over whilst lying on the ground. Traces of blood were found on D's car, and although D admitted to running her over he claimed it was an 'accident'. Although a sentence of ten year's or life imprisonment would normally be passed in a case of murder, the lower sentence was justified by D's age and mental and physical condition, the Court of Appeal held.

Another major difference in Swedish law is that in addition to a causing death offence under the Penal Code, there is also an offence of causing injury under Chapter 3, section 8:

> A person who through carelessness causes another to suffer bodily injury or illness not of a petty nature, shall be sentenced for causing bodily injury or illness to a fine or imprisonment for at most six months.
>
> If the crime is gross, imprisonment for at most four years shall be imposed. If the act was committed by driving a motor vehicle, special consideration shall be given, in assessing whether the crime is gross, to whether the sentenced person was under the influence of alcohol or other substance.

This offence mirrors the causing death offence in its requirements, although the maximum penalty on conviction is much lower. It provides prosecutors with an offence to charge in cases where carelessness in traffic might be difficult to prove and although the victim was lucky enough to survive the collision, suffered some degree of injury equating to the English notion of 'grievous bodily harm'. In England and Wales such a case could only be prosecuted as either careless driving or dangerous driving, depending on the degree of negligence involved, with the government having rejected calls to widen the causing death offences to include causing serious injury (see Chapter 2). As with the causing death offence, this offence is available in all contexts of causing injury through negligence, in particular accidents in the workplace.

An example of this offence being successfully prosecuted where the charge of carelessness in traffic failed is the Court of Appeal case *RH 2003:53*. D had been driving in a bus lane when he hit and injured a pedestrian who walked out into the lane. The Court found that D had been negligent in causing the pedestrian's injury, but that he had not failed in the care and caution required to such an extent that he could be found guilty of carelessness in traffic.

These offences under the Penal Code of causing another person's death or injury allow luck to play a central role in the criminal liability of negligent drivers in Sweden. The role luck plays is in fact even more crucial than that which it plays in England and Wales, since if D's driving can be described as negligent but is not sufficiently bad to fall within the meaning of carelessness in traffic, D can be prosecuted under the criminal law only if the driving results in a collision causing death or serious injury.

Some might prefer the Swedish position on the basis that a driver who has driven carelessly should be held liable for the result, whether that be death or serious harm. But as will be argued in Chapter 7 in relation to causing death by careless driving, if the aim of the law is to improve road safety it is the underlying endangerment offence which is arguably most important in having the potential to improve bad driving. The fact is that in Sweden there is no equivalent to the endangerment offence of careless driving, since carelessness in traffic requires a similar degree of negligence to that of dangerous driving. The Swedish law appears to be entirely retributive in nature in that it punishes only once carelessness results in harm, and does not seek to employ a utilitarian rationale by punishing risk-taking in the absence of harm. Where no serious injuries or deaths are caused through what English law would classify as mere carelessness, it may be that D can be prosecuted for some underlying traffic offence such as running a red light (although the same is true in England and Wales). Although some might see this as problematic, there are also elements of appeal in this position, in that the law can be used to concentrate the driver's mind on exactly what it is that they have done wrong (whether that be tailgating, running a red light or failing to give way). Despite the law on causing another's death or injury appearing to be retributive, sentences for the offence are low in practice, rarely exceeding a couple of years' imprisonment. Terms of imprisonment known in England and Wales for causing death by dangerous driving at the higher end of the scale are unheard of even in the worst cases of causing another's death in Sweden.

## Policy: Vision Zero

Whatever a country's substantive law on traffic offences, the success or otherwise of the law in reducing casualties on the road will depend on how the law is enforced. As noted in the Chapter 1 of this book, enforcement is just one of the three Es often used in road safety policy, the others being engineering and education. Sweden has gone one step further in coordinating its road safety policy and taking account of these different methods of casualty reduction. In 1997 the Swedish parliament adopted a new road safety policy known as 'Vision Zero' (*Nollvision*). Whilst Sweden has been consistent in reducing its road death rate since the 1970s, the authorities have not been complacent in their success and have taken the attitude that even the comparatively small numbers of deaths on Sweden's roads are unacceptable.

Traffic safety has had a high priority in Sweden ever since 1967, the year that the country changed from left- to right-hand traffic. The inherent dangers involved in such a significant alteration to driver behaviour were highlighted by the authorities. Very low speed limits helped to reduce these dangers and, initially at least, kept fatality rates low. Between 1975 and 1983 fatalities reduced from 1200 to 700 and it was only once Sweden's national economy improved in the late 1980s that fatalities began to increase once more, with a figure of 900 in 1989 (Koornstra et al. 2002, 9).

The essence of Vision Zero is that it takes a holistic view of road safety policy. Whilst the central premise on which Vision Zero is founded, that the only acceptable figure for the number of fatalities and serious injuries in traffic is zero, may be criticized as political rhetoric and wholly unrealistic or unattainable, the strategy itself incorporates interesting and promising ideas:

> Vision Zero alters the view on responsibility. Those who design the road transport system bear the ultimate responsibility for safety: road managers, vehicle manufacturers, road transport carriers, politicians, public employees, legislative authorities and the police. It is the responsibility of the individual person to abide by laws and regulations. Prior to this, practically all the responsibility had been put on the individual road user.
>
> Vision Zero is composed of several basic elements, each of which affects safety in road traffic. These concern ethics, human capability and tolerance, responsibility, scientific facts and a realization that the different components in the road transport system interact and are interdependent. (Vägverket 2006, 5)

Vision Zero recognizes that all drivers make mistakes, but suggests that it is wrong that these may be 'punishable' by death through the occurrence of fatal road traffic collisions (ibid.). Although the goal is to achieve zero fatalities on the road, the method for achieving this is not seen to be the prevention of all collisions, as collisions are seen to be inevitable, but the aim is to minimize the harm caused in collisions so that they do not result in death or serious injury. This, it is claimed, can be achieved by designing safer cars to protect their occupants, and Vision Zero suggests that any development in vehicle design must also be accompanied by a harmonization of road environment design. A key feature of Vision Zero is that a major share of responsibility for road safety is shifted to those who design the road transport system (ibid., 6).

> At the core of the Vision Zero is the biomechanical tolerance of human beings. Vision Zero promotes a road system where crash energy cannot exceed human tolerance. While it is accepted that crashes in the transport system occur due to human error, Vision Zero requires no crash should be more severe than the tolerance of humans. (Whitelegg and Haq, 2006a, 7)

On the road engineering front, Vision Zero has resulted in greater use of roundabouts and central median barriers, and the removal of trees from the side of rural roads to help prevent fatal collisions when vehicles leave the road. On the education front, a Road Traffic Inspectorate was established in 2003, the first of its kind in Europe. This inspectorate is a supervisory authority with a similar role to that of the Health and Safety Executive, albeit without law enforcement powers. Currently with a staff of only sixteen but with plans to increase this to two thousand in coming years, the tasks of the Inspectorate are:

1. To monitor and analyse conditions that could substantially affect the design and functioning of the road transport system through taking a holistic view of the road safety goals adopted by public authorities, municipalities and others.
2. In dialogue with the organizations referred to above, work to ensure that they apply a systematic procedure to prevent road accidents that result in death or serious injury.
3. To co-operate with other players to improve traffic safety on roads.

4. To initiate research and development within the road safety sector and monitor research of importance to the operations at the Inspectorate. (Vägtrafikinspektionen 2003)

The Inspectorate's work includes visiting the premises of companies who employ drivers as part of their business, such as haulage companies and companies with fleets of company cars, to advise managers of best practice and encourage management systems to be established in relation to driving tasks. The Inspectorate's role is to develop a dialogue with such organizations, as well as with system designers, to promote road safety as a priority.

The Vision Zero policy has been celebrated as a groundbreaking policy, attracting huge interest from other jurisdictions keen to replicate the success in road safety achieved in Sweden. The UK has itself researched the possibility of adopting a similar strategy, with a report by the Stockholm Environment Institute commissioned by the Department for Transport examining the desirability and cost of replicating the policy in the UK. The conclusions were that

> Swedish interviewees were convinced that Vision Zero binds together disparate stakeholders with a common, highly motivated, 'can do–will do' mentality. There is more focus, more cohesion and more targeted effort across all agencies. … The over-riding conclusion … is that there is a great deal to gain from moving in this direction and hardly anything at all to lose. (Whitelegg and Haq 2006b, 6)

Blackpool has become the first local authority in Great Britain to implement its own version of Vision Zero with a launch on 12 September 2007 (Marshall 2007). However, from the publicity surrounding that launch the version of Vision Zero being communicated to the public seems to have overlooked the fundamental basis of the Swedish Vision Zero: road users are just one element of those who must share responsibility for road safety. The Council's press information stated that 'this vision of shared responsibility reflects Blackpool's underlying view that "Road Safety is Everyone's Responsibility" and as part of the campaign Blackpool Council and the [Primary Care Trust] will work with members of the community, emergency services and local figureheads towards a reduction in deaths and injuries on Blackpool's roads using publicity and education as a means to communicate the relevant messages'. Although education is an essential ingredient of the success of any road safety policy, Vision Zero is a policy requiring far more than just education.

The approach taken in Blackpool seems to be that all drivers must face prosecution for traffic infringements whereas in Sweden, up until recently, Vision Zero has had little impact on the 'driver on the street' and has been concentrating on the role of the system designers in reducing the likelihood of fatal and serious collisions through other means. Some might be concerned that Vision Zero has been interpreted to mean that the blame for fatalities in the road system is assigned to the failure of the road system rather that the road user (Whitelegg and Haq 2006a, 7), but this demonstrates that the central thesis of Swedish Vision Zero can be easily misunderstood. It may be that the UK will find it difficult to adopt the

Swedish policy in its entirety, since the danger is that it may have a negative effect on road users if not carefully explained. It would not be beneficial to encourage an attitude amongst drivers that no matter what risks they take they should not be held responsible for subsequent harm caused because responsibility should lie with the road designers. However, this is not in fact the premise on which Vision Zero is based. Road design can only be successful in reducing casualties in so far as road users abide by the rules of the road.

In a survey of British stakeholders, 62 per cent of respondents thought it unhelpful to have a policy that establishes a vision of zero fatalities or serious injuries, and 79 per cent thought that the UK should not adopt the Swedish Vision Zero policy (Whitelegg and Haq 2006a, 45). The tradition in the UK has been to set targets, such as to reduce the number of people killed and seriously injured on the roads by 40 per cent by the year 2010 (DETR 2000), which is seen by many as far more achievable than a general vision of zero deaths or serious injuries. Interviews with road safety professionals in the UK suggest that Vision Zero would not be accepted by the British people or the UK political system because it would not fit the 'British psyche' (Crawford 2007, 19). However, the Parliamentary Advisory Council for Transport Safety (PACTS) has drawn on some of the elements of Vision Zero in recommending that the UK take a more integrated and holistic approach to road safety (ibid.). This will be discussed in more detail in Chapter 7 below.

## Practice

Ten years after its introduction, Vision Zero is starting to affect the work of the police in terms of law enforcement policy. In early 2007 the police began to implement a new road safety policy, designed alongside policy strategists from Vision Zero to help in the goal to further reduce road traffic fatalities and casualties. The number of traffic officers has reduced significantly in recent years, and there has been a problem of inconsistency in the enforcement of traffic offences. The new policy seeks to introduce a uniform way of working in this area, with a focus on intelligence-led policing in traffic. It encourages an increase in the number of controls carried out by uniformed police officers 'as an integral part of combating crime' (Rikspolisstyrelsen 2007, 3). One major obstacle to achieving such a goal is the common attitude amongst police officers (other than traffic officers), as well as the public, that traffic offences do not amount to 'real' crime, an attitude shared to a greater or lesser degree across Sweden. The European survey of public attitudes to road safety found that when asked to assess the effectiveness of the system in detecting and punishing the majority of driving offences Swedish drivers rated the Swedish system as being far less effective than British drivers rated the British system (Dahlstedt 2006, Table 103).

The new enforcement strategy in Sweden seeks to change this. It requires all officers on patrol to carry out traffic enforcement initiatives, and to use their power to impose on-the-spot fines when they come across violations. There are four priority areas for collision prevention measures by the police:

- Speed
- Drink-driving
- Use of seat belts, child restraints and helmets
- Aggressive driving. (Rikspolisstyrelsen 2007, 9)

In relation to speed, the police have in the past been very inconsistent in the tolerance level of their reporting limit. The new policy lowers the reporting limit to 6 kmph above the legal limit, when in the past it used to be as high as 15 kmph above the limit. No matter the speed limit, whether it is 30 kmph or 100 kmph, the police will fine those who drive at 6 kmph or more above that limit. The difficulty is, however, in motivating police officers who do not see speeding at this level as truly criminal to implement the policy. In particular, it was suggested in interview that those using hand-held speed detectors may be concerned about stopping a driver who has driven at 76 kmph in a 70 kmph limit and in doing so missing an opportunity to detect the next vehicle that races past at a far higher speed such as 90 kmph.

The SUNflower project found that speed limits on inter-urban roads (A-roads and motorways) are higher in Britain than in Sweden. However, the actual mean speeds on these types of roads are higher in Sweden than in Britain (Koornstra et al. 2002, 99). This indicates that speed limits have not been enforced effectively in Sweden, where speeding is commonplace. As in England and Wales, one of the challenges in promoting observance of speed limits is the degree to which the validity of a particular speed limit is accepted by drivers. With this in mind, the Swedish Road Administration (*Vägverket*) has conducted pilots of variable speed limits. This allows a variable statutory or a recommended maximum speed limit to be displayed on adjustable electronic road signs depending on the prevailing road conditions at any particular time. These have been trialled at intersections, and the results show a positive result in reducing average speeds and also in compliance to speed limits (Vägverket 2006b).

Unlike speeding, drink-driving has long been a priority for the police in Sweden. As noted above, under Swedish law the police are entitled to use random testing and regularly set up road blocks to carry out ‘drink-driving controls’, where all drivers are stopped and must submit to a breath test. Figures show that in Sweden there is one test a year per four cars whereas the rate in Great Britain is one in 26.5 cars (Koornstra et al. 2002, 49). This high rate of testing is made possible by the use of mobile evidential breathalysers carried in the back of police vans, avoiding the need to accompany any suspected offender to a police station to obtain an accurate breath analysis. In addition, all drivers stopped by the police, for whatever reason, are subjected to a breathalyser test, and each uniformed officer carries his or her own personal breathalyser for this purpose.

A key aspect of Vision Zero is the cooperation between different players in the system. Using the law to punish drink-drivers is only one way to deal with the problem. The holistic view of Vision Zero encourages the police to liaise with other service providers to combat drink-driving by dealing with the underlying problem of alcoholism or drug addiction. To prevent known offenders re-offending alcohol interlocks can be installed in their vehicles, physically preventing the driver from starting the vehicle without providing a clear breath test. Sweden has taken the lead here, with Britain following (provisions for interlocks have been made in the Road Safety Act 2006: see Chapter 3 above). Such interlocks are also used by companies employing drivers to guarantee that their workforce is not driving whilst impaired.

Another change under the new policy is that responsibility for traffic enforcement now rests with the commissioner of each county police department and operational management, rather than with the traffic police chiefs and Swedish Road Administration, as was previously the case. Part of the impetus behind this has come from the current National Police Commissioner who is seen to be far more interested in and supportive of the police role in traffic safety than his predecessor.

Another individual who has assisted in bringing traffic offences, such as speeding, to the fore in public debate is Sven-Erik Alhem, Chief Public Prosecutor in the Malmö region and Head of the Prosecution Development Centre there. He is keen to optimize the deterrent effect of the law and, in particular, to try to apply the same element of educative deterrence successful in cases of drink-driving to other offences such as speeding. He is all too aware of the dichotomies presented by a law where the outcome of a piece of bad driving will dictate the seriousness with which the offender is dealt.

However, although, as noted above, the role luck plays in establishing criminal liability is prominent under Swedish law, the approach taken to investigating collisions is different to that in England and Wales. Unlike the English experience, where a police force is likely to either employ a civilian collision investigator or specially train a number of police officers for that purpose, in Sweden there are no specialist collision investigators employed by the police to attend the scene of serious traffic collisions. The first police officers on the scene should take steps to secure basic evidence such as photographs of the scene and record any marks appearing on the road surface, but there is far less use of expert evidence in reconstructing a collision for the purpose of establishing liability in Sweden. It is not usual, for example, for a road to be temporarily closed in order that such evidence can be preserved. The advice provided by the Prosecution Development Centre to police is that they should ensure that thorough investigations are made of all severe collisions, whether fatal or not, since whether a death has occurred may be a matter of coincidence. However, in interview prosecutors noted the poor quality of police reports in many of the cases referred to the Centre by victims and families appealing against the local prosecutor's decision not to prosecute. In many of these cases essential evidence has not been collected or has been lost. For example, it may be the case that the cars involved in a serious collision have been crushed before first being examined. This then makes it extremely difficult to alter the original prosecutor's decision, since it will often be impossible to establish criminal liability without such evidence.

Although the quality of investigations of fatal collisions by police is unreliable, such collisions are also investigated by the Swedish Road Administration (*Vägverket*). Under Vision Zero it is the responsibility of the State to improve road conditions to reduce the risk of collisions, and investigations are carried out with a view to implementing this policy. There are no inquests in Sweden, but the investigations carried out by *Vägverket* might result in the same kind of recommendations that a coroner will be able to make once reforms are introduced in England and Wales in terms of identifying collision black-spots (see Chapter 7 below). In-depth studies of fatal collisions lead to 'OLA' projects, with OLA standing for 'Objective data, List of solutions/actions and Addressed action plans' (Vägverket 2006a, 12). System designers use the data collected from the investigations to discuss possible prevention of future collisions.

Factors contributing to fatal collisions are categorized into three groups:

- excessive force – when the road-users have done their best to follow traffic regulations and have used safety equipment. They have however made an error that resulted in fatal collision forces, due to the design of the road environment in combination with the prevailing speed limit;
- excessive risk – when road-users are injured due to insufficient personal protection. The most common scenario is not wearing a safety belt. Another example is cyclists not using cycle helmets;
- beyond system restrictions – when the road-users have consciously and seriously violated regulations that have a great bearing on the severity of the collision. The most common scenario is greatly exceeding the speed limit.

According to *Vägverket*, two-thirds of fatal injuries in Sweden occurring 1997–99 were due to excessive force. However, an analysis of these investigations in 2000 suggested that such studies could be improved by the inclusion of estimations of vehicle pre-crash and crash speeds, suggesting the absence of such data prior to 2000 (Sagberg and Assum 2000), which possibly undermines the conclusions reached by *Vägverket*. Without the closure of roads at collision sites the ability accurately to establish the cause of a serious collision can be brought into question, and whilst *Vägverket* hold responsibility for such investigations there appears to be less pressure on the police to ensure thorough investigations of fatal collisions are conducted. The view held by those involved appears to be that without evidence of a criminal offence there is no need to conduct a criminal investigation of a collision. This can be contrasted with the position in England and Wales, where a thorough investigation is carried out in order to establish whether a criminal offence should be suspected.

## Conclusions

Sweden has had a history of success in reducing its road casualty rate and currently has a similar fatality rate to that of Great Britain. The Swedes see themselves as having a tradition of good road safety dialogue, and are keen to continue the trend with the implementation of the Vision Zero initiative. It should be noted that different factors may be contributing to deaths on Swedish and English roads. For example, 'dark and snowy winters with elks crossing the roads' (Koornstra et al. 2002, 4) play a part in Sweden, and statistics show that almost 2 per cent of fatalities in Sweden result from collisions with wild animals (ibid., 28). Factors which may assist in the low fatality rate, on the other hand, include the fact that geographically Sweden covers a much larger area than Great Britain (449,760 $km^2$ as opposed to 244,046 $km^2$). As a result, the smaller population is spread out to a greater degree (with the exception of the three main cities of Stockholm, Malmö and Göteborg), and whilst there is a population density of 238 per $km^2$ in Great Britain, the population density in Sweden is only 20 per $km^2$. This would suggest that there is less likelihood of vehicles coming into conflict with one another, supported by the fact that there are 23.6 metres of road length per capita in Sweden compared to 6.6 metres in Great Britain (ibid., 22). If one looks at the fatality rates per billion vehicle kilometres, Great Britain actually has a better safety rate than the other SUN countries with the rate being 10–15 per cent lower than in Sweden and the Netherlands (ibid., 38).

The fact remains, however, that Sweden, along with the UK and the Netherlands, has a very good road safety record in comparison to other European countries. It would appear that up until now it has been geographical and cultural factors, rather than law enforcement, that have played a vital role in achieving the success of a low road traffic fatality rate in Sweden. The one exception to this is with regards to drink-driving, an area of law and law enforcement in which Sweden can be held up as a model for other European countries, including England and Wales. The attitude that prevails in Sweden seems to be that resources and attention should be directed towards detecting and punishing cases of drink-driving, and that it would be wrong to divert such resources and attention to other dangerous driving activities and risk undermining the achievements gained thus far in the drink-driving sphere.

A common concern for those interviewed in Sweden was the need to change attitudes to driving offences shared by the public and those with the responsibility of enforcing traffic offences to bring them more in line with the attitude that already prevails in relation to drink-driving. If drivers' normative view of speeding could be altered to the extent that it became socially unacceptable, this would surely contribute considerably to Vision Zero's goal. This normative view of traffic offences will be discussed as the key to unlocking better compliance to traffic laws in England and Wales in subsequent chapters, with reference to the work of psychologists and criminologists. One country in which change is currently rife is France. France has seen a rapid improvement in road safety, with fatalities falling by 32 per cent between 2001 and 2004 as a result of road safety becoming a top priority for President Chirac in his second term in office (ETSC 2006, 56). There has been a huge increase in the number of automated speed cameras used and attitudes to speeding are reported to have undergone drastic change, with 68 per cent of drivers declaring that they had reduced their speed on motorways in the two years prior to 2005, although records show that 48 per cent of vehicles still exceeded speed limits in 2004 (ibid., 57). However, starting from such a poor observance rate France has achieved admirable results in a comparatively short period, and if the trend continues it may become a model for other countries.

# Chapter 6

# The Role of the Criminal Law in Promoting Road Safety

## Introduction

In considering how the law relating to traffic offences ought to be reformed in 1988, the North Committee reasoned that:

> Courtesy, common sense, habit and self-interest go a long way to encourage people to observe the regulations, but without the sanction of the criminal law more people than already do so would break the rules, and the benefits they bring would be gradually lost. (Department of Transport 1988, para.2.11)

Chapters 2–4 above have set out and discussed the various driving offences forming the subject matter of this book. Chapter 5 considered what contribution law enforcement may have made to achieving a good road safety rating in Sweden. Since shortly after the motor vehicle entered modern society, it has been assumed that the criminal law can and should be used to temper the thrill-seeking attractions and inherent dangers of the car. The body of legislation regulating this mode of transport in England and Wales has swelled over the past century, providing courts and lawyers with a constant stream of work. There seems no danger of the law in this area becoming stagnant, with new offences and proposals being introduced at frequent intervals. Regulation of drivers and vehicles has as its goal the improvement of road safety and the prevention of harm on the roads. However, as may be seen in relation to speeding offences, this laudable aim is frequently unrecognized by those to whom it applies. Other methods of minimizing the harm caused by vehicles include education and improved engineering of both roads and vehicles. The question is how far we can expect the law to go in achieving these aims and how to formulate offences that are most likely to succeed.

Dealt with in the criminal courts and leading to criminal punishments, driving offences form part of the criminal law, although they are often not seen as 'real' crime. Is it right that driving offences are seen as some lesser kind of offence? If not, how might the status quo be changed? The starting point is to examine what it is that society is trying to achieve in criminalizing bad driving, what are some of the aims of punishment in the criminal law generally, and which of those aims are sought to be achieved in punishing bad drivers in particular. One aspect of punishment, as will be seen, is retribution. What is unclear, however, is the extent to which any harm caused by bad drivers should affect the amount of punishment they deserve and whether it is only those drivers who cause harm who deserve punishment. It will be seen that the treatment of drivers by the criminal law is dichotomous. The role of the law in criminalizing bad drivers generally seems to be quite different to the role it takes in criminalizing bad drivers who kill. The harm caused by drivers is currently central to their criminalization, and whilst causing death by dangerous driving (CDDD) is widely accepted as a criminal offence, this is not true of the lesser offences of careless driving and speeding. The one exception to this is that drink-driving is, even in the absence of harm caused, usually viewed as criminal. It may be that there are lessons to be learnt from social attitudes to this offence that can be used elsewhere to improve driver behaviour. (This will be explored further in Chapter 7.) In order to establish how the law could be improved to maximize the potential to change drivers' behaviour through application of the criminal law, it is first necessary to look at what dictates how a driver behaves. There is much that can be learnt about how we can influence drivers through the use of the criminal law by looking to the field of psychology, since there has been substantial work done within that discipline to understand the way in which thought processes when driving are developed. The psychology of aberrant driving behaviour could uncover potential for using the criminal law to better effect in achieving road safety aims.

## Criminalization and Punishment

Why is it that the criminal law, rather than some other branch of law, should deal with preventing wrongful conduct on the roads? Criminal law can be distinguished from civil law in that those breaching the criminal law face stigmatic punishment, whereas, although breach of the civil law may lead to sanctions, these do not normally involve public censure of the individual for his or her failure to meet the requirements of the law (Clarkson et al. 2007, 2). A crime is committed not only against the individual victim who may have suffered harm, but against the State. It is the State that accepts responsibility for prosecuting and punishing those who have breached the criminal law. In establishing in advance who ought to be punished, the State must decide what conduct merits criminalization and therefore punishment.

### *Making Bad Driving Criminal*

According to Hart, the aim of criminal legislation is to denounce certain types of conduct as something not to be practised (Hart 1968a, 8). Many agree that criminal law leads to punishment and punishment: 'is the deliberate imposition of a burdensome liability on an individual for some blameworthy conduct in order to censure that conduct' (Lamond 2007, 621). The reason why society wishes to censure certain types of conduct is that they are wrong or harmful. If it is accepted that the aim of the criminal law is to prevent harm to others, it is necessary to establish what is meant by 'harm'. Feinberg has defined harm as the 'thwarting, setting back or defeating of an interest' (Feinberg 1984, 33). It is uncontroversial to include physical injury and death within the meaning of harm, and essentially it is this type of harm which driving offences, particularly the offence of dangerous driving, seek to prevent. However, driving offences are often seen as controversial. Essentially, this is because, although they seek to prevent physical harm, they lack the characteristics of paradigmatic crime. There are two essential elements to paradigmatic crime: harm and blame (Clarkson 2005, 4). Taking the requirements of some driving offences at face value, it can be argued that they represent a double departure from this paradigm (ibid., 131).

Firstly, the offences discussed in Chapters 2 and 3 of this book (careless driving, dangerous driving, drink-driving and speeding) do not require that physical harm has been caused before criminal liability can be established. They are what are known as endangerment offences, which exist to punish those who take risks, whether or not such risks result in physical harm. Risk-taking is a wrong in itself because of the possibility that it can result in harm, and can be seen as a kind of second-order harm (Gross 1979, 125). Finkelstein has explained this by stating that people have a legitimate interest in avoiding unwanted risks and that 'a person who inflicts a risk of harm on another damages that interest, thus lowering the victim's baseline welfare' (Finkelstein 2003, 966). Duff identifies the wrong in endangering others as that of creating an unreasonable or unjustified risk of harm which 'manifests our lack of proper concern for the interests of those we endanger' (Duff 2005, 53).

Secondly, unlike paradigmatic crime such as violent crimes, the driving offences of careless and dangerous driving do not require the blameworthiness of the defendant to be proved in terms of subjective *mens rea*. It is sufficient that an objective test of blameworthiness in the form of negligence (carelessness or dangerousness) be proven. The difficulty is that some have argued that punishment for negligence cannot be justified (for example, Williams 1961, 122–3), and that only conduct which is committed with the actor's awareness of the risk of harm should be criminalized. According to this point of view, negligence is not a form of *mens rea*, since it involves no cognitive element of knowledge or foresight. However, Hart argues that negligence can be included within the meaning of *mens rea* and that there is no reason why criminal liability should not be founded on such a state of mind (Hart 1968b). That negligence can provide the *mens rea* of even serious criminal offences has been confirmed on a number of occasions recently, with, for example, the Sexual Offences Act 2003 introducing a *mens rea* requirement of negligence for rape. In some situations, those who fail to think about the outcome of their actions may be just as blameworthy as those who foresee an outcome before taking a risk, provided that those who fail to think had the ability to have thought and to have acted differently. In relation to driving offences, only those who have the capacity to meet the standard of the competent and careful driver are entitled to drive, so that if they fail to meet the standard there should be no bar to their responsibility. Thus although the offences of careless and dangerous driving fail to incorporate the paradigmatic form of blameworthiness (subjective *mens rea*), there should be no objection to their criminalization in requiring an element of objective fault.

Speeding and drink-driving, on the other hand, require no element of fault whatsoever. Strict liability offences form a growing body of law and are usually justified on utilitarian grounds: 'In favour of strict liability, it is claimed that the interests of the public require that the highest possible standards of care be exercised by people engaged in certain forms of conduct. This, in utilitarian terms, is the greater good to be achieved by occasionally convicting someone who may have taken all reasonable care to abide by the law' (Clarkson et al. 2007, 222). This does not, however, overcome the problem that many members of the public, and even those responsible for enforcing such laws, see them as falling outside the scope of offences deserving censure which, as noted above, is the characteristic of criminal law which is most important in differentiating it from other bodies of rules. Somehow, however, drink-driving has overcome this obstacle to successful deterrence and, despite the fact that there is no requirement to prove that D knew that D was under the influence of drink or drugs when setting out to drive, results in real stigma attaching to any person convicted of the offence.

The vehicular homicide offences discussed in Chapter 4, in contrast to the offences in Chapters 2 and 3, do not constitute double departures from the paradigm of criminal liability. In this regard, CDDD, causing death by careless driving (CDCD) and causing death by careless driving whilst under the influence of drink or drugs (CDCDUI) need to be considered separately from causing death by unlawful driving (CDUD) and causing death by aggravated vehicle-taking. CDDD, for example, can be seen as a partial departure from the paradigm in that although it requires the same fault element as dangerous driving, and therefore fails to live up to the paradigmatic view of 'blame', it does meet the requirement of harm in its paradigmatic sense. The same can be said of CDCD and CDCDUI in that although, in terms of *mens rea*, both only require negligence to the degree of carelessness, this seems to be offset by the fact that death has been caused. As noted in Chapter 4, however, CDUD does not require any form of *mens rea* and can be described as an offence of strict liability. The fact that death is involved has been used, however, to create a serious homicide offence. The involvement of death in all these offences appears to be the main reason why they are more readily accepted by some as 'true' crime, but, as will be discussed in the next section, it is questionable whether the additional punishment levied on drivers who kill is either justified or achieves any additional aims of the criminal law.

### *Aims of, and Justification for, Punishment*

If the aim of criminal legislation is to denounce conduct, then it could be argued that upon criminal conviction no further action on the part of the State against the convict is required, since labelling D as a wrongdoer may be sufficient to communicate society's censure. Thus, Hart argues that punishment requires justification over and above this (Hart 1968a). Justification for punishment is often divided into two types: utilitarian, or reductivist, and retributive. There is no consensus as to how much weight, if any, should be given to each type of justification, with much disagreement amongst those contributing to the debate. Hart argues that there is one general justifying aim of punishment, which is that it leads to beneficial consequences, but that retribution plays a part in helping to establish how much punishment is justified in any one case (ibid.). Others, such as Moore, argue that the only reason why punishment is justified is that offenders deserve it, and there is no need to find other benefits of punishment (Moore 1998).

Under the law of England and Wales a number of purposes of sentencing have been set out under section 142 of the Criminal Justice Act 2003:

> 142 (1) Any court dealing with an offender in respect of his offence must have regard to the following purposes of sentencing –
> (a) the punishment of offenders,
> (b) the reduction of crime (including its reduction by deterrence),
> (c) the reform and rehabilitation of offenders,
> (d) the protection of the public, and
> (e) the making of reparation by offenders to persons affected by their offences.

In practice a sentence would be unlikely to implement all of these purposes at once, with the judge having to choose which to apply in the particular circumstances. The first of the listed purposes amounts to retribution, whilst the other four can all be described as utlitarian.

*Utilitarian justifications* Williams states that the reason for punishing negligence (of which careless driving and dangerous driving are examples) is the utilitarian one, that we hope thereby to improve people's standards of behaviour (in this case their driving) (Williams 1983, 91). This was recognized at a Law Society conference in 1964 at which it was said that 'the vast mass of traffic offences were temporary lapses of ordinary men and women and the aim therefore was not so much retribution as making them more careful drivers' (quoted in Hood 1972, 97). Utilitarian justifications can be seen as the only ones applicable to crimes of strict liability such as speeding.

Punishment can be designed to improve behaviour in a number of ways. Firstly, the threat of punishment may deter all drivers from driving badly (general deterrence). Secondly, having been convicted of an offence and suffered the consequences, a driver could be deterred from re-offending in the future (specific or individual deterrence). Some have argued that deterrence fails to operate in relation to driving offences, since if D is not deterred from taking a risk by the immediate threat of physical harm to him or herself, or damage to D's property, D will not be deterred by any other consequences which could ultimately result. Schulhofer notes that: 'With respect to reckless or negligent conduct, the motivation to desist is probably very strong in any event; the actor, to the extent that he is aware of the danger at all, will still wish to avoid tort liability for injury to others, not to mention the possibility of injury to himself' (Schulhofer 1974, 1521). Williams argues that although this is true, driving offences can add to the pressure to make bad drivers change their habits and in the last resort, to give up driving (Williams 1983, 93). In an earlier work, he more persuasively argued that 'just as it is possible for punishment to cause a person to exercise greater control over his acts in view of the known dangers, so it is possible for punishment to bring about greater foresight, by causing the subject to stop and think before committing himself to a course of conduct' (Williams 1961, 123).

For a prospective offender to be deterred from committing himself or herself to a particular course of conduct, he or she must be able to identify that course of conduct as one that the law seeks to prevent. D must know the nature of driving which is criminalized, and must recognize that D's own driving may fall within that definition. Drivers should be aware of the speed limit in force on a particular stretch of road and stay alert to any changes in the limit to avoid commission of a speeding offence. Vehicles are equipped with speedometers that make this task an easy one to achieve. Drivers should also know that they must not drive when under the influence of alcohol and, if they do choose to drink before driving, should familiarize themselves with the amount that is permitted under the current blood alcohol concentration (BAC) limit. Drivers also know that they should not drive dangerously or without due care and attention. One possible problem of achieving the aim of deterrence in relation to careless and dangerous driving, however, is that prospective offenders do not necessarily identify their own actions with those prohibited by those offences. This issue will be returned to later.

It can be argued that all forms of punishment available to sentencers in cases involving driving offences offer some deterrence. In fact, Ashworth points out that in some cases it is the process of prosecution, not just the resulting sentence, which is the punishment (Ashworth 2000, 67). This is confirmed by Pearce, whose research found that the predominant feelings of offenders attending court on charges of careless or dangerous driving were 'nervous, embarrassed and ashamed' (Pearce 2004, 28). Such punishment by process will be lacking in cases of speeding dealt with by fixed penalty notices, since there is no public process to be experienced by the offender. The same is also true of cases of careless driving where D does not attend court but pleads guilty by letter. The cost of having to pay a fine may or may not deter careless and speeding drivers, depending on their financial circumstances, but perhaps a more effective deterrent is the threat of losing one's licence as a result of immediate disqualification or points which accumulate under the 'totting-up' system. For example, Walker states that motorists are more anxious to avoid disqualification than fines (Walker 1991, 18). However, Mirrlees-Black notes that disqualification will only work as a deterrent if potential offenders are aware of the penalty. She found that many of the first-time offenders she interviewed had not known that they could be disqualified for their offence. This affects the law's ability to achieve general deterrence. However, most of those offenders interviewed claimed that their experience of disqualification would deter them from future offending, meaning that disqualification seems to be a success in terms of individual deterrence (Mirrlees-Black 1993). Harland and Lester also found that the penalty most frequently mentioned by offenders when interviewed was disqualification. Half of offenders said they thought they would be deterred by disqualification and a quarter thought they would be deterred by a fine (Harland and Lester 1997).

Imprisonment is not a sentence available in cases of careless driving or speeding, but may result from a conviction for drink-driving or dangerous driving, and will be the normal result of a conviction for CDDD or CDCDUI (*Cooksley* 2004). The maximum sentence available for CDDD is considerably higher than that for dangerous driving, however, and in the case of careless driving the fact of death now leads to a potential period of imprisonment for CDCD where none is available for the underlying offence. This cannot be justified on the basis of deterrence. As noted above, if the possibility of killing oneself or others does not deter a dangerous driver, it is unlikely that possible criminal penalties will. What one is attempting to deter is risk-taking. However, the possibility of apprehension leading to criminal penalties adds a further dimension to the equation involved in the taking of risks and the effectiveness of deterrence. This requires further explanation.

If there were no criminal penalties for driving badly, drivers would only have to assess whether to accept a risk of causing harm to themselves or others. One might expect that this risk would be enough to deter drivers from bad driving. As noted by Åberg, 'It is difficult to understand why traffic safety rules should be necessary to change behaviour. If they were behaving in a rational way, drivers who learn that their behaviour is associated with increased risks should avoid performing that behaviour and then traffic safety rules would not be necessary' (Åberg 1998, 209). Groeger argues that although a driver's own safety is one of the goals D has, is not particularly influential. Instead, D's aspirations are 'to reach destinations, avoid obstacles, minimize delay and driving time, enjoy driving, feel in control etc. It is the concrete expression and realization of these goals, rather than more abstract principles such as safety, that has real impact on behaviour' (Groeger 2000, 189). If D can be persuaded of the need to avoid punishment for driving offences as one of the goals, the law might act as a deterrent to bad driving. In a jurisdiction where bad driving is a criminal offence leading to penalties, D will likely assess the risk of causing harm but will also assess the further risk of whether D is likely to be penalized for D's bad driving. Therefore, the function of traffic laws, Åberg suggests, is to provide drivers with new risks, with higher probabilities, than the ordinary safety risks of traffic (Åberg 1998, 209). The risk of being detected while violating a rule must be perceived as high enough to ensure compliance in order for it to be effective.

For the offences of careless and dangerous driving the assessment of the risk of getting caught and the risk of causing harm to oneself or other road users must be carried out separately, since prosecution is not dependent upon occasioning a collision. However, D may be ignorant about the *actual* probability of either of these risks materializing. For the offence of CDDD, for which D faces a maximum of fourteen years' imprisonment, D must first assess the risk of causing death. If D discounts the risk of causing death, D will also discount the risk of being punished for doing so. Schulhofer expresses it thus:

> [I]t would seem that the deterrent effect of a penalty imposed only for causing harm would tend to diminish as the risk of harm (in terms of circumstances of which the actor should be aware) diminishes and as the extent to which the actor actually adverts to this risk diminishes .... [T]his tendency to diminish as the degree of risk and the degree of the actor's advertence to the risk diminishes will presumably be reinforced

> by the natural tendency of many people to discount such contingencies. (Schulhofer 1974, 1541)

There are a number of psychological reasons which will be discussed later in this chapter as to why drivers discount the risk of being involved in a collision, but two are worth mentioning here just briefly. 'Subjective risk' of a collision is reduced because individuals do not see themselves as belonging to the same population as the 'victims of accidents' and because most drivers rate themselves as better-than-average (Näätänen and Summala 1976, 69).

Schulhofer concludes that penalties applicable only in the event of a fatality (such as 14 years' imprisonment for CDDD or five years' imprisonment for CDCD) seem to add nothing to the deterrence achieved by penalties applicable to the underlying offence (in this case dangerous or careless driving) (Schulhofer 1974, 1544). Thus, whilst drivers may be deterred from driving dangerously, they will not be deterred from causing death thereby. And for drivers to be deterred from driving dangerously they must believe that the threat of unpleasant consequences (whether they be physical harm or criminal punishment) is strong enough to persuade them not to take the risk. The same is true of careless driving. It is unknown what the success rate in apprehending dangerous and careless drivers is. However, the assumption must be that it is low. Anecdotal evidence given to researchers at the Transport Research Laboratory suggests that prosecutions in the absence of a collision are rare (Pearce et al. 2002, 33). Thus, unless D suspects that there is more than a minimal risk that D will cause a collision, or that there may be police presence in the area to witness D's dangerous driving, it is unlikely that D will be deterred from taking the risk.

To summarize, motorists can only be deterred from driving dangerously or carelessly, not from causing death, since they have no control over the outcome of their actions. As far as individual deterrence is concerned, most drivers convicted of CDDD or CDCD will be deterred from continuing to take risks whilst driving, not so much by the penalty they receive, but by the very fact that they have caused the death of another human being. This point was made by Pearce et al. in their research for the government (Pearce et al. 2002, 96), and is supported by research into the deterrence of joyriding (which often involves dangerous driving) in Australia, which indicates that young people see the possible death of either an innocent bystander or a friend as being a more important deterrent to joyriding than the possibility of being sent to a detention centre (McDonagh et al. 2002).

Returning to the ways in which punishment can reduce offending, a second way in which punishment aims to bring about a change in behaviour is through incapacitation. The difficulty with this utilitarian justification for punishment is that the effects only last as long as the sentence. Unlike deterrence or rehabilitation which aim to alter permanently an offender's behaviour, incapacitation can only aim for a temporary change. Disqualification is one way of incapacitating bad drivers. However, unfortunately it is not always an effective penalty because some drivers continue to drive even though disqualified. Corbett and Simon carried out a survey in which 27 per cent of respondents disqualified from driving admitted that they had driven whilst disqualified (Corbett and Simon 1992a, 50). Imprisonment also provides a way of incapacitating offenders. It would be difficult, however, to justify the imprisonment of bad drivers on the basis of incapacitation alone. The frugality principle, attributed to Bentham, suggests that since punishment is undesirable for its own sake it can be justified only by necessity and should be no greater than is required to achieve its goal (reproduced in part in von Hirsch and Ashworth 1998, 56). It is difficult to justify the imposition of imprisonment on drivers who have carried out the driving task negligently through driving dangerously or carelessly, if one is to respect the frugality principle. Long-term disqualification (with perhaps greater enforcement against disqualified driving) and possibly the obligatory surrender of an offender's vehicle would, on the other hand, achieve incapacitation without violating the frugality principle.

A third utilitarian justification for punishment is rehabilitation. This is often rejected as a valid justification on the basis that efforts to rehabilitate criminals have failed. However, in relation to bad drivers the prospects for successfully improving a driver's behaviour are greater. As seen in Chapters 2–4 above, the law now offers a range of initiatives aimed at improving bad drivers. In some cases these are offered as an alternative to prosecution (for example, the National Drivers Improvement Scheme and speed awareness courses) whilst others exist to complement other forms of punishment (such as the High Risk Offenders Scheme).

*Retributivist justifications* Having examined how the utilitarian goals of punishment can apply to traffic offences, the discussion now turns to consider retribution as a justification for punishment. The meaning of retribution has perhaps altered over time. Schulhofer distinguishes retribution from retaliation or vengeance (Schulhofer 1974). Retribution can be seen as a theory of punishment based on moral blameworthiness, according to which offenders should be punished proportionately to their offence. The difficulty is in determining what factors ought to influence an offender's moral blameworthiness. More precisely, there is disagreement over whether the result of D's actions affects D's moral blameworthiness, or whether moral blameworthiness depends solely on state of mind. This question is central to the issue of whether any of the constructive vehicular homicide offences discussed in Chapter 4 are justified in punishing more severely a bad driver who has caused death than one who has not. Schulhofer argues that the culpability of an offender guilty of negligence must stem from his having taken a forbidden risk, and any result of his risk-taking should not affect his penalty (ibid., 1517).

The modern form of the retributivist account of punishment is just deserts theory, pioneered by von Hirsch. Unlike Schulhofer, von Hirsch attaches considerable importance to the occurrence of harm in determining criminal liability. Von Hirsch and Jareborg have developed what they have called a 'living-standard analysis' to aid the assessment of how much punishment someone deserves for their offence (von Hirsch and Jareborg 1991). This is an attempt to develop criteria for judging the seriousness of an offence. They argue that seriousness of crime has two dimensions: harm and culpability (ibid., 2), and of these it is the former which is addressed by the living-standard analysis. It grades different harms in seriousness according to the level at which it affects the victim's living-standard, with the most serious level of harm threatening subsistence (ibid., 17). Applying this to driving offences, it can be seen that this highest level of living-standard may be threatened by conduct prohibited by the offences, since they are designed to reduce injuries and fatalities on the road. In the case of vehicular homicide offences it is clear that subsistence is destroyed and therefore the conduct has the highest harm-rating. Once the harm-rating has been established, that rating must be applied to a harm-scale which further assists in the assessment of desert. At this stage in the analysis the authors argue that discounts need to be made for risked or threatened harm (ibid., 30). Thus, whilst CDCDUI would remain at the top end of the harm-scale, drink-driving would fall in a lower harm category because the risk of death is fairly remote. This would equally apply to the offences of CDDD and CDCD and their corollary endangerment offences.

There is no explanation as to why a discount should be given in cases where the harm is only risked and not caused. It is clear that killing someone by drink-driving is more harmful than merely creating a risk of killing by drink-driving. Apart from anything else, in the former case an individual becomes the victim of the driving, whereas in the latter case only a general class of other road users whose lives have been put at risk are directly affected. But this does not explain why a driver who kills deserves more punishment than one who does not, given that whether or not a driver kills depends on chance.

Since its creation in the middle of the last century, the offence of CDDD has been described as 'illogical' by some (for example, MacKenna 1970). The illogicality of the offence is caused by the central role that luck plays in the offence. As noted by Willett in relation to non-fatal traffic offences: 'it is often a matter of chance whether the damage done is great or not. It is ... frequently the skill of other drivers or the alertness of the police that prevents more serious consequences' (Willett 1973, 71). Improvements in medical care and technology over time increase the role luck has to play, since many collisions which in the past could have been fatal no longer lead to death if the victim is fortunate enough to receive the necessary care (see Noland and Quddus 2004). As will be discussed in Chapter 7 below, it is not clear that the chance occurrence of death means that a dangerous or careless driver *deserves* more punishment than one who, due to any number of factors beyond his or her control, causes serious injury falling short of death.

If we are to punish offenders according to just deserts, surely they only deserve punishment for that over which they have control? This brings us back to the question of what modern desert theorists see as being the benefit of punishment. The advantage of one desert-based conception of punishment is that it relies on the emphasis of the communicative features of punishment (von Hirsch 1998, 169). Although desert theorists reject utilitarian justifications for punishment, they also recognize that if punishment had no usefulness in preventing crime there would be no need for it, since society would devise other methods of expressing censure (ibid., 171). It is arguably this which is central to the reason behind the punishment of bad driving. In punishing a driver who has taken risks (whether advertently or inadvertently) the law is not just trying to deter future offending by the offender or by others through the threat of imprisonment, disqualification or fines; it is expressing censure. When the law expresses censure it does so in the hope of modifying future conduct. Duff claims that the aim is not merely to bring about a change in attitudes and conduct, but to persuade D to modify D's future conduct by encouraging D to recognize that the conduct which is criminalized is wrongful (Duff 1998, 162). In doing so, the law also sends the message to others that such conduct is wrong. There remain, however, some obstacles to achieving these goals, given that few accept the message that offences such as speeding are 'wrong'.

## The Problem: Perceiving Driving Offences as 'Real Crime'

The previous section explored some of the possible reasons for criminalizing and punishing bad driving, although no conclusion as such was reached as to whether a utilitarian or retributive stance should be taken. Some have argued, however, that it is not a question of a choice between the two, and indeed that punishment must be justified both on grounds of retribution and crime reduction (utilitarianism) by taking a 'dualist' approach (Wood 2002). The difficulty is that unless drivers recognize that the law is justified in punishing those who drive badly, the law will fail in its aims and any censure it attempts to express will fall upon deaf ears. Attitudes towards traffic offences are often that they are not 'true' crimes and that any punishment awarded as a result of offending behaviour is unwarranted. The exception to this general problem, though, comes in relation to the vehicular homicide offences where the public seem all too ready to penalize drivers who kill, displaying a divergence of views towards crime which could be seen as quite illogical.

An example of this illogical attitude can be seen in one particular tabloid, *The Sun*, particularly in two campaigns run by the newspaper since 2004. On the one hand it has campaigned against the use of speed cameras, complaining that they victimize drivers and can only be justified if used at 'accident black-spots'. On the other hand it launched its 'Campaign for Justice', which argues that tougher sentences are needed for drivers who kill, and that such drivers should face a single charge of manslaughter, whatever the standard of their driving. On the same day that it launched this campaign on page 17, it ran a story on page two complaining about the use of speed cameras which were to replace speed humps (*The Sun*, 16 April 2004). The editors seem blind to the contradiction between their two campaigns. They seem not to categorize speeding as a criminal offence and are of the opinion speeding drivers should not be penalized, whilst at the same time arguing that speeding drivers who kill should face punishment for manslaughter.

Driving offences such as speeding and careless driving are often seen as 'social conventions' rather than as crimes. This view is even shared by those involved in enforcing the laws and punishing the offenders, such as traffic police officers and magistrates. Corbett et al.'s research found that some police officers tend only to treat speeding as a 'real' criminal act when negative consequences ensue (Corbett et al. 1998, 38), and 47 per cent said that how they dealt with speed-limit violators depended on the attitude of D when stopped. In some cases a warning would be sufficient, whereas in other cases education is seen as a waste of time and there is a perceived need, on behalf of the officer, for punishment to result (ibid., 36). Magistrates held similar views, with only 9 per cent being of the opinion that breaking *any* speed limit was 'really a crime' (ibid., 40).

Corbett's experience of research in this area has led her to contend that: 'in Britain speeding has been socially constructed as almost a "non-crime", or at least as not "real" crime' (Corbett 2000, 34). This social construction of speeding and other driving offences as not 'real' crime is extremely problematic. As noted by Elliott and Street, official proscription of conduct is not enough on its own for the citizen to regard it as criminal (Elliott and Street 1968, 137). The difficulty is that where no harm is caused as a result of bad driving or speeding, people seem reluctant to classify the conduct as criminal, whereas where harm is caused they quite readily identify that a crime has been committed because the harm is evident. On the one hand, CDDD can be seen as an aggravated form of dangerous driving and therefore a traffic offence. On the other hand, because a death has been caused, it can be classified as a homicide offence alongside manslaughter. This hybrid nature of CDDD means that unlike other traffic offences it is more likely to be viewed by members of the public as a 'real' crime. This is also true of vehicular homicide offences requiring a lower degree of blameworthiness, such as CDCD and CDUD.

This view of 'causing death' offences as 'real' crime does not depend upon the label given to an offence; rather it seems to be determined by the fact that physical harm has been caused irrespective of the extent to which the driver departed from a safe standard of driving. Brook carried out a survey of attitudes to road traffic law in which he asked a representative sample of the public to rank eight traffic and non-traffic offences in order of seriousness. Injuring a pedestrian whilst driving carelessly was ranked the most serious of the eight offences, while driving after drinking too much was placed second. The non-traffic offences of burglary, vandalizing and shoplifting were placed in third, fifth and seventh place respectively. Speeding (driving at 50 mph in a 30 mph limit) was seen as the least serious of the eight offences, and driving whilst disqualified and driving through a red light were placed fourth and sixth. One reason for this mix of rankings of seriousness amongst traffic offences possibly relates to the extent to which the respondents themselves were likely to have committed each of the offences. Although the respondents may have driven carelessly in the past (with or without realizing it), no doubt very few of them had ever caused injury as a result. Similarly, they are unlikely to have committed burglary, criminal damage or to have shoplifted. On the other hand, it has been found that a high percentage of drivers break the speed limit. In a study of drivers carried out by Corbett and Simon 88 per cent admitted exceeding the 30 mph speed limit by up to 10 mph (Corbett and Simon 1992a, 15). As many as 16.8 per cent admitted to driving over 50 mph in a 30 mph area (ibid.).

Corbett and Simon divided drivers into four groups with different opinions as to what types of traffic breaches constitute a 'crime'. The first group thought a breach of any traffic rule was a crime, although no information is given as to how many interviewees fell within this group. The second group thought that breaches with the potential to cause harm were crimes. The third group required harm to have been caused before they categorized an act as a crime. Finally, the fourth group did not perceive any traffic offence as a crime, supporting this view by the fact that any harm caused by such offences is not intended (ibid., 39).

Evidently, public opinion with regard to drivers who kill is by no means consistent. Brook's findings are particularly surprising in that often, although it may be true that most members of the public have never injured or killed whilst driving carelessly, they may harbour a feeling of 'there but for the grace of God go I'. This was the reason for the creation of a separate offence of CDDD in 1956. However, it should also be recognized that public opinion is constantly changing. There has been little recent research into the public's view of motor manslaughter and CDDD in the UK, but in Victoria, Australia, a public attitude survey was conducted in 1991 in order to inform reform of the law in this area (Law Reform Commission of Victoria 1992, Appendix 3). Respondents were given three scenarios and asked whether the appropriate charge in each would be manslaughter or some lesser offence.

The first scenario was of a drunk-driver knocking down and killing a pedestrian on a pedestrian crossing. According to 89.9 per cent of respondents, the appropriate charge in such a case would be manslaughter. In the second scenario a person who is running late for work overtakes near the crest of a hill, without thinking and ignoring the double white lines, and kills the driver of an on-coming car. In this case 68.1 per cent thought that the driver should be charged with manslaughter, whilst 28.5 per cent thought that a lesser charge would be appropriate. The final scenario was a non-vehicular homicide involving a person who jokingly points a gun at another person without first checking to see if it is loaded. By accident, the gun goes off and the other person is killed. In this instance, 56.1 per cent of respondents thought that manslaughter should be charged. The Law Reform Commission used the results to suggest that the community of Victoria was willing to equate very bad driving causing death with manslaughter, casting doubt on the argument often used to counter such suggestions. It is impossible to say whether the cultural situation in Victoria is sufficiently similar to that in England and Wales to be able to use this as evidence of a universal change in public opinion. However, it does suggest that without testing public opinion we cannot presume that it would continue to provide a reason for a separate offence of CDDD. These arguments will be returned to in the next chapter.

How can this divergence in opinions about traffic offences and their acceptance as 'true' crime be explained? Wells notes that a similar attitude is displayed towards offences regulating other activities, such as health and safety legislation in the workplace (Wells 2001). She explains that 'what appears to lie behind the "true" crime/"quasi" crime distinction is an unarticulated argument that, if an activity was not traditionally a matter for the criminal law, then it cannot achieve the status of a "true" crime' (ibid., 7). Corbett echoes this argument and takes it one step further. Not only is traffic crime a fairly recent invention, its historical background further explains why it has failed to achieve the status of 'true' crime. Her argument is that the car began as a luxury and novelty for the rich. When traffic laws were deemed necessary they were introduced with only minimal sanctions because the lawmakers were among the car-owning minority who dealt sympathetically with others amongst their class indulging in new-found driving pleasures (Corbett 2003, 30). There was, according to Emsley, a pervading attitude that 'ordinary' drivers did not commit motoring offences because they were by definition respectable members of society (Emsley 1993, 369). This attitude was possibly perpetuated by the benefits accrued by the elite in supporting the car-manufacturing industry in this country, and the desire not to discourage the use of cars through harsh penalties for bad driving (Corbett 2003, 30). Added to this was the fact that most of the victims of motor vehicles were pedestrians and pedal cyclists from the working classes (Perkin 1976, 138). At that time many collisions were attributed to human error, but this meant error by the victim rather than the driver, whilst other causes were seen to be bad roads and acts of God (ibid., 139). Now that driving is no longer reserved for the elite but is engaged in by the majority of the electorate, most of whom break some of the traffic rules, Corbett argues that there are political reasons for not 'criminalizing the majority' (Corbett 2003, 33; 2000, 36).

In focusing on speeding as one acceptable form of offending, Corbett suggests that because speeding has been constructed as a 'consensual activity seen as legitimate by the majority' it would be a contradiction for it to be seen as 'deviant' behaviour in the way that most other crime is categorized (Corbett 2000, 36). The historical reasons for downgrading speeding as a 'criminal' offence still prevail in modern times, in that unlike other crimes which are seen as deviant behaviour carried out by 'the poor', it is a behaviour committed by the majority of the electorate. A knock-on effect of the prevalence of speeding is that the system has had to adapt to cope with the sheer number of violations, allowing violators to accept fines or plead guilty by post, meaning that they do not go through the normal stigmatic procedure of attending court to be sentenced (ibid., 38). It is not surprising that speeding fines have, as a result, become seen as administrative, rather than criminal, penalties.

## The Psychology of Driving: Who Offends and Why?

Although it is true that speeding is often a 'consensual' activity, and one accepted by far more members of the public than are most other criminal offences, it would be wrong to suggest that it is an offence committed by all drivers, and it would be even less accurate to suggest that drivers can be viewed as one collective group who behave identically. Some drivers commit driving offences and others do not and, of those that do, some commit more offences than others. If the law is to be successful in reducing the number of driving violations committed on the roads it would be helpful to have some understanding of who it is that is more likely to commit driving offences and what motivates them in doing so. Conversely, what are the reasons for drivers' compliance with the law and can the law capitalize on those reasons? Fortunately a great deal of work has been carried out in attempting to answer some of these questions in the field of cognitive psychology. Such research is often used to help inform innovations in driver training, but could equally provide legislators and lawyers with useful information for the drafting and enforcement of driving offences.

### *Identifying Motoring Offenders*

Criminologists and psychologists have approached the task of identifying drivers who commit driving offences in different ways. Criminologists often start by analysing records relating to convicted offenders to establish whether they also have convictions for other types of offences. Psychologists, on the other hand, tend to use self-report methods which employ questionnaires given to a sample of drivers asking them to estimate how often, if ever, they engage in a number of offending behaviours. There are clear weaknesses in using either methodology, and the combined results give an unclear picture of who it is that commits driving offences.

Back in 1964 Willett attempted to divide motoring offenders into two categories: abnormal offenders, who could be seen as deviant in all walks of life, and normal offenders, who were otherwise law-abiding but committed traffic offences because they did not consider them to be crimes (Willett, 1964). Previously it had been thought that traffic offenders were otherwise law-abiding citizens, and so some found it surprising that about 23 per cent of the offenders in Willett's sample had convictions for non-motoring offences (ibid., 299). However, Steer and Carr-Hill questioned this finding, arguing that most motoring offenders were in fact 'respectable citizens' (Steer and Carr-Hill 1967). They took a different approach in analysing Willett's statistics to show that 'normal' motoring offenders commit 'driving' offences such as CDDD and drink-driving, whilst 'abnormal' motoring offenders commit 'dishonest' offences such as driving whilst disqualified or without insurance.

More recently Rose and Broughton have both conducted studies looking at the identity of driving offenders. Rose used three methodologies, one of which was to analyse the Home Office Offenders Index to compare those convicted of serious traffic offences with other groups of offenders (Rose 2000). Three driving offences are classed as 'standard list' offences, which qualify to appear on the Offenders Index: dangerous driving (including CDDD), drink-driving and driving whilst disqualified. It was found that females were involved far less in serious traffic offending than they were in other kinds of offending (ibid., 13). As for the age of offenders, disqualified and dangerous drivers fell within a similar age group to mainstream offenders, whilst drink-drivers were significantly older (ibid., 16).

The study also examined the nature of multiple convictions and found that 15 per cent of disqualified drivers and dangerous drivers were also convicted of a mainstream offence at the court appearance in question (ibid., 29). Previous convictions were most common in disqualified drivers (78 per cent), least common in drink-drivers (40 per cent), whilst 52 per cent of dangerous drivers had previous convictions (ibid., 36). The study also subdivided dangerous drivers into those with previous convictions for car theft and those with other previous convictions. This showed that car theft was an important factor in indicating the relative criminality of dangerous drivers, the implication being that those convicted of dangerous driving may be a mixture of Steer and Carr-Hill's 'driving offenders' and 'dishonest offenders' (ibid., 48).

The main conclusion of Rose's report was that traffic police officers play an important role in apprehending mainstream criminals through enforcing traffic offences. More relevant to the current discussion was the finding that: 'The evidence shows that serious traffic offenders cannot be thought of as otherwise law-abiding members of the public' (ibid., 68). The clear weakness with the methodology of this study was that it relied on a conviction having been obtained in order for a case to come within the sample. It may well be that more mainstream offenders who happen to commit driving offences are detected and prosecuted than otherwise law-abiding members of the public who commit driving offences. The attention of the police may be more readily drawn to the driver of a stolen car who, as a result, is likely to drive in a dangerous manner in trying to evade police arrest. This could result in a disproportionate number of mainstream criminals being convicted of serious motoring offences compared to other members of the public who do not figure in the conviction statistics because they are not apprehended.

Broughton's 2007 study linked offence data from two sources: the Transport Research Laboratory's archive of driving licence information, which includes details of motoring convictions supplied by the DVLA, and the Home Office's Offenders Index. Broughton found that almost 70 per cent of males convicted of one of the three driving offences in 1999–2003 had no conviction for a non-motoring offence during that period (Broughton 2007, 279). This would suggest that the majority of driving offenders, even of serious driving offences, are not otherwise criminally active. However, the research confirmed that unlicensed and disqualified drivers are more likely to have convictions for non-motoring offences. Three-quarters of drivers who committed at least nine non-motoring offences were disqualified at some time between 1999 and 2003 (ibid.). On average a male driver with one conviction for a non-motoring offence committed about seven times as many serious motoring offences as a driver with no convictions (ibid., 280). What Broughton's research seems to confirm is that whilst most convicted driving offenders do not necessarily involve themselves in other types of criminal activity, mainstream offenders are far more likely than the average driver to engage in offending behaviour on the roads (with the exception of speeding). This is unsurprising, since an individual who is willing to commit what is seen to be 'real' crime is unlikely to be deterred from committing offences which are seen to be far less serious by most members of the public.

In conducting research on how the Road Traffic Act 1991 has operated in practice, Pearce's questionnaire of offenders convicted of careless driving, dangerous driving and CDDD included information concerning D's background.

Unlike other research, these questions included details of D's occupation (see Table 6.1).

**Table 6.1 Occupation of offenders**

| Occupation | Careless driving (No.) | Careless driving (%) | Dangerous driving (No.) | Dangerous driving (%) |
|---|---|---|---|---|
| Senior managerial, administrative, professional | 102 | 23 | 46 | 17 |
| Junior managerial, administrative, professional | 77 | 17 | 31 | 12 |
| Supervisory or clerical | 25 | 6 | 15 | 6 |
| Skilled manual work | 91 | 20 | 89 | 33 |
| Semi-skilled or unskilled manual work | 48 | 11 | 29 | 11 |
| Student | 15 | 3 | 10 | 4 |
| Housewife | 13 | 3 | 2 | 1 |
| Unemployed | 17 | 4 | 26 | 10 |
| Retired | 61 | 14 | 19 | 7 |
| Total | 449 | 100 | 267 | 100 |

*Source*: Pearce 2004, 20.

Interestingly, a total of 40 per cent of careless driving offenders classified themselves as in managerial, administrative or professional roles, which one would expect not to have convictions for other criminal offences. Respondents were not asked about their previous convictions, other than their prior driving offences. Twenty-seven per cent of careless driving offenders and 20 per cent of dangerous driving offenders said that they had received penalty points for a speeding offence during the previous four years (Pearce 2004, 21). Eight per cent of careless driving offenders and 18 per cent of dangerous driving offenders had previously been convicted of drink-driving (ibid.).

Corbett and Simon were aware of the problems of using convictions as the basis of a sample to measure unlawful driving behaviour (Corbett and Simon 1992a, 2). They chose to rely on self-report data to measure levels of offending, although this in itself has obvious weaknesses, given that it relies on respondents admitting their involvement in crime. However, this weakness was recognized by the authors, who thought it probable that the respondents underreported their more serious offences (ibid., 12). In addition to this, Corbett and Simon's sample was unrepresentative in that those involved in collisions and young drivers were overrepresented. Despite this, the authors argue that the study goes some way towards describing drivers' patterns of behaviour and their reasons for such behaviour. Respondents were asked to admit whether they 'sometimes' committed any of twenty-five unlawful actions and were allocated offending scores according to their responses. It was found that:

- offending score decreased with age, and within each age group males had higher scores than females;
- there was no relationship between offending score and socio-economic status;
- there was a positive correlation between offending score and mileage driven in the last year;
- respondents with less than 10 years' driving experience had higher offending scores than those with 10 years' or more (this would be largely correlated with the age relationship);
- drivers living in large cities had higher scores than those living in small towns or villages, but offending score was unrelated to the types of roads (motorways, built-up areas, rural) on which the respondent had done most driving in the last year;
- offending score was slightly related to the type of vehicle normally driven (motorcyclists were not included in the sample). Those who drove sports cars had the highest scores, whilst those who drove small saloons had the lowest (ibid., 19).

Although it is clear that driving offenders are far more likely to be male than female, Corbett warns that there seems to be a 'ladette' culture emerging in recent years, based on the fact that the number forming the minority of female driving offenders is gradually increasing (Corbett 2007). Although the number of licensed female drivers increased by only 6 per cent between 1998 and 2003, Corbett found that there was a disproportionate rise in the number of women convicted of offences such as dangerous driving (an increase of 39 per cent), speed limit convictions (an increase of 24 per cent) and drink- and drug-driving (an increase of 19 per cent) (ibid., 252). Corbett notes that it is possible that these increases could be caused by greater enforcement activity rather than a rise in female criminality behind the wheel, but doubts that this is the case given that, with the exception of speeding, offences are detected as a result of collision investigation (ibid.).

Despite the proportion of women committing driving offences increasing, it remains clear that men are far more likely to commit driving offences than women. Krahé and Fenske attempted to measure characteristics likely to induce aggressive driving. Aggressive driving is prone to involve traffic violations such as exceeding the speed limit or dangerous overtaking, and they found that aggressive driving was significantly more common among younger drivers, drivers endorsing a 'macho personality pattern', and drivers owning high-performance cars (Krahé and Fenske 2002). So, although men are more likely to commit driving offences it is those men who can be described as 'macho' and who, for example, emphasize aspects of car speed and sportiness in deciding to buy a car, who are more likely to engage in aggressive driving than 'non-macho' men who are guided by safety considerations in buying a car.

Lawton et al. used a self-report questionnaire to measure the relationship between road traffic violations, social deviance and collision involvement (Lawton et al. 1997a). They also found that men violate to a greater extent than women and, as a result, are involved in more collisions. In addition to gender, mileage is likely to affect the degree to which a driver violates traffic rules, with high violators being more likely to be those drivers who have a high annual mileage. Lawton et al. suggest that this might mean that males commit more violations than females in part because they drive more and thus have more opportunity to do so. Another characteristic which affects both propensity to violate and collision involvement is age. Young drivers were found to be more likely to commit driving violations and be involved in collisions (ibid., 257). There was also a significant relationship between social deviance and violations which, the authors suggest, means that violating behaviour on the roads may be one way in which social deviance manifests itself, although it does not imply that all violators are socially deviant (ibid., 258). This confirms the research conducted by those such as Broughton who use conviction rates to assess the relationship between motoring offenders and mainstream offenders (see above).

### *Understanding Motivations of Driver Behaviour*

We have seen that those who violate traffic rules are not necessarily deviant in other walks of life, but are more likely to be male and young than female or old. Research by psychologists has gone further than identifying who it is that constitutes the offending population, and has tried to discover what it is about people that makes them more or less likely to commit a driving offence. For example, Yagil's findings suggest that the reason why women are less likely to violate traffic rules is that they have a more positive view than men of the content of traffic laws and feel a stronger obligation to abide by them without questioning their validity (Yagil 1998, 131). On the other hand, young men tend to evaluate traffic laws negatively and feel justified in breaching them on the basis that they are illogical, old-fashioned or redundant (ibid.).

Corbett and Simon conducted a study to assess the various reasons for adhering or breaching traffic rules and found that they differed between those who admitted a high-rate of offending and those whose offence rate was much lower (Corbett and Simon 1992b). The top five reasons given by drivers for offending were:

1) confidence in one's own skill and control;
2) a wish to decide driving actions for oneself rather than be bound rigidly by rules;
3) safety: perceiving the action as carrying little risk of a collision;
4) being in a hurry or under pressure (from work);

5) inadvertence: offending without realizing it; not concentrating; not thinking about it; misjudgement. (This reason for offending was offered more by low-rate offenders than by high ones.) (Ibid., 541.)

The top five reasons for not offending were:

1) safety: perceiving action as carrying a risk of accident (especially in relation to drink-driving and red-light-running);
2) fear of the penalty (especially drink-driving);
3) chance of being caught;
4) offence (drink-driving and speeding) would reduce driver's control;
5) consideration for other road users.

In sixth place was: 'Morality, respect for law, wish to stick to rules' (ibid., 542).

Many of these reasons are interlinked. For example, Corbett and Simon note that those who are more likely to break the rules are able to justify this on the basis that to do so is not 'immoral' because the driver feels in control and is confident that no-one else's safety will be put at risk (ibid., 544). Those who abide by the rules, on the other hand, see committing a breach as creating a safety risk for others and so rationalize that to do so would be immoral. However, this issue of morality was not in itself enough to determine whether an individual would breach a traffic rule or not (ibid.). The risk of getting caught was seen as central to the decision of whether to go ahead with the breach or not, meaning that a driver's perception of the risk of getting caught was a principal factor in the decision. This research suggests that there are two separate motivations for desisting from committing driving offences: fear of getting caught and attitude towards the morality of offending. If drivers could be persuaded that (a) they are likely to get caught if they offend and (b) whether or not they get caught offending is wrong because it creates a risk to other road users, then offending might be reduced. However, the latter reason for adhering to the rules will be difficult to instil in drivers, given that many reject the suggestion that their offending could harm others.

Indeed, sometimes drivers have been found to argue that committing a particular violation would be safer than adhering to the law. Forward found that drivers who intended to speed in an urban area believed the outcome would be positive and, of these violators, some described themselves as a better and safer driver if they followed the flow of the traffic rather than the speed limit (Forward 2006, 416). Underlying the view that committing a driving offence is a 'safe' thing to do is, however, the fact that drivers are seemingly incapable of assessing their own driving ability realistically. Svenson found that drivers tend to estimate their ability as better than average (Svenson 1981). It is impossible that the majority of drivers are better than the 'average' driver, and this finding is central to the understanding of justifications for driving violations. It has been found that even drivers with advanced training (advanced police drivers) hold the opinion that they are better drivers than other expert drivers who have received the same level of training (Waylen et al. 2004).

McKenna et al. asked drivers to make judgments of their own and the average driver's skill in 20 different driving scenarios (McKenna et al. 1991). The results showed that males tend to rate themselves higher than females rate themselves with little difference between the sexes on their rating of the average driver (ibid., 48). Drivers seemed to have a fairly uniform view of how skilful the average driver would be in different situations, with both men and women in agreement that the average driver is skilled when carrying out a simple manoeuvre such as a hill start. Similarly, there was agreement that the average driver is relatively poor in adapting to adverse conditions (ibid., 49). However, in looking at how drivers perceived their own driving behaviour in relation to the 'average' driver, Manstead et al. found a degree of false consensus in the number of violations committed (Manstead et al. 1992). They found that those who commit traffic violations overestimate the number of other drivers who also commit such violations, whilst those that did not commit such violations underestimated how many others did commit such violations (ibid., 522).

Corbett and Simon's number one reason for violating a traffic rule, 'confidence in one's own skill and control' (Corbett and Simon 1992b), can be explained by this prevailing opinion that drivers tend to see themselves as possessing a degree of skill over and above that of the average driver. If the rules of the road are designed for the average driver, whose ability to adapt to the prevailing road conditions is poor, then D may feel that they have no application to D's own driving since, unlike the average driver, D is far more capable at adapting to the prevailing road conditions (for example). Corbett et al. have applied this theory to speeding and found that Ds feel that their accident risk is the same when speeding as when keeping to the limit, provided that they feel in control (Corbett et al. 1998, 48). Ds can justify their offending to themselves on the basis that they have not created a risk to other road-users since their own skill can ensure that any risk is avoided. A clear theme emerges from psychologists' research suggesting that drivers are comfortable to violate traffic rules as long as they feel in control.

McKenna has found that what he terms the 'illusion of control' is the key factor explaining why people tend to think that negative events such as collisions only happen to other people (McKenna 1993). He conducted two experiments, the results of which suggested that first, individuals perceived themselves to be much less likely to be involved in an accident when they were driving then when they were a passenger (ibid., 43) and second, that what is important is the level of control the individual perceives as a driver because drivers believe that through the exercise of personal skill they can create relative immunity to collisions (ibid., 47). The difficulty this creates is that if individuals perceive that particular negative events are less likely to happen to them then it is possible that they will pay less attention to risk-related information and be less motivated to engage in self-protective behaviour (ibid., 44). Corbett and Simon concur:

> The problem is that the feeling of control may have something of an illusory quality to it. ... Convincing drivers that there can be a disjunction between perceived and actual control, such that even above-average drivers are not immune from accidents,

could prove difficult .... Countless offences are reinforced by the lack of an accident .... (Corbett and Simon 1992b, 547)

Even where D has overestimated the degree of control and skill D possesses and a collision results, D may be reluctant to recognize or admit that D's driving was the cause of the collision. People generally, it has been suggested, are more likely to assign responsibility to someone for an accident as the consequences of the accident become more serious. Walster tested this hypothesis and purported that the results of her experiment supported it, suggesting that people are more likely to attribute a collision to the victim in more serious cases because this is reassuring in that they can be distanced from the victim, and thus the likelihood of experiencing such a negative event themselves in future, on the basis that they are different from the victim and would have behaved differently in the circumstances (Walster 1966). This theory became known as the 'defensive attribution theory'.

However, Walster's conclusions were questioned by Shaver, who was unable to replicate her findings in similar experiments, and who herself came to the conclusion that 'avoidance of *blame* for an accidental occurrence is more important than avoidance of the outcome itself. Thus responsibility is attributed not to the person potentially at fault but to "chance"' (Shaver 1970, 112). Shaver's research suggested that whether a collision would be attributed to the fault of someone involved in the collision or to chance would depend on who it was that was making the judgement. This was confirmed more recently by Stewart, who reported that drivers generally attribute the responsibility for their crashes to other drivers and are more likely to make such attributions when their crashes involved injuries that necessitated medical treatment (i.e. were more severe) (Stewart 2005, 686). It was also shown that drivers are more likely to accord factors beyond their control, such as weather and road conditions, greater responsibility in crashes for which they accepted responsibility compared to crashes that were attributed to other drivers (ibid., 687).

The fact that drivers, as human beings, tend to attribute negative events to factors outside their control (whether that be the environment or other drivers) means that even when over-confident drivers are involved in collisions, suggesting that their confidence is unfounded, they may still be unwilling to accept that their own driving can be blamed for the collision. Pearce's research found that 36 per cent of careless drivers and 37 per cent of dangerous drivers claimed that the incident leading to their conviction was caused or made worse by another person's actions (Pearce 2004, 23). Perhaps in the case of fatal collisions, where a full police investigation into the causes of the collision are able to highlight D's contribution to the event and where a court of law can use such evidence to attribute the collision to D's driving, the message can be brought home to D that D is at fault and ought not to continue to drive in that manner. However, in cases where luckily a fatality has been avoided it may be that D will feel able to continue to drive as before and will not learn from the event. Unfortunately Pearce's findings are unable to confirm whether this is the case, given that the figures for careless driving offenders do not identify which were involved in fatal collisions, and the number of respondents convicted of CDDD was too low to be representative. Her findings did show, however, that 74 per cent of those who blamed the collision on someone else were surprised to be convicted at court (ibid., 30). Respondents reacted in very different ways to the collisions they were involved in, with some respondents (for example, 34 per cent of dangerous driving offenders) feeling miserable or devastated for over a year (ibid., 25).

Other research has looked at what, if anything, is likely to reduce drivers' risk-taking behaviour.

*Risk homeostasis theory* Wilde argued that individuals each have their own preferred level of risk and will adjust their behaviour to correlate with that desired level (Wilde 1982). Thus in the case of driving, a D will likely accelerate to such a speed that D feels subjectively matches the level of risk with which D is comfortable, or will slow down if that level is exceeded. The significance of the 'risk homeostasis theory' for road safety is that it suggests that the only way to reduce the collision rate is to increase drivers' desire to feel safe; other countermeasures such as traffic laws, safer vehicles and ergonomically designed roads (for example, speed humps), are unlikely to have the desired effect. All that is important is the subjective risk perceived by drivers.

Adams notes that objective measures of risk are elusive (Adams 1995). In a similar vein to Wilde he argues that because of the phenomenon of 'risk compensation', laws may be ineffective in promoting road safety. One example he provides is that of the seat-belt law introduced in England in 1983. Adams doubts the actual effectiveness of the law in preventing road deaths, arguing that although seat belts may be effective in saving lives in the event of a collision, the very existence of the law may have contributed to drivers taking more risks so that they are now more likely to have a collision. He argues that the added sense of security provided by belts encourages more heedless driving, so that although the driver him or herself may be safer in the event of a collision, other road users, particularly pedestrians, are put at greater risk (ibid., 121). Risk compensation also operates in relation to engineering improvements introduced to improve the safety of roads and vehicles. If drivers feel that the environment in which they are driving is safer, this produces a behavioural response in the driver who then creates more risks when driving (ibid., 141).

Others, however, have rejected Wilde's risk homeostasis theory and Adam's risk compensation theory. McKenna argues that the fact that the collision rate has been continuously falling, particularly following the introduction of seat-belt legislation, fundamentally undermines risk homeostasis theory (McKenna 1988). McKenna claims to have adduced evidence which contradicts the theory and discusses methodological issues surrounding this, but also provides theoretical reasons for why the risk homeostasis reason is wrong. First, he argues that the theory is 'unable to capture the complexity of human risk perception', since people do not have the required sensitivity to low probability events to be able to adapt their behaviour to their desired level of risk (ibid. 479). The difference between perceived risk and objective risk is too great. Secondly, he argues that the theory cannot be correct since collisions frequently occur when D is unaware of risk-taking. Risk is an *outcome* of decision-making, not a *goal*. If most drivers consider themselves safer and more skilful than the average driver, as found by Svenson, and they also think that collisions are negative events that happen to other people, they are unlikely to behave in a way that is solely influenced by considerations of risk (ibid.).

Fuller, on the other hand, suggests that Wilde was to some extent right in claiming that feelings of risk are a critical determinant of driver behaviour, but that what is more important in influencing driver behaviour is task difficulty (Fuller 2005). Task difficulty is determined by two groups of factors: those affecting driver capability (which include biological characteristics as well as training and experience) and those affecting the driving task demand (such as environmental factors and other road-users). The main way that drivers adapt their task difficulty is by adjusting their speed, which is likely to decrease when other variables arise to increase the difficulty of the driving task (ibid.). This explains why drivers tend to slow down when they talk on their mobile phones whilst driving, since the increase in task difficulty caused by having to concentrate on a telephone conversation needs to be offset by decreasing the task difficulty by way of adjustment in speed.

*The theory of planned behaviour* Whilst there is some disagreement over the validity of risk homeostasis theory, another theory has been widely accepted as being valid in discussions of what affects drivers' behaviour. Ajzen was the first to develop the theory of planned behaviour (TPB) (Ajzen 1985), building on Fishbein and Ajzen's theory of reasoned action (Fishbein and Azjen 1975) and, although it has been criticized for lack of clarity of meaning, it has a high degree of support (Forward 2006, 413). The TPB assumes that people engage in behaviours if the expected outcome is perceived to be of benefit to the individual, and can be likened to rational choice theory espoused by criminologists. According to the TPB, intention or willingness to perform certain behaviour is determined by a combination of attitude, subjective norm and perception of control. The TPB has been applied to driving violations by a number of researchers including Parker et al., who provide a clear indication of how the theory operates in this area (Parker et al. 1992b).

Parker et al. tested the TPB against four driving violations in interviews: drink-driving, speeding (40 mph in a 30 mph limit), close following and dangerous overtaking. It was found that respondents had a negative attitude towards all four violations, although speeding was viewed less negatively than the other three (ibid., 120). In terms of subjective norm, which measures the individual's perception of the normative pressure on him or her to perform the behaviour, it was found that respondents thought that almost all their significant others would disapprove of the violations, with the exception that young drivers thought that their peers would approve of most of the violations (ibid., 121). It was also the case that males felt less normative pressure to avoid drink-driving than women did and all respondents felt more normative pressure to speed at night than in the day (ibid., 124). In terms of control beliefs, this factor measures an individual's perception of the degree to which performance of the behaviour is under his or her volitional control. Parker et al.'s results showed that older respondents felt it was easier to refrain from committing the violations than did younger respondents and felt more in control. Females rated it easier to refrain from drink-driving and speeding than males did, but males found it easier to avoid driving too close to the car in front than women did (ibid.).

In building on this research, Parker et al. found that perceived behavioural control was the most important single predictor of drink-driving and speeding (Parker et al. 1992b). They found that those who felt less in control of their own actions rated themselves as more likely to commit violations (ibid., 100), implying that drivers would not take responsibility for their offending. Parker et al. suggest that the implications for driver training and road safety are that the message needs to be conveyed to drivers that it is possible to make progress on the roads without committing violations, and that drivers have to take responsibility for their own driving behaviour (ibid., 99). The main use to which the TPB has been put, however, is in creating a typology of driver behaviour, distinguishing primarily between 'violations' and 'errors' through the development of the Driver Behaviour Questionnaire.

*Distinguishing errors and violations* The Driver Behaviour Questionnaire (DBQ) was developed in Manchester and first used by Reason et al. (1990), since when it has been modified by numerous researchers. The original DBQ was developed to explore possible distinctions between aberrant driving behaviours, based on a distinction of violations and errors which Reason developed in writing about human error in other contexts such as major accidents in transport and the workplace (Reason 1990). Error is defined as a: 'generic term to encompass all those occasions in which a planned sequence of mental or physical activities fails to achieve its intended outcome, and when these failures cannot be attributed to the intervention of some chance agency' (ibid. 9). Errors encompass slips, lapses and mistakes. Slips and lapses result from a failure to execute a plan, whilst mistakes are failures in the judgemental and/or inferential processes involved in planning and action (ibid.). Violations can be distinguished from errors on the basis that violations involve deliberate deviations from rules (ibid., 195). An example of a violation when driving would be to become impatient with a slow driver in the outer lane and overtake on the inside, whilst to underestimate the speed of an on-coming vehicle when overtaking would amount to an error (Reason et al. 1990, 1318).

The DBQ used to test this distinction in the context of driving contained 50 'items' or scenarios covering a range of behaviours incorporating different examples of errors and violations. Each item was also allocated one of three risk categories: A – no risk to other road users, only embarrassment or inconvenience for the perpetrator; B – some possibility of risk to others; C – a definite risk to others (ibid., 1319). Respondents were asked if they had experienced each of the items, and the results demonstrated differences in the commission of dangerous errors and violations. This distinction, although not one that can be described as 'hard and fast' (ibid., 1316), has become crucial to the understanding of driver behaviour in subsequent research. It was shown in this first DBQ that violations declined with age and were thus more likely to be committed by the young, whilst errors were not predicted by age. Men were found to commit more violations than women, whilst women seemed to be more error prone than men, although the type of errors committed by women tended to be harmless lapses. Of most interest was the finding that those who reported the most violations also tended to rate themselves as particularly skilful drivers, suggesting that these subjects:

> [B]elieve that a good driver is someone who can 'bend the rules'. Drivers who violate may see themselves as skilful enough to take risks (or, perhaps, to behave in ways which would be risky only for 'less skilful' drivers). Alternatively, drivers who violate may come to think of themselves as good drivers because they get away with what they do. (Ibid., 1330)

Reason et al. suggested that the implications of these findings were that:

> If it can be said that errors and lapses on the roads involve failures of cognitive competence (e.g., failures of the effective deployment of attention as a result of inadequate training, bad habits, or the distracting effects of mood), and that violations on the roads involve motivational factors (e.g., trading the risk of a violation against the benefits of rapid progress, driving in accordance with a valued social image, or of indulging in self-expressive driving), then it would seem that the design of remedial strategies could benefit from taking this cognitive/motivational distinction into account. (Ibid., 1331)

So, whilst training courses could be used to help reduce the number of errors committed on the roads, violations would require alternative countermeasures. The suggestion was that violations amongst young male drivers may stem from peer group values, and so would need to be countered by altering the attitudes of targeted age groups to specific kinds of violations (ibid.).

Subsequent research explored this distinction between errors and violations, sometimes adapting the definition of the terms to take into account new empirical results. Many of the findings described above relating to the identity of traffic offenders and the motivations behind such offending were obtained through use of the DBQ. Lawton et al. made a distinction between 'ordinary violations' (breaches of the Highway Code) and 'aggressive violations' (Lawton et al. 1997b), whilst Mesken et al. distinguished between 'interpersonal violations' (which included aggressive violations and behaviours such as overtaking on the inside and pushing in at the last minute) and 'speeding violations' (fast driving and making progress) (Mesken et al. 2002). It was found that these last two types of violations result from different motives. Interpersonal violations are likely to be caused by a lack of respect for other road users' rights, and a possible intention to cause harm (either physical or psychological). In legal terminology it would be useful to subdivide this category into those interpersonal violations that merely display a lack of respect for others and those that involve intention to harm, since the latter would, in law, amount to an offence against the person such as assault, whilst the former would only amount to a driving offence. It was found that speeding violations, on the other hand, are mainly committed because D wants to get to D's destination in time or because speed causes positive feelings (ibid., 481).

In the same research Mesken et al. distinguished between 'active crashes' and 'passive crashes' and explored whether errors or violations could be seen as predictors of either type of crash. Active crashes are those in which D takes responsibility for being a primary cause of the collision, whereas passive crashes are those where D blames a third party. It is important to note that the methodology used required participants to make their own assessment of the crashes they were involved in, in that an objective assessment of the cause of the crash might not tally with that provided. The results surprisingly suggested that errors may be predictors of active crashes whilst interpersonal violations can predict passive crashes, a finding that conflicts somewhat with Parker et al.'s results showing a link between violations and active loss-of-control accidents (Parker et al. 1995b, 579). Mesken et al. explain this by suggesting that those who report errors also see themselves more easily as the 'guilty party', whilst those who commit interpersonal violations consider themselves to be 'error free' and are not likely to take responsibility and therefore report less active crashes, blaming the other party for a crash (Mesken et al. 2002).

Parker et al. found a clear link between the self-reported tendency to commit violations and collision involvement (Parker et al. 1995a, 1044). Conversely, they found no evidence for the existence of a clear link between reported error-proneness and collision involvement. This would suggest that violations are particularly dangerous and are the behaviours that drivers must be dissuaded from committing. Parker et al. agreed with the conclusions of the original DBQ that violators are likely to need persuading to desist from committing violations in order to change their behaviour, since training is unlikely to be effective (ibid., 1045). These findings will be used in the following chapter to help inform suggestions for law reform in the field of driving offences.

## Achieving the Aims of the Criminal Law in Improving Road Safety

Research by criminologists has shown that drivers who violate traffic rules do so because they reject the validity of the rules, which they do not accept as constituting 'real' crime or wrongful behaviour. They value the feeling of control and prefer to apply their own code of conduct when driving rather than adhering to one that they feel must have been designed for the 'average' driver, who is less skilful than they are themselves. As long as the road conditions and speed at which they are driving do not surpass a level of task difficulty with which they feel comfortable, they are unmotivated to adhere to the rules of the road. These drivers, whose violating may well lead to collisions, require interventions to change their attitude towards driving in order to alter their behaviour, and can be distinguished from drivers who inadvertently engage in risk-taking through the commission of errors, who may hold positive attitudes towards traffic rules but who require remedial training to reduce their bad driving. The suggestion implicit in these findings is that the criminal law should treat these two categories of drivers differently.

If it is agreed that punishment must seek both to reduce offending behaviour and satisfy retributivist considerations, then it can be seen that the current law fails in its task at various levels. The first problem is that the law is failing in its primary task of educating the public through censure because traffic offences are not seen as 'real' crime. To take von Hirsch's concept of the preventive function of the criminal sanction, which is that it supplies a prudential reason that supplements the normative reason not to engage in the proscribed conduct (von Hirsch 1993, 13), it can be seen that currently drivers have, insofar as they perceive a risk of detection, the prudential disincentive not to drive badly, but do not recognize the normative reason, since they do not accept the sanction's message that bad driving is reprehensible.

In relation to the question of retribution and desert theory, drivers will not be seen as 'deserving' punishment for bad driving if driving offences are not seen as 'real' crime. The exception to this comes with the vehicular homicide offences, since in contrast to the normal view of bad drivers, those who cause death are seen as deserving a high degree of punishment to reflect that death has been caused. It has been argued above that punishment based on retribution must focus on the blameworthiness of the driver through the taking of risks, rather than on the chance occurrence of harm. If drivers are to be seen as deserving of punishment, attitudes towards driving offences need to be altered in order to highlight the moral wrongness in creating danger to others on the roads, whether or not the risk materializes.

In relation to the question of deterrence, the problem is that under the current system deterrence is only likely to work once harm has been caused due to the occurrence of a collision, by which time it is too late. Motorists may well be deterred by the current penalties available for dangerous driving, if they believe it likely that their dangerous driving will be detected and prosecuted. However, two obstacles to the achievement of such deterrence present themselves. Firstly, unless death or serious injury results from a piece of bad driving it is unlikely that it will be detected. Secondly, there is some disagreement amongst those involved in the prosecution of cases as to what behaviour amounts to dangerous and careless driving (see Chapter 2 above). The implication is that the standard of the 'competent and careful driver' is not readily identified, either by the police, lawyers and the courts, or by members of the driving public. If potential offenders are ignorant as to the meaning of the offence, how can they be deterred from committing it? The final chapter of this book will explore ways in which the law should be changed in order to deal with these difficulties.

Chapter 7

# The Future of Road Traffic Offences

## Introduction

Earlier chapters of this book gave an account of the law on various driving offences, then Chapter 6 explored what the criminal law ought to be striving to achieve in criminalizing bad driving and what is known about those drivers who currently flout the law. This chapter will firstly attempt to employ the knowledge provided by researchers in the field of criminology and psychology in order better to define the general offences of dangerous and careless driving and increase the potential for the law to achieve the aims set for it in improving road safety. The focus here is on the offences discussed in Chapter 2 which, from the empirical work conducted by the author amongst others, appear to cause prosecution lawyers the most difficulties in bringing drivers to justice. Whilst the law on drink-driving can be improved, primarily by way of reducing the legal blood alcohol concentration (BAC) level from 80 mg/100 ml to at most 50 mg/100 ml and by introducing random breath testing in order to increase drivers' perceptions of the likelihood of getting caught, it is generally accepted that attitudes to the law on drink-driving are positive, and that drivers recognize normative motives for desisting from drink-driving (although a caveat should be added in that there is a need to maintain and reinforce the message directed at younger drivers).

Speeding, on the other hand, does not induce anywhere near the same degree of moral censure amongst the motoring public, and attitudes towards the offence require manipulation in order that drivers recognize the normative reasons for not speeding. However, it is likely that education and training have far more potential to achieve this goal than any amendment to the law on speeding itself. Politically it is a sensitive issue, and whilst speed cameras can increase the perceptions of the likelihood of getting caught they can at the same time damage relations between drivers and the police. Whilst it is common to hear the justification for placing a speed camera as relating to the location of an 'accident black spot', the danger is that motorists will only be deterred from speeding in such locations and will continue to offend in locations they know to be camera-free. A policy of secretly placing cameras at random locations in order to instil in drivers the fear that they could be caught anywhere could prove effective in promoting a more uniform observance of the speed limit, but the danger is that this could alienate drivers even further. It is also important that cameras do not replace police patrols on the roads altogether, since other forms of bad driving can only be detected by human observation.

This is particularly true of bad driving that may amount to careless or dangerous driving: offences which commonly are detected following the occurrence of a collision providing evidence of a departure from the acceptable standard of driving. Physical evidence obtained from the scenes of collisions may be one of the best ways of proving these offences, but eyewitness evidence from police officers (particularly if supported by video camera evidence) is another effective method of securing convictions. Readers are reminded that the test for careless driving is driving that falls below the standard of a competent and careful driver, whilst the test for dangerous driving is driving that falls *far* below that standard, and creates a risk of injury or serious damage to property. These tests are entirely objective. Part of the difficulty is, however, that the standard of driving required of the 'competent and careful' driver is not readily identifiable and this issue will be the focus of the first part of this chapter. Once a proposal for reforming the law of careless and dangerous driving has been put forward, the discussion will turn to the question of how the law should deal with bad drivers who cause death. It will be argued that there is little need for separate vehicular homicide offences, since the main aim of the criminal law in this area is to improve road safety and reduce risk-taking on the roads, and the focus in determining liability should be on the blameworthiness of drivers.

## Reform: Deterring and Educating Motoring Offenders

Given that many serious traffic offenders are otherwise law-abiding people, it would seem that one of the best ways in which to improve compliance with the law would be to encourage a change in attitude towards driving offences in order to bring them within the realm of 'real' crimes. This was something advocated by both Willett (1973) and Macmillan (1975), and since these authors' publications a huge shift has occurred in public attitudes towards the offence of drink-driving. Little change has occurred in attitudes towards other offences such as careless driving, dangerous driving and speeding, however. As noted by Parker et al.: 'The long, expensive but ultimately quite successful campaign to change drink-driving attitudes and behaviours in the UK provides an instructive example of how much time and effort will need to be expended in order to change attitudes towards other driving violations' (Parker et al. 1995a, 1045).

In Chapter 6 it was noted that researchers have found that drivers tend to have their own personal code of driving standards quite separate from the rules imposed on them by statute and the Highway Code, a finding similarly presented by Dix and Layzell in a study of police responses to offending behaviour on the roads (Dix and Layzell 1983, 29). Such hypotheses cast doubt on the potential effectiveness of the current tests for the offences of dangerous and careless driving, which require an offender's driving to be measured against that of the 'competent and careful' driver. As was also seen in Chapter 6, most drivers assess themselves as being more skilful than the average driver, and this is particularly true of those who commit violations, who also tend to overestimate the number of other drivers who likewise offend. Since drivers who offend tend not to judge their driving as anything less than above average, and therefore see themselves as more than competent, they do not identify themselves with others who, in carrying out the same manoeuvre, might be judged to be less than competent simply because they do not possess the same degree of skill. Thus, the first problem is that the definition of the offences is likely to fail to deter those who are most likely to offend because, even if they are aware of the offence definitions (which in itself seems unlikely), they will not see the offence as applicable to them. An additional problem is that where an offence is committed, those decision-makers within the criminal justice system whose responsibility it is to decide whether there is a realistic prospect of conviction in order to charge (Crown prosecutors) and whether they ought to convict (magistrates and juries) are likely to find the application of the objective test difficult without comparing D's driving with their own and it will necessitate some degree of subjective judgement (Pearce et al. 2002, 35). In essence, the problem has been summarized by District Judge Wallis, who has described the concept of the 'competent and careful driver' as 'mythical' (DJ Wallis, quoted in *Milton v DPP* 2007 at para.11).

Duff has similarly identified this problem as one that relates to offences of endangerment generally (whether driving offences or otherwise):

> The drawback is that, unless we can rely on some quite specific shared understandings of what counts as an 'unreasonable risk', and of what kinds of care people should take, in a range of contexts, the standards that courts have to apply will not be the polity's shared standards, but the individual standards of each court and its members – which generates the familiar defects of uncertainty in the law's content, and unpredictability and inconsistency in its application. (Duff 2005, 60)

Drink-driving taking the form of driving with excess alcohol under section 5 of the RTA 1988 avoids this problem by setting a concrete, measurable limit above which an offence will be committed, promoting certainty, predictability and consistency. This may have contributed to the success of drink-driving as an offence. Whilst education has probably played a major part in changing attitudes to drink-driving, it has also been argued that the law itself has been used as a tool to manipulate the morality of drink-driving which, when first introduced as an offence, was not seen as 'wrong'. In Chapter 5 it was seen that there is even less tolerance of drink-driving in Sweden, probably because of the strict approach taken by the law from an early time. This has been somewhat of a Scandinavian tradition. In 1966 in Norway the legal BAC had already been set at 50 mg/100 ml, and Andenaes reported that the courts were extremely consistent in giving prison sentences for violations (Andenaes 1966). This, he suggested, was the source of differing attitudes to drink-driving amongst Norwegians and Americans: 'It is … my feeling – although I am here on uncertain grounds – that the legislation has been instrumental in forming or sustaining the widespread conviction that it is wrong, or irresponsible, to place oneself behind the wheel when intoxicated' (ibid.). At that time the message had not permeated American society because, Andenaes asserted, the law there took a far less strict approach to drink-driving.

The message has now got through to most of the citizens of Western countries, through what Braithwaite labels 'effective shaming'. 'Effective shaming' is perhaps another term for 'educational deterrence', and has been directed at offences such as drink-driving, which did not traditionally fall within the category of behaviours deemed to be criminal or immoral (Braithwaite 1989). This, he suggests, 'has for many adults integrated new categories of wrongdoing (for which they had not been socialized as children) into the moral frameworks pre-existing from their childhood' (ibid., 79). Bottoms similarly contends that although traditional crimes involve acts that are considered to be impermissible by society, some criminal laws when first passed do not reflect positive reality but are created in order to change behaviour through their deterrent effect. He argues that:

> the fact of the prohibition, and citizens' evolving response to it, can influence the development of a new strand of positive morality. Something very like this seems to have occurred in relation to drinking and driving: in Britain there is now substantially greater moral disapproval of such behaviour than was the case thirty or so years ago when it was first made a criminal offence. (Bottoms 2002, 25)

Bottoms continues by explaining how this can be achieved, providing a schema of mechanisms underpinning legally compliant behaviour. He identifies four main forms of compliance: instrumental or prudential compliance, constraint-based compliance, normative compliance and compliance based on habit or routine. Of these four mechanisms, he sees normative compliance as pivotal. The suggestion here is that normative compliance is probably the most effective way of reducing the number of traffic offenders, since what is needed is a change in attitude towards the law. Those psychologists who have applied the theory of planned behaviour to the driving task have similarly highlighted the importance of subjective norms in determining driving behaviour, given that this is one of the determinants of behaviour under the theory. For example, Parker et al. have suggested that violations should probably be dealt with by attempting to change attitudes, beliefs and norms (Parker et al. 1995a, 1037). Åberg has specifically noted that an important difference between the attitudes to drink-driving and to speeding is the influence of social norms (Åberg 1998, 212). He argues that in relation to drink-driving social norms are important influences on evaluations of sanctions, attitudes and intentions. In contrast, he was unable to find such an influence of norms among factors affecting drivers' decisions to speed or not (Åberg 1993). It is thus useful to examine more closely how normative compliance can be promoted.

Bottoms identifies three subtypes of normative compliance. Firstly, normative compliance will be achieved through acceptance of or belief in a social norm. The examples he gives are the norms against assaulting others or taking their property without their consent. In relation to traffic offences it can be argued that the relevant norm is the norm against endangering the lives and safety of others. It is important that others' safety is seen to be endangered, since drivers may feel entitled as a question of autonomy to take risks if it is only their own safety they see as being at risk. Although a norm against endangering the lives of others is probably generally accepted by members of the public, the problem is that they do not necessarily associate what they see to be fairly minor traffic offences with the endangerment of others. As identified by Riley, education of the public was necessary before many drivers accepted that drink-driving was indeed dangerous (Riley 1985).

Bottom's second subtype of normative compliance is what he terms 'attachment leading to compliance'. This involves the offender forming a relationship to a particular person, group or institution which hold non-criminal values. This is perhaps something over which the authorities have little control, the difficulty being that young drivers perceive less pressure from their peers to avoid committing driving violations than do older drivers (Parker et al. 1992a). The third subtype is legitimacy. This relies on the potential offender recognizing the power of the authority imposing the prohibition. This might be one of the reasons for non-compliance with traffic offences. Although the offences are created through legislation, as are other criminal offences, the way they are enforced may differ throughout the country (Dix and Layzell 1983). In particular, in relation to speed limits, it is the local authorities who determine what the speed limit on a particular stretch of road should be. A further problem is that if those enforcing speed limits fail to abide by them, as has been found (Corbett et al. 1998), this will also undermine the legitimacy of the offence.

Thus, a change in public attitude towards the worst driving offences is needed in order to achieve normative compliance with the law. A combination of normative compliance and instrumental compliance will be most effective, the latter taking place in the form of deterrents such as imprisonment, penalty points, disqualification and fines. In order to improve normative compliance, however, the public need to be better educated about the dangers in driving in certain ways and about the law itself. Burgess has used the work of Blair in relation to psychopaths to illustrate the need to encourage compliance with road traffic law. In exploring the cognitive development of psychopaths, Blair distinguishes between moral transgressions and social conventional transgressions (Blair 1995). The former are defined by their consequences for the rights and welfare of others, whilst the latter are 'violations of the behavioural uniformities that structure social interactions within social systems' (ibid., 5). Usually people judge moral transgressions as more serious than conventional transgressions. Moral transgressions are not dependent on prohibiting rules to influence behaviour, while conventional transgressions are judged permissible if there is no rule prohibiting them. According to Blair, the moral/conventional distinction has been found in children from the age of 39 months (ibid., 6).

Burgess suggests that traffic laws may be perceived as moral or conventional transgressions, depending upon the viewpoint of the individual concerned (Burgess, unpublished). He provides the example of a speed limit in a built-up area, which may be considered as a convention agreed upon by 'Society' as being arbitrarily 'safe'. However, the implications for breaking the speed limit become more morally based when the increased potential for harm to other road-users and pedestrians is taken into account. The suggestion is that emphasis on the moral justification for traffic law is needed in order to promote observance of the law, which in effect means changing drivers' normative attitude to the law.

Blair's distinction between moral and social conventions brings to mind the distinction drawn by lawyers between *mala in se* and *mala prohibita*. Whilst this distinction is commonly recognized, it has been described as 'elusive' (Husak 2005, 66). A general description of *mala in se* is that they are crimes that are morally wrong in themselves and do not depend on their legal status to suggest that they ought not to be committed. *Mala prohibita*, on the other hand, have been described by Husak as offences proscribing conduct which is not wrongful prior to or independent of the law that defined it as criminal (ibid.). Traditional crimes which have existed for a long time such as murder, theft and assault are accepted as *mala in se*, whilst regulatory offences, particularly those that are strict liability requiring no *mens rea,* are usually categorized as *mala prohibita.* One of the reasons why driving offences are not seen as 'real' crime may be the fact that they are often seen to fall into the category of *mala in prohibita.* This is not true of all driving offences: Duff states that dangerous driving is a *malum in se* on the basis that it is a public wrong (Duff 2005, 54), and even suggests that careless driving (driving without due care and attention) is also a *malum in se* because it exposes others to the unjustified risk of harm (Duff 2002, 102). However, it is not clear the public itself identifies this to be the case.

Norström categorizes drink-driving as *mala in se* because he sees strong moral attachment to the offence, whilst he suggests that speeding is *mala prohibita* (Norström 1981). This is on the basis that moral attachment has no impact on speeding, other than in a reverse direction: drivers tend to rationalize their speeding behaviour on the basis that speeding is not morally wrong (ibid., 60). If offences such as speeding can successfully be portrayed as *mala in se* this might lead to drivers feeling a normative reason to desist from committing them, although Norström suggests that moral attachment may be a rationalization of speeding behaviour, rather than a cause of it (ibid., 64). To achieve such a shift in attitudes would be extremely difficult. Norström's conclusion is that whilst there is now little need for the law to act as a deterrence for drink-driving, since compliant behaviour is ingrained in drivers, more needs to be done to deter speeding since the public mores are insufficiently inhibiting to affect speeding behaviour.

Duff, on the other hand, classifies drink-driving in the form of driving whilst over the legal BAC limit (RTA 1988, section 5) as a kind of 'hybrid' offence combining elements of *mala in se* and *mala prohibita* (Husak 2005), on the basis that the offence is created in order to prevent drivers endangering others, despite the fact that in some cases a D who was technically over the limit could be capable of driving safely (Duff 2002, 102). In such an instance the case would be one of *malum prohibitum*, whereas the offence under section 4 of the RTA 1988, given that it requires impairment of D and thereby creates a risk to others, would amount to a *malum in se*. Speeding similarly hovers between the two categories under Duff's model, since in some cases the offence will be wrong because it creates a real risk to others whilst on other occasions (one supposes where D is driving alone at night with no other road-users around) speeding could be committed 'safely' (ibid.). Thus under Duff's model, an offence is not *mala in se* or *mala prohibita per se*, it requires a value judgement in order to assess whether a particular instance of the offence was wrong because it in fact led to the creation of a risk. However, in classifying careless driving as *mala in se* Duff fails to recognize that the offence definition does not in fact require a risk to have materialized, only that D drove below the standard of a competent and careful driver. Careless driving, then, should also fall within his category of hybrid offences.

Duff has developed his thesis to distinguish between *implicit* and *explicit* endangerment offences (Duff 2005, 59). Explicit endangerment offences are those, such as dangerous driving, which specify the relevant risk in the offence definition (ibid.). For dangerous driving the relevant risk is one of injury or serious damage to property (RTA 1988, section 2). Implicit endangerment offences, whilst created in order to deter risk-taking, can in fact be committed without creating a risk (Duff 2005, 59). One might be tempted to say that the distinction between explicit endangerment offences and implicit endangerment offences equates to the distinction between *mala in se* and *mala prohibita*. However, yet again drink-driving proves to be the exception to the rule here, falling within the category of implicit endangerment offences (the offence can be proved if D was in charge of a vehicle when over the prescribed limit, whether or not there was a risk of D actually causing harm in the particular circumstances) but also being seen as a *malum in se*. Careless driving would come within the same category as speeding, an implicit endangerment offence, given that it does not require a specific risk to have been created. Given that the two offences of careless and dangerous driving are so closely linked, it could be argued that they should be defined in such a way that they *both* fall within the category of explicit endangerment offences. This might help careless driving be seen as *mala in se*, since the creation of a risk would mean that it should amount to a moral transgression. The problem is that, although some such as Duff recognize dangerous driving as a *malum in se*, few seem to agree that it should be seen as 'real' crime.

If driving offences which are currently seen to be social conventions rather than moral transgressions are to succeed in deterring aberrant driving behaviour, it is important that drivers are aware of what constitutes such offences and what are the penalties attaching to them. Dix and Layzell argued for better education about the average or maximum penalties available for traffic offences (Dix and Layzell 1983) and, although the Highway Code now goes some way towards implementing this suggestion by containing a table giving the maximum penalty for various offences, the problem is that many drivers fail to refer to the Code after passing their driving test. Given that the law in this area is continually changing, it is important that enough is done to keep drivers abreast of legislative changes if increased or new penalties are to be an effective deterrent.

More importantly, perhaps, if the key to changing behaviour is to instil normative reasons for desisting from such behaviour (as has occurred with drink-driving), rather than relying purely on punitive deterrence, it needs to be communicated to drivers that there are valid moral reasons why offences such as speeding, careless driving and dangerous driving ought not to be committed. This communication might best be effected through campaigns and other educative means, although there is perhaps potential for the law itself to provide a clearer moral message in the offence structure. One way to do this could be by importing into the definition of offences the concept of *mens rea*, or more specifically, intention, on the basis that this would help identify a transgression as a serious offence. It is suggested that the offences of dangerous and careless driving are in need of reform for the additional reason that they are currently insufficiently defined and fail to communicate to drivers what behaviour it is that each offence criminalizes. The fact that most drivers judge themselves to be better than average and more than 'competent and careful' means that no matter how much effort is given to educating drivers on the wrongness involved in committing dangerous or careless driving, they are unlikely to identify their driving with the prohibited behaviour.

Duff recognizes this mindset that is prevalent amongst drivers and suggests that this can provide a justification for implicit rather than explicit endangerment offences: 'given the risks involved in the activity concerned, given our proneness to misjudgement, we should follow relatively simple rules ("Don't drink and drive"; "Don't exceed the speed limit"), rather than allowing ourselves to decide on each occasion how fast to drive or how much to drink before driving' (Duff 2005, 61). What is being proposed here is that the law could make use of such implicit endangerment offences in defining explicit endangerment offences. Duff explains that under the current law 'the implicit offences lay down rules that are intended to capture part of the content of the standards declared in the explicit offences' (ibid.). If the law could make this connection more explicit, it might be better able to achieve a deterrent effect. Since the aim of the criminal law in this area is to prevent the taking of risks and consequently the causing of harm, the law should concentrate drivers' minds on driving safely and in accordance with the Highway Code. As suggested to the North Review, it might be possible to enact a list of separate offences similar to infringements of the Highway Code. The North Report recognized that such offences might be easier to prove, but the problem as the Review saw it was that such offences would not obviate the need for general bad driving offences (Department of Transport 1988, para.4.19). There might, however, be potential to combine the two approaches to create general offences based on infringements of the Highway Code. It would not be enough to say that all infringements of the Highway Code could be prosecuted as a general driving offence such as dangerous driving, but if this was combined with a further indication of blameworthiness it might be that such an approach could be strengthened.

Pearce et al. argued that in practice the current law operates by distinguishing between those who deliberately take risks and those whose risk-taking is not deliberate (Pearce et al. 2002). This is supported by the CPS *Policy for Prosecuting Cases of Bad Driving*, which lists, for example, 'disregard of traffic lights and other road signs, which, on an objective analysis, would appear to be deliberate' as an example of conduct that would normally support a charge of dangerous driving (CPS 2007b, para.5.27), whilst 'inadvertently driving through a red light' is an example of careless driving (ibid., para.5.32). This is not how the law was designed to operate, since the tests for dangerous and careless driving are entirely objective, but it may be inevitable that in practice people *do* judge those who take deliberate risks differently from those who do not. One reason why driving offences are not seen as 'real' crime is that serious criminal offences usually require intention, or at least foresight of a risk of harm. As has been seen, driving offences are able to depart from this tradition because of their categorization as endangerment offences designed to improve road safety. However, there is scope for treating those who deliberately infringe the law more seriously than those who do so inadvertently. It is generally accepted that intentionally committing an act is more blameworthy, and therefore more wrong, than doing so recklessly or negligently.

Not only is there an instinctive tendency for us to blame drivers who deliberately take risks more than those who do so inadvertently, there are also, as was seen in Chapter 6, good remedial reasons for distinguishing between these types of risk-taking. The distinction between violations and errors, stemming from Reason et al.'s original Driver Behaviour Questionnaire research (Reason et al. 1990), is based on whether the driver intended to breach a traffic rule or not. Psychologists have suggested that because violations and errors involve different psychological processes they need to be dealt with in different ways. A logical extension to this argument is that the law itself should distinguish between violations and errors, in order to exploit this knowledge and improve the law's potential effectiveness in attempting to reduce offending. Merry and McCall Smith have suggested in the context of determining criminal and civil liability for medical accidents that findings from research by psychologists have a role to play: 'legal inquiries are about justice and social utility, and these goals would be greatly assisted if the law were to pay adequate attention to what this information can tell us about how people behave and, most importantly, how they can realistically be expected to behave' (Merry and McCall Smith 2001, 42).

Merry and McCall Smith use Reason's taxonomy of error and violations to construct a classification of five levels of blame to assist in determining whether a medical practitioner should face liability under either tort law or criminal law for harm caused in the course of medical treatment (ibid., Chapter 5). Whilst their second level of blame, based on Reason's concept of errors, could lead to liability under civil law, they present an objection to adopting it for the purpose of determining punishment. A violation should be required for criminal liability, they conclude (ibid.). The central thesis of Merry and McCall Smith's book is that medical incidents currently defined as negligence leading to liability under civil and criminal law do not always involve significant blameworthiness, suggesting that the law too readily holds medical practitioners liable for their mistakes. It is not suggested that the same is entirely true of liability for bad driving, since there is much to distinguish the two activities of driving and treating patients. First, as noted by Merry and McCall Smith, medical practitioners can be contrasted with drivers on the basis that the former act with the intention of helping, whilst a driver who knocks over a pedestrian has no intent either way (to help or to harm) in relation to the particular individual (ibid., 27–8). Secondly, medical practitioners will only face criminal liability if their negligence leads to death, since there are no endangerment offences of negligent treatment the equivalent of careless or dangerous driving. However, Merry and McCall Smith's underlying message that the law must take account of how the human brain works is a valid one.

### *A New Offence Structure Based on Violations and Errors*

As errors by their very nature cannot be deterred, it is common sense that we should not try to use the criminal law to deter them. Note that psychologists' definitions of violations and errors do not depend upon the legal status of particular behaviours, since it may be a rule of the Highway Code that has been intentionally breached in commission of a violation, rather than a particular offence, such as speeding. The law could, however, use the Highway Code as a foundation for creating new general driving offences reflecting the distinction between violations and errors, based on the existence or otherwise of an intention to infringe the rules contained therein (Cunningham 2007).

Where D intentionally breaches a rule, amounting to a violation in psychology terms, this could form the more serious of two general offences. In the absence of such intention, where an 'error' is committed, this could lead to prosecution for a lesser offence. Each of these offences would lead to different legal interventions to reflect the different psychological processes involved in their commission. Errors would normally result in court orders to attend training sessions similar to those currently provided under the National Driver Improvement Scheme as an alternative to prosecution. Unlike the current NDIS, however, the proposed system would require the courts to make the order so that the offence maintains its criminal status. This is a development already provided for by sections 34 and 35 of the Road Safety Act 2006, which allows attendance on training courses to reduce the period of disqualification or number of penalty points imposed for careless driving.

Violations, on the other hand, would result in punishments that are intended to have a deterrent effect, namely disqualification from driving and, in the very worst cases, imprisonment. These could be combined with some educational initiatives with a view to attempting to change offenders' attitudes to their crimes, but the primary aim of the offence would be to convey to offenders the message that they deserve punishment for their wrongdoing and will suffer if they do not heed the warning. The harshness of the penalty should not depend so much on the outcome of the violation (whether a collision or not was caused and, if so, what injuries or fatalities resulted), as much as the severity of the risk taken.

In their research on bad driving offences, Pearce et al. used their own categories, based on the above distinctions, to analyse the distribution of offence charges and convictions. In addition to violations and errors they included lapses and aggressiveness to make a total of four categories. They found that, broadly speaking, violations and aggressiveness normally resulted in charges for dangerous driving, whilst errors and lapses were normally charged as careless driving (Pearce et al. 2002, 46). This would suggest that the proposed offences would fit well with current practice. However, some care would be needed in categorizing bad driving as errors or violations. In Pearce et al.'s discussion of cases not following the general trend a more detailed explanation was given of cases that had been categorized by the authors as violations or errors. Three of the four cases described as 'errors' would seem to be better described as 'violations', since they involved infringements such as overtaking on a bend and knowingly exceeding a 30 mph speed limit by 20 mph (ibid., 48). In one case it was noted that a clear case of a violation (driving at nearly twice the speed limit in a town centre) resulted in the jury convicting D of careless instead of dangerous driving (ibid.). Clearly a new offence structure would have to be defined precisely in order to try to avoid such anomalies in practice.

The predecessor of dangerous driving, the offence of reckless driving, was abolished primarily due to the perception that it was difficult to prove because of the subjective element of the *mens rea* requirement of the offence. In proving recklessness, it was necessary to prove whether D had considered the risk or not and this was said to be too difficult. Dangerous driving was introduced with a purely objective test of negligence in order to avoid such difficulties. Some might object to the proposal of replacing dangerous driving with a 'violation' offence on the basis that this will reinstate the problems experienced in relation to reckless driving because it will require proof of D's state of mind. However, proving *mens rea* in relation to any criminal offence is just one of the elements with which prosecutors might encounter problems and, whilst there are good policy reasons for doing away with the *mens rea* requirements in relation to 'errors' or other offences such as speeding, it can be argued that those reasons do not apply to a serious criminal offence carrying with it threat of imprisonment. Given that 'dangerousness' for the purposes of section 2 of the Road Traffic Act 1988 has itself proved difficult to establish, there seems little to be lost in re-introducing in the most serious driving offence a requirement of *mens rea*, since this may be no more difficult to establish. In the important case relating to recklessness of *G and Another* (2004) Lord Bingham suggested that in cases where *mens rea* is denied, the jury (or bench of magistrates) is able to infer intention 'from all the circumstances and probabilities and evidence of what the defendant did and said at the time' (*G and Another* 2004, para.39). Similarly, the Law Commission has recognized that in some cases the task for the jury in finding intention or recklessness to cause harm is easier than applying the current test for dangerousness of falling far below a certain standard (Law Commission 1996, para.5.33).

If the proposal for an offence based on 'violations' were brought in, the task for the prosecution would be quite different to that faced in relation to reckless driving. There would be no need to prove that D was aware of the risk D had created, only that D was aware that D was breaching a pre-existing traffic rule. This proposal is very similar to one offered by Spencer in response to the North Report in 1988 (Spencer 1988, 713). He was pessimistic about the likely success of the Review's suggestion for the offence of dangerous driving because he saw the proposed test as too vague and predicted that the courts would have difficulty in defining it (ibid.). He noted that:

> Experience amply shows us that it is unworkable to have a vague offence of bad driving, with a *mens rea* requirement that forces the prosecution to prove that the driver realised his behaviour actually created a risk for other road users. But if the offence

> were defined at a low level of abstraction, so that it included driving in any one of a number of ways which are generally recognized as being unacceptably dangerous, a *mens rea* requirement would surely not be unworkable at all. (Ibid.)

Spencer suggested that an offence be:

> drafted in general terms, but incorporating a partial definition expressly putting a number of recurrent cases within the general clause for the avoidance of future doubt: racing another vehicle, overtaking on a blind corner, driving when seriously under the influence of drink or drugs, driving a vehicle with seriously defective steering or brakes, etc. (Ibid.)

However, in order to avoid a statutory provision for an exhaustive list of rules to form the basis of the new offence, it would arguably be simpler for a new statutory provision to refer to the rules in the Highway Code. Although D would not need to have foreseen any risk, what D would be punished for is in fact the taking of a risk, since the rules of the Highway Code exist in order to prevent risk-taking. It is thus justified to punish drivers for the intentional violation of a rule which creates a real danger to others, since in doing so they have created a second-order harm in the form of risk of harm. Given that it is unpredictable whether a particular case of risk-taking will result in harm, the offence would be punishable whether or not a collision resulted. This type of offence construction is preferable to one which relies solely upon the objective question of risk-taking or of falling below a certain standard of driving, because Ds see themselves as sufficiently skilful to commit an action which is objectively risky because they believe they can rule out, or at least minimize, the risk through their own skill. If Ds are instead told that they MUST NOT violate a traffic rule on pain of criminalization, the fact that they do not recognize that their action has created an objective risk does not matter – they should be deterred nevertheless.

Some care would be needed in drafting this law, however, in order to include within the meaning of 'violation' all those acts which warrant punishment. For example, in the case of dangerous overtaking one would want to avoid D using as a defence the argument that D honestly thought that there was sufficient room to complete the manoeuvre without creating a risk to others. In order to include such conduct in the definition of the offence, it would have to be clear that all that was required was that D intended to overtake a vehicle at the particular place where it was prohibited. On the other hand, the law would need to exclude from the offence cases which might technically amount to a violation but where there would be little acceptance that criminal liability for a serious criminal offence was warranted. Merry and McCall Smith suggest that although exceeding the speed limit by one mile per hour would be a violation, few people would describe it as 'reckless' (the level of blame which Merry and McCall Smith argue should be required for criminal liability), whereas most would say that exceeding the speed limit by 50 mph would be 'seriously reckless' (Merry and McCall Smith 2001, 102). The difficulty is in determining how bad a violation would need to be in order for it to warrant criminal liability. Whilst it would be advantageous for the law to be able to establish a clear line that must not be crossed on pain of liability, it may be impossible in practice to enforce such a law. This is a weakness in the proposed offence, particularly given that one of the main reasons for suggesting it is that it would send out a clear message to drivers about what behaviour is unacceptable. However, given that drawing fine distinctions is a ubiquitous problem for the criminal law, this problem should not be insurmountable.

It is suggested that in addition to a subjective *mens rea* element to the offence, an additional test would be that the violation was objectively dangerous. This would equate to the secondary test under the current law that it would be obvious to a competent and careful driver that driving in that way would be dangerous. However, it is suggested that there is no need for a reference to the 'competent and careful driver' and that it would suffice to require that the driving created a risk of harm to others. This would avoid the problem that all cases of intentional speeding, for example, would constitute a violation. Only in cases where speeding created a risk of harm to others would the more serious offence be committed, whilst the offence of speeding would remain to penalize all those who exceeded the speed limit. This though leads to further possible problems. First, a lot of work might be made for the courts in establishing that D's act was objectively dangerous. The presumption is, however, that any breach of the Highway Code is likely to carry with it a risk of danger to others and that only in exceptional cases would D be able to rely on a defence that the breach was safe in the circumstances. Secondly, it is common for drivers to drive within the speed limit, but at a speed that creates a risk because it is inappropriate for the conditions. The new law would have to make it clear that contravention of the rules set down in the Highway Code concerning driving at safe speeds (Rules 125 and 126) would constitute a violation.

For the new law to succeed, the Highway Code would have to be rewritten. Currently, some of the rules within the Highway Code are also statutory requirements, and are identified as such by the words 'MUST'/'MUST NOT'. Others are merely advisory, but some are clearly intended as orders. For example, rules 125 and 126 direct drivers as to the need to reduce speed and allow sufficient stopping distances, whereas rule 124 refers to the legal requirement to drive within the speed limit. It might be desirable that the Highway Code be redrafted to give some rules the status to allow them to form the basis of the new offence, even if they are not themselves proscribed by statute. It would have to be made clear within the Code which rules were relevant to the 'violation' offence.

It would also be necessary for the law to include instances of dangerous driving which under the current law are committed when D drives a vehicle in a dangerous condition. Rules 113–16 provide the law on lighting requirements and rule 98 sets out towing and loading requirements, whilst other regulations appearing in legislation such as the Road Vehicles (Construction and Use) Regulations 1986 may not be mentioned in the Highway Code but, if violated, could cause danger to others and thus fall within the suggested offence. In addition, drink-driving and other forms of impaired driving leading to the creation of risks would be covered by the offence although, as with speeding, drink-driving itself would continue to cover all cases of driving under the influence of alcohol or drugs, allowing the police to step in to prevent harm before any risks are taken.

Given the seriousness of the offence in terms of the risk of harm created (and perhaps caused) in its commission and the blameworthiness of an offender in intending to violate the law, the offence would warrant a fairly high maximum prison sentence, in addition to a mandatory term of disqualification from driving. It is difficult to set the upper limit of such a penalty, but it would warrant a sentence exceeding the current two-year maximum for dangerous driving. The government has suggested raising the maximum sentence for dangerous driving to five years' imprisonment (Home Office 2002) and, although this proposal has not been enacted, five years might be an appropriate maximum for a 'violation'. As for giving the offence a label, 'dangerous driving' could be retained, given that the violation must cause danger to others.

'Negligent driving' might be a suitable label for the offence of committing a driving 'error', although alternatives might be deemed more suitable. Negligent driving would differ substantially from dangerous driving in that there would be no requirement to prove a subjective state of mind. The question then becomes, however, whether the offence should require that a risk of death or serious harm was created, as would be required for dangerous driving. If it was decided that no such risk must have been created this would maintain the distinction present under current law that dangerous driving falls within Duff's category of explicit endangerment offences, whilst careless driving amounts to an implicit endangerment offence. This would further mark out the difference in seriousness between the two offences, justifying the difference in penalty. However, there would then be a problem in distinguishing negligent driving from underlying moving traffic offences such as driving through a red traffic light or speeding. It is therefore suggested that there is a need to incorporate a risk of harm into the definition of negligent driving in order to justify the law taking a different response and to bring the two offences of dangerous and negligent driving into line with one another under the umbrella of explicit endangerment offences.

Negligent driving would exist to encourage drivers to take care in their driving and to remain alert and pay attention at all times. One difficulty that might arise is that, as with careless and dangerous driving, a case of negligent driving is unlikely to come to the attention of the police in the absence of a collision. There seems little that can be done about this. However, it should be reiterated that as an endangerment offence, the police should not shy away from prosecuting in cases where no harm has actually been caused, if sufficient evidence exists. Disqualification would serve as a deterrent in such cases, but, as noted by Parker et al., the main purpose of the law should be to retrain and educate offenders who commit errors (Parker et al. 1995a). In the worst cases a term of disqualification, the length of which would depend upon the severity of the error, could be combined with compulsory attendance on the NDIS. Only once the NDIS had been attended and perhaps a driving test passed would D be able to recover D's licence. It seems that the key to reducing errors is to change drivers' habits through retraining, given that Pearce found that 44 per cent of those guilty of careless driving under current law said that they had been driving in the way that they normally did at the time of their offence (Pearce 2004, 23). Such drivers were more likely to be surprised to be convicted of the offence (ibid., 30), suggesting that they require education concerning what is wrong with their driving.

It is hoped that the suggested offences would achieve the goals of the criminal law in focusing offenders' attention on what exactly they should not do, having the knock-on effect of reducing the amount of risk-taking on the roads. The rules in the Highway Code and other regulations exist to discourage the creation of risk. If a change in the law along the lines suggested here took place, the status of the Highway Code would change considerably. At present an infringement of the Highway Code is not an offence in itself, although it could provide evidence to support a charge of careless or dangerous driving. As a result of this change in status the suggested law would require further educative efforts to be made alongside enforcement of the law. Drivers who may not have referred to the Highway Code since passing their tests would have to become re-acquainted with its contents in order to avoid committing an offence. It might be economically beneficial to distribute new copies of the Highway Code free of charge to all drivers registered with the DVLA. Drivers would then have no excuse not to know the rules and, if the law succeeded in reducing risk-taking, less public money would need to be spent in dealing with road deaths. The benefit of this would far outweigh the cost and inconvenience caused. Those who currently take risks inadvertently would hopefully become more aware of their actions, reducing the number of errors they committed. Those who commit violations would be discouraged from doing so by the penalties that they could face, and, in time, it is hoped that this would lead to a change in attitudes towards the law, as occurred with drink-driving.

Would it work in practice? If one were to apply the proposals to some of the problematic cases within the author's study of road deaths, would the problems be lessened? Taking a case involving excess speed as an example, C18 was a case in which witnesses described D as travelling at speeds of up to 100 mph. D lost control on a dual carriageway when he had to swerve to avoid a car that was crossing the dual carriageway, and collided with a car travelling in the opposite direction. D admitted to exceeding the speed limit (although claimed he did not go above 80 mph) and clearly created a danger to other road users. The prosecution should therefore be capable of proving him guilty of the proposed 'violation' offence (D in this case was in fact only prosecuted for careless driving).

More problematic, however, would be cases involving driver fatigue and inattention. Rule 91 of the Highway Code advises drivers to, amongst other things, 'make sure you are fit to drive. Do not begin a journey if you are tired. Get a good night's sleep before embarking on a long journey'. It is difficult to imagine, however, how such advice could form the basis of a prosecution for the proposed dangerous driving offence. Some of the cases in the author's study of road death incidents might cause difficulties under the proposed offence. In cases such as C23 and C51 involving HGV drivers who failed to see stationary vehicles ahead of them which were visible for periods of at least 20 seconds, the Ds clearly warranted conviction for dangerous driving. In some cases where drivers' hours regulations have been breached, this violation could form the basis of the proposed offence, but in cases where D is merely tired or loses concentration, or is a car driver, it is difficult to see how the prosecution could construct a case against D based only on D's failure to see something in D's path.

Would it then be necessary, or even possible, to create a separate offence of driving when fatigued? Corbett notes that under the current law drivers may feel that the act of driving when tired cannot be serious because it is not unlawful (Corbett 2003, 93–4). She questions what (if any) controls should be placed by legislators on fatigued driving, but is unable to answer the question herself (ibid., 97). It is indeed difficult to provide a solution to this problem. Jones et al. have proposed that a specific offence could be constructed in one of three ways:

1) a general prohibition of dangerous driving while impaired due to fatigue;
2) defining dangerous driving while fatigued as constituting a *prima facie* breach of an existing crime (e.g. that driving while fatigued can be considered reckless); or
3) an offence making it illegal to drive when fatigued over a certain level (Jones et al. 2003, 356).

As was seen in Chapter 2, the second of these has formed the basis of 'Maggie's Law' in New Jersey, where driving with no sleep in the prior 24 hour period is deemed to amount to recklessness. However, any rule requiring a driver to have a certain amount of sleep within a certain time period prior to setting out on a journey would seem unworkable. So too would a rule prohibiting anyone who felt 'tired' from getting behind the wheel of a car, since the issue is far too subjective to form the basis of a prosecution. Jones et al. suggest that the last of their three models would be based on the same rationale as drink-driving laws, but would require the development of a test to do the same job as a breathalyser (ibid., 357). Whilst no such test is currently available, they are confident that research may bring such initiatives in future (ibid.). A study has recently been carried out for the Department for Transport to assess the available sleepiness detection devices on the market (Wright et al. 2007). These are, however, designed to be used by drivers (or commercial drivers' employers) to warn them that they are too tired to drive, rather than by the police to diagnose fatigue in the investigation of a collision. Some of these measure eye activity or head or wrist movement, while others use alternative physiological measures. It is unclear whether there is scope to develop a detection device for enforcement purposes, but at the moment it has been concluded that 'no single method exists that is commonly accepted to detect driver fatigue in an operational context' (ibid., 14). It would clearly be desirable to bring drivers such as Hart, the driver in the Selby rail crash, and some of the defendants in the author's sample, within the realms of the proposed serious offence. Further consideration would be needed as to how this could be achieved.

It is hoped that in time this suggested offence structure would bring enhanced respect for the law of traffic offences. Those guilty of the more serious crime would merit the stigma attached to the label of 'criminal', with the requirement of intention to violate the law, bringing the offence closer to the paradigmatic nature of crime. For those who committed errors and were guilty of negligent driving, their re-education as part of their sentence would hopefully reinforce the justification for their punishment by illustrating to them the necessity to adhere to the rules of the road and the risks involved in failing to adhere to them. Overall, contempt for traffic offences would hopefully lessen, risk-taking on the roads would reduce, and the number of people killed or injured would decrease. The law would not of course eliminate offending altogether, but it would perhaps mean that otherwise law-abiding citizens would desist from offending, leaving offenders who engage in all forms of criminal conduct to become the main perpetrators of traffic crime. An additional and important benefit would be that police and prosecutors would find a real distinction between the two offence levels, solving many of the problems faced by decision-makers in preparing cases for trial under the current law.

### *The Relevance of Consequences*

The proposal to redefine the general driving offences, which are offences of endangerment, does not itself address the issue of how drivers who cause death or injury falling short of death should be dealt with by the criminal law. As explained in Chapter 4, the offence of CDDD was created because of reluctance on the part of juries to convict of manslaughter motorists who killed whilst driving in a grossly negligent manner. The North Review was unable to establish the degree to which the fear of juries failing to convict of manslaughter was justified in 1988 (Department of Transport 1988, para.6.13) and there remains little evidence on this today. In Victoria research has revealed that this fear may be unfounded (Law Reform Commission of Victoria 1992), and there have been suggestions that the same is true in the UK. In its consultation exercise the North Review received conflicting views on whether a separate offence of CDDD should be retained, with the main issue being whether it is appropriate in law to concentrate on the results of bad driving when such results may be fortuitous (Department of Transport 1988, para.6.8).

More recently, in considering the possibility of creating a new offence of causing death by careless driving (CDCD), the government suggested that 'The law in this area can and should demonstrate ... the seriousness with which society takes bad driving and its consequences. There is some evidence that the public is taking a more serious view of these matters. National newspaper campaigns have highlighted the perceived inadequacies in the law' (Home Office 2005a, para.2.20). To support this assertion it referred to an AA survey which found that 81 per cent of people think the law is weak on drivers who kill (ibid.). This indicates that there truly has been some change in public opinion and that it has become more punitive towards drivers who kill. However, this change in opinion seems to have swung too far in the opposite direction, leading to parliament creating an offence which, as seen in Chapter 4, departs from the principles of criminal law generally applicable to serious homicide offences.

The government, in consulting on the possibility of creating CDCD, accepted some of the conclusions that have been drawn in this book. For example, it recognized that, in relation to the capacity for the general offences of dangerous and careless driving to work as a deterrence:

> The apparently strong correlation between prosecution for these offences and involvement in a crash or collision implies that few drivers will be induced to drive more safely merely by weighing up the likelihood of being charged and convicted of the general offences, since they do not expect to crash in the first place. (Ibid., para.2.19)

Having accepted this proposition, it seems contradictory that the government should proceed to propose the creation of an offence, prosecution for which will depend on a driver crashing. The new offence, then, will exercise a retributive rather than deterrent role, attempting to address the perceived problem that: 'The limited penalties available for the lower level offence (driving without due care or reasonable consideration) make it virtually impossible to take account of the consequences of the bad driving at that level. This problem is at its most severe when bad driving at that lower level has caused death' (ibid., para.1.14). The central question for the government was whether the consequences of bad driving ought to be capable of being taken into account in not only sentencing an offender, but in providing a more severe offence label. Given that drivers are unlikely to be deterred by the more severe penalties because they do not foresee a likelihood of crashing (Cunningham 2007), the key to answering this question is to determine whether the contribution of 'luck' or 'chance' in leading to consequences should affect a driver's culpability.

The question of how luck should influence criminal liability is one which pervades much of the criminal law, with commentators taking a view as to whether or not consequences should be relevant to liability. On the one hand, Ashworth argues that the role of the criminal law is to express censure and that the law 'should censure people for wrongs, not misfortunes' (Ashworth 1993, 120). It can be argued that the wrong in the offences of CDDD and CDCD is to have driven dangerously or carelessly, and that the misfortune is to have caused death. On the other hand, there are those who argue that any harm caused by a defendant who has broken the law should be attributed to D in allocating responsibility on the basis that D has 'made his own luck' (Horder 1995). A similar justification for imposing criminal liability for death in the context of constructive manslaughter where death was not foreseen is that in committing a criminal offence, such as an assault, D has changed his or her 'normative position' towards the victim and deserves to be held responsible for the result (Gardner 1998; Clarkson 2000). The author has argued elsewhere that these arguments, even if accepted in relation to assaults, should not be translated into the driving context, on the basis that a driver who commits dangerous or careless driving, unlike a defendant who has committed assault, has not necessarily chosen to break the law, since liability for the underlying offences is based on negligence rather than intention (Cunningham 2007). If, however, the proposal put forward in this chapter to distinguish between violations and errors were taken forward, it could be argued that the deliberation required for a violation would allow for the application of the 'change in normative position' argument to justify a 'causing death by violation' offence. In response, it is suggested that because the intention required for a violation relates to the breach of a traffic rule and not to the creation of a potentially fatal risk, it would remain inappropriate to describe D as changing his or her normative position towards the deceased victim of an ensuing collision in the same way that a defendant charged with manslaughter based on assault changes, in engaging in violent conduct, his or her normative position towards the victim.

The government, in considering whether a new offence of CDCD ought to be created, took a rather inconsistent approach to the role luck ought to play in criminal liability, providing a mishmash of arguments and contradicting itself as to their application. The following quotation from the Consultation Paper starts by seemingly agreeing with Ashworth's point that what is important is the risk-taking involved in bad driving, then brings into the equation the view that drivers' luck is not 'pure', echoing Horder's thesis, before admitting that any number of factors beyond the driver's control might determine whether a collision results in a fatality or not, but concludes by dismissing such factors as irrelevant to determining the law.

> Why should the culpability of bad drivers extend to the consequences of their bad driving, as well as the bad driving itself? For the following reasons. All bad driving involves the taking of risks. Drivers either know, or should know, that they are taking those risks. The culpability lies in the risk taking. The driver who overtakes on a blind bend and manages to avoid a collision is as culpable as the driver who does the same, collides with an oncoming vehicle, and kills its driver. Chance has entered into which driver killed, but it was predictable that, if the manoeuvre were repeated often enough, disaster would result. It is not 'bad luck' for the driver who killed. The driver who did not kill was simply fortunate. In practice, it would be neither right nor practical to deal equally severely with both drivers. The full weight of the law must be reserved for those whose risk taking has its predictable results. Many factors will bear on the outcome of a piece of bad driving. Whether an injured victim dies may turn on how soon the emergency services are able to arrive, or the age and health of the victim. The severity of the injuries, and the likelihood of death, may turn on the age of the vehicle and its safety devices. It is impossible to legislate for all eventualities. The broad framework of the law can justifiably hold drivers to account for the consequences of their actions, however, as well as the criminality of the actions themselves, and fatal consequences are uniquely dreadful. (Home Office 2005a, para.3.24)

It is the uniqueness of the harm of death that is central to the creation of offences such as CDCD (Cunningham 2008), in that instinctively one feels the need to punish a driver far more harshly for the fatal outcome of a collision than for some lesser harm (even if that is paralysis for life), despite the outcome being beyond the driver's control and dependant on a multitude of factors. Whilst it is true that drivers *ought* to know that bad driving can always create a risk of death, the relevant point to make in law is that the offence on which CDCD is constructed does not require foresight of that risk or indeed of any risk to the safety of others.

The fact that it is instinctive to wish to punish those who have caused harm more severely than those that have only risked harm can be explained by the psychological literature discussed in Chapter 6 in relation to 'defensive attribution theory' (Walster 1966). Merry and McCall Smith refer to the natural desire to attribute blame in cases of death as 'outcome bias' (Merry and McCall Smith 2001, 163). They argue that, rather than concentrating on those medical errors which have caused death in order to exact retributive punishment, the law should seek to identify errors of all kinds, whether leading to harm or not, in order to take preventive measures by addressing the problems of those whose behaviour, if left unaddressed, could cause (further) harm in future. The same is true of drivers who commit errors: they do not deserve punishment for the misfortune of death but require retraining. Rather than simply responding to harmful consequences and near misses with the instinctive 'look what you did'/'look what you might have done' response (Duff 2008), the law should be used to good effect in not only pointing out to the offender what he or she 'might have done' but ensuring that a lesson is learnt for the future. This can be done through retraining rather than punishment.

At present offence labels under criminal law only take account of the results of bad driving if they amount to death, reflecting the views of society on the sanctity of life. The one exception to this is the offence of wanton and furious driving under section 35 of the Offences Against the Person Act 1861, which requires that bodily harm has been caused. As seen in Chapter 2, however, this offence is reserved for cases where dangerous driving cannot be charged for one reason or another, and is rarely used. So far suggestions that dangerous driving resulting in serious injury should be provided for in a separate offence have failed to make it past the consultation stage of any review of the law. Here luck also plays a part. A collision may result in serious injury where death might have otherwise been caused were it not for the quick response of emergency services or the presence of safety measures in the victim's vehicle. On the other hand, serious injury might be caused in other cases where, had the victim been luckier, he or she could have walked away with minor injuries. Given that serious injury was not within the contemplation of D, and any injuries can operate as an aggravating factor in sentencing for dangerous driving, it seems to have been accepted that a separate offence is not warranted. Serious injury does not result in the same response as does the harm of death, and this is true whether it results from bad driving, medical malpractice or some other 'accident'. It seems unlikely that this position will change in the near future, or that it should. The nature of the harm of death is so final and unique that the criminal law operates in an entirely different way in deciding whether to allocate responsibility for its cause (Fletcher 2000).

Where death is caused and D's driving is so bad that it can be said to fall within the definition of 'gross negligence' in *Adomako* (1995), then D is deserving of punishment for manslaughter and ought to be charged with that offence. The question is whether there ought to be available to the prosecution other charges for those drivers whose driving cannot be said to have involved a clear risk of death. The question of whether the law should rely on a single offence of manslaughter to cater for those whose risk-taking results in death, or whether a number of offences, including but not confined to vehicular homicide offences, should be retained or created to deal with killing in specific contexts has attracted recent attention (Clarkson and Cunningham 2008). Many of the issues discussed above are relevant to this question. Ashworth summarizes the arguments for and against having separate 'nominate' offences for different contexts of killing:

> Three arguments in favour of nominalism stand out – that it is much more communicative, thereby emphasising the special duties of citizens in certain roles or positions; that the circumstances of some types of case are so unlike others that a separate category is a more accurate label; and that, if there were not a nominate offence for certain conduct, the law might be misapplied by juries. (Ashworth 2008)

If we take each of these arguments and apply them to the offences of CDDD and CDCD it has already been argued that the main reason for creation of CDDD, that juries were reluctant to convict drivers of manslaughter, is probably no longer valid. The second argument, that the circumstances of some types of case are so unlike others that a separate category is a more accurate label has been put forward by some, such as Clarkson, who argue that drivers who kill should be treated differently to other killers because driving is such a widespread activity that we identify with their actions more than with those of, for example, negligent surgeons (Clarkson 2000). Their wrong is 'situationally relevant' to ourselves. This term was first used by Shaver, who conducted experiments to test Walster's defensive attribution theory (see Chapter 6). Shaver found that whether or not fault would be attributed to a driver involved in a collision depended on whether the person making the judgment was in a similar situation to that of the driver. The greater the relevance of the driver's situation to that of the person making the evaluation, the more lenient the evaluation would be (Shaver 1970, 112). Lloyd-Bostock in turn drew on the work of Walster and Shaver in discussing the psychological issues involved in attributing blame in the legal process (Lloyd-Bostock 1979), and was cited by Clarkson in putting forward the argument that situational relevance applies when determining liability for manslaughter or causing death by driving (Clarkson 2000).

As noted by Blom-Cooper and Morris: 'That there are millions of drivers of motor vehicles, most of whom do not indulge in the kind of driving that results in death, is no reason why the law should make special provision for them when others are harmed by their unlawful actions' (Blom-Cooper and Morris 2004, 153). There may be strong psychological reasons why people who drive demonstrate such an attitude, but this in itself does not explain why someone whose blameworthiness meets the standard of gross negligence ought to be tried for an offence with a different label to manslaughter and with a lower maximum penalty (see further Cunningham 2008).

The last argument in favour of nominalism was that having separate vehicular homicide offences is much more communicative, thereby emphasizing the special duties of citizens in the particular role as drivers. It can be seen that all these arguments are interlinked, but are not necessarily consistent with each other. One reason why the argument of 'situational relevance' might be rejected is that it could be seen as approving of an attitude that taking risks when driving is somehow less bad than other forms of gross negligence leading to death. This might in itself undermine the message that driving is a dangerous activity that must be carried out in accordance with the Highway Code. If that were true then the communicative effect the law would be having would be the opposite of that intended. In any case, it is unlikely that separate offences of CDDD and CDCD will succeed in any desire to communicate to the pubic their duties as drivers, given what we know about driver behaviour and the tendency for offenders to see the Highway Code as applying to other ('average' or 'below average') drivers who need to comply with the rules because they are less skilful than themselves. Even if the proposal for reformulating dangerous and careless driving as violations and errors were adopted, it would still be the case that drivers would be unlikely to be deterred by the harsher penalties attaching to a causing death offence, since they do not expect to crash.

The most forceful argument in favour of nominate offences of CDDD and, more recently, CDCD seems not to have been any of the above but, instead, public opinion (Cunningham 2007). One of two main factors contributing to the North Review's recommendation that a causing death offence ought to be retained was that there was strong public acceptance that where death results from a culpable act, that consequence should lead to a more serious charge (Department of Transport 1988, para.6.9). In accepting this factor the Review recognized that it was rejecting the more logical arguments against retention of such an offence in favour of reliance on public expectations of the law.

The same factor was instrumental in the government's decision to create CDCD: '[there is] no adequate justification (save, arguably, that of appeasing public opinion) for creating an offence of causing death by careless driving when the fault requirement is so very low' (Ashworth 2008). Although public opinion is important in creating new laws, in that it may be difficult to enforce a law with which the public does not agree, and the government may be tempted to pass laws to win the loyalty of voters, commentators have opined that it should not be the determining factor in law-making policy. Writing several years before the North Report, Alldridge stated that: 'it is not a principle of English jurisprudence that offences ought to be named palliatively so as to increase the conviction rate, nor is it just that one who kills with a car should be exposed to a lower maximum penalty than one who, no more culpably, kills otherwise' (Alldridge 1980, 571). Writing in 1994 on the subject of the Law Commission's proposals to reform the law of manslaughter (Law Commission 1994), Wasik stated that: 'there is now a significant academic literature addressing the underlying issues of culpability and harm in criminal law, so that policymakers need no longer resort to hunches about public opinion' (Wasik 1994, 893).

Roberts and Hough point out that little effort is invested in exploring the nature of public attitudes to punishment, or in informing or consulting the public in a rational manner (Roberts and Hough 2002, 1). Stalans notes that people's inner attitudes can only be assessed through sophisticated surveys, but that simple opinion surveys only test surface attitudes (Stalans 2002). Not only is it difficult to assess the nature of public opinion, there are also problems in relying upon it when many of the public are ignorant about criminal justice issues and tend to be informed mainly by the media, who are selective in their reporting on such issues and fail to put news items in context and perspective (Ashworth and Hough 1996, 779). As noted by Hough et al., members of the public form views based on the very worst cases imaginable:

> If members of the public were asked about the typical offender convicted of a driving offence resulting in death, it is likely that they would describe a young male driver who had been drinking, driving recklessly and who had a history of similar offences. The loss of life resulting from these offences is likely to eclipse, in the public mind, consideration of the offender's level of culpability. The public appear to endorse a model of case seriousness in which the harm assumes primordial importance. For all these reasons, it is not surprising that the spontaneous reaction of members of the public to sentencing offenders of these crimes is often quite punitive. The challenge for researchers is to move beyond this level to explore the true nature of public opinion. (Hough et al. 2008, 1)

Where researchers are able to go beyond knee-jerk or spontaneous reactions the response may be quite different. Hough et al. recently took up the challenge of exploring the 'true nature' of public opinion in preparing research on public opinions to sentencing in driving causing death cases for the Sentencing Advisory Panel (SAP). The findings are interesting, in that when research participants were asked to give an initial opinion about sentencing in causing death by driving cases in general, more than 50 per cent believed that sentences are normally too lenient (SAP 2008, para.10). However, when given details of specific sample cases and the chance to discuss the impact of various aggravating and mitigating factors, the majority of participants came to the conclusion that the sentences proposed by the Sentencing Advisory Panel (which are not far removed from current sentencing practice) were broadly acceptable (ibid.). This suggests that the public, when able to spend time thinking objectively about appropriate responses to specific examples of offending, are less punitive than first impressions may suggest.

In summary, the law should be able to rely on the common-law offence of manslaughter to punish and label appropriately those who cause death by driving. If a driver's culpability does not meet the test for gross negligence manslaughter, perceived public opinion should not act to justify the creation or continued existence of serious homicide offences that seek to impose retributive punishment on such drivers. The underlying offences of bad driving should be relied upon to punish, deter and rehabilitate bad drivers and, if reformed as suggested here, could arguably improve road safety considerably.

### *The Victim's Experience*

Many members of the public responding to the 2005 consultation exercise considering the creation of CDCD were relatives of victims of road death incidents with a clear motivation in responding to the consultation. The fact that relatives of victims will have had the impetus to voice their opinions on the level of justice they received following their loss is something that must not be ignored by government. In dealing with such a sensitive issue it is, however, difficult to strike a balance between the needs of the victim and justice for the defendant. There is strong support for offences such as CDCD from those who have personal experience of the carnage bad driving can bring, but it is not necessarily appropriate for homicide offences to attempt to help the grieving process for relatives of victims of road death incidents. There is a requirement for their needs to be met in a public setting, however, and some suggestions are made as to how to improve their experiences.

Road safety groups such as BRAKE and RoadPeace, who represent families of victims of fatal road traffic collisions, have been amongst the most vociferous supporters of increased penalties for drivers who kill, with suggestions that a new concept of motor manslaughter ought to be introduced to ensure that the focus for the criminal law is on the fact that death has been caused rather than the standard of D's driving (Home Office 2005b). Whilst their proposals do not find full support here, in that there is no justification for punishing a driver for manslaughter unless the requirements under the current law and the case of *Adomako* are present, it is quite understandable that those who have been the victim of bad driving and suffered the worst loss known to humankind should hold such views. Some victims may feel a strong desire for retribution and those needs may be impossible to meet under the modern justice system. Others, however, seek something different from the public arena in which the criminal law operates. It is worth considering whether there are any changes that can be made to improve the experience of those who currently feel let down by the justice system.

The publication by the Sentencing Guidelines Council (SGC) of its consultation guidance for sentencing cases of driving causing death offences (SGC 2008) met with a great deal of media attention. The media were keen to report on the response to the guidelines from those who had experienced the loss of a relative through bad driving. Cynthia Barlow's daughter died in June 2000 when she was knocked from her bicycle and run over by the driver of a concrete mixer lorry turning left across her path. Whilst Ms Barlow argues that the main issue is to make drivers accountable for their actions, and that they should face trial at a court higher than the magistrates' court, her comments reveal that there is an additional underlying reason for these views:

> We do think that they should always go to a higher court, so there is a more thorough investigation, a better standard of prosecution so that at least families can know the facts, which at the moment they don't with a magistrates' court hearing. (*BBC News Online* 9 January 2008)

For many relatives, their expectation is that a criminal trial will provide them with detail of the circumstances leading to V's death, which they hope will enable them better to come to terms with their loss. If D pleads guilty to the offence charged, however, not only will families likely face disappointment relating to a lesser penalty imposed in recognition of the plea, but they are also unlikely to hear evidence providing an explanation of the crash. The SAP research into attitudes to sentencing included 11 in-depth interviews with relatives of victims, who it was found tended to express dissatisfaction with all stages of the criminal justice process, not just the sentences imposed (SAP 2008, para.12). The results of this research closely matched those of an earlier survey of victims (Pearce 2004).

Whilst the police, and particularly family liaison officers, received positive comments and were seen as more helpful and sympathetic than other agencies within the system (Pearce 2004, para.5.11; Hough et al. 2008, 65), the CPS was criticized by a large proportion of victims and seen as unsympathetic and lacking in their consideration for the victims (Pearce 2004, para.5.13). Much of this criticism seems to stem from the victims' experience that they were not kept informed about the progress of the case (ibid., para.5.11), and were distressed by court delays (ibid., para.5.15). Both pieces of research found that a common complaint was that when a case got to court, relatives of the victims often had to sit close to relatives of the defendant in the public gallery, causing further distress (Pearce 2004, para.5.15; Hough et al. 2008, 63).

The CPS is aware of the criticism levelled at it by relatives of victims, and notes that in the past five years steps have been taken to 'champion justice and the rights of victims' (CPS 2007b, 28). The first initiative, introduced in 2001 and included within the *Code of Practice for Victims of Crime*, has been to write to bereaved relatives to inform them of any decision to discontinue a case or substantially alter a charge and to offer the bereaved victims to meet a CPS lawyer to explain the decision (ibid., para.6.4). In addition to the *Code of Practice for Victims of Crime*, the CPS has also made promises to victims about how cases will be dealt with in its Prosecutor's Pledge, published in 2005. Efforts to keep those promises include setting up Witness Care Units to assess the needs of witnesses and provide information relating to the progress of a case directly to the victim, or their family, or via the police Family Liaison Officer (ibid., para.6.6), and introducing the Victim Focus Scheme for cases heard at the Crown Court (ibid., para.6.7). The Victim Focus Scheme involves a prosecutor meeting with relatives to explain charging decisions and answer questions about the court process. It is also the way in which victims will learn about victim personal statements, first introduced in 2001.

Under the *Consolidated Criminal Practice Direction*, updated in 2007, victims are provided with a formal opportunity to say how the crime has affected them (Her Majesty's Court Service 2007). This statement may be read out in court and enable the court to take account of the statement in determining sentence. That said, it is not for the victim to give a view as to the appropriate sentence in the statement. The *Practice Direction* makes it clear that it is the impact of the offence on the victims, rather than their opinions as to sentence, which may inform the sentencing task, and if victims choose to present opinions as to sentence despite being advised of this, then the court should pay no attention to them. This might explain why several of the victims interviewed as part of the SAP research said that they were disappointed by the fact that their victim impact statement was not read out in court (Hough et al. 2008, 62). Perhaps victims are not being accurately informed as to the purpose of the statement.

For the interviewees in the SAP research, a common complaint was that court proceedings were geared around the needs of the offender rather than being focused on the impact of the crime (Hough et al. 2008, 61), and the trial was all about the defendant rather than the victim (ibid., 62). That this is the case is inevitable, given that criminal punishment is an expression of public condemnation of the crime and the Crown is prosecuting on behalf of the state rather than the victim. The wrong committed by D is a 'public' wrong in that it merits recognition and condemnation by the polity because D has threatened harm to the collective (Duff 2005, 54). That the criminal law is seeking to address a public wrong is something that victims may find it difficult to come to terms with: it is they who have suffered as the result of the defendant's actions and they naturally feel the desire to experience some 'ownership' of the trial. When this fails to materialize they will feel disappointment at least, if not anger. But this is the very reason why the criminal justice system attempts to exact justice in an objective, if perceivably cold manner; victims of crime are emotionally involved in events and will find it difficult to retain the necessary objectivity in deciding D's fate.

Nevertheless, the various initiatives introduced by the CPS and other agencies may go some way to improving the experience of victims within the court system, and every effort should be made to keep victims informed of the process and limit their distress as far as possible. Whilst a criminal trial approaches the incident causing death from the perspective of D in order to determine D's culpability, it may be that there is scope for other courts within the legal system to focus more on the experience of the victims. Victims may be able to sue D under the law of tort in the civil courts and it may be that inquests could play a more prominent role in meeting the needs of bereaved relatives (Cunningham 2008).

An inquest should be opened whenever a death appears to be unexplained, allowing the coroner to examine evidence to come to a conclusion as to how V's death came about. In doing so the coroner, unlike a jury or magistrates in the criminal courts, is not determining whether a particular individual is to blame for the death and, unlike a criminal trial the proceedings are not adversarial in nature with two sides pitted against each other. In cases where careless driving has been charged, the inquest should normally be concluded before the criminal trial commences (*Smith v DPP* 2000). However, in cases where D has been charged with CDDD or CDCDUI, the inquest should be adjourned until after the criminal trial, and will only be resumed by the coroner if there is 'sufficient cause' to do so (section 16 of the Coroners Act 1988). In many cases the inquest will not be resumed (Matthews 2002, para.10.55), which is unsurprising given that if resumed the coroner must take cognisance of the rule that the finding of cause of death must not be inconsistent with the outcome of the criminal proceedings (Coroners Act 1988, section 16(7)). ACPO suggest that an inquest may be resumed in cases where a charge of CDDD has been reduced to one of careless driving, when the coroner may consider that public testing of the evidence is appropriate (ACPO 2004, para.8.2).

Inquests do, however, play an important role, and it has been suggested that that role could be further enhanced (Cunningham 2008). One of the benefits of the inquest system is that it provides the police with an incentive, beyond that of collecting evidence suggesting that a criminal offence has been committed, to conduct a thorough investigation of all road deaths. The police will prepare a separate file for the coroner, although in practice the file will not differ greatly from the file prepared for the prosecution (ACPO 2004, para.2.11.5). ACPO provide the following guidance on what should be included in the coroner's file:

> It is considered good practice to include for example details of the amount of hours spent on the inquiry, the number of actions raised, the number of people interviewed and other such relevant information. If any actions have been identified which could help to prevent similar occurrences, they should be included in the file submitted to the coroner. Typically these will be such matters as road design, layout or signing. Such traffic management issues may need expert advice and a meeting with local authority or Highways Agency representatives may be beneficial and will show that positive action has been taken. (Ibid.)

The *Road Death Investigation Manual* states that the senior investigating officer should keep the coroner updated on the progress of the investigation on a regular basis (ibid., 131), and notes that coroners may wish to attend the scene of high-profile fatal collisions (ibid., para.8.1).

In its consultation process regarding charging policy, the CPS asked whether respondents thought that it would be beneficial for the case prosecutor to attend the inquest. Twenty-eight of the 40 responses to this question agreed that it would be beneficial (CPS 2007a, 11). This has led the CPS to state that: 'Where it is considered beneficial to do so, the reviewing lawyer will attend an inquest where the related criminal proceedings have still to be concluded' (CPS 2007b, para.6.11). This might prove helpful in some cases where the evidence is equivocal, since it may give the prosecutor a better idea of how evidence is likely to be interpreted in the criminal trial, and if any decision regarding charge needs to reviewed as a result. It would be unlikely, however, for a charge of careless driving to be raised to one of CDDD on the strength of the inquest, since such a change would normally face challenge from the defence as an abuse of process. The value of the CPS attending the inquest is more likely to be that it will show bereaved relatives that the case is being taken seriously.

The government has for some time been considering making changes to the system of inquests, and expressed a commitment to reforming the coroner service in June 2006 (DCA 2006b, para.107). A Draft Coroners Bill is designed to provide bereaved people with a right to contribute to coroners' investigations and to bring their concerns to coroners even where a death certificate has been issued (ibid., para.108). There will be a Charter for Bereaved People providing rights to participation, including the right to view post-mortem reports and any other investigations (DCA 2006a, 120–21). The use of narrative findings, rather than the simple findings of 'accident', 'misadventure', 'unlawful killing', etc. would be expanded, providing the coroner with:

> the power to make a report to a person who may have the power to prevent similar events happening in future. This power could, for example, be used by the coroner to report to a local authority the fact that several deaths have occurred in similar circumstances on the same stretch of road. It would then be up to the local authority to consider what action, if any, they should take. (DCA 2006a, Clause 12(2))

Under the current system coroners may already make recommendations to whichever authority is in a position to take remedial action, such as the highways authority in cases where there was a problem with road layout or signs (Pearce et al. 2002, 66). However, the proposal would formalize these powers. Such reforms may be beneficial to the relatives of road death victims, who may be able better to come to terms with their loss if provided with comprehensive information concerning the events leading to the collision. This, it has been argued, may reduce the demands currently made on the criminal justice system to provide relatives with an explanation of what happened, but could go further (Cunningham 2008). The Parliamentary Advisory Council for Transport Safety (PACTS) has recently proposed that the current Coroner's Rules ought to be amended to provide coroners with powers similar to those enjoyed by the sheriff in Scotland to highlight the importance of preventing work-related deaths (Crawford 2007, 66). This would apply only when V was killed while driving in the course of undertaking employment duties, and would allow the coroner to determine how the death might have been avoided and any defects in the system of working which contributed to the death (ibid.).

**The Future Focus for Road Safety Policy**

The government's current strategy, established in 2000, set a target of a 40 per cent reduction in all killed and seriously injured (KSI) casualties and a 50 per cent reduction in child KSIs on Britain's roads by 2010 (DETR 2000). By 2007, the government reported that the number of KSI casualties had dropped by 33 per cent (DfT 2007c, para.45) and the number of child KSI casualties had been reduced by 49 per cent (ibid., para.52). This is clearly positive, but the government admits that there is still work to be done. The government attributes what reductions there have been to improvements in road infrastructure, technology within cars and speed management (ibid., para.29). However, it notes that driver behaviour is the main contributor to casualty numbers and plans to increase enforcement activity and enhance publicity campaigns.

The figures presenting a reduction in casualties do not tell the whole story; although the government appears to be on track regarding killed *or* seriously injured casualties, if those casualties are split up the figures show that the number of deaths has reduced by only 11 per cent (ibid., para.65). What reductions there have been are mostly in relation to pedestrian deaths, which have dropped by 33 per cent (ibid., para.74), whilst car occupant deaths have decreased by only 5 per cent (ibid., para.69), and motorcyclist deaths have actually increased by 22 per cent (ibid., para.71).

The government identifies a number of problem areas on which it intends to focus: those, particularly young drivers, who continue to drink-drive; single-vehicle collisions, where the primary cause is loss of control; speeding, which remains a 'significant problem'; motorcyclists; young drivers; and those who drive for work. In relation to those who drive for work, it is unsurprising that driver fatigue, being under pressure of time (perhaps leading to speeding behaviour) and in-car tasks such as hands-free mobile phone conversations were identified as contributing to the fact that around 1,000 fatalities a year involve someone who is driving for work (ibid., 24). A new Think! campaign promotes best practice for employers, and the government also stresses that the threat of prosecutions under health and safety legislation will also hopefully motivate employers to ensure safe driving by employees (ibid., 42). Since the government' strategy was set out, the Corporate Manslaughter and Corporate Homicide Act 2007 has been passed, increasing the motivation for senior managers (see Chapter 4 above). PACTS has suggested that more should be done by the Health and Safety Executive in preventing road deaths at work, and recommends that the HSE should establish a road death investigation unit to investigate road deaths that are suspected to have occurred while at work (Crawford 2007, 65). The HSE is criticized on the basis that it takes an inconsistent approach: 'whereas it has a commendably strong role in upholding health and safety laws in other sectors, it chooses to overlook work-related road safety issues and it should take up its rightful role overseeing this area as a matter of priority' (ibid.). The difficulty that would have to be overcome if this were to be implemented, however, is the issue of resources. The HSE is already under-resourced, and far more money would be needed to create a road death investigation unit. Arguably the better approach is for the police to investigate all road deaths and to forward to the HSE any evidence of breaches of health and safety legislation that come to light.

Another approach being taken to promote safe driving, particularly in the commercial sector, is to stress the benefits for the environment in terms of the fuel efficient effect of safe driving style. Anticipating hazards early so as to avoid unnecessary braking and acceleration reduces fuel consumption and reduces carbon dioxide emissions, which is desirable in terms of climate change (DfT 2007c, para.109), and this will also benefit employers who can save on fuel bills. There are thus dual benefits in promoting courses such as SAFED (the safe and fuel efficient driving course) (ibid., para.150). A similar initiative has been introduced in Sweden, where a policy has been developed to use energy efficiency for speed management following a calculation that achieving a 100 per cent compliance rate with speed limits could reduce $CO_2$ emissions by 700,000 tons per year (Tingvall 2007).

Young drivers are more at risk because they commit more offences such as speeding and drink-driving, and drive older cars with fewer secondary safety features (DfT 2007c, 25). The government intends to tackle this with changes to driver training and testing, and by looking at the attitudes that children develop before they learn to drive, with a view to providing relevant road safety education in schools and encouraging parents to set a good example in their driving (ibid., para.136). The House of Commons Transport Committee recently produced a report on novice drivers highlighting the extent of the problem (HoC Transport Committee 2007). Statistics provided in evidence to the committee included:

- one in eight driving licence holders is aged under 25, yet one in three drivers who die in a collision is under 25, and almost one in two drivers killed at night is under 25;

- 27 per cent of 17–19 year-old males are involved in a road collision as a driver in their first year of driving;
- 1,077 people died in 2005 in crashes involving a driver aged 17–25 (of whom 377 were drivers aged 17–25) (ibid., para.7).

The committee noted that there have been a number of initiatives to improve driving tests over the past few years, including theory tests and hazard perception tests, but that these have only had a marginal effect on novice driver safety (ibid., para.14). One of the main problems with the current system of learning to drive was identified as being that it encourages people to seek to pass their test in the minimum time possible, rather than to learn to drive safely, and people distinguish between learning to drive and learning to pass their test (ibid., para.22). The committee recommended the introduction of a minimum 12 month learning period, which would increase the minimum age at which someone is entitled to a full driving licence to 18 years (ibid., para.49). In addition, it would be stipulated that a specified number of hours of professional tuition would have to be undertaken within that 12 month period to ensure that learners gain experience of driving in various weather and lighting conditions and do not bunch their tuition into a short space of time (ibid., para.50). This minimum learning period would be accompanied by the introduction of a structured syllabus for learning to drive, requiring a number of modules to be completed and signed-off before a learner could take his or her test (ibid., para.58). In order to encourage the right attitude to driving, the committee recommended that the syllabus should include group-based learning to cover driving theory, risks, hazard perception, self-assessment and traffic law (ibid., para.73). There has been considerable research conducted on the driver behaviour of young drivers, much of it by psychologists whose work was referred to in Chapter 6 of this book. There is insufficient space to consider in full the findings of that research here, but it is a positive aspect that the committee has been able to draw on the work of those such as McKenna, Stradling and Meadows in considering what improvements can be made to driver training.

As was seen in Chapter 3, drink-driving is committed primarily, but not exclusively, by young drivers. It has been reported that 17 per cent of road deaths occur when someone was driving over the legal limit, and evidence suggests more fatal drink-drive collisions occur in urban areas than in rural areas (DfT 2007c, 27). The government has stated that it will consider random testing (ibid., 47) and will keep the present drink-drive limit under review (ibid., para.163). Arguably, a stronger commitment to lowering the legal BAC to 50 mg/100 ml would go a long way, if evidence from other countries is considered. A reduction from 80 mg/100 ml to 50 mg/100 ml took place in Switzerland on 1 January 2005. At the same time as random breath testing was introduced. This combination appears to have led to a 20–25 per cent reduction in road deaths from 2004 to 2005 (ETSC 2006, 10). The government has also failed to adopt the House of Commons Transport Committee's recommendation to introduce a separate lower legal BAC of zero or 20 mg/100 ml for novice drivers.

In relation to speeding, the government notes that it has issued new guidance to traffic authorities with regards to the setting of speed limits. Traffic authorities have been asked to review the speed limits in accordance with the guidance and make any changes by 2011 (ibid., para.206). This will hopefully be beneficial in improving the consistency with which decisions as to the speed limit to be set for a particular road is made across the country, which may help in persuading drivers that limits are 'fair' and lead to better acceptance and, as a result, compliance.

In addition, the government plans to develop a national speed limit database (ibid., para.225). This will in future enable the use of intelligent speed adaptation systems. Intelligent speed adaptation (ISA) is a recent concept developed to help change drivers' behaviour and stop speeding, the aim of which is to adapt drivers' speed to a particular speed limit through different techniques ranging from advisory to intervening (Wallén and Åberg 2006, 427). Wallén and Åberg tested one particular ISA device in Sweden which used global positioning systems (GPS) to track where the car was, its speed and whether it was exceeding the speed limit on that road. It informed the drivers of the speed limit and if they exceeded the limit it warned the driver using flashing lights and sound signals, and logged the drivers' behaviour. The authors warn that such devices must be acceptable to drivers if they are to succeed in changing driving behaviour. They concluded that ISA devices could be a useful tool in reducing speeding behaviour (ibid., 432). The main obstacle for implementing such a system in the UK is that it requires a national digital map to be developed, incorporating speed limits. It is therefore a major step forward for the government to have agreed to the development of a speed limit database. This will be one of the major costs in implementing ISA, but other savings would be made in the long term. If a mandatory system were implemented to make it impossible for vehicles to exceed the speed limit it has been estimated that it could reduce injury collisions by 20 per cent and fatal collisions by 37 per cent (Carsten and Tate 2005). In addition to reductions in casualties, road calming measures would be extremely cheap to introduce since they would only require a change to the speed database (ibid.). On a cost–benefit analysis such a system could pay back up to 15 times the amount spent on it (ibid.).

In terms of enforcement, the number of operational traffic officers in England and Wales fell between 1999 and 2004 by 21 per cent. PACTS has expressed concern over the marginalization of roads policing, in particular the fact that attention has been shifted away from roads policing in the form of casualty reduction and emphasis given to work tackling terrorism (Crawford 2007, 70). In 2002–2003 there were 6,902 police officers whose primary role was roads policing and in 2004–2005 this increased slightly to 7,104 (DfT 2007c, para.287). As with many other areas of policing, roads policing will become subject to the government's setting of targets under a new Roads Policing Strategy and a national Policing Performance Assessment Framework. One of the component indicators used to measure police performance within this framework is the number of people killed or seriously injured in road traffic collisions per 100 million vehicle–kilometres travelled (ibid.). Given that, as recognized under Sweden's Vision Zero policy, road safety is the responsibility of a number of stakeholders, it is not clear that the setting of such indicators is a fair measure of police performance in the area of road traffic.

As in many other areas of government, there is increasing involvement of the EU in road safety issues. The EU's target is to reduce road deaths across Europe by 50 per cent by 2010, a target adopted in a White Paper on the Common Transport Policy in 2001 (ETSC 2006, 7). The European Transport Safety Council (ETSC) has said that the long-term target is to reduce road casualties as much as possible (ibid., 29). This is based on the Swedish Vision Zero policy that, as seen in Chapter 5, states that responsibility for traffic safety cannot solely be on the user. While the final responsibility for safe behaviour will always be on the individual user, all actors – including public authorities and industry – have to accept their share in responsibility for this. The ETSC states that public authorities should devise a road transport system that limits the scope for individual errors leading to death and injury, and that industry should design motor vehicles in a way that unsafe behaviour is largely excluded. As noted in Chapter 5 the danger, however, is that drivers will see such a policy as absolving them of responsibility if it is not carefully explained to them.

In the UK the Parliamentary Advisory Council for Transport Safety (PACTS) has carried out a consultation exercise to consider the application of a Vision Zero policy here (Crawford 2007). As noted in Chapter 5, although many interviewees admired the aspirational nature of the policy, they did not think it would translate effectively into British culture (ibid., 19). However, PACTS has recommended the development of an 'engagement plan' to involve organizations that have not traditionally worked in road safety as part of a future strategy (ibid., 16). This should be achievable, it is suggested, on the basis that death and injury as a consequence of road traffic collisions is a public issue and also involves environmental issues (ibid.). Those stakeholders responsible for these tangential issues can help to contribute to a vision if they believe they also have something to achieve from it (Claes Tingvall, quoted in Crawford 2007, 16). There is therefore scope to link efforts to improve road safety, obesity and climate change, given that establishing a safe road traffic system which is conducive to active travel in the form of walking and cycling clearly has health and environmental benefits (Crawford 2007, 29). PACTS sets out a number of recommendations which would aim to improve the experience for pedestrians and cyclists, thereby reducing car usage and road traffic casualties. These range from a default speed limit of 20 mph in built-up areas to subjecting new residential developments to a 'pint of milk test' (can a resident reach a shop for a pint of milk in under ten minutes without using a vehicle).

PACTS recommends that beyond 2010 further targets for reducing road casualties are adopted, but rejects the ultimate target of Vision Zero in favour of one that would reduce the likelihood of being killed whilst using the road from 8.5 times greater than other everyday activities to twice that experienced elsewhere in everyday life (Crawford 2007, 19). This would be achieved through a more integrated and holistic approach to road safety, drawing on the work of Vision Zero. However, it would also draw on the Dutch model of Sustainable Safety, which would involve a physical adaptation of much of the existing system of local roads, and PACTS' own 'pragmatic vision', which recognizes the need to balance an acceptable level of risk on the roads with an acceptable limit on road user's feelings of freedom.

Whilst the government has not gone as far as adopting a holistic approach similar to that in Sweden, it has stated that it plans to form a new national Road Safety Delivery Board that brings together representatives of 'key delivery partners' to monitor progress in delivering the strategy to achieve the government's targets by 2010 and to sort out problems and issues, to assist in developing closer partnerships and to spread good practice (DfT 2007c, para.40). This may go some way to integrating policy as suggested by PACTS, provided that it is given the opportunity to do more than add another layer of bureaucracy and can have a positive effect on developing road safety policy.

## Conclusions

The Audit Commission recently identified the main issue for improving road safety as: 'the need to shift emphasis from targeting accident black spots and dangerous stretches of road, to influencing the behaviours of all road users. This will be best achieved through coordinated activity by all the agencies involved, working at local, regional or national level as appropriate' (Audit Commission 2007, para.81). As has been argued in this book, changing driver attitudes to road traffic offences is key to influencing the behaviour of drivers. It is unlikely that 'car culture' (Corbett 2003) within England and Wales will change dramatically in future, even with any improvements to public transport which might be implemented, and a large proportion of the public are likely to continue to value driving as a symbol of independence, spontaneity, wealth and power (Crawford 2007, 23). Education is a critical component of a successful strategy to change attitudes to driving offences, and should be used to reinforce and complement enforcement policy.

As one of the three Es of road safety, enforcement has, however, been the focus of this book. We have seen that the current law can be complex and difficult to interpret, and there is scope for improvement in its definition and implementation. Dangerous and careless driving, as the general offences criminalizing bad driving, have been designed to penalize those who objectively demonstrate levels of risk-taking that can be deemed blameworthy. It has been seen however, that offenders are unlikely to identify their behaviour with commission of an offence and, due to the way in which drivers' behaviour is informed by normative attitudes, are unlikely to be influenced by the existence of such offences. Inevitably, given that there is no agreement about the skill and care required of a 'competent and careful' driver, the law is also difficult to apply. The results of the author's empirical study on criminal charges brought in cases of road death incidents have illustrated the inconsistent approach taken by police, prosecutors and courts, particularly in relation to cases involving fatigue and excess speed. Although the government has recently ruled out reform of the substantive law in relation to general driving offences, there is scope for improvement. The work of psychologists seems to provide scope for constructing a new definition of general driving offences, based on the distinction between violations and errors.

In the worst collisions, where bad driving unluckily results in death, the government hopes that the distinction between careless and dangerous driving, whilst blurred, will be of less importance once the new offence of CDCD comes into force. This will allow offenders to be labelled as causers of death, whether they have committed dangerous or careless driving. It will also enable careless drivers who cause death to be sentenced to periods of imprisonment, although as seen in Chapter 4 the Sentencing Guidelines Council suggests that in many cases a community sentence will be more appropriate. This is as it should be, given the low level of culpability displayed by those guilty of careless driving. However, in those cases where a driver displays a high degree of culpability, there is little reason why manslaughter should not be charged on the basis of gross negligence. Although the CPS has not amended its policy on charging manslaughter in driving cases to any large extent, it is hoped that prosecutors can be encouraged to increase the cases in which manslaughter is charged, where that charge is warranted. The fact that historically there has been a reason for the creation of a statutory offence of CDDD does not mean that the more serious common-law offence should not be utilized where possible.

Chapter 3 demonstrated the contrast between two offences that penalize those who drive above certain limits. Driving when above the legal BAC is seen as a serious offence both by (most) drivers and by the police, whilst driving in excess of the speed limit results in far less stigma. It was interesting to see in Chapter 5 that in Sweden, another country in which road safety policy has proved successful in reducing casualty rates, the dichotomy in attitudes is even greater. Whilst the police have wider powers to enforce a more stringent law on drink-driving, resulting in zero tolerance of the offence amongst members of society, speeding has until recently been under-enforced, meaning that attitudes to the offence are far more lax. The same is true of England and Wales. Continued enforcement may go some way to helping change attitudes, particularly with the use of speed awareness courses in response to offending, and other forms of education may help.

It is hoped that this book has provoked some thought as to how best the law can be used to achieve the role set for it in the road safety agenda. There is plenty more work to be done in this area, particularly in researching prosecutorial practice. Anecdotal evidence suggests that careless and dangerous driving are rarely charged in the absence of collisions, but there is no concrete research to assess the accuracy of this conjecture. Further research will also be needed to assess the way in which the new vehicular homicide offences operate, and the impact of amendments to policy in police and CPS practice.

# References

All websites last accessed 4 February 2008 unless otherwise stated.


Åberg, L. (1993), 'Drinking and driving: intentions, attitudes and social norms of Swedish male drivers' *Accident Analysis and Prevention* 25, 289–96

Åberg, L. (1998), 'Traffic rules and traffic safety' *Safety Science* 29, 205–15

ACPO (Association of Chief Police Officers) (2001), *Road Death Investigation Manual* (Bramshill: National Operations Faculty)

ACPO (2004), *Road Death Investigation Manual* Version 2 (Centrex)

ACPO (2006), *Guidance for the Introduction of a National Speed Awareness Course*, available from <http://www.acpo.police.uk/asp/policies/Data/National_speed_awareness_course_website.doc>

Adams, J. (1995), *Risk* (London: UCL Press)

Ajzen, I. (1985), 'From Intentions to Actions: A theory of planned behaviour' in Kuhl, J. and Beckmann, J. (eds) *Action Control: From cognition to behaviour* (Berlin: Springer-Verlag)

Åklagarmyndigheten, *Prosecutor – a Part of the Legal System*, downloaded from <http://www.aklagare.se/upload/Dokumentsamling/Informationsmaterial och nyhetsbrev/Prosecutor – a part of the legal system.pdf>

Åklagarmyndigheten (2007), *Trafikbrott – vårdslöshet i trafik och vållandebrott i 3 kap. Brottsbalken Promemoria (Traffic Law Prosecutors' Memorandum)* (Malmö)

Alldridge, P. (1980), 'Manslaughter and Causing Death by Driving Recklessly' *Justice of the Peace* 144, 569–71

Andenaes, J. (1966), 'The General Preventive Effects of Punishment' *University of Pennsylvania Law Review* 114, 949

Ashworth, A. (1993), 'Taking the Consequences' in Shute, S., Gardner, J. and Horder, J., *Action and Value in the Criminal Law* (Oxford: Clarendon Press)

Ashworth, A. (2000), *Sentencing and Criminal Justice* 3rd ed. (London: Butterworths)

Ashworth, A. (2007), 'Commentary to *O'Halloran and Francis v UK*' *Criminal Law Review* 897–900

Ashworth, A. (2008), '"Manslaughter": Generic or Nominate Offences?' in Clarkson, C.M.V. and Cunningham, S. (eds), *Criminal Liability for Non-Aggressive* Death (Aldershot: Ashgate) (forthcoming)

Ashworth, A. and Hough, M. (1996), 'Sentencing and the Climate of Opinion' *Criminal Law Review* 776–87

Ashworth, A. and Redmayne, M. (2005), *The Criminal Process* 3rd ed. (Oxford: OUP)

Association of National Driver Improvement Scheme Providers website: <www.driver-improvement.co.uk> accessed 25 October 2007

Audit Commission (2006), *Neighbourhood Crime and Anti-Social Behaviour*, cited in Audit Commission (2007), *Changing Lanes: Evolving roles in road safety* available from www.audit-commission.gov.uk

Audit Commission (2007), *Changing Lanes: Evolving roles in road safety* available from <http://www.audit-commission.gov.uk/Products/NATIONAL-REPORT/A199BBC7-6F37-4f0d-A99B-E291497C0C72/Changing Lanes.pdf>

Auld, L.J. (2001), *Review of the Criminal Courts of England and Wales*, (London: The Stationery Office)

Austrian Road Safety Board (Kuratorium für Verkehrssicherheit) (2003), *Preventive Measures to Prevent Driving While Under the Influence of Alcohol/Drugs: Literature study for the Swedish National Road Administration* available from <http://www.vv.se/filer/35555/the_study.pdf>

*BBC News Online* 'Killer Drivers Could Avoid Jail' 9 January 2008: <http://news.bbc.co.uk/1/hi/uk/7178120.stm>

*BBC News Online* 'Drivers Face New Phone Penalties' 27 February 2007: <http://news.bbc.co.uk/1/hi/uk/6399407.stm>

*BBC News Online*, 'Haulage Boss Jailed over M1 Crash' 3 December 2004: <http://news.bbc.co.uk/1/hi/england/4066331.stm>

Bird, S. (2007), 'Home Office Minister Fined for Using his Mobile whilst Driving' *The Times* 3 November 2007

Blair, R.J.R. (1995), 'A Cognitive Developmental Approach to Morality: Investigating the psychopath' *Cognition* 57, 1–29

Blom-Cooper, L. and Morris, T. (2004), *With Malice Aforethought: A study of the crime and punishment for homicide* (Oxford: Hart)

Bottoms, A. (2002), 'Morality, Crime, Compliance and Public Policy' in Bottoms, A. and Tonry, M. (eds), *Ideology, Crime and Criminal Justice* (Cullompton: Willan Publishing)

BRÅ (Swedish National Council for Crime Prevention), *Cleared-up Offences, 2005* (Table 170) downloaded from <www.bra.se>

BRÅ (Swedish National Council for Crime Prevention), *Cleared-up Offences, 2006* (Table 170) downloaded from <www.bra.se>

BRÅ (Swedish National Council for Crime Prevention), *Persons Found Guilty of Criminal Offences, 2005* (Table 420) downloaded from <www.bra.se>

BRÅ (Swedish National Council for Crime Prevention), *Persons Found Guilty of Criminal Offences, 2006* (Table 420) downloaded from <www.bra.se>

Braithwaite, J. (1989), *Crime, Shame and Reintegration* (Cambridge: Cambridge University Press)

Briscoe, S. (2004), 'Raising the Bar: Can increased statutory penalties deter drink-drivers?' *Accident Analysis and Prevention* 36, 919–29

Brook, L. (1987), *Attitudes to Road Traffic Law* (Transport and Road Research Laboratory CR 59)

Broughton, J. (2007), 'The Correlation between Motoring and Other Types of Offence' *Accident Analysis and Prevention* 39, 274–93

Broughton, J., Buckle, G.S., Buttress, S. and Pearce, L.M. (2005), *The Effects of the National Driver Improvement Scheme on Re-offending Rates* TRL Report 649, (Crowthorne: Transport Research Laboratory)

Burgess, C. (c.2000), 'The Wilful Traffic Offender Profile and its Implications for Education and Training' unpublished manuscript found at <http://www.people.ex.ac.uk/cnwburge/pages/edqsum.html>

Burgess, C. and Webley, P. (2000), 'Evaluating the Effectiveness of the United Kingdom's National Driver Improvement Scheme' unpublished work available at: <http://www.ex.ac.uk/~cnwburge/pages/ndis03.html>

Carsten, O.M.J. and Tate, F.N. (2005), 'Intelligent Speed Adaptation: Accident savings and cost-benefit analysis' *Accident Analysis and Prevention* 37, 407–16

Centre for Corporate Accountability <http://www.corporateaccountability.org/manslaughter/cases/convictions.htm>

Clarkson, C.M.V. (2000), 'Context and Culpability in Involuntary Manslaughter: Principle of instinct?' in Ashworth, A. and Mitchell, B. (eds), *Reforming the English Law of Homicide* (Oxford: Oxford University Press)

Clarkson, C.M.V. (2004), 'Necessary Action: A new defence' *Criminal Law Review* 81–95

Clarkson, C.M.V. (2005), *Understanding Criminal Law* 4th ed. (London: Sweet and Maxwell)

Clarkson, C.M.V. and Cunningham, S. (2008), *Criminal Liability for Non-Aggressive Death* (Aldershot: Ashgate) (forthcoming)

Clarkson, C.M.V., Keating, H.M. and Cunningham, S.R. (2007), *Clarkson and Keating: Criminal law text and materials* 6th ed. (London: Sweet and Maxwell)

CLRC (Criminal Law Revision Committee) (1976), *Working Paper on Offences Against the Person* (London: HMSO)

CLRC (1980), *Fourteenth Report on Offences Against the Person*, Cmnd 7844

Coleman, K., Jansson, K., Kaiza, P. and Reed, E. (2007), *Homicides, Firearm Offences and Intimate Violence 2005/2006* Home Office Statistical Bulletin 02/07 (Supplementary Volume 1 to *Crime in England and Wales 2005/2006*) (London: Home Office)

Collins, G. (2007), 'Eight Years of Average Speed Enforcement – What Has Been Achieved?' paper given at *Road Safety Expo 2007* (London)

Conner, M. and Lai, F. (2005), *Evaluation of the Effectiveness of the National Driver Improvement Scheme* Road Safety Research Report No.64 (London: Department for Transport)

Cooper, S. and Orme, M. (2008), *Blackstone's Police Manual 2008 Volume 3: Road Policing* (Oxford: Oxford University Press)

Corbett, C. (1995), 'Road Traffic Offending and the Introduction of Speed Cameras in England: The First Self-Report Study' *Accident Analyses and Prevention* 27:3, 345–54

Corbett, C. (2000), 'The Social Construction of Speeding as Not "Real" Crime' *Crime Prevention and Community Safety: An International Journal* 33–46

Corbett, C. (2003), *Car Crime* (Cullompton: Willan Publishing)

Corbett, C. (2006), *Research and Policy: Have we got the balance right?* Occasional Research Report (London: Parliamentary Advisory Council for Transport Safety) available from www.pacts.org.uk/research

Corbett, C. (2007), 'Vehicle-related Crime and the Gender Gap' *Psychology, Crime and Law* 13, 245–63

Corbett, C. and Simon, F. (1992a), *Unlawful Driving Behaviour: A criminological perspective* TRL Contractor Report 301 (Crowthorne: Transport Research Laboratory)

Corbett, C. and Simon, F. (1992b) 'Decisions to Break or Adhere to the Rules of the Road from the Rational Choice Perspective' *British Journal of Criminology* 32:4, 537–49

Corbett, C. and Simon, F. (1999), *The Effects of Speed Cameras: How drivers respond* Road Safety Research Report No. 11 (DETR)

Corbett, C., Simon, F. and O'Connell, M. (1998), *The Deterrence of High Speed Driving: a Criminological Perspective*, TRL Report 296, (Crowthorne: Transport Research Laboratory)

CPS (Crown Prosecution Service) (1996a), *Driving Offences Charging Standard* (London: CPS)

CPS (1996b), *An Explanatory Memorandum for use in Connection with the Code for Crown Prosecutors* (London: CPS)

CPS (1996c), Press Release (002/96) dated 7 March 1996, quoting Barbara Mills QC

CPS (2004), *Code for Crown Prosecutors* 5th ed. (London: CPS)

CPS (2006), *Prosecuting Bad Driving – A Consultation on CPS Prosecution Policy and Practice* (London: CPS)

CPS (2007a), *Prosecuting Bad Driving – A Consultation on CPS Prosecution Policy and Practice: Response to Consultation* (London: CPS)

CPS (2007b), *Policy for Prosecuting Cases of Bad Driving* (London: CPS)

Crawford, E. (2007), *Beyond 2010 – a holistic approach to road safety in Great Britain* (London: PACTS) available from <http://www.pacts.org.uk/>

Crown Prosecution Service Legal Guidance online: <http://www.cps.gov.uk/legal/section9/chapter_b.html>

Crundell, D., Bains, M., Chapman, P. and Underwood, G. (2005), 'Regulating conversation during driving: a problem for mobile telephones?' *Transportation Research Part F* 8, 197–211

Cunningham, S. (2001), 'The Reality of Vehicular Homicides: Convictions for murder, manslaughter and causing death by dangerous driving' *Criminal Law Review* 679–92

Cunningham, S. (2005), 'The Unique Nature of Prosecutions in Cases of Road Traffic Collisions' *Criminal Law Review* 834–49

Cunningham, S. (2007), 'Punishing Drivers Who Kill: Putting road safety first?' *Legal Studies* 27:2, 288–311

Cunningham, S. (2008), 'Vehicular Homicide: Need for a special offence?' in Clarkson, C.M.V. and Cunningham, S. (eds), *Criminal Liability for Non-Aggressive Death* (Aldershot: Ashgate) (forthcoming)

Dahlstedt, S. (2006), *The SARTRE 3 Tables: Another set of opinions about traffic and traffic safety of European drivers*, VTI report 541/541A, 2006 available at <www.vti.se/publications>

DCA (Department for Constitutional Affairs) (2006a), *Coroner Reform: The Government's Draft Bill improving death investigation in England and Wales* Cm 6849

DCA (2006b), *Draft Coroners Bill: Regulatory Impact Assessment* available from <http://www.dca.gov.uk/risk/ria_coroner_ draft_bill.pdf>

Dennis, I. (2002), *The Law of Evidence* 2nd ed. (London: Sweet and Maxwell)

Dennis, I. (2007), 'Sentencing for Causing Death by Driving Offences' (Editorial) *Criminal Law Review* 253–4

Department of Transport and Home Office (1988), *Road Traffic Law Review Report* (North Report), (London: HMSO)

DETR (Department for the Environment, Transport and the Regions) (1998), *Combating Drink-driving: Next steps: A consultation paper* (London: The Stationery Office)

DETR (2000), *Tomorrow's Roads – Safer for Everyone*, 2000

DfT (Department for Transport) (1999), *The Effects of Speed Cameras: How drivers respond (No.11)* available from: <http://www.dft.gov.uk/pgr/roadsafety/research/rsrr/theme4/theeffectsofspeedcamerashowd4779>

DfT (2006a), *Road Casualties Great Britain 2005* (London: The Stationery Office)

DfT (2006b), *Vehicle Speeds in Great Britain 2005*, Statistics Bulletin SB (06)21 (London: DfT)

DfT (2007a), *Road Casualties Great Britain: 2006* (London: TSO)

DfT (2007b), *Traffic Statistics 2006: Traffic, Speed and Congestion* Transport Statistics Bulletin 20/07 (London: TSO)

DfT (2007c), *Tomorrow's Roads – Safer For Everyone: The second three-year review* (London: DfT) available from <www.dft.gov.uk/pgr/roadsafety/strategy targetsperformance/2ndreview>

Department of Transport, Local Government and the Regions (2001), *Road Accidents Great Britain: The Casualty Report 2000* (London: The Stationery Office)

Dix, M.C. and Layzell, A.D. (1983), *Road Users and the Police* (London: Croom Helm)

DPP (Director of Public Prosecutions) (2007), *Guidance to Police Officers and Crown Prosecutors Issued by the Director of Public Prosecutions under S37A of the Police and Criminal Evidence Act 1984,* 3rd edition, available from <http://www.cps.gov.uk/publications/docs/dpp_guidance.pdf>

Duff, R.A. (1998), 'Desert and Penance' in von Hirsch, A. and Ashworth, A. (eds) (1998), *Principled Sentencing* 2nd ed. (Oxford: Hart)

Duff, R.A. (2002), 'Crime, Prohibition and Punishment' *Journal of Applied Philosophy* 19:2, 97–108

Duff, R.A. (2005), 'Criminalizing Endangerment' in Duff, R.A. and Green, S.P. (eds), *Defining Crimes: Essays on the Special Part of the Criminal Law* (Oxford: Oxford University Press)

Duff, R.A. (2008), 'Whose Luck is it Anyway?' in Clarkson, C.M.V. and Cunningham, S. (eds), *Criminal Liability for Non-Aggressive Death* (Aldershot: Ashgate) (forthcoming)

Edwards, I. (2005), 'An Analysis of the National Driver Improvement Scheme by Referral Type' in Dorn, L. (ed.), *Driver Behaviour and Training Volume II* (Aldershot: Ashgate)

Elliott, D.W. and Street, H. (1968), *Road Accidents* (Harmondsworth: Penguin)

Emsley, C. (1993), '"Mother, What *Did* Policemen Do When There Weren't Any Motors?" The Law, the Police and the Regulation of Motor Traffic in England, 1900–1939' *The Historical Journal* 36:2, 357

ETSC (European Transport Safety Council) (2006), *Traffic Law Enforcement across the EU: An Overview* (Brussels) available from <http://www.etsc.be/documents/Traffic_Law_Enforcement_in_the_EU_An_Overview_May_2006_ETSC.pdf>

European Road Safety Observatory website: <http://www.erso.eu/knowledge/content/05_alcohol/the_legal_limit.htm>

Feinberg, J. (1984), *The Moral Limits of the Criminal Law: Harm to others* (Oxford: Oxford University Press)

Fell, J. and Voas, R. (2006), 'The Effectiveness of Reducing Illegal Blood Concentration (BAC) Limits for Driving: Evidence for lowering the limit to 0.5 BAC' *Journal of Safety Research* 37, 233–43

Finkelstein, C. (2003), 'Is Risk Harm?' *University of Pennsylvania Law Review* 151, 963–1001

Fionda, J. (1995), *Public Prosecutors and Discretion: A comparative study*, (Oxford: Clarendon Press)

Fishbein, M. and Ajzen, I. (1975), *Belief, Attitude, Intention and Behaviour: An introduction to theory and research* (Reading, MA: Addison-Wesley)

Fiti, R., Murray, L. and Giraud, W. (2006), *Offences Relating to Motor Vehicles England and Wales 2004: Supplementary tables* (Home Office: London)

Fletcher, G. (2000), *Rethinking Criminal Law*, (Oxford: Oxford University Press)

Foreman-Peck, J. (1987), 'Death on the Roads: Changing national responses to motor accidents' in Barker, T. (ed.), *The Economic and Social Effects of the Spread of Motor Vehicles* (London: Macmillan)

Forward (2006), 'The Intention to Commit Driving Violations – A Qualitative Study' *Transportation Research Part F* 9, 412–26

Fuller, R. (2005), 'Towards a General Theory of Driving Behaviour' *Accident Analysis and Prevention* 37, 461–72

Fuller, R., Bates, H., Gormley, M., Barbara, H., Stradling, S., Broughton, P., Kinnear, N. and O'Dolan, C. (2006), 'Inappropriate High Speed: Who does it and why?' in DfT, *Behavioural Research in Road Safety 2006: Sixteenth Seminar*

Fylan, F., Hempel, S., Grunfeld, E., Connor, M. and Lawton, R. (2006), 'Evidence-based Behavioural Change for Speeding Drivers' in DfT, *Behavioural Research in Road Safety 2006: Sixteenth Seminar*.

Gardner, J. (1998), 'On the General Part of the Criminal Law' in Duff, A. (ed.), *Philosophy and the Criminal Law* (Cambridge: Cambridge University Press)

Gibb, F. (2008), 'Careless drivers who kill could avoid jail' *The Times* (9 January 2008)

Glidewell, I. (1998), *The Review of the Crown Prosecution Service: A Report*, Cm 3960

Greenaway, D. (2004), *Uninsured Driving in the United Kingdom* Report for the Secretary of State for Transport (London: HMSO)

Groeger, J.A. (2000), *Understanding Driving: Applying cognitive psychology to a complex everyday task* (Hove: Psychology Press)

Gross, H. (1979), *A Theory of Criminal Justice* (New York: Oxford University Press)

GRSP (Global Road Safety Partnership) (2007), *Drinking and Driving: A road safety manual for decision-makers and practitioners*, (Geneva) available at: <http://www.grsproadsafety.org/themes/default/pdfs/Drinking Driving Manual.pdf>

Haglund, M. and Åberg, L. (2000), 'Speed Choice in Relation to Speed Limit and Influences from Other Drivers' *Transportation Research Part F* 3, 39–51

Hansard, HC vol. 450 (9 October 2006)

Hansard, HC vol. 461 (4 June 2007)

Hansard, HC vol. 463 (3 Sep 2007)

Hansard, HL vol. 675 (22 November 2005)

Harbluk, J.L., Noy, Y.I., Trbovich, P.L. and Eizenman, M. (2007), 'An On-road Assessment of Cognitive Distraction: Impacts on drivers' visual behaviour and braking performance' *Accident Analysis and Prevention* 39, 372–9

Harland, D.G. and Lester, J. (1997), *Does Retesting Deter Dangerous Driving?* TRL Report 252 (Crowthorne: Transport Research Laboratory)

Hart, H.L.A. (1968a), 'Prolegomenon to the Principles of Punishment' in *Punishment and Responsibility* (Oxford: Clarendon Press)

Hart, H.L.A. (1968b), 'Negligence, Mens Rea and Criminal Responsibility' in *Punishment and Responsibility* (Oxford: Clarendon Press)

Her Majesty's Court Service (2007), *The Consolidated Criminal Practice Direction* (last updated 27 April 2007) available at: <http://www.hmcourts-service.gov.uk/cms/files/ccpd_260407.pdf>

HM CPS Inspectorate (2002), *Report on the Thematic Review of the Advice, Conduct and Prosecution by the Crown Prosecution Service of Road Traffic Offences Involving Fatalities in England and Wales*, available from <http://www.hmcpsi.gov.uk/reports/RoadTrafficReport0302.pdf>

HoC (House of Commons) Transport Committee (2004), *Traffic Law and its Enforcement* 16th Report of Session 2003–04 (London: The Stationery Office)

HoC (House of Commons) Transport Committee (2007), *Novice Drivers: Seventh Report of Session 2006–07, Volume 1* HC 355-I (London: The Stationery Office)

Home Office (1989), *The Road User and the Law*, CM 576 (London: HMSO)

Home Office (2000a), *Reforming the Law on Involuntary Manslaughter: The Government's Proposals*

Home Office (2000b), *Offences Relating to Motor Vehicles England and Wales 1999: Supplementary Tables*

Home Office (2001), *Offences Relating to Motor Vehicles England and Wales 2000: Supplementary Tables*

Home Office (2002), *Report on the Review of Road Traffic Penalties* (London: Home Office Communication Directorate)

Home Office (2004), *Drink-driving: Prevalence and attitudes in England and Wales 2002* Home Office Research Findings 258

Home Office (2005a), *Review of Road Traffic Offences Involving Bad Driving: A Consultation Paper*

Home Office (2005b), *A Summary and Next Steps: The Review of Road Traffic Offences Involving Bad Driving*

Home Office (2006), *Motoring Offences and Breath Test Statistics England and Wales 2004* Home Office Statistical Bulletin 05/06

Home Office (2007), *Explanatory Note to the Corporate Manslaughter and Corporate Homicide Act 2007*, available at <http://www.opsi.gov.uk/acts/acts2007/en/ukpgaen_20070019_en.pdf>

Hood, R. (1972), *Sentencing the Motoring Offender* (London: Heinemann)

Horder, J. (1995), 'A Critique of the Correspondence Principle' *Criminal Law Review* 759–70

Horne, J. and Reyner, L. (1995), 'Sleep-related Vehicle Accidents' *British Medical Journal* 310, 565–7

Horne, J. and Reyner, L. (1999), 'Sleep-related Vehicle Accidents: A review' *Occupational and Environmental Medicine*, 56:5, 289–94

Horne, J. and Reyner, L. (2001), 'Sleep-related Vehicle Accidents: Some guides for road safety policies' *Transportation Research Part F*, 4, 63–74

Hough, M., Roberts, J., Jacobson, J., Bredee, A. and Moon, N. (2008), *Attitudes to the Sentencing of Offences Involving Death by Driving* Sentencing Advisory Panel Research Report 5 available from <http://www.sentencing-guidelines.gov.uk/docs/death-by-driving-attitudes-report.pdf>

House of Lords Select Committee on the European Union (2002), *Drinking and Driving* Session 2001–2, 24th Report, HL Paper 140 (London: The Stationery Office)

Husak, D. (2005), '*Malum Prohibitum* and Retributivism' in Duff, R.A. and Green, S.P. (eds), *Defining Crimes: Essays on the Special Part of the Criminal Law* (Oxford: Oxford University Press)

Inwood, C., Buckle, G., Keigan, M. and Borrill, R. (2007), *Extended Monitoring of Drink-drive Rehabilitation Courses. Final Report* TRL Report 662 (Crowthorne: TRL)

James Committee (1975), *Report on the Distribution of Criminal Business between the Crown Court and the Magistrates' Courts* (Cmnd 6323)

Jones, C., Dorrian, J. and Dawson, D. (2003), 'Legal Implications of Fatigue in the Australian Transportation Industries' *The Journal of Industrial Relations* 45:3, 344–59

Judicial Studies Board (2007), *Crown Court Bench Book: Specimen Directions*

Koornstra, M., Lynam, D., Nilsson, G., Noordzij, P., Pettersson, H., Wegman, F. and Wouters, P. (2002), *SUNflower: A comparative study of the development of road safety in Sweden, the United Kingdom and the Netherlands* (Leidschendam: SWOV Institute for Road Safety Research) available from <http://www.swov.nl/rapport/Sunflower/Sunflower.pdf>

Krahé, B. and Fenske, I. (2002), 'Predicting Aggressive Driving Behavior: the Role of Macho Personality, Age, and Power of Car' *Aggressive Behavior* 28, 21–9

Lamble, D, Kauranen, T., Laakso, M. and Summala, H. (1999), 'Cognitive Load and Detection Thresholds in Car Following Situations: Safety implications for using mobile (cellular) telephones while driving', *Accident Analysis and Prevention* 31:6, 617–23

Lamond, G. (2007), 'What is a Crime?' *Oxford Journal of Legal Studies* 27:4, 609–32

Law Commission (1985), *Report on the Draft Criminal Code*, Report No. 143

Law Commission (1994), *Involuntary Manslaughter* Consultation Paper No.135

Law Commission (1996), *Legislating the Criminal Code: Involuntary Manslaughter* Report No.237

Law Commission (2005), *A New Homicide Act for England and Wales?* Consultation Paper No.177

Law Commission (2006), *Murder, Manslaughter and Infanticide* Report No.304

Law Reform Commission of Victoria Report No. 45 (1992), *Death Caused by Dangerous Driving*

Lawton, R., Parker, D., Stradling, S.G. and Manstead, A.S.R. (1997a), 'Predicting Road Traffic Accidents: The role of social deviance and violations' *British Journal of Psychology* 88, 249–62

Lawton, R., Parker, D., Manstead, A.S.R. and Stradling, S.G. (1997b), 'The Role of Affect in Predicting Social Behaviours: The case of road traffic violations' *Journal of Applied Social Psychology* 27, 1258–76

Lloyd-Bostock, S. (1979), 'The Ordinary Man, and the Psychology of Attributing Causes and Responsibility' *Modern Law Review* 42, 143–68

McDonagh, E., Wortley, R. and Homel, R. (2002), 'Perceptions of Physical, Psychological, Social and Legal Deterrents to Joyriding', *Crime Prevention and Community Safety: An International Journal* 4:1, 11–25

MacKenna, B. (1970), 'Causing Death by Reckless or Dangerous Driving: A suggestion' *Criminal Law Review* 67–71

McKenna, F.P. (1988), 'What Role Should the Concept of Risk Play in Theories of Accident Involvement?' *Ergonomics* 31:4, 469–84

McKenna, F.P. (1993), 'It Won't Happen to Me: Unrealistic optimism or illusion of control?' *British Journal of Psychology* 84, 39–50

McKenna, F.P., Stanier, R.A. and Lewis, C. (1991), 'Factors Underlying Illusory Self-assessment of Driving Skill in Males and Females' *Accident Analysis and Prevention* 23, 45–52

Macmillan, J. (1975), *Deviant Drivers* (Westmead: Saxon House)

Magistrates' Association (2004), *Magistrates' Court Sentencing Guidelines*, available from < http://www.jsboard.co.uk/downloads/acbb/section2a.pdf>

Mannering, F.L. and Grodsky, L.L. (1995), 'Statistical Analysis of Motorcyclists' Perceived Accident Risk' *Accident Analysis and Prevention*, 27:1, 21–31

Manstead, A.S.R., Parker, D., Stradling, S.G., Reason, J.T. and Baxter, J.S. (1992), 'Perceived Consensus in Estimates of the Prevalence of Driving Errors and Violations' *Journal of Applied Social Psychology* 22:7, 509–30

Marshall, T. (2007), 'Vision of Zero Road Deaths' *Blackpool Citizen*, 12 September 2007

Matthews, P. (2002), *Jervis on the Office and Duties of Coroners* 12th ed. (London: Sweet and Maxwell)

Merry, A. and McCall Smith, A. (2001), *Errors, Medicine and the Law* (Cambridge: Cambridge University Press)

Mesken, J., Lajunen, T. and Summala, H. (2002), 'Interpersonal violations, Speeding Violations and their Relation to Accident Involvement in Finland' *Ergonomics* 45, 469–83

Mirrlees-Black, C. (1993), *Disqualification from Driving: An effective penalty?* Research and Planning Unit Paper 74 (London: Home Office)

Moore, M. (1998), 'The Moral Worth of Retribution' in von Hirsch, A. and Asworth, A. (eds), *Principled Sentencing* 2nd ed. (London: Hart)

Näätänen, R. and Summala, H. (1976), *Road-user Behavior and Traffic Accidents* (Amsterdam: North-Holland Publishing Company)

Noland, R.B. and Quddus, M.A. (2004), 'Improvements in Medical Care and Technology Reductions in Traffic Related Fatalities in Great Britain' *Accident Analysis and Prevention* 36:1, 103–13

Norström (1981), *Studies in the Causation and Prevention of Traffic Crime* (Stockholm: Almqvist and Wiksell International)

O'Connell, S. (2006), 'From Toad of Toad Hall to the "Death Drivers" of Belfast' *British Journal of Criminology* 46, 455–69

Ormerod, D. (2005), *Smith and Hogan: Criminal Law* 11th ed. (Oxford: OUP)

Ormerod, D. (2006), 'Commentary to *R v Pleydell*' *Criminal Law Review* 426–7

Parker, D., Manstead, A.S.R., Stradling, S.G. and Reason, J.T. (1992a), 'Determinants of Intention to Commit Driving Violations' *Accident Analysis and Prevention* 24, 117–31

Parker, D., Manstead, A.S.R., Stradling, S.G., Reason, J.T. and Baxter, J.S. (1992b), 'Intention to Commit Driving Violations: An application of the theory of planned behaviour' *Journal of Applied Psychology* 77, 94–101

Parker, D., Reason, J.T., Manstead, A.S.R. and Stradling, S.G. (1995a), 'Driving Errors, Driving Violations and Accident Involvement' *Ergonomics* 38, 1036–48

Parker, D., West, R., Stradling, S. and Manstead, A.S.R. (1995b), 'Behavioural Characteristics and Involvement in Different Types of Traffic Accident' *Accident Analyses and Prevention* 27, 571–81

Parker, D., Stradling, S. and Manstead, A. (1996), 'Modifying Beliefs and Attitudes to Exceeding the Speed Limit: An intervention study based on the theory of planned behaviour' *Journal of Applied Social Psychology* 26:1, 1–19

Parker, D., Manstead, A., Stradling, S. and Senior, V. (1998), *The Development of Remedial Strategies for Driving Violations* TRL Report 300 (Crowthorne: Transport Research Laboratory)

Patten, C., Kircher, A., Östlund, J. and Nilsson, L. (2004), 'Using Mobile Telephones: Cognitive workload and attention resource allocation' *Accident Analysis and Prevention* 36, 341–50

Pearce, L.M. (2004), *Drivers Convicted of Dangerous and Careless Driving and Victims: What they think of driving offences and penalties* Road Safety Research Report No.46 (London: Department for Transport)

Pearce, L.M., Knowles, J., Davies, G.P. and Buttress, S. (2002), *Dangerous Driving and the Law*, Road Safety Research Report No.26 (Crowthorne: Transport Research Laboratory)

Peek-Asa, C. (1999), 'The Effect of Random Alcohol Screening in Reducing Motor Vehicle Crash Injuries' *American Journal of Preventive Medicine* 16, 57–67

Perkin, H. (1976), *The Age of the Automobile* (London: Quartet Books)

Pidd, H. (2008), 'One-week Ban for 10 mph Drive on Motorway' *The Guardian* 5 January 2008

Radun, I., Ohisalo, J., Radun, J., Heikki, S. and Tolvanen, M. (n.d.) 'Fell Asleep and Caused a Fatal Head-on Crash? Multidisciplinary In-depth Analysis vs. the Court' unpublished paper supplied by author

Reason, J. (1990), *Human Error* (Cambridge: Cambridge University Press)

Reason, J., Manstead, A., Stradling, S., Baxter, J. and Campbell, K. (1990), 'Errors and Violations on the Roads: A real distinction?' *Ergonomics* 33, 1315–32

Redmayne, M. (2007), 'Rethinking the Privilege Against Self-Incrimination' *Oxford Journal of Legal Studies* 27:2, 209–32

Rikspolisstyrelsen (Swedish National Police Board) (2007), *The Swedish Police Road Safety Policy* (Stockholm)

Riley, D. (1985), 'Drinking Drivers: The limits to deterrence' *The Howard Journal* 24:4, 241–56

Roberts, J.V. and Hough, M. (2002), *Changing Attitudes to Punishment* (Cullompton: Willan Publishing)

Robinson, D. and Campbell, R. (2006), *Contributory Factors to Road Accidents* (London: DfT)

Rose, G. (2000), *The Criminal Histories of Serious Traffic Offenders*, Home Office Research Study No. 206

Rothengatter, T. (2002), 'Drivers' Illusions – No More Risk' *Transportation Research Part F* 5, 249–58

Sagberg, F. and Assum, T. (2000), *In-depth Road Accident Investigations: Aggregated results from 196 fatal accidents in Mälardalen, Sweden, 1977–99 (Summary)*, (TØI report 499/2000) (Oslo: Institute of Transport Economics)

SAP (Sentencing Advisory Panel) (2007), *Consultation Paper on Causing Death by Driving Offences* available from <http://www.sentencing-guidelines.gov.uk/docs/Cons-2007-01-09.pdf>

SAP (2008), *Advice to the Sentencing Guidelines Council: Driving Offences – Causing Death by Driving* available from <http://www.sentencing-guidelines.gov.uk/docs/death-by-driving-advice.pdf>

Schulhofer, S.J. (1974), 'Harm and Punishment: A critique of emphasis on the results of conduct in the criminal law' *University of Pennsylvania Law Review* 122, 1497

Sexton, B., Tunbridge, R., Board, A., Jackson, P., Wright, K., Stark, M. and Englehart, K. (2002), *The Influence of Cannabis and Alcohol on Driving*, TRL Report 543 (Crowthorne: Transport Research Laboratory)

SGC (Sentencing Guidelines Council) (2008), *Causing Death by Driving: Consultation Guideline* available from <http://www.sentencing-guidelines.gov.uk/docs/death-by-driving-cons-guideline.pdf>

Shaver, K.G. (1970), 'Defensive Attribution: Effects of severity and relevance on the responsibility assigned for an accident' *Journal of Personality and Social Psychology* 14:2, 101–13

*Sheffield Today* 9 September 2007 'Boyfriend Let Kirsty Die after Car Crash': <http://www.thestar.co.uk/news/Boyfriend-let-Kirsty-die-after.1682845.jp>

Shute, S. (1999), 'Who Passes Unduly Lenient Sentences? How Were They Listed? A Survey of Attorney-General Reference Cases, 1989–1997' *Criminal Law Review* 603–26

Smith, J.C. (1997), 'Commentary to *Roberts*' *Criminal Law Review* 209

Smith, J.C. (2002), *Smith and Hogan: Criminal Law* 10th ed. (London: Butterworths)

Spencer, J.R. (1985), 'Motor Vehicles as Weapons of Offence' *Criminal Law Review* 29

Spencer, J.R. (1988), 'Road Traffic Law: A Review of the North Report' *Criminal Law Review* 707

Spencer, J.R. (2004), 'Road Traffic Notes' *Magistrates' Court Practice* 8:7, 6

Stalans, L.J. (2002), 'Measuring Attitudes to Sentencing' in Roberts, J.V. and Hough, M. (eds), *Changing Attitudes to Punishment* (Cullompton: Willan Publishing)

Steer, D.J. and Carr-Hill, R.A. (1967), 'The Motoring Offender – Who is He?' *Criminal Law Review* 214

Stewart, A.E. (2005), 'Attributions of Responsibility for Motor Vehicle Crashes' *Accident Analysis and Prevention* 681–8

Svenson, O. (1981), 'Are We All Less Risky and More Skilful Than Our Fellow Drivers?' *Acta Psychologica* 47, 143–8

*The Guardian* 'Tougher Speeding Penalties Planned' 9 November 2007

*The Sun* 16 April 2004

Tingvall, C. (2007), 'How the Latest Innovations and Advance are being Better Deployed to Improve Traffic Safety in Sweden', paper presented at RoadExpo '07

TRL (Transport Research Laboratory) (2001), *Blood Alcohol Levels in Road Accident Fatalities for 1999 in Great Britain*, Leaflet No. LF2084, October 2001

TRL (2002), *Blood Alcohol Levels in Road Accident Fatalities for 2000 in Great Britain*, Leaflet No. LF2086, October 2002

Tunbridge, R., Keigan, M. and James, F. (2001), *The Incidence of Drugs and Alcohol in Road Accident Fatalities* TRL Report 495

Vägtrafikinspektionen (Swedish Road Traffic Inspectorate) (2003), *Sweden Now Has an Inspectorate with Responsibility for a Safer Road Traffic Environment*, (Borlänge)

Vägverket (Swedish Road Administration) (2006a), *Safe Traffic – Vision Zero on the Move*, 2nd ed. (Borlänge) available from <http://publikationswebbutik.vv.se/shopping/ShowItem.aspx?id=1317>

Vägverket (Swedish Road Administration) (2006b), *Variable Speed Limits: Evaluation at intersections*, available from <http://publikationswebbutik.vv.se/shopping/ShowItem____2700.aspx>

Voas, R., Tippetts, A. and Fell, J. (2003), 'Assessing the Effectiveness of Minimum Legal Drinking Age and Zero Tolerance Laws in the United States' *Accident Analysis and Prevention* 35, 579–87

von Hirsch, A. (1993), *Censure and Sanctions* (Oxford: Clarendon Press)

von Hirsch, A. (1998), 'Proportionate Sentences: A desert perspective' in von Hirsch, A. and Ashworth, A. (eds), *Principled Sentencing* 2nd ed. (Oxford: Hart)

von Hirsch, A. and Ashworth, A. (eds) (1998), *Principled Sentencing* 2nd ed. (Oxford: Hart)

von Hirsch, A. and Jareborg, N. (1991), 'Gauging Criminal Harm: A living-standard analysis' *Oxford Journal of Legal Studies* 11, 1

Walker, N. (1991), *Why Punish?* (Oxford: Oxford University Press)

Wallén Warner, H. and Åberg, L. (2006), 'Drivers' Decision to Speed: A study inspired by the theory of planned behaviour' *Transport Research Part F* 9, 427–33

Wallis, P., McCormac, K., Brown, P. and Swift, K. (eds) (2005), *Wilkinson's Road Traffic Offences* 22nd ed. (London: Sweet and Maxwell)

Walster, E. (1966), 'Assignment of Responsibility for Accident' *Journal of Personality and Social Psychology* 3:1, 73–9

Wasik, M. (1994), 'Form and Function in the Law of Involuntary Manslaughter' *Criminal Law Review* 883–93

Waylen, A.E., Horswill, M.S., Alexander, J.L. and McKenna, F.P. (2004), 'Do Expert Drivers Have a Reduced Illusion of Superiority?' *Transportation Research Part F* 7, 323–31

Wells, C. (2001), *Corporations and Criminal Responsibility* 2nd ed. (Oxford: Oxford University Press)

*Westlaw*: <www.westlaw.co.uk> accessed November 2007

Whitelegg, J. and Haq, G. (2006a), *Vision Zero: Adopting a target of zero for road traffic fatalities and serious injuries* (Stockholm: Stockholm Environment Institute)

Whitelegg, J. and Haq, G. (2006b), *Vision Zero: Adopting a target of zero for road traffic fatalities and serious injuries: executive summary* (Stockholm: Stockholm Environment Institute)

Wilde, G.J.S. (1982), 'The Theory of Risk Homeostasis: Implications for safety and health' *Risk Analysis* 2, 209–25

Willett, T.C. (1964), *Criminal on the Road* (London: Tavistock Publications)

Willett, T.C. (1973), *Drivers After Sentence* (London: Heinemann)

Williams, G. (1961), *Criminal Law, The General Part* 2nd ed. (London: Stevens)

Williams, G. (1983), *Textbook of Criminal Law* 2nd ed. (London: Stevens)

Wood, D. (2002),'Retribution, Crime Reduction and the Justification of Punishment' *Oxford Journal of Legal Studies* 22:2, 301–21

Wright, N.A., Stone, B.M., Horberry, T.J. and Reed, N. (2007), *A Review of In-Vehicle Sleepiness Detection Devices* TRL Published Project Report PPR157 (Crowthorne: Transport Research Laboratory)

Yagil, D. (1998), 'Gender and Age-related Differences in Attitudes toward Traffic Laws and Traffic Violations' *Transportation Research Part F* 1, 123–35

Zila, J. (2006), 'The Prosecution Service Function within the Swedish Criminal Justice System' in Jehle, J.-M. and Wade, M. (eds), *Coping with Overloaded Criminal Justice Systems: The rise of prosecutorial power across Europe* (Heidelberg: Springer)

# Index

For Product Safety Concerns and Information please contact our EU representative GPSR@taylorandfrancis.com
Taylor & Francis Verlag GmbH, Kaufingerstraße 24, 80331 München, Germany

www.ingramcontent.com/pod-product-compliance
Ingram Content Group UK Ltd.
Pitfield, Milton Keynes, MK11 3LW, UK
UKHW010958180926
475701UK00004B/438

* 9 7 8 1 1 3 8 3 7 8 9 9 5 *